Dyslexia Research and its Applications to Education

Dyslexia Research and its Applications to Education

Edited by
George Th. Pavlidis
Senior Research Fellow
Department of Psychology,
University of Manchester

and

T. R. Miles

Professor of Psychology,
University College of North Wales, Bangor

JOHN WILEY & SONS
Chichester · New York · Brisbane · Toronto

British Library Cataloguing in Publication Data:

Dyslexia research and its applications to education.
  1. Dyslexia
  I. Pavlidis, George Th.
  II. Miles, T. R.
  371.9′14   LB1050.5   80–49975

  ISBN 0 471 27841 6

Photosetting by Thomson Press (I) Ltd, New Delhi
and Printed in the United States of America.

(For love exacts what is possible rather than what is due: what is due is sometimes impossible, as, for instance, in the case of the honour due to . . . parents; for no one could ever pay all his debt to them)

Aristotle, *Nicomachean Ethics*, VIII, 14, 4.

ΣΕ ΣΑΣ ΜΑΝΑ ΚΑΙ ΠΑΤΕΡΑ   To the memory of my parents

                                                            T. R. M.
To my mother and father
with all my love and respect

              G. Th. P.

List of Contributors

BAKKER, D. J.   *Professor of Psychology, Free University Pedological Institute, Amsterdam, Netherlands.*

BOUMA, H.   *Professor of Psychology and Director of the Institute for Perception Research, Eindhoven, Netherlands.*

CRITCHLEY, M.   *President Emeritus, The World Federation of Neurology.*

ELLIS, N. C.   *Lecturer in Psychology, University College of North Wales, Bangor, UK.*

LEGEIN, CH. P.   *Ophthalmologist and part-time Research Associate, Institute for Perception Research, Eindhoven, Netherlands.*

MASLAND, R. L.   *Professor Emeritus of Neurology, Columbia University, USA.*

MEUDELL, P.   *Lecturer in Psychology, University of Manchester, UK.*

MILES, E.   *Director of Teaching, Dyslexia Unit, University College of North Wales, Bangor, UK.*

MILES, T. R.   *Professor of Psychology, University College of North Wales, Bangor, UK.*

NAIDOO, S.   *Headmistress, Dawn House School, Rainworth, Nottinghamshire, UK. Former Director of the Word-Blind Centre for Dyslexic Children, London, UK.*

PAVLIDIS, G. TH.   *Senior Research Fellow and Director of Dyslexia Project, Department of Psychology, University of Manchester, UK.*

RAWSON, M. B.
Former Editor of the Bulletin of the Orton Society; now Editor-in-Chief for the Orton Society. Formerly Associate Professor of Sociology, Hood College, Frederick, Maryland, USA.

SCHROOTS, H. J. F.
Netherlands Institute for Preventive Medicine, Leyden, Netherlands.

ZANGWILL, O. L.
Professor of Psychology, University of Cambridge, UK.

Contents

Foreword*

Although an apparently specific disability in learning to read ('word blindness') was first described by Hinshelwood nearly a hundred years ago, the modern era in the study of this grave educational handicap may be said to have begun with the work of S. T. Orton in the twenties and thirties of the present century. Orton's work clearly showed that dyslexia is 'specific' in the sense that it is due neither to want of intelligence nor to lack of educational opportunity, and that it is not uncommonly associated with mildly defective articulation, clumsiness, and retarded acquisition of simple motor skills. Furthermore, it is much more common in boys than in girls and seems frequently to be associated with left or mixed handedness and with backwardness in reading in other members of the family. These observations have led many people to suppose that the syndrome so exhaustively described by Orton is essentially genetical in origin. ——*genetic*

The present book is concerned with dyslexia in the light of contemporary research. As the editors make clear in their Preface, its purpose is to forge links between the three disciplines most closely concerned in its study and treatment, namely neurology, experimental psychology, and education. All too frequently, alas, these disciplines have pursued their respective paths with scant concern for one another's existence and, as the editors rightly point out, dyslexia is above all an interdisciplinary subject.

In a much-needed effort to break down the barriers between these three disciplines and to help bring about a measure of integration in research on reading and its disorders, the editors have brought together a number of papers contributed to three symposia on dyslexia held recently in the University of Manchester and added to them a small number of invited papers from research workers overseas. The resulting book is intended neither as a systematic text nor as a comprehensive review of current work in its field: its aim could best be

---

* Dr G. Th. Pavlidis's chapter was not available to the author (apart from an outline) when he wrote this foreword.

described as a forum for presentation of some recent work on dyslexia and for discussion of modern theoretical approaches to its understanding and treatment. In spite of considerable differences in viewpoint and approach, the editors consider that there is a very fair measure of common ground and that the various views expressed in the chapters of their book are in large degree complementary.

Although the writer of this Foreword has not himself been active in dyslexia research for some years, he is confident that the policy espoused by the editors has much to commend it. He feels, therefore, that the most helpful way in which he can introduce the book is to indicate where the major differences in outlook or interpretation lie between workers in the different disciplines and the ways in which one may hope that they can be resolved by interdisciplinary enquiry.

As dyslexia was first recognized by medical men, it is perhaps to the discipline of neurology that we should first turn. In this volume, clinical neurology is represented first by Dr Macdonald Critchley, whose efforts on behalf of the dyslexic child have won him international renown, and secondly by Professor R. L. Masland, a clinical neurologist who takes a particular interest in language and its disorders in both children and adults. Although a psychologist by trade, Dr Peter Meudell has specialized in the study of those organic disorders of the nervous system which present primarily at the psychological level; and his chapter, though largely psychological in style and content, should be viewed as closely related to neurological issues. Needless to say, such issues are also touched upon by several other contributors, notably Professor Miles and Dr Ellis, and by Mrs Naidoo.

Dr Critchley (Chapter 1) leaves us in no doubt that he fully shares the editors' belief that dyslexia is an interdisciplinary subject in which cooperation between the neurologist and the remedial teacher is indispensable in any attempt to alleviate the disability. He further lays stress on dyslexia viewed as a constitutional disorder, probably of genetical origin, and considers that its characteristics differ appreciably from comparable reading difficulties attributable to injury of the brain at birth or in early infancy. Although his view is entitled to great respect, it must be admitted that, at all events in so far as the reading and spelling troubles are concerned, the two syndromes resemble one another very closely and such differences as may exist between them appear to have but little importance from the point of view of remedial teaching.

Both Professor Masland (Chapter 3) and Dr Meudell (Chapter 4) lay stress on a number of common factors in the acquired and developmental dyslexias. Dr Meudell, in particular, specifies several similarities between the two conditions which may or may not prove to have a bearing upon issues of aetiology. At all events, his substantial chapter suggests that careful study from the point of view of neuropsychology may shed important light on certain defects of cognitive function which may underlie dyslexia irrespective of its origin.

Rather little is said by the contributors to this book, whether they write primarily from the neurological or psychological standpoint, about the possible relation of dyslexia to issues of laterality and cerebral dominance. As is well known, Orton put great emphasis on letter and word reversals in both the reading and writing of dyslexic school children and attempted to explain them in terms of failure to establish unequivocal cerebral dominance in the acquisition of motor and linguistic skills. While Orton no doubt attached excessive significance to questions of handedness and greatly over-estimated the incidence of reversal errors, it is difficult to believe that issues of unilateral cerebral dominance are wholly without relevance to specific learning disabilities in school children.

In spite of the fact that this book contains no chapter specifically devoted to the issue of cerebral dominance, the matter is touched upon in passing by several of the contributors. Dr Meudell, for example, raises the issue of cerebral asymmetry in the representation of expressive and receptive speech respectively. While it is now known that the dominant hemisphere is exclusively in control of propositional speech, the right hemisphere, while virtually mute, has none the less been found to possess appreciable powers of understanding. This is particularly the case as regards lexical comprehension. These differences in linguistic potential between the two hemispheres have raised the interesting possibility that, in dyslexic subjects, the phonological encoding of visual information is deficient or even absent altogether. Further analysis of this deficiency may do much to bring closer the neurological and psychological modes of approach to reading and its disorders.

Professor Miles and Dr Ellis (Chapter 9) likewise call attention to the parallels which have been adduced between the effects of certain focal lesions of the brain in adults and the somewhat similar patterns of disability not uncommonly observed in dyslexic children.

In view of the fact that both editors and a majority of the contributors are psychologists, it is not surprising to find that experimental psychology is the dominant discipline represented in this book. The psychological chapters, however, are by no means without links with other chapters concerned primarily with neurological or educational issues and their authors make no attempt to view dyslexia as a problem falling exclusively within the domain of psychology.

The study by two Dutch psychologists, Professor D. J. Bakker and Dr H. J. F. Schroots (Chapter 5) on temporal order raises an issue which has been much discussed in relation to backwardness in reading. It derives from an idea advanced some years ago by Karl Lashley that temporal order is to be viewed as an element in nervous integration of the utmost importance to the evolution of adaptive behaviour in animals and man. The experiments which these authors report leave little doubt that perception of temporal order or sequence is poorly developed in some children who, though undeniably backward readers, may or may not have been classed as dyslexic in a strict sense. At the same time, it is not entirely clear whether this deficiency is limited to serial order generally or whether it is symptomatic of some more circumscribed failure in phonetic encoding. In view of the obvious importance of correct serial order in both reading and spelling, a further analysis of what is loosely called 'sequencing difficulty' would appear a high priority.

Dr G. Th. Pavlidis (Chapter 6) is likewise concerned with sequencing but mainly with regard to saccadic eye movements. Although the study of eye movements in reading is an old-established preoccupation of experimental psychologists, it is odd how little work has been done on eye movements in recent years on subjects who exhibit reading problems. In Orton's day, it is true, several investigators reported an increased frequency of regressive eye movements ('back-tracking') in dyslexic subjects, which might suggest an inborn preference for ocular scanning from right to left. More commonly, however, 'back-tracking' has been explained in terms of an attempt to compensate for poor comprehension or limited short-term memory. Although doubt has been thrown on this latter interpretation by (among others) Zangwill and Blakemore (1972), Professor Miles and Dr Ellis (Chapters 8 and 9) appear to subscribe to such a view. This is clearly a controversial matter calling for further analysis.

The experiments reported by Dr Pavlidis are of particular interest in so far as he finds clear-cut differences between subjects who are poor readers and those who in addition meet the stricter criteria required for a diagnosis of dyslexia. If confirmed, this method may find useful application to the diagnosis of developmental dyslexia and its differentiation from poor reading due to limited intelligence or inadequate schooling. As the oculo-motor anomalies, moreover, do not appear to be wholly confined to reading, it might seem that deficit in acquiring and maintaining rapid and correct directional eye movement sequences in reading may reflect a primary deficit rather than a compensatory strategy.

In another study from the Netherlands, Dr Legein and Professor Bouma (Chapter 7) describe experiments on the recognition of letters and words exposed briefly in either foveal or parafoveal vision. Their subjects included both dyslexics and normal controls, all of whom had their reading level determined by a standard scholastic attainment test. The dyslexics, moreover, underwent a complete ophthalmological examination—a precaution all too rarely taken in psychological inquiries. While the dyslexics were found to perceive and process the stimuli as adequately as the controls, they appeared to be significantly slower in naming the presented letters or words; in other words 'phonological encoding' was in some degree deficient. These findings may perhaps find a measure of interpretation along the lines discussed above in connection with Dr Meudell's chapter. They also support the view expressed by Professor Miles and Dr Ellis that speed of lexical encoding is a critical factor in governing the reading rate.

What might perhaps be called the *pièce de resistance* of the entire book is the contribution by Professor Miles and Dr Ellis on dyslexia conceived as a deficiency in lexical encoding (Chapters 8 and 9). Although the work is clearly collaborative, it may be surmised that Dr Ellis took the major responsibility for the writing of Chapter 8, which adduces experimental evidence for the authors' view and generates two tentative models in terms of which the nature of the deficiency might be explained; Professor Miles, in his turn, appears to have taken the lead in the writing of Chapter 9, which deals with a variety of clinical observations of high relevance to dyslexia and which are believed by the authors to find explanation in terms of the explanatory framework adumbrated in the preceding chapter.

Although the propriety of viewing human performance in terms of information processing is now generally accepted in experimental psychology, this approach is still relatively unfamiliar to doctors and educationalists. It should be explained that the approach evolved from the massive advances in communications and control engineering and computer technology which took place during and after the last war and which inevitably influenced biological thinking at many points. At the same time, it cannot be said that the models which have been put forward on the basis of information processing are always easy to relate to the more traditional concepts and theories of clinical neurology and the earlier, though not necessarily wholly outdated, formulations of experimental psychology. None the less, physiologists and others ignore information processing models of human performance at their peril. Although the models of cognitive processes espoused by information theorists often appear oversimplified and lacking in relevance to the findings of neurology, they may well direct attention to important aspects of human cognition and its modes of deficiency or breakdown. These two chapters provide an excellent example of how distinctively an approach along cognitive lines can contribute to our understanding of reading and its disorders.

While the first of these chapters (Chapter 8) will be of interest mainly to experimental psychologists whose interests lie in cognitive processes in general and the power of models in particular, Chapter 9 is likely to attract a wider readership in so far as it takes into account many of the phenomena of dyslexia very familiar to neurologists and remedial teachers. These include limitations of short-term memory, slow and incomplete verbal learning, bizarre errors of spelling, and deficiencies in the sphere of naming. With devastating logic, the authors criticize the explanations given by Orton and others of the incidence in dyslexia of directional confusion, mirror reading and writing, and failure correctly to identify individual fingers of the two hands (so-called finger agnosia). Their conclusion is that all these features, by no means uncommon in children with reading handicaps, can be more plausibly explained in terms of inadequate verbal labelling or encoding than in terms of specific neurological deficits in the sphere of gnosis or praxis. They further offer an explanation of the difficulties encountered in articulating certain words (usually polysyllables) in some dyslexics in terms of an acoustic confusion between phonemes superimposed upon a specific retardation in the process of lexical encoding.

In spite of the care and skill with which this informational model of dyslexic handicap has been conceived, the present writer may be forgiven if he expresses some doubts as to its adequacy to explain all aspects of dyslexia. For example, the sequencing difficulty which appears to lie at the root of the oculo-motor abnormalities described by Dr Pavlidis seems to indicate a sensori-motor rather than an intellectual disability. As has been suggested above, it may result from a constitutional bias towards 'sinistrad scanning' rather than from a strategy to counter slow and uncertain lexical or semantic processing. Again, the slow learning and rapid forgetting of spelling may imply an accelerated rate of forgetting rather than a failure in initial encoding of the appropriate sequence of letters. But in spite of these and other objections, the information processing model is undoubtedly contributing to our understanding of reading disability and will no doubt in time come to be placed upon its neurological foundation. Professor Miles and Dr Ellis have convincingly demonstrated that this 'new wave' of cognitive psychology is not only intellectually stimulating but has convincing practical applications.

Last, though certainly not least, are three chapters which deal with educational issues. These are by Mrs Margaret Rawson, Mrs Elaine Miles and Mrs Sandhya Naidoo. Owing to the fact that Mrs Rawson's chapter extends well beyond remedial teaching to embrace a number of general issues, my review of it will be postponed to the end.

Needless to relate, Mrs Miles (Chapter 10) has been closely associated with the work of her husband, Professor Miles, at the University College of North Wales and has largely built up the work of the Dyslexia Unit attached to his Department. Not only has this work been closely linked with the research programme initiated by Professor Miles but it has indeed been largely based on the theoretical position which he and his colleagues have evolved. Yet Mrs Miles's chapter makes clear that she not only has unrivalled experience in the tuition of dyslexic children but that she also has decided views of her own. While accepting the view that dyslexia reflects a constitutional disability in encoding symbolic visual material, she none the less insists that only if this theory stands up, given the tough pragmatic test of educational utility, can its validity be justified.

Everyone who has been concerned with dyslexia will be aware of the frustration which is produced in school children, more especially if they are talented and ambitious, by failure to pass examinations, largely on account of slow writing and composition, poor organization of material, and, above all, grossly defective spelling. Although good spelling is today regarded as less essential than once it was, Mrs Miles is right in pointing out how important it is for talented school children to master the English spelling system. While it is well known that the reading of dyslexic children as a rule improves spontaneously during adolescence whether or not they receive remedial teaching, spelling almost always lags behind and bad spelling not infrequently constitutes the major scholastic handicap when the child grows up. Appropriately, therefore, Mrs Miles concentrates particularly on difficulties in learning to spell and considers in a most interesting way the extent to which spelling difficulties can be understood in terms of poorly developed encoding skills.

In this connection, Mrs Miles rightly criticizes the undue emphasis which has been placed in some quarters on visual factors in relation to difficulties in reading and spelling. Her own emphasis is plainly on the phonic element and she advocates a structured phonic programme for teaching spelling, insisting that the teacher should be 'clear and explicit about irregular words'. She also provides a most useful classification of some of the more common inconsistencies in English orthography. As many have found, it is not poor reading that critically disables the grown-up dyslexic but laboured composition and abysmal spelling. Inadequate composition and hopeless spelling have been the downfall of many highly intelligent and promising young men who have set their sights at a university career. In conclusion, Mrs Miles remarks on the close association between teaching basic skills in reading and writing and the teaching of music. This is a challenging and thought-provoking statement and it is a pity that she does not spell out the analogy in greater detail.

Mrs Naidoo (Chapter 11), is an educational psychologist and a former Director of the Invalid Childrens Aid Association's Word-Blind Centre in London. She is now Headmistress of one of the Association's Schools for Aphasic Children. In this chapter she presents a full and informative survey of remedial teaching methods suitable for use with dyslexic children and the principles upon which they are ostensibly based. Her concerned, yet critical, survey will be found most instructive to those without experience of remedial teaching and indicates the range of both our knowledge and our ignorance in the remedial sphere. Her chapter should provide a much-needed stimulus to the development of new methods of remedial teaching in the basic school subjects.

Lastly, we may turn to Mrs Margaret Rawson's essay (Chapter 2) on 'A Diversity Model for Dyslexia'. For convenience's sake, this may be grouped with the chapters on education though the author in fact ranges discursively over a broad field, from indisputably pathological deviance to the limits of normal variability, from Orton and the brain to cultural diversity, and from remedial teaching to wide issues of individual growth and development. In dyslexia, as she tellingly puts it, 'the diagnosis is clinical; the treatment educational'. This treatment issues not in the 'cure of a disease' but 'in a way of learning and living matched to the individual's whole personal configuration'. While such respecters of humane values as Mrs Rawson monitor our science, there is little danger of its degenerating into a mere consortium of techniques and models that strip the individual, whether literate or otherwise, of his distinctively human qualities. Although her chapter appears early in the book, it in many ways sums up the whole interdisciplinary endeavour.

The Psychological Laboratory   O. L. ZANGWILL, F. R. S.
University of Cambridge

REFERENCE

Zangwill, O. L. and Blakemore, C. (1972) Dyslexia: reversal of eye movements during reading. *Neuropsychologia*, **10**, 371–373.

Editors' Preface

Much of the material in this book was originally presented at three 3-day symposia on dyslexia which were organized by Dr G. Th. Pavlidis and Mr John Shaw and held at Manchester University in 1978, 1979, and 1980. Among the invited speakers were Dr Critchley, Professor Masland, Dr Meudell, Professor and Mrs Miles, Dr Pavlidis, Mrs Rawson, and Professor Zangwill. Quite early on, however, the editors decided that the proposed volume would gain in interest and depth if it also included the ideas on dyslexia of other workers in the field, and we were very pleased when Professor Bakker, Professor Bouma, Mrs Naidoo, and Dr Legein, Dr Schroots, and Dr Ellis all accepted our invitations to contribute.

Dyslexia is an interdisciplinary subject, and the chief purpose of the book is to show how the three main disciplines concerned—neurology, experimental psychology, and education—provide a body of evidence whose parts are interlocking and mutually supportive.

Having chosen our contributors we made it a firm point of editorial policy to give each a free hand; and no attempt has been made to iron out disagreements or differences of emphasis. That there is a fair measure of agreement—or at least compatibility—between the different chapters is of course in part due to the way in which the contributors were selected; but we still wish to claim that the book forms a coherent whole and that in the dyslexia field the criticism that there are *tot homines quot sententiae*—as many different opinions as there are workers in the field—is entirely invalid.

To set the stage it seemed appropriate that Professor Zangwill's Foreword should be followed by two chapters—those by Dr Critchley and Mrs Rawson—which commented on the dyslexia scene as a whole. An important theme which unites these two papers is that of definition. Mrs Rawson calls attention to the fact that the area over which a word is applicable does not always have precisely specified limits; thus, to cite her dramatic example, the boundaries of Jimmy's new word 'd'b'm' were by no means clearly drawn at first. One is reminded in this connection of the thesis of Waismann (1945) that language has 'open-texture' and also of the dictum of Wittgenstein (1953, p. 220 e) that we should let the use of a word teach us its meaning. It is certainly no argument against the value of a concept to point out that the limits of its applicability are imprecisely specified, and indeed very few of our everyday concepts would be serviceable if that were so. In the case of 'developmental dyslexia' it is a striking feature of Dr Critchley's proposed definition—based on a lifetime's experience—that it allows for the retention of a suitable degree of 'open-texture' (as do all medical terms in Dr Critchley's view) while strongly emphasizing that the concept is not a mere 'rag-bag' one.

These two introductory chapters are followed by Professor Masland's comprehensive survey of recent neurological evidence. Next comes Dr Meudell's paper on the similarities and differences between acquired and developmental reading failure, which in its turn is followed by the account by Professor Bakker and Dr Schroots of their researches into the deficiencies shown by their subjects in temporal order perception. In Chapter 6 Dr Pavlidis reviews the literature and presents evidence showing that erratic oculomotor sequencing is displayed by dyslexics in both reading and non-reading sequential tasks, and he argues that use of the non-reading task could lead to an early objective diagnostic test of dyslexia. This would be independent of reading ability, memory, intelligence, and indeed of environmental and linguistic factors in general.

One of the striking developments in recent years has been the approach to dyslexia through the study of information processing. This approach is represented in Chapter 7 by Dr Legein and Professor Bouma and in Chapters 8 and 9 by Dr Ellis and Professor Miles. Finally, Mrs Miles in Chapter 10 draws on her experience both as a language specialist and as a teacher of dyslexic children to demonstrate why it is that they need a structured phonic programme, while Mrs Naidoo in Chapter 11 carries out a comprehensive review of a range of such programmes, pointing out the many similarities and the relatively small differences between them.

The position of those who still doubt the value of the concept of 'dyslexia' seems to us to be rendered particularly uncomfortable not only by the remarkable coherence of the evidence from different disciplines but also by the fact that those working in the same discipline have independently arrived at similar conclusions. Thus the evidence from genetics (see, for example, Owen, 1978) is independent of the evidence from neurology, while both are independent of studies of information processing and short-term memory; and Dr Pavlidis's discovery that in both reading and non-reading sequential tasks dyslexics display erratic eye movements not found even in backward readers of the same chronological and reading age gives further support to the view that dyslexic phenomena are coherent and relatively homogeneous. In addition, it should be noted that the very similar conclusions reached by Dr Legein and Professor Bouma and by Dr Ellis and Professor Miles as to the nature of the information processing deficiency in dyslexia were the result of totally independent in-vestigations. Finally, it is clear from the evidence in Chapters 9, 10 and 11 not only that teachers in different parts of the world have independently reached similar conclusions as to how dyslexic children can best be taught but that the methods which have evolved are precisely those which enable children with an information processing deficiency to use compensatory strategies. The convergence of evidence presented from these different areas, particularly if considered in conjunction with the detailed case studies and other complementary data which have appeared in the literature over the years, seems to us sufficient to refute any overall scepticism about the value of the dyslexia concept. This, however, is a matter about which readers must form their own judgements.

We should like to thank the Department of Extra-Mural Studies, Manchester University, and the staff of Holly Royde College for providing the facilities for making the original symposia possible. We should also like to express our appreciation of the generous and unfailing help which has been given to us by Mrs C. Bird and the rest of the staff of John Wiley and of the financial support for our research into dyslexia which has been given to both of us at different times by the Social Science Research Council. In addition we should both like to express particular gratitude to Professor Zangwill for his personal support and encouragement over many years.

Finally, we would like to thank the contributors themselves and those many individuals who took part in the research and whose behaviour is described or summarized in this book.

G. Th. P.
T. R. M.
1980

REFERENCES

Owen, F. W. (1978) Dyslexia: genetic aspects. In A. L. Benton and D. Pearl (eds.) *Dyslexia: An Appraisal of Current Knowledge*, New York: Oxford University Press, pp. 265–284.
Waismann, F. (1945) 'Verifiability', *Aristotelian Society*. Supplementary Volume XIX, 119–150. Reprinted in A. G. N. Flew (ed.) *Logic and Language* (1950), Oxford: Blackwell, pp. 117–144.
Wittgenstein, L. (1953) *Philosophical Investigations*, tr. G. E. M. Anscombe, Oxford: Blackwell.

CHAPTER 1

Dyslexia: An Overview

MACDONALD CRITCHLEY

> As felicitous an instance of futile classicism as can well be found, is the
> conventional spelling of the English language. English orthography
> satisfies all the requirements of the canons of reputability under the law
> of conspicuous waste. It is archaic, cumbrous and ineffective; its
> acquisition consumes much time and effort; failure to acquire it is easy
> of detection.
>
> *Thorstein Veblen*

In an attempt to unfathom the unfathomable, to unscrew the inscrutable, I will
try and analyse something which according to the critics, is incapable of being
defined—despite a number of excellent attempts over the past half-
century—namely, dyslexia.

Of course, delay in learning to read may be due to causes other than dyslexia.
While it is agreed that at least 10% of the school population are reading, writing,
and spelling less well than they should be, dyslexic children make up only a
proportion of these. The exact prevalence has not yet been established. Much
depends upon the skill of the one who is testing, the extent of his experience with
the intricacies of the problem, and his freedom from the shackles of personal
prejudice. Many have never been taught what to look for, how to observe, and
how to interpret what they find.

To define, then, the indefinable:

Developmental dyslexia is a learning disability which initially shows
itself by difficulty in learning to read, and later by erratic spelling and by
lack of facility in manipulating written as opposed to spoken words.
The condition is cognitive in essence, and usually genetically determined. It is not due to intellectual inadequacy or to lack of socio-
cultural opportunity, or to emotional factors, or to any known
structural brain-defect. It probably represents a specific maturational
defect which tends to lessen as the child grows older, and is capable of

1

considerable improvement, especially when appropriate remedial help is afforded at the earliest opportunity.

(Critchley and Critchley, 1978)

The expression 'specific reading retardation' is sometimes put forward as an alternative, but is it really appropriate? In great Britain, a certain reluctance to accept the term 'dyslexia', diminishing it is true, lingers in the corridors of those responsible for the organization of learning. It stems from the prejudice begotten of ignorance, for rarely are civil servants medically or educationally qualified. In the ponderous Bullock Report of a committee convened by the Government (1975), we were confronted with a document of 600 pages in which dyslexia was dismissed in a mere seventeen lines. Within the cursory comments are at least two blatant fallacies: (1) that dyslexia is incapable of precise operational definition; and (2) that a more helpful term is 'specific reading retardation'. Nothing could be more unwarranted.

Dyslexia implies vastly more than a delay in learning to read, which is but the tip of the iceberg. The etymology of the term dyslexia' expresses admirably a, difficulty—not in reading—but in the use of words, how they are identified, what they signify, how they are handled in combination, how they are pronounced, and how they are spelt. All these constitute a handicap to a dyslexic, and it usually happens that mere reading difficulties are later submerged by the many other defects. The natural history of a dyslexic schoolboy is usually one of steady improvement in his ability to read, but the other troubles or epiphenomena are then highlighted. The term 'specific reading retardation' is, therefore, not appropriate as it indicates an isolated symptom, whereas developmental dyslexia is a complex syndrome.

When one realizes that the costs of the Bullock Commission with its report amounted to £95000 one feels tempted to say, as Cromwell did, 'My brethren by the bowels of Christ, I beseech you bethink you that you may be mistaken!'

Another unfortunate tendency still exists, namely a confusion of specific developmental dyslexia with those learning disabilities resulting from dysfunction due to structural lesions of the brain. In cases of developmental dyslexia no neurological abnormalities are to be found on examination and there is usually a family history of similar problems with reading, writing and spelling. The situation is different in cases of learning disabilities due to minimal brain dysfunction. Here, there is no family history, and neurological defects can usually be discovered on examination. Usually, too, there is a clear story of perinatal trauma, anoxia or ill-health.

I have always insisted that the diagnosis of specific developmental dyslexia is a medical responsibility. This view is not popular among certain educational psychologists, but its truth can scarcely be denied. To isolate specific developmental dyslexia from the mishmash of late readers requires the ability to eliminate those children in whom faulty apprehension of sense-data is responsible, to analyse the emotional problems and distinguish those which are causal from those which are clearly reactionary. Tasks like these may be far from simple or straightforward and are beyond the skills of the inexperienced. A particularly exacting and yet important duty devolves upon the diagnostician to separate clearly the cases of learning disability due to minimal brain dysfunction, from those which are constitutional; in other words, to differentiate the true cases of specific developmental dyslexia from those late developers with obvious structural lesions of the brain.

Is it necessary or even worthwhile to make such a distinction? Indeed it is. Treatment may not be the same; prognosis certainly differs. Confusion between these two disorders is reflected in much of the literature and impedes research.

The earliest piece of evidence predicting an impending dyslexia is that the child lags behind his peers in his first steps in reading. Here rises the initial suspicion that all is not well.

Gradually this gap widens, and in the young child often provokes frustration, either overt or masked.

The child is late in learning to name the letters of the alphabet, whether by way of a 'phonic' approach, that is, *ah. . . buh. . . kuh. . .* or by 'alphabetical analysis', in other words, *ay. . . bee. . . see. . . .*

The child remains confused as to the correct orientation of individual letters and numerals. Hence the numerous reversals, inversions, and rotations which persist long after they should have gone.

It is important to realize that even in normal circumstances the later processes of learning which go to make up the education of a young child are complicated indeed. It is convenient to analyse them into a series of component stages, namely:

(1) The recognition of individual letters which, it must be remembered, is not a matter of memorizing 26 symbols but a far larger number of graphemes made up of upper case, lower case, script and even many other typefaces.

(2) The juxtaposition of letters so as to form short words, orientated correctly, that is, from left to right, and not mirrorwise.

(3) The task of learning to copy, not only in a slavish fashion from upper case to upper case, but also to transcribe from upper case into lower case as well as into script.

(4) At some time the child becomes able to link, or 'join up', letters in script. Incidentally, this is a trick which may not be learned by a dyslexic until well into adulthood. During this operation, conflict may arise between the rôles of phonic as opposed to 'whole-word' or 'sight-word' recognition.

(5) The mastery of the little words; realization of the value of contextual cues; and the studied avoidance of proleptic guesswork.

(6) The steady rise of serial thinking and automatic recall as particularly applied to numerals, and to the placement of letters within the alphabet; then

multiplication tables, then knowledge of the succession of days of the week and the months of the year. This may take many years. The achievement of reading a clock comes later, and the confusion engendered by digital clocks as opposed to dials must be overcome.

(7) The correlation of grapheme with phoneme, that is to say, the relation of the sound of a symbol to its visual appearance, must also be accomplished. Conflicting regional accents often complicate this operation.

(8) Then comes the two-fold task of reading aloud not only with correct articulation, but also with simultaneous understanding. The two activities may be split. Considerable anxiety may attend and impair the act of reading aloud in the presence of others.

What a complicated contrivance is this seemingly straightforward business of learning to read. Not quite the miracle of learning to *talk*, but just as intricate. No wonder that a dyslexic stumbles in his progress. Let us examine the various facets of his personal difficulty with words, or, to use the terminology of science, his dyslexia.

I shall enumerate below the various characteristics which attend the bookwork of the dyslexic who presents himself around the age of puberty or perhaps a little later.

It is obvious to all who are close to him that the dyslexic youngster, though not incapable of reading, is a conspicuously unwilling reader. Rather than sit down with a book, he prefers either to do things with his hands, or indulge in outdoor activities. Sometimes this reluctance is extreme, and one may witness a veritable aversion to the printed page. Some have spoken of a hatred, or even a fear of words.

Even when this reluctance has been overcome, which in itself constitutes an epochal surmounting of a hurdle, a turn of the tide, the resolving dyslexic is still a slow reader. He cannot be hurried, for if pressurized he falters and loses accuracy. Moreover he fails to hoist in the connotation of what it is he is scrambling to decipher. Allied to this disinclination to read and an associated slowness, is a similar avoidance of the act of writing. In a homely setting this shows itself in a dislike of writing 'thank you' letters, or seasonal greetings. In a classroom context, essays constitute a considerable problem. Though the dyslexic may know his work, and may have a head full of ideas, imaginative and penetrating, the task of committing them to paper is too much. He is painfully slow, being held up by a search even for words that are within his capacity to spell. Moreover, grammar, punctuation, and, of course, literary style, are all imperfect, and often too the handwriting is atrocious. This inadequate and laboured written work contrasts vividly with his ability to express his abundant ideas verbally, his diction probably being logical, crisp, restrained, concise and impressive.

A dyslexic's slowness in writing is not confined to spontaneous composition. It applies also to the mechanical task of simple copying. Furthermore the taking down of notes dictated by the teacher, or proclaimed by a lecturer, is rarely satisfactory.

Without losing sight of these fundamental handicaps occasioned by reluctant reading and writing, and slowness in both activities, let us examine a little more closely the manner of mistakes which are likely to mar the performance of a young dyslexic when he reads aloud. This is an experience which calls for more than a cursory evaluation. It requires a close and careful analysis of exactly what it is that a dyslexic utters as he struggles to surmount a reading test of increasing difficulty. His silences are as eloquent as his mistakes.

To scrutinize his performance we must keep a look out for, and make specific note of, the following:

(1) An overall slowness of performance, punctuated by hesitancies when an unfamiliar or polysyllabic word is encountered.

(2) Confusion of mirror-opposite letters. A common example is met with when the dyslexic child misreads *boy* as *dog*, or vice versa.

(3) Omission of short words like the articles, particles, conjunctions and prepositions. Grammarians speak of these as 'filler' words, 'empty', 'cementing', or 'utility' words. They are notoriously tricky. To anyone striving to learn a foreign language they present particular difficulty. Their rôle is far more abstract than the wholly concrete nouns, adjectives and verbs, and, therefore, less easy to manipulate. It is not surprising that they are stumbling blocks for a dyslexic. The apprentice reader, like everyone else, projects his gaze ahead of the word he is uttering. Sometimes he discerns a longish word—one recently learned. In his eagerness to say it aloud, he may omit the preposition or article which precedes it. Or he may misread the word as *the* instead of *a*, or *this* instead of *that*.

(4) A common fault is the pluralization of a singular noun; or, *per contra*, the omission of the plural suffix, which is usually a terminal *s*.

(5) The abbreviation of a rather lengthy word, for example, *walk* for '*walking*'; *adolsent* for *adolescent*. This commonplace defect appears when a dyslexic is struggling to read a sentence which is close to the ceiling of his performance. In a language such as German with its fantastic portmanteau words of ridiculous length, a dyslexic really comes to grief. Thus, a word such as *Strassenbahnhaltestelle* (tramstop) might take a dyslexic ten times as long to enunciate as anyone else, if indeed he were bold enough to try. Even in the schoolrooms of Italy, where it has been claimed that the language is too logical to permit dyslexia, the word *precipitevolissimevolmente* might shatter their complacency.

(6) Far less often do we find a dyslexic reader incorrectly lengthening a word, even though this type of misreading was specifically described by Charles Dickens.

(7) A minor type of error commonly made by a dyslexic, is mispronunciation. In determining the reading age, this type of fault should not be regarded as a

frank error, particularly so if the mispronunciation does not imply that the dyslexic reader fails to understand the word in question. The phenomenon of mispronunciation is most often seen when a dyslexic, in reading a rather lengthy word, puts the accent, or stress, on the wrong syllable. As, for example, when he says *miscellanous* instead of *miscellaneous*; *colloneeal* for *colonial*.

A word of caution is necessary. The mispronunciation may be the norm for the child's socioeconomic class, and not necessarily a hallmark of dyslexia. I should emphasize that I am talking about British English, where Standard, Southern, Received English is the accepted model from which deviations are evidence either of regional influences or of socioeconomic background and educational standards. In north America or Australasia it is probably quite different.

(8) Among the detectable errors one must include examples of guesswork. The word read aloud usually shares with the model the same initial letter. Common examples encountered when a child reads the Holborn Reading Scale are *officer* for *official*; *approximate* for *appropriate*; *fingers* for *fringe*.

(9) I would like to draw special attention to an unexpected type of misreading which has for some time impressed me when testing dyslexic children. This is the phenomenon whereby the reader, confronted with a word, substitutes another which is more or less synonymous although it might differ considerably in form. Thus the dyslexic might say *beer* instead of *ale*; *alive* for *healthy*; *buy* for *bought*. It is almost as though the dyslexic child had read the word silently, had interpreted it, but for some obscure reason, supplies an alternative. This type of error has occasionally been observed in adult cases of aphasia and described by the unsatisfactory term 'deep dyslexia'. When met with in cases of developmental dyslexia, I prefer to speak of the symptom as a 'narremic substitution', a 'narreme' being a unit of meaning.

(10) When the reader is approaching the limit of his reading ability, unfamiliar or longish words may be totally misread, or not attempted. We are now in sight of the dyslexic's 'reading age'.

It is often noticeable that the dyslexic reader does not recognize the error in a written or printed word which happens to be misspelt. This is particularly striking in an older age dyslexic who has achieved a certain academic maturity. Indeed the word in question is often one which he can spell with confidence, and yet the mistake perpetrated by someone else completely deceives him; a triumph of plausibility over appraisal.

The literary potential of an adult, well-educated and intelligent dyslexic forms in itself an interesting chapter for discussion, as I have undertaken elsewhere (Critchley, 1973). But worthy of mentioning here at this point is the unorthodox manner of rapid reading in such an individual. Thus, still a relatively infrequent reader, he may find it far from simple to detect and comprehend the nub or core of a lengthy, rather complicated document, especially if it is of an official character, or a paper dealing with business, legal, or technical matters. This problem naturally adds to the inherent reluctance to read at all.

May we pause for a moment to consider the movements of the eyes made by a dyslexic during the act of reading. It is the brain, of course, and not the eye which is responsible for absorbing information. But an immobile stare at the page of an open book is not enough. The gaze has to sweep from left to right, then descend to the beginning of the next line, and the lateral performance repeated. By employing one of many technical devices, it is possible to make an exact recording of the ocular movements. Not surprisingly they are usually very abnormal. A diversity of anomalies may be uncovered, according to such factors as the length of the lines, the size of the type, the content of the text and the words entailed. We begin to understand now why it is that some dyslexics read large print better than small. Other dyslexics say the diametrically opposite. It is interesting to ponder why such as a diversity occurs. Perhaps the answer ties up with another interesting clinical experience, namely that dyslexics sometimes find poetry easier to read than prose. Then there are factors of a personal nature, the age and experience of the reader, and his cultural and intellectual status.

Ocular studies take note of the number and duration of pauses (*stations de regard*), of regressions (or backward movements) of the eyes, and the length of the span encompassed by each successive lateral sweep, as well as little *mouvements inutiles*, and rapid saccadic jerks.

Years ago it was thought by some that these faulty ocular movements observed in dyslexics were responsible for the imperfect reading. This led on to a vogue for 'treating' dyslexics by protracted and costly courses of eye exercises. This topsy-turvy way of thinking grew so as to constitute something of a scandal until it was eventually rejected by opticians themselves.

At an ophthalmological congress in the United States, one forthright speaker proclaimed in unambiguous terms that

> an increasing number of parents are being bilked out of large sums of money by charlatans who have made a travesty of the eyes' role in reading. Much of this activity is centred around the phenomenon of 'eye dominance'. The belief that this can be at the root of so profound and broad a human problem as a reading or learning disability is both naive, simplistic and unsupported by scientific data.

Erratic eye-movements are the product, and not the cause, of imperfect reading.

Recently there has been a revival of interest in the subject of eye-movements while reading. In Manchester, Dr Pavlidis (1979) is currently examining this question in great detail, being impressed by the very early appearance of demonstrable faults in the tracking movements of the eyes following moving lights. He believes they may be not only of diagnostic but even of some predictive value in the setting of dyslexia. In New York, Drs Denckla, and Rudel (1976) have been intrigued by what the former terms RAN, or 'rapid automatized naming'. This is a test procedure where a child identifies and names a succession of stimuli set out horizontally before him. It was claimed that learning disabled children performed less well than others, and that developmental dyslexics fared worse still. This type of research is also currently being carried out by my wife and myself, using even more elaborate techniques of visuo-naming and elimination. Our work is still under way and it would be premature to comment on the results at this stage, except to say that the problem is far more complicated than has been realized so far. In other words, this particular chapter in the study of developmental dyslexia cannot yet be regarded as closed.

I have lingered perhaps too long upon the complexity of the reading process. I will now get off that tip of the iceberg to comment briefly upon what lies deeper. I have glossed over the fact that when the growing dyslexic puts pen to paper, which he does very unwillingly, his efforts are visibly marred by erratic and inconsistent spelling. This is a symptom which is probably never 'cured' in the strict sense of the word, so that even late in adulthood, when the dyslexic has achieved an acceptable competence in reading, his spelling is still capricious. There are many underlying explanations, but time will not permit a detailed analysis.

An ever-present handicap to a dyslexic is his weakness in visual imagery as far as letters and words are concerned, leading to shortcomings in his serial thinking and recall. This means that he cannot rapidly consult a dictionary or a telephone directory; as a filing clerk, for example, the ex-dyslexic is a failure. One shrewd adolescent patient of mine picks up the telephone and asks for 'directory enquires' rather than take the trouble to search through the bulky telephone book. His rapport with the operator eventually became so friendly that he would often consult her when he was in doubt as to how a word should be spelt. The syndrome of the cured or adolescent dyslexic is an interesting study in itself.

At this point, however, I shall make one observation which is not widely recognized by most of those who work in the field of learning disorders. I refer to the fact that there exist incomplete cases of dyslexia—dyslexia-variants. In other words, the triad of late reading, poor spelling, and inability to communicate easily on paper, does not of necessity always occur in combination.

Formes frustes of dyslexia are quite often encountered among the relatives of a person who is known to be a fully fledged dyslexic. Without an adequate knowledge of the family history, some of these atypical or incomplete variant cases are liable to be missed altogether, or their essential nature go unrecognized.

Then there is the teasing question of handedness. Ever since the work of Orton (1925), we have been aware that dyslexics not infrequently betray an infirm one-sided cerebral dominance. That is to say, they are not 100% right-handed, right-footed, right-eyed, and right-eared. For that matter, no one is, but the incidence of hemispheric ambivalence seems to be higher among dyslexics than non-dyslexics. Some enthusiasts have taken their thinking and their terminology to extremes, using the term 'crossed laterality' as though it were some malignant entity, to be obliterated at all costs if the child is to succeed in reading.

However interesting the speculation behind the matter of cerebral dominance or hemispheric compromise, one practical outcome can be affirmed. Leave matters alone, and let nature take its course. Nothing but harm and frustration will follow meddling manoeuvres and attempts to alter manual or ocular preferences.

Of far more practical importance is the question of prognosis. Some dyslexics do extremely well and attain academic distinction; at the other end of the scale, a few seem to be resistive to all attempts at remediation. Is it feasible at an early age to foretell which dyslexic child is likely to succeed, and which will not? I believe it *is* possible. My wife and I have isolated what we call a 'prognostic pentagon', comprising five favourable factors, which, in combination, augur well for the future (compare Critchley and Critchley, 1978).

(1) High intellectual calibre. Other things being equal, the higher the IQ, the more likely is the dyslexic to do well.

(2) The earlier the diagnosis is made, the better. It is better that the condition be recognized for what it is at the age of 6, rather than at 12, or 16.

(3) A sympathetic, enlightened and encouraging attitude on the part of both the parents and the teachers.

(4) The availability of skilled, sympathetic, intensive tuition, that is, individual coaching at the hands of a teacher who is trained and experienced in the modern techniques for helping dyslexics. A rapport of warmth and understanding is vital, and is rarely lacking in my experience.

(5) Lastly, and perhaps most important of all, a personality trait on the part of the patient; sheer dogged determination to succeed in mastering the difficult and boring chore of reading and spelling. This is what American psychiatrists call ego-strength; in Great Britain we prefer the simpler term 'guts'.

On the other hand, there are unfavourable indications which suggest that a dyslexic might prove recalcitrant, and unresponsive to remedial teaching. First, the existence of some or all of the *converse* of the five favourable factors. Thus we should feel uneasy in the combination of (1) a low IQ; (2) a belated recognition of the true nature of the scholastic non-achievement; (3) lack of sympathetic understanding on the part of teachers and parents; (4) non-availability of skilled, qualified, remedial teachers; and (5) lack of motivation in the dyslexic, an attitude of despair or of submission to the inevitable.

In addition there are some environmental circumstances which must be rated not as causal but as unpropitious. They include:

(1) A polyglot or even bilingual background.

(2) Inconsistent schooling, owing usually to the parents being uprooted due to the father's profession.

(3) Absenteeism because of, for example, serious illness or frequently recurring ill-health.

(4) Inadequate techniques of teaching. I write with diffidence about this, being only a doctor. But I believe I have good reason to deplore the early employment of 'Look and Say' techniques, or i.t.a. These unorthodox methods of teaching reading may not hamper the child who is naturally a good reader, but they retard the progress of a dyslexic.

(5) Lastly, and as a doctor, I can assert that a dyslexic's progress is impeded if his general health is unsatisfactory. The sickly child who is chronically anaemic, or a prey to frequent allergies and infections, laid low by migrainous headaches, is working against an ever-present handicap. And yet as a medical man I never cease to wonder at the sheer resilience which youngsters show in the face of batterings of both physical ill-health and mental stress.

My remarks have been confined to diagnosis because I am not an educationalist, but I firmly believe that the rational remedy of developmental dyslexia is not psychotherapeutic nor optometric, but educational, and entails the early and judicious employment of intensive techniques on a one-to-one basis at the hands of a patient, sympathetic, and highly qualified teacher experienced in helping dyslexic children.

As with many other disorders and handicaps in the developing child, the door is wide open for false prophets, purveyors of fringe medicine, riders of remedial hobbyhorses, and practitioners who are either mad or bad or even perhaps a touch of both. It is a lush Tom Tiddler's ground, ripe and ready for drastic prescriptions and still more drastic proscriptions; curious dietetic regimes and fantastic exercises. Occasionally, benefit seems to accure, but for all too short a time. It is what is called the 'Hawthorne effect', that is, a temporary betterment often, alas, ill-sustained, due to the fact that attention has at long last become focused upon the child's handicap. It was found at the Hawthorne works (Roethlisberger and Dickson, 1939) that increased work-output on the given task can for a while follow any change in environmental conditions irrespective of the *type* of change.

Years ago Herbert Spencer proclaimed that human opinion passes through three phases, 'The unanimity of the ignorant, the disagreement of the inquiring, and the unanimity of the wise. It is manifest that the second is the parent of the third.' One likes to think that today we are witnessing the steady maturation of this grandchild.

REFERENCES

Critchley, M. (1973) Some problems of the ex-dyslexic. *Bull. Orton Soc.*, **23**, 7–14.

Critchley, M. and Critchley, E. A. (1978) *Dyslexia Defined.* London: Heinemann Medical Books Ltd.

Denckla, M. B. and Rudel, R. G. (1976) 'Rapid automatized naming' (RAN): dyslexia differentiated from other learning disabilities. *Neuropsychologia*, **14**, 471–479.

Department of Education and Science (The Bullock Report). (1975) *A Language for Life.* London; HMSO.

Orton, S. T. (1925) World-blindness in school children. *Arch. Neur. Psychiat*, **14**, 581–615.

Pavlidis, G. Th. (1979) How can dyslexia be objectively diagnosed? *Reading*, **13**(3), 3–15.

Roethlisberger, F. J. and Dickson, W. J. (1939) *Management and the Worker.* Cambridge, Mass.: Harvard Press.

Dyslexia Research and its Applications to Education
Edited by G. Th. Pavlidis and T. R. Miles
© 1981 John Wiley & Sons Ltd.

CHAPTER 2

A Diversity Model for Dyslexia

Margaret B. Rawson

How shall we look upon the phenomena we group as dyslexia? What is the human significance of this condition? Is it 'real'? How can we obey the injunction, 'Define your terms'? Before we ask what the word really means, perhaps we should ask what it means to be a word. Where do any words come from and how do they get their meanings? Let us follow the life history of Jimmy's word '*d'b'm*', for it is typical of the basic process.

One september, many years ago, when Jimmy had just rounded his first birthday, he was beginning to find, usually to coin, one-word labels for the experiences he was identifying. Oscar's friendly collie made overtures and produced a joyous, 'd'b'm!' Then, as the family started on a long car journey Jimmy recognized, named and waved a farewell to, 'D'b'm', so the parents knew the boy had a new word. On the trip, every dog, cat, cow, horse and sheep, and a small host's white mouse, was excitedly identified by the now inclusive common noun as a 'd'b'm'. As the weeks wore on, all living creatures, every stuffed toy and even a strip of fur ('big, 'ong d'b'm') joined the category. Clearly the experiences were specific but the concept was open-ended, the boundaries loosely defined. Santa brought a teddy-bear, taken to the heart as '*I* [*my own*] d'b'm!' Gradually specific words, *horse*, etc., replaced the general term, but 'D'b'm' remained for years the proper name of the beloved bear-companion. Then, one night when Jim was eight he said firmly, 'Put that bear away. I don't need him anymore, and besides, his name's not D'b'm', either!' Years later, the old friend was retrieved with pleasant memories, and Jim provided each of his children with a d'b'm to love. And so a word was born a label, became a consciousness-filling concept, was refined by definition, made personal and emotionally significant and moved into the background of consciousness where it was available to memory and for cultural transmission.

Observation suggests that this is an elemental pattern for the acquisition of interrelated words and concepts, progressing from the unknown and hence non-conscious to recognized globality, to the definition of embedded related

13

specificities, and finally to assimilation into the personal linguistic matrix, once more out of conscious awareness but now available on triggered demand for memory and the mind's creative or personal and social uses. (For a mentally stimulating analysis of this kind of 'holographic' provocation of thought through language, see Pribram, 1971, p. 370.)

The growth of an abstract concept like 'dyslexia' and its symbolic formulation is similar but more complex. Its way into assimilation by both individuals and societies may be rapid and easy or beset with obstacles to understanding and acceptance. First one has many experiences, large and small, personal and distant, significant to one's self and casual, specific and ill-defined. They are not thought of as related. If we bother to explain them, each may be from a world more or less its own. Some have names, like 'stubbornness', some do not; some are loosely grouped with others, like 'reading and spelling failure', while some are thought of as individual 'quirks', like being confused by 'turn right' (directional) but not by 'make a right turn' (a physical manoeuvre). Something in our own lives or someone else's puzzling problem, like 'Peter's five-year failure to learn to read', may be instrumental in bringing a new term into our awareness and leading us to relate many hitherto unrelated phenomena. A further result may be the taking of a new vocational direction by the individual or the development of something new in the scientific, technological or therapeutic spheres, with an open-ended future of possibilities.

There are two contrasting tendencies in people's initial reaction to new terms: to accept and go along with them, or to reject and deny them. These start chain reactions in other people, who may want to be 'open-minded' but not to 'get carried away', to hunt for categorical solutions or to be made uneasy by change, and to react, as a habit, simplistically to the words themselves. Upon reflection, however, one realizes that what is important is not so much what one says as what one means by one's words and what meanings they have to the person who hears them. Just now we are trying to get away from the effects of tying 'badness' labels to groups of people either by denying that individuals can be grouped at all or by changing the labels to others that are benign or neutral.

Whatever our motives, neither extreme course will be likely to have a useful outcome. If we refuse to categorize, we may miss the essential point of understanding and helping, by becoming sentimentally confused about our students' or clients' needs and our responsibilities or, on the other hand, by being overwhelmed by the complexities and giving up or applying shotgun remedies. In the second case—the changing of labels—since there has been no fundamental reorientation toward the labelled persons, the speaker (who favours them) may be trying to mollify the hearer's attitudes, while the listener, if he accepts the new term at all, merely shifts his language while retaining his old opinions and feelings about the subject and the persons. The new term soon becomes as objectionable as the old; the change is in the wrong place—the word rather than the mind.

Dyslexia, like the 40 or so terms related to it, has in many places been involved in such semantic confusions (Rawson, 1978). Most definitional arguments avail little to improve life for the learners affected. It is true that the etymology of this Greek term, dyslexia (initially used by Berlin in 1887 and discussed by Thompson in 1966, and others), points to an entity, a syndrome or an area of meaning: *dys* (poor or inadequate) and *lexis* (language, as words, related to speech and to lexicon). Or, as 10-year-old Alfred put it to me, 'I can think OK, but what's wrong is my words. I forget them and I can't manage them.'

The 'humane' and 'informed' thing to do just now is to call Alfred a 'language-different child'. In a sense, he is just that. His problem is not general, for his physical and intellectual equipment and his general maturity are 'within the normal range'; his emotional state and his social and cultural background are 'unremarkable'. The range of advantageous and disadvantageous factors which go to make up the unique Alfred would not make him stand out among 10-year-old American boys. Only, and specifically, in his encounters with his mother tongue is he clearly distinguishable as 'different'. We may properly call him 'dyslexic'—he has so described himself. His history (see Rawson, 1972) makes 'developmental dyslexia' appropriate and more than suggests the constitutional nature and familial, probably genetic, origin of this aspect of his makeup.

He is in trouble with language learning because he is 'different'. This is obviously true, but what is different about him and from whom does he differ? Is he unique in these respects or is he part of a group? Is this a large or a small part of the human race? Do all its members differ in the same ways and to the same degrees from the rest of humanity and from each other? Does 'different' mean 'deficient', 'damaged' or 'defective'? Always, sometimes, never? Can similar signs point to different differences? Is it important whether we substitute 'language–learning–different' for 'dyslexic' or for the (by our criteria) non-synonymous term 'learning disabled'? What differences will ensue in our attitudes towards the *subject matter* and the *subject persons*—our understanding and treatment of them? What changes of fundamental attitudes are involved and, finally, what difference does it all make?

In the first place, when we say a person is 'different' we need to ask 'from whom, and who is saying so?' Is the word used simply descriptively or denotatively, as we recognize that all persons (even, in minor ways, identical twins) are unique? To this we readily agree, while we also agree that people can be grouped in terms of certain characteristics or patterns of characteristics. It is in this sense that many of us have no semantic discomfort in saying that the problems we name 'dyslexia' are real, and experienced by real people we handily call dyslexic. So considered, especially in our modern, literate world, dyslexia is certainly 'real'. If you doubt it, ask the person who has these characteristics. So the Alfreds are different in their makeup and needs from people who pick up language skills without apparent effort or can be taught them relatively easily by teachers who themselves were in most cases facile language learners. For most such teachers and the linguistically successfully opinion-framers generally, to be different from themselves is a 'deviance from the norm'. Such a deviance, if not reprehensible or indicative of inferiority, is at least unfortunate and should be 'remediated' by especially effortful and skilful teaching (no quarrel with that!), using 'sound educational principles'—and directed by 'sound' school principals!

This is entirely understandable. For instance, fish and cetaceans (whales and dolphins) are equally skilful in getting about and supporting themselves in the sea. One might imagine the tuna, the mackerel and the perch looking on the minority, whale-like, species as somehow deficient because they must surface periodically to—'what is it they do up there? breathe?' Perhaps with instruction, determination and practice they could become independent of surfacing and live like 'real fish'. They are different from fish, all right, and disadvantaged if circumstances require that they stay too long submerged—as any whaler could testify. On the other hand, from the whale–dolphin viewpoint, it is the fish who are different, at a disadvantage above water, and deprived of the joys of breathing air and enjoying activities and experiences that the two-world life makes possible. If either part of the sea population were in charge of the basic or remedial education of the other, 'different', meaning 'deviant', could lead not to 'correction of an oxygen intake problem' but to ecological disaster. Or we could vary the analogy by thinking of dolphins as less like fish than like men with a constitutional walking disability, or men as like dolphins whose writing is superior but whose swimming is rudimentary. It is enough to note that innate differences do make a difference in how one learns to live in the world!

Historically speaking, in America it was Dr. Samuel T. Orton (1925) who first gathered together the threads from the past (Kerr, 1897; Morgan, 1896; Hinshelwood, 1896; fragmentary case histories), and the findings of neurologists and psychologists up to the mid-1920's (see Thompson, 1966; and Critchley and Critchley, 1978, *inter alia*). Orton integrated these findings with his own clinical and laboratory experience, with his theoretical analyses and with his physician's commitment to helping his patients. He formulated hypotheses as to causes, devised treatment strategy, enlisted associates and students, refined and tested his own diagnostic and educational knowledge, presented his formulations, and encouraged colleagues and successors, with full recognition of their areas of superior competence. This began a multidisciplinary collaboration and a field of professional specialization. Work was carried on in several independent schools and clinics, and in private practices, continuing steadily, although on a numerically small scale, from 1925 until Orton's death in 1948. His medical and pedagogical successors, notably his wife, June L. Orton, several medical associates including Paul Dozier, and that scholarly, practical team Anna Gillingham (psychologist), and Bessie Stillman (teacher), and others, continued and developed his already successful approaches to diagnosis and treatment. They worked out materials, refined procedures, taught teachers, and, in 1949, founded the Orton Society (see, for instance, Childs, 1969; Cox, 1974; J. L. Orton, 1966, 1973; Rome and Osman, 1972; Slingerland, 1971).

The Orton Society was alone in its field and is still, in the United States, the only open-membership, largely professional association devoted exclusively to the problems of language learning disorders. It has provided a confluence point for the several concerned professions, and through its activities, journals and other publications it has exerted influence far beyond its relatively small but growing membership. Other, much larger, agencies—the Association for Children with Learning Disabilities, the Council for Exceptional Children and the International Reading Association, especially—have recently been giving increasing attention to dyslexia, by one name or another, although their major commitments lie elsewhere. There is, happily, a growing tendency to transcend barriers in the common interest of services to children.

Early treatment efforts were primarily centred on remedial education of school-age children and were, as we have said, carried on in independent (that is, private) schools or by tutors or therapists working alone or in non-public facilities. More recently, there has been increasing concern with young children's development of the listening and speech components of the basic language continuum. Early screening and preventive teaching of vulnerable children is becoming less rare. More public (state supported) schools have classroom and individual programmes than was the case, say, a dozen years ago, but the coverage is spotty in both availability and excellence. Recently enacted federal laws make mandatory the provision of 'free public education' for every child in accordance with his needs, but the administrative and pedagogical resources of the schools are not yet anywhere near ready to meet the laws' demands. Still, 'dyslexia' is now specifically designated as one of the recognized areas requiring the deployment of educational resources. The United States is a large and pluralistic society with a high degree of autonomy in its educational structures; it is far less easy to secure near-universality of provisions here than in smaller, more homogeneous societies.

Since both language and the difficulties of its learning are universal, whatever the differences in specific languages, it is not surprising to find both understanding and action running parallel courses in several languages and cultures. There comes to mind the work of several authorities: in Czechoslovakia, from Heveroch (1904) to Matějček (1977); in Denmark, of Hermann (1959) and Norrie (1939; in England, of Critchley (1975) and Critchley and Critchley (1978), and many others including contributors to this volume; of Bakker (1972) in the Netherlands, and Smelt (1976) in Australia; and so on. One group focuses on one 'hot spot' in the field, while others take hold elsewhere, each seeing or relating especially to what he or she has experienced as important, 'true' or significantly troubling, but with much in common. It would, of course, be surprising if this were not true, man and language being what they are. And yet, it is taking a long time for these similarities to emerge in the face of variations in the disciplinary, rather than the national, modes of thought. The neurologist, the psychologist, the linguist, the psychiatrist, the educator and each of the many others who share interest in the problem may or may not be aware of the interrelatedness of the phenomena and disciplines involved. Despite the variations resulting from their several world views and fields of practice, each has had to come to grips with the learning of his own language and the necessity of his country's children to do so. With the widening and deepening of experience and study, the fundamental unity of the human predicament and its solution must become more apparent. It is not that the differences often felt so strongly, are 'merely semantic', although semantic they truly are in part, nor that there is 'one true answer' nor certainly a simplistic one.

Take, for example, those proverbial blind men and their elephant. Each man was sure he 'knew' the whole animal, extrapolating from the part he felt. 'It's a rope' (the tail); 'No, a moving tree trunk' (the leg); 'A leathery wall' (the side); 'A big leaf' (the ear); 'A hard, smooth prong' (the tusk); 'You are *all* wrong! It's a writhing boaconstrictor,' said the sixth man as he was lifted from his feet by the trunk. Each of us has a part of that ponderous pachyderm to feel, to feed, to groom or train, and to name in his or her working model, but if we share our world views we can talk together better about the whole.

Although I speak most securely about the English language and its American users and learners, I believe that what is said here applies to a much broader world.

Certain facts may be accepted as almost axiomatic. Symbolic, verbal language and verbal thinking as major components of cultural interchange and transmission are an almost distinctively human capability. Spoken languages have been developed in every human society. Language is potential in each new human being, but it is not instinctive; it must be learned and is taught, however informally, by the culture which surrounds the child. Language is phylogenetically late in the development of the race, and ontogenetically perhaps the last characteristic to be established in the growing individual, the specific neural myelinization on which it depends being the fast myelinization to occur in the child. Written or graphic language has come about even later in the development of the race and the individual, and literacy is not universal, either on the globe or within those cultures which have written language. In evolution, it seems, the later and the more complicated the function involved, the greater the variation in its degree of perfection, its universality in the species and the individual facility in its achievement, as for example in the acquisition of language skills. And yet, given appropriate circumstances, the basic potentiality, at least in language, is there to be developed.

There is, and as far as we know always has been, wide individual variation in language learning and use, as there has been in the learning and practice of any other skill. Some of these differences have been the results of history and opportunity; the swineherd, the vintner, the tailor, the sailor, the warrior and the prince are among the not necessarily language-facile cases in point. Of old, if a person lacked aptitude or opportunity in one field, many others were available.

Increasingly, however, the openings in the modern technological world require not only the verbal or visual memory which sufficed for the bard or the steward but also literacy, so that aptitude for learning the skills of written language has become more and more critical. It is not enough to have spatial, mechanical, practical or social skills; one must also use the media of language from moderately well to maximally if one is to avoid the failure, frustration and despair resulting in and from one's unused, unusable potential in almost all spheres of life. It is said (Saunders, 1977) that in the United States already about 85% of occupations require some degree of literacy, and the percentage is rising. If someone should say, 'Well, he can at least dig ditches', the speaker's next assignment should be a few minutes watching a mechanical back-hoe and tamper. The neglected illiterate, be he dyslexic or simply unschooled, is almost sure to be at a crushing disadvantage in any society dependent on tools or machines and the print one needs to cope with them.

An initial question about language almost always concerns the prevalence of its hampering disorders. How many dyslexics are there? The answers vary from country to country to some extent, but much more from respondent to respondent. A range of incidence estimates from about 3% to 25% or more suggests that not everyone is talking about the same thing or people, or is equally well informed, and perhaps *nobody* knows just what he himself is talking about. Figures at the low end of the estimates are those we expect in the case of a defect or disability, such as mental retardation, hearing loss, epilepsy and the like, but language learning problems make trouble for more people than that, As a conservative estimate, experienced teachers and large-scale surveys put the fraction of those in major scholastic difficulty at 10% to 15% in English, Danish and some other language communities. Numbers seem somewhat lower where sounds and symbols are more simply related as, for instance, in Czech or Spanish. Nobody is sure of these figures, and some place them much higher, especially in certain disadvantaged populations. My own experience suggests that the better we get to know language-based phenomena and the more discriminatingly we observe language behaviour, the larger becomes the percentage of those having trouble, with, it seems, almost everybody doing now and then what dyslexics do commonly and with failure-inducing results. With data of this kind, perhaps the preponderance of cases can more acceptably be explained as showing normal constitutional variations in the evolutionarily 'unfinished' human race. *The differences are real; make no mistake about that!* When not understood and not properly provided for, they make for serious difficulties which can lead to disabilities, even to disaster. At the 'severe' end of the line a clear diagnosis of specific language disability is quite in order, but still with prognostic optimism. Even when they are not cripplingly severe, the problems may interfere tellingly with enthusiasm for securing full educational, professional and personal development. Distaste for school, a sense of inadequacy, and early discontinuance of study are common. On the other hand, if appropriately dealt with the difficulties can be challenges to be surmounted, and can undergird the achievement of diversity and its enrichment of our cultures. Masland (1976), discussing this kind of diversity, spoke of, 'The potential advantages of being the kind of person who might have difficulty learning to read'.

There are, of course, other types of language learning difficulty which look very like the several 'syndromes of specific dyslexia' (Klasen, 1972; Rawson, 1978). They have appeared in the clinic and the literature since the nineteenth century, often inextricably mixed into the general problem population. It may take considerable neurological sophistication to identify true brain damage. Often, too, the treatment is the same as for the extreme dyslexic, though slower progress and less complete alleviation are likely. In known or unknown ways, the 'head count' of these people has, as we say, 'thickened' or 'enriched' the low end of the incidence curve. The patients are there for different reasons but unknowingly help one another. Aphasias of traumatic origin helped Orton and his successors to bring together patterns of language disorders which led to recognizing *developmental* delays and dissonances which he characterized with strong conviction as normal variations of neurophysiological functioning. So, too, with the study of victims of birth injury, endocrine or organic brain malfunction and other conditions, the insights gained from the pathologically based disorders help to define normal variations. The prognoses may differ, but the treatment plans are often mutually suggestive.

When all is said and done, however, we can allocate each language learner to a part of what we might call the 'lexis continuum'. At one end are the 'eulexics', those to whom the mastery of words (*lexis*) comes well (*eu*) and readily. At the other end are the ones whose language is poor or inadequate (*dys*), and learned with difficulty, the 'dyslexics'. On a language learning facility scale those who are specifically dyslexic may be at the low end because of extreme difficulty with one type of language skills, say auditory, visual, kinaesthetic, or with intermodal organization. Alternatively, less severe problems in two or several modalities, not in themselves too hampering, may add up to a major, temporarily insurmountable, roadblock. Again, secondary, concurrent difficulties—intellectual, emotional, physical or environmental—may interact with language learning ineptitudes, each intensifying the others in a baffling entanglement. If the language problem is a significant feature in the complex, we may call the person dyslexic, but whatever the diagnostic judgement, attention to language skills is often the most productive place to start untying the knot which holds him in its grip.

If it is part of a continuum with ill-defined points of limitation, can we think of and treat dyslexia as an entity, a diagnosable condition? Money's (1962) medically phrased statement is clarifying:

> It is not at all rare in psychological medicine, nor in other branches of medicine, that a disease should have no unique identifying sign, that

uniqueness being in the pattern of signs that appear in contiguity. Out of context, each sign might also be encountered in other diseases, or, in different intensities, in the healthy. Specific dyslexia is no exception in this respect. A good example of this is the matter of reversals and translocation of letters . . . . Thus, it appears that the diagnosis of specific dyslexia will continue not to depend on a single tell-tale sign, or signs, but on the clinical appraisal of the whole configuration of symptoms and test findings.

Using this criterion, and after experience with my own hundreds and my colleagues' thousands of patients and students, I feel confident in holding dyslexia to be both real and diagnostically identifiable. The surest and most productive diagnosis is still individual and clinical, but simple identification can often be quick and reliable. One need only ask, 'Are his language learning skills, by test or school achievement, disproportionately lower than his apparent intelligence and other learning, the degree of his physical intactness, his environmental opportunities and his reasonable aspirations?' Such a degree of disparity calls for therapeutic intervention.

Between the optimum and the rule-of thumb in diagnostic procedures one makes what compromises one must, with the ideal in mind but not waiting for perfection at the cost of getting to work helping the student. In general, expert diagnosis facilitates treatment; the more expert the diagnostician and the available teacher the less elaborate need be the initial testing and the more reliance can be placed on the clinical judgement of diagnostician and therapist.

With the more severely dyslexic individual the assessment often seems unequivocal, unless there is a question of the primacy of some secondary or concurrent cause of learning disorder or deficiency. But what of those with less severe problems, those who stand higher on the language facility scale? How far up the curve shall we draw the line of diagnostic categorization? When is a difference nameable and when is it 'just diversity'? The answer seems to me to call for the flexibility of open-ended judgement. As with any other complex and relatively independent trait or phenomenon, most instances lie between the extremes. Unless it is a matter for true dichotomy (one cannot be moderately pregnant, for example!), the distribution tends to be describable by a bell-shaped curve, perhaps somewhat skewed. Language learning seems to be a case in point.

This is one place (treatment is another) where it seems to me that viewing dyslexia as a normal, expectable variation in the human condition makes a positively productive difference. Accordingly, a shift from a deviance, or even a difference, model to one emphasizing diversity and normal variation seems in order. Orton recommended this in the 1920s, but it has been hard to keep it in mind as a guiding principle when the urge to classification is strong.

Let us say that everyone is 'lexic'—a language learner (since he or she is not born skilled), a language user (by reason of being human), and part of a society or culture. However gifted, he is still part of that unfinished species, *homo sapiens*. He may be a silver-tongued orator with a phenomenal verbal memory, or a fluent reader with generally perfect spelling and multilingual understanding, but under stress, or perhaps as a personal idiosyncrasy, he may make some errors characteristic of his equally brilliant dyslexic companions. Is he being, or acting, 'dyslexic'? Or he may have a particular *bête noir*, say a tendency to frequent speech reversals, Spoonerisms like *cashing the greats* (instead of *crashing the gates*) or saying '*Segundheit!*' (when his sneezing friend might expect '*Gesundheit!*'). Perhaps his penmanship is laboured, with legibility rivalling his doctor's prescriptions. Is he, then, 'one of those dyslexics'? When do we call his language by some categorical name? Is it reprehensible, or pitiable, or a somewhat endearing personal quirk which may sometimes be a nuisance? Does he need corrective treatment, understanding sympathy, a bit of mirth, polite ignoring, or a touch of self-knowledge which can improve his insight into his blood brotherhood with a 'true' or 'more' dyslexic fellow man? Does he 'have it' and is 'it' a problem?

Perhaps the answer is that it *is* a problem when it *makes* a problem for *him*, subjectively or practically or both. The 140 IQ medical student who is flunking out because of his spelling and his confusion in taking written tests does have a problem which may prevent him from becoming the gifted surgeon to which future his other aptitudes point. He may need to have dyslexia explained to him, to his dean and to his professors, who may then see their way to making adjustments in his examination conditions so they will know they are testing his knowledge of subject matter, not his writing skill and speed. He may find it profitable to take some time out for intensive skill-improvement tutoring.

The driver of 20-ton trailer truck with the same language aptitude pattern may say he 'couldn't care less', though he has to read road and mechanical information and somehow produce adequate logs for his boss. He and the medical student, however, would be relieved to know, whatever they do about it, that this is something real which can be understood and is no reflection on their intelligence, character, stability or potential as roadmaster or surgeon. If the two men share a 'failing', this, as well as their mechanical, spatial superiority, is another common characteristic of their brotherhood in valuable human diversity. They are the people whom Masland was referring to in his statement quoted above. They can say, 'Some of us are wired up that way. Nothing wrong with that! What, if anything, we need to do about it depends on where we're headed.' Demonstrably true and good for the ego, it makes a *real* difference when we cast our thinking in these terms.

Using the medical-model parlance, we have said, 'The diagnosis is clinical; the treatment is educational', not 'cure' but rather a way of learning and living matched to the individual's whole personal configuration, with all its internal variables and its time-and-space singularities. We plan our strategy and tactics, we say, to 'teach the language as it is to the person as he is', and if we do it well it will be effective and lasting. Let us see what this means, what is our base of operations and what is our practice.

First 'the language as it is', whichever one it is. Each language, be it oriental or occidental, however it be organized, spoken or written, and so forth, has system and order as part of its nature. A set of constraints is necessary for its use, is known by its users and is transmitted to their juniors and to others who join their language community. Teachers of any language must, in some usable sense, 'know' that language, whether this knowledge be conscious or not. Its transmission may be deliberate or it may be casual—apparent only to a somewhat detached observer, a learning that 'happens' as part of the new generation's experiential acquisition of his culture.

The capacity to learn language is part of the inheritance of the human species, but it is the cultural setting which determines the specific language which will be, literally, the mother tongue of each new individual. Those who pass it on to him, whatever their methods of teaching, have made part of themselves the sounds and speech patterns of their language, its grammar and syntax, its vocabulary and semantic forms of expression. If it has a written form, there is also the graphic system to teach and to learn a bit later in childhood, with the interrelationships of the written code to the basic spoken language. To be a competent teacher, one must know 'the language as it is'.

One must also know one's pupil, 'the person as he is' of the formula. In what ways can be learn best? This depends on his nature as a human being and his constitution and history as an individual.

One of the seeming paradoxes of life is that human beings are all alike and also all different. The structure and functions of the central nervous system provide a constant, generally dependable frame of reference and mode of operation for all of us, a manageable, describable organization. We learn as human beings, not as amoebas, aardvarks, or even apes, much as we have in common with each of them. But individual persons are the resultants of so many and such complex constituents that each is unique. Each combines hereditary traits, inherent developmental patterns and responses to environmental stimuli, making almost infinite diversity of outcomes inevitable, yet still within the limitations of the species. This diversity is of adaptive and creative value to the person, the culture and the race. It should be cherished as a resource; hence the value of the 'diversity model' for education as a whole and for language learning in particular.

But diversity is most useful if understood and, at least in some respects channelled, not rigidly, but with enough organization to make its creative potential adaptively available. Part of knowing the individual learner as he is, in the light of the understandings of the 1970s, presumably the 1980s, requires consideration of the right and left brain hemisphere cortical functions and their interactions, specifically with respect to the language function and its development.

Samuel T. Orton, following his neurological forebears as far as the knowledge and technology of his time permitted, proposed and validated hypotheses which are still exerting seminal influence. The recent advances in brain science and their applications to education are consonant with these earlier formulations and are important extensions and additions to them.

The nature of the language-dominant (usually the left) hemisphere is being further explored and elaborated. Its ways of dealing with life as rational, sequential, linguistic, analytical and the controller of verbally mediated consciousness are easily comprehensible, because that is the kind of person each of us recognizes himself or herself as being. We tap into, use and educate these aspects of life through the medium of verbal language.

The language function as centred in the left hemisphere is summarized in Figures 2.1 and 2.2; the accompanying text is taken from Rawson (1975):

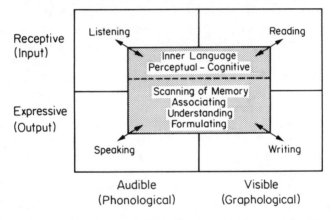

Figure 2.1. Analysis of verbal language (after Rawson, 1968). Reproduced by permission of York Press Inc.

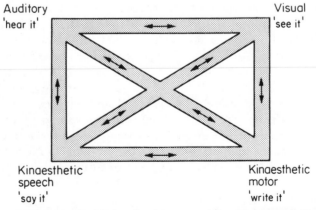

Figure 2.2. Sensory associations in language learning (after Wolff, 1970). Reproduced by permission of York Press Inc.

There is order and plan in every child's acquisition of verbal language. The diagram [Figure 2.1] shows its fractions and their complex interactions. On the left are the audible or phonological components, the basic language of listening and speech, common in some tongue to every known culture. Spoken language is first to develop and almost inevitable in each child's life. On the right of the scheme are the visible or graphological components, reading and writing. These are taught and learned later, at what we call 'school age', in literate cultures, and often they are mastered with difficulty. Cut the other way, the diagram shows, above, the receptive or input language (listening and reading) and, below, the expressive or output language (speaking and writing). All of these fractions interact continuously, as indicated by the arrows, through the mediation of the perceptual and cognitive processes of inner language, which go on inside the brain. . . . [Figure 2.2] modified from one originated in England by Agnes Wolff [Wolff, 1970], shows the multisensory intersensory linkages for learning of the language modalities. If we superimpose it upon [Figure 2.1], it is easy to see how well the two models fit each other—language, and its learning.

The positive functional specialization of the other (usually the right) hemisphere was only guessed at in Orton's time but has recently come most illuminatingly to the fore. Only in the past twenty years or so (see Benton, 1965, and his sources: Sperry, 1974; Pribram, 1971) has this 'other' hemisphere emerged from its former role as the subordinate, somewhat mysterious, 'silent partner' which was known to have some alternative or residual language potential and suspected of often intruding this activity confusingly into consciousness, especially among dyslexics. With its emergence has come an identifiable home for those abilities which we call spatial, global, synthesizing and in many ways artistically creative. Still mysterious, and at least presently fundamentally inexplicable, as is all work of the mind, this kind of function is no longer to be vaguely ascribed to inspiration of unknown origin. The right hemisphere provides, if not the fully understood source, at least the primary instrument, as the left hemisphere does for the most part in the area of verbal language.

It has been suggested to me by Edith Gollan (1979) that the apparent recent increase in language learning difficulties may in part be real, and explainable in terms of hemispheric differentiation. We, in the dyslexia field, have generally pointed to the increased necessity for literacy in the modern world, to the practice of compulsory academic education of children in many countries, and to the egalitarian ideal of potential upward social mobility for everyone. People both expect and demand more success in education; the public is more aware of the phenomenon of dyslexia; and we are somewhat more ready to believe that where there is a problem a solution can be found. All these are valid observations still, I believe, but Gollan's new component enriches the explanation.

Language learning, she reiterates, requires automatic linear sequencing of symbols which are learned, patterned, and dependent on conscious analysis and ordered structure—a left hemisphere activity par excellence. Such learning was the backbone of a great deal of home and school teaching of the past. In contrast, consider how different is the world of the modern child. He is bombared by tonality—and atonality—from the air and, especially, by the rapid succession of 'total experiences' of television, often more continuous than sequential, beginning in his prelinguistic infancy. Perhaps he is being 'right hemisphere stimulated' to a high degree and so, unless his left hemisphere aptitudes are strong, he finds their cultivation less comfortable than the spatial, holistic modes. Moreover, he may be more confused by the welter of his experiences and the problem of coordinating them with one another than were his elders in sensorially simpler times. In either case, he may be one who finds the world of words less assimilable and manageable and thus may be more likely to be characterized as dyslexic. It is a challenging idea.

As Whittrock (1978) emphasizes, '. . . the cortical hemispheres overlap greatly. . . . No dichotomy of function does justice to the sophistication and complexity of the human brain.' And so we have still not completed the picture, for man as a living system functions as a dynamic whole. To walk, for instance, he needs both legs, and the component parts of each one, working in synchrony. To grow, to think, to act, and to *be* he needs both of his asymmetrically specialized brain hemispheres to be developed individually and coordinated in their functioning through the instrumentalities of neural networks and action systems and across the corpus callosum. His education as a person should nourish the whole in whatever ways each part requires. Pribram (1971) summarizes the ways man uses language, and hence must learn to use it, in these terms, ' . . . as a tool to accomplish his purposes. . . [that is] to express his existence . . . to obtain information from or to achieve control over his environment . . . to explore and achieve control over his World Within' in which service 'it becomes thought'. Further discussing thought, he says, 'My hypothesis is that *all* thought has, in addition to sign and symbol manipulation, a holographic component. Holographic representations, in which the whole is contained in each of its fragments, are, he says, 'the catalysts of thought', being the associative mechanisms which perform the cross-correlations so available in instantaneous memory and creative recombination of ideas.

As the person develops throughout life, he needs to acquire knowledge, the raw materials of thought, action and creativity, and to develop skills with which to implement his knowledge. Each is a necessary, but neither alone is a sufficient, condition of human fulfilment. Leonardo da Vinci worked diligently to learn anatomy, mechanics and the skills of painting to use in the service of his inspirations and his notebook formulations of theory. Both elements and their mutuality were needed to produce the 'bi-hemispheric' genius that was Leonardo. In modern education, too, we hear much about the 'whole child' and specifically of late about 'educating both hemispheres of the brain'. We know empirically from the experience of generations that this 'whole child' emphasis brings rewarding results with all children, whatever their special needs, and we forget its implications at both the youngsters' cost and our own.

Within the population the person we recognize as generally dyslexic or as having marked dyslexic subtraits is often (though not always) gifted in 'right-hemisphere' aptitudes. He may (but may not) be strong in the use of basic, spoken language and in linguistic thinking. To serve his other aptitudes in all areas, he needs language *skills* which depend heavily on the organized sequential memory and processing of linguistic symbols, primarily a left-hemisphere attribute. This need has been abundantly spelled out by many writers, but no one has yet, I think, said it better than did Samuel T. Orton in 1937: ' . . . the process of reading is a . . . complex activity requiring the physiological integrity and interplay of many brain areas although the angular gyrus and its adjacent cortex in the dominant hemisphere still bear a critical relation to this function. . . ' .

The naturally facile language learner picks up these skills with only moderate effort, but it is the hallmark of the dyslexic that in several or a crucial few ways he cannot do so without specific, often highly skilled teaching. This need for organization, ordering and overlearning on the part of the student determines the approach to instruction for skill development. For the dyslexic the teaching seems most effective when it is structured, systematic, sequential, cumulative, thorough, multisensory and appeals to the intellect as a guide to comprehension in practice. A supportive therapeutic climate and programme flexibility adapted to individual needs should permeate the whole, whatever the language or culture (Dr Lucius Waites, 1966).

For users of English (as well, doubtless, as of other languages with which I am less familiar) many people have applied these principles and written well about them, especially since 1925, the year of Orton's landmark first paper on the subject. Monroe (1932), Gillingham and Stillman (1956, 1960), and others were soon at work with him, but their effectiveness has been due in considerable part to Orton's treatment directives, which still read with a convincing modernity. His summary statement, published in 1937, reads as follows:

> Our experiences in teaching reading to those children who have suffered from a delay or defect in learning this subject have pointed to the importance of sequence building in such cases and in our experiments in the other syndromes this has led us to look for such units as the child can use without difficulty in the field of his particular disability and to direct our training toward developing the process of fusing these smaller, available units into larger and more complex wholes.

In practice, this dictates concentration on the speech sounds (in English about 44 phonemes) and the symbols by which they are represented (in English 26 alphabetic letters singly and in a few graphemic groupings). The student blends units together for reading and analyses words into their components for spelling and writing. The load on his unreliable memory is thus reduced to a minimum, while his reliance on the system and its employment utilizes his relatively strong intelligence. These two practices make it possible for him to retrieve forgotten words or work out still unfamiliar ones. Since he can now 'afford to forget', his reduced anxiety actually facilitates his memory, and with practice promotes, as a highly desirable accompaniment, an increasing degree of automaticity and fluency.

One of the most crucial aspects of this approach is its reliance on simultaneous multisensory reinforcement in learning, as shown in Figure 2.2. Sight hearing and the muscular awareness of speech and the hand in writing are the sensory bridges between 'the world out there' and the mind which perceives and understands incoming messages, formulates thought and gives it expression. The whole is a dynamic system, a unity, *homo symbolicus* (as Kinget 1975 characterizes him), busy at his highest left-hemisphere skill. The senses need to be functioning clearly, smoothly, reliably and in synchrony with one another if language is to become a vehicle for rapid, automatic transmission of symbolic thought from one mind to another. The capacity thus to perform is evolution's gift to man. The development of innate capacity into functioning ability is a primary aim of man's education—that is, his training in organized language skills. He needs both education for understanding and training for mastery; richness in experience and organized practice for achievement of readily usable skills are partners in the mutual enterprise of growing a man or woman (see Jemicy School, 1972). It is especially here that the person with dyslexic tendencies in his learning needs most help, not to the neglect of his general education but to permit his full utilization of his whole self. It makes sense, therefore, to build into the pedagogical schema, from the start, occasions for repeated practice to develop multisensory, intersensory skills, in ways adapted to his individual needs. Hence, we say, 'Hear it, say it, see it, write it. Let each sensory servant learn well and support the others. They can help each other when one forgets, or when they come up against something new. As they become more and more skilful, you can let them work automatically while your thinking mind attends to the messages you are getting or sending, but always your mind is the master, in time of trouble and to decide what you want to do. That's what it's all about!'

While structure, system, sequence and order, which come almost naturally to some people, must be deliberately taught to and purposefully learned by the dyslexic person, each student is unique. Orton (1937) emphasizes this point as follows: 'We have tried to avoid overstandardization lest the procedure become too inflexible and be looked upon as a routine method applicable to all cases of non-readers, which would be clearly unwise in view of the wide variation in symptomatology and hence in training needs which these children exhibit'. The wealth of detail and the recommendations of empirically tested procedure in the manuals and guides published for the help of teachers by Gillingham and Stillman, by June L. Orton, and by their many able juniors over the past decades, then, are to be understood as facilitators in a 'structured but not programmed' plan, to be used flexibly by tutors and teachers with as rich background and as much wisdom as can be found. This is no task for the unprepared, however well they mean, nor for the person dependent on authority or tied to the necessity of following a guidebook ritualistically!

The student will progress faster and more securely if he understands his own nature and the relationship between his makeup and the way he is being taught. His intelligent participation and immediate or gradual assumption of responsibility for his own education, including its training aspects, are powerful motivational factors, as are the recognized achievement of steps towards competence and the formulation of goals which are appropriate and reachable. Goals should not be limited by factors related to dyslexia, but only to degrees of giftedness and opportunity, as is the case with other young people. Of course, the general goal of education for everybody is assumed to be to make the most of given talents and to provide within the culture the greatest degree of liberation for these talents, however far we may fall short of this ideal in practice. Facing the problems of dyslexia often makes both planners and participators in education face the larger issues and their practical interrelationships with the special problems to be solved. To the extent that this occurs, both aims will be forwarded. Not only in particular, with student and mentor, but as a general principle we re-emphasize, 'Mind is the master'.

That literacy and its achievement have many important individual and cultural values is undeniable. One reads, and writes, in the service of practical utility and of personal enjoyment and enrichment which accompanies the assimilation of one's culture. Dyslexics share the interests, desires and capacities of their peers, differing only in the ease and rate with which they acquire language skills. If the ultimate goals are kept in mind while their special needs are being met their progress and satisfaction will be enhanced. Accordingly, we not only have students reading books appropriate to their ages and interests just as soon as possible, but recommend that students be read to, and where appropriate be exposed to non-print media, at the levels of their intelligence, practical and scholastic needs and personal interests. It has been our experience that they will rely on external aids only as long as and to the extent that they need to, if they are being appropriately taught. The urge to independence is normally great, often particularly so if a student needs to prove his competence to himself and others and comes to feel that, indeed, he can do so. When skills are adequate, comprehension of content and motivation to achievement are limited only by intelligence and experience (a prime reason for keeping the dyslexic student abreast of his peers through supplementary reading to him and the like). Motivation usually takes care of itself or is amenable to the sorts of stimulation effective with everyone else. All this is another strong reason for viewing dyslexia—a temporary impediment only rather than a disability—as an aspect of acceptable diversity, not of divisive deviance, or even 'difference from the rest of us'. Imperfections we all have; this one is amenable to correction or adequate alleviation.

From the mental health or self-concept point of view, too, the attitudes of all concerned are important. If, for example, one follows the psychosocial development schema of Erik H. Erickson (see Rawson, 1974), one centres on the psychosocial 'work' of Erickson's Stage IV, appropriate to the school-age child. At this point, if previous stages of growth have taken place appropriately, the child is concerned primarily with the establishment of competence in the acquisition of skill-dependent aspects of culture, many of which are taught and learned in school, and with the reality-based sense of himself as a competent person. He needs to feel that he is 'like everybody else' in important ways, and also that he is entitled to his personalized differences, that the latter do not set him apart as undesirably 'different', but are a part of what makes him himself—good, desirable, full of justification for present happiness and future fulfilment. If the earlier stages of his growth have been hamperingly inadequate, psychotherapy may be essential, but in many cases the designedly therapeutic climate of the kind of educational treatment we have outlined as appropriate for the dyslexic student may be enough to liberate him emotionally also. If true competence is achieved, or is so well on the way that he can have confidence in his progress, the young person can tackle the establishment of identity, towards which the adolescent especially works, and the later stages of developing maturity when their time comes. If he comes into the clinical and 'remedial' picture at one of the later ages, the work of competence-building and its self-enhancing correlates must be done, along with the support and growth of the later stages.

No matter what the emotional problems appear to be (and most often they are the result of learning failures and unfulfilled learning potentials rather than their causes), the education and training necessary to competence and the realization of its achievement cannot be short-circuited. In literate cultures, and to a considerable extent in the technologically influenced non-literate world, one seldom finds a truly happy or effective person to whom the ways of language are largely closed, one to whom written symbols are literally a closed book from which he is excluded. There are those who claim that 'everyone has the right *not* to read'. No one would quarrel with that, but only with the assumption that a person is free to exercise his right if, in fact, he cannot read. Everyone with even a modicum of intelligence can learn to read; experience tells us this. It is society's responsibility to provide the opportunity for this learning, and also for the development of the ability to write, even if only on a functionally minimum level. If the first steps have been taken, the learner knows that all the rest is within the realm of possibility. For his self-concept, and hence his mental health, he can profitably think of dyslexia as a facet of diversity. In some ways it is a nuisance but perhaps also it is the other side of some of his most valuable attributes—his adaptability and flexibility. It is a part of himself to which he is entitled by nature, rather than by our sufferance. He can come to terms with it as a challenge he is capable of meeting successfully, and even turning to advantage. Our acceptance of this as a society can influence his outlook as a person.

It seems to many of us that we have reason to believe that everyone can learn to read up to the limit of his innate intelligence, to spell understandably if not always conventionally, and to write at least legibly. Many, many case histories, some published but more still nestled in the files of practitioners, and a small but increasing number of group statistical studies attest to this. The attitudinal and instructional approach which is here summarized is effective, and those of us who use it do so because it seems best suited to the dyslexics whom we know, that is, to be theoretically and practically sound. The test of the approach, with its careful structure flexibly utilized, is to be found in the histories of students as they first respond and then, growing older, go on to further schooling and into adult life. With very few exceptions our follow-up contacts and studies find our former students doing 'what was in them to do', as they would have had they not found language skills initially so difficult to master as to justify our thinking of them as 'dyslexic'. My own generation-long follow-up study covering life histories known since 1935 (Rawson, 1968), has been joined by a few others, like Enfield (1976), and Palatini (1976). Others are in preparation, notably a longitudinal study of a sampling of graduates of a school established some 45 years ago especially for dyslexics, and an intensive scrutiny of the genetic background and current history of the whole population of a more recently established school with the kind of total educational programme envisioned by this author as approaching the ideal. These studies are the work in progress of Barton Childs and his group at the Johns Hopkins Hospital Department of Pediatrics in Baltimore.

My former students who are represented in my study have all done well, surprisingly enough a degree better than their non-dyslexic schoolmates, also studied. With a couple of successful 'blue collar' exceptions, they have graduated from college or university and most of them have gone to graduate school, many having taken advanced degrees, with one-fourth of them having achieved the doctorate or gone bevond it. Occupationally, also, they are functioning well in those walks of life which other aptitudes and their interests indicate as suitable. Dyslexia, authentically diagnosed, occasionally slowed them down a bit but did not stop them. They are by no means unusual, except in having been subjected to statistical study, for histories like theirs have been repeated many times over by individuals whom we know and have worked with, some of them far exceeding our initial estimates of their potentialities. There are, alas, uncounted numbers of others, some identified and some not, who have not had the needed help. Some have won through 'the hard way', often with psychological scar tissue which might have been avoided, but many others have not, swelling the ranks of personal and social casualties. For all our need for more knowledge and refinements of skill, it appears that among us here in North America and elsewhere (as shown later in this volume) we have made a very promising beginning in the past 55 years or so in solving this very troubling problem. Whether or not any of our successful students reach the degree of eminence attained by da Vinci, Einstein, Niels Bohr, Hans Christian Andersen, Auguste Rodin, Woodrow Wilson, Nelson Rockefeller and a long list of others who struggled with language learning problems, they are contributing to their own productive lives and society's well-being with deserved satisfaction and, it is to be hoped, a comparable sense of self-worth.

People of their kind of constitution, whatever difficulties they may have, are not to be thought of as victims of pathology, I believe, but as examples of the diversity that is to be expected in the present state of the evolution of the human species. Placed in a larger context, they are very often recognized as being especially capable of adaptability and of the creative contributions which we all need. This is the view which we need to take of those among us who function in these ways: our task is not to treat a disability but to provide the opportunities for their optimum development. Such an outcome would, I believe, be fostered by a change of mental set which considers dyslexia as an example of diversity, for the ways we view people and the ways we speak of them can make profound differences in the ways we act toward them. We influence both ourselves and others by the ways in which we use language in talking about language and in meeting the challenges which it presents to its learners and to those who teach them. The concept of *dyslexia as diversity* can be both liberating and productive.

REFERENCES

Bakker, D. J. (1972) *Temporal Order in Disturbed Reading: Developmental and Neuropsychological Aspects in Normal and Reading-Retarded Children.* Rotterdam: Rotterdam University Press.

Benton, A. L. (1965) The problem of cerebral dominance. *The Canadian Psychologist,* **6A:4**. Reprinted in *Bull. Orton Soc.,* **16**, 38–54.

Berlin, R., (1887) *Eine Besondere Art von Wortblindheit (Dyslexie)*, Wiesbaden: Verlag von J. F. Bergmann.

Childs, S. B., (ed.) (1968) *Education and Specific Language Disability: The Papers of Anna Gillingham, M.A., 1919–1963.* Monograph 3, Towson, Md.: The Orton Society.

Cox, A. R. (1974) *Structures and Techniques: Remedial Language Training for use with Alphabetic Phonics.* Cambridge, Mass.: Educators Publishing Service.

Critchley, M. (1975) Developmental dyslexia: its history, nature and prospects. In D. D. Duane and M. B. Rawson (eds.). *Reading, Perception and Language,* pp. 9–14, Baltimore: York Press.

Critchley, M. and Critchley, E. A. (1978) *Dyslexia Defined*, London: Heinemann Medical Books.

Enfield, M. L. (1976) *An Alternate Classroom Approach to Meeting Special Learning Needs of Children With Reading Problems.* Unpublished thesis, University of Minnesota. (Copyright, University of Michigan, Ann Arbor, Michigan).

Gillingham, A. and Stillman, B. W. (1956, 1960) *Remedial Training for Children with Specific Disability in Reading, Spelling, and Penmanship.* Cambridge, Mass.: Educators Publishing Service.

Gollan, E. B. (1979) Personal communication. Ottawa.

Hermann, K. (1959) *Reading Disability*. Springfield, Ill.: Charles C. Thomas.

Heveroch, A. (1904) About specific reading and spelling difficulties in a child with excellent memory [in Czech]. *Publikováno v Paedagogický*, Rozhledech.

Hinshelwood, J. (1896) A case of dyslexia: a peculiar from the word-blindness. *Lancet*, **2**, 1451–1454.

The Jemicy School, A Philosophy, (1972) *The Jemicy School, Owings Mills, Md.*

Kerr, J. (1897) School hygeine in its mental, moral and physical aspects. *Roy. Stat. Soc.*, **60**, 613–680.

Kinget, G. M. (1975) *On Being Human*, New York: Harcourt, Brace, Jovanovich.

Klasen, E. (1972) *The Syndrome of Dyslexia*, Baltimore: University Park Press.

Masland, R. L. (1976) The advantages of being dyslexic. *Bull. Orton Soc.*, **26**, 10–18.

Matějček, Z. (1977) Specific learning disabilities, *Bull. Orton Soc.*, **27**, 7–25.

Money, J. (1962) *Reading Disability: Progress and Research Needs in Dyslexia*. Baltimore: The Johns Hopkins University Press.

Monroe, M. (1932) *Children Who Cannot Read, University of Chicago*.

Morgan, W. P. (1896) A case of congenital word-blindness. *Brit. Med. J.*, **2**, 1378.

Norrie, E. (1939) *Om Ordblindhed*, Copenhagen.

Orton, J. L., (ed.) (1966) *Word-blindness in School Children and Other Papers on Strephosymbolia (Specific Language Disability—Dyslexia), 1925–1946, by Samuel Torrey Orton, M.D.*, Monograph 2. Towson, Md.: The Orton Society.

Orton, J. L. (1973) *A Guide to Teaching Phonics*. Cambridge, Mass.: Educators Publishing Service.

Orton, S. T. (1925) 'Word-blindness' in school children. *Arch. Neurol. Psychiat.*, **14**, 581–615. Also in J. L. Orton (ed.) (1966) cited above, 17–51.

Orton, S. T. (1937) *Reading, Writing and Speech Problems in Children*. New York: W. W. Norton.

Palatini, L. (1976) *Informal Study of Early/Intervention Aspects of Learning Disability Program*. Unpublished, Cambridge, Mass., Public School Bureau of Public Services.

Pribram, K. H. (1971) *Languages of the Brain: Experimental Paradoxes and Principles in Neurophysiology*, Englewood Cliffs, NJ: Prentice-Hall.

Rawson, M. B. (1968) *Developmental Language Disability: Adult Accomplishments of Dyslexic Boys*. Baltimore: Johns Hopkins University Press. (Reprinted in paperback) 1978, Cambridge, Mass.: Educators Publishing Service.

Rawson, M. B. (1972) Langauge learning differences in plain English, *Acad. Ther.*, **7**, **4**, 411–419. Also *Reprint #40*, Towson, Md: the Orton Society.

Rawson, M. B. (1974) The self-concept and the cycle of growth. *Bull. Orton Soc.*, **24**, 63–76.

Rawson, M. B. (1975) Developmental dyslexia: educational treatment and results. In D. D. Duane and M. B. Rawson (eds.) *Reading, Perception and Language*, pp. 231–258, Baltimore: York Press.

Rawson, M. B. (1978) Dyslexia and learning disabilities: their relationship. *Bull. Orton Soc.*, **28**, 43–61.

Rome, P. D. and Osman, J. S. (1972) *Language Tool Kit*, Cambridge, Mass.: Educators Publishing Service.

Saunders, R. E. (1977) Personal communication.

Slingerland, B. H. (1971) *A Multisensory Approach to Language Arts for Specific Language Disability Children*. Cambridge, Mass.: Educators Publishing Service.

Smelt, E. D. (1976) *Speak, Spell and Read English*, Victoria, Australia: Longman Australia Pty Ltd.

Sperry, R. W. (1974) Lateral specialization in the surgically separated hemispheres. In F. O. Schmidt and F. G. Worden (eds.) *The Neurosciences: Third Study Program*, pp. 5–19, Cambridge, Mass.: MIT Press.

Thompson, L. J. (1966) *Reading Disability: Developmental Dyslexia*, Springfield, Ill.: C. C. Thomas.

Waites, L. (1966) Personal communication.

Whittrock, M. G. (1978) Education and the cognitive processes of the brain. In J. S. Chall and A. F. Mirsky (eds.) *Education and the Brain*, University of Chicago Press, Chicago: National Society for the Study of Education.

Wolff, A. G. (1970) The Gillingham–Stillman programme, In A. W. Franklin and S. Naidoo (eds.) *Assessment and Teaching of Dyslexic Children.* London: Invalid Children's Aid Association.

Dyslexia Research and its Applications to Education
Edited by G. Th. Pavlidis and T. R. Miles
© 1981 John Wiley & Sons Ltd.

CHAPTER 3

Neurological Aspects of Dyslexia

Richard L. Masland

My purpose in this chapter is to review both old and new knowledge regarding the structure and function of the brain as they relate to language, and to consider ways in which they may be different in persons with dyslexia. The older knowledge is derived largely from studies of brain-damaged adults and from animal studies. The function of a structure is inferred from observing the deficits which develop when that structure is damaged or diseased. Some information has been gained from observations made during electrical stimulation of the brain under operation. More recently, information has been developed by studying responses of normal and atypical individuals to various types of sensory experiences, and by recording not only behaviour but electrical responses of the brain. These latter studies have been especially valuable for comparing the relative effectiveness of the two sides of the brain in the analysis of simultaneously presented visual, auditory or cutaneous stimuli. It is such studies which are adding greatly to our understanding of the differences of function of the left and right sides of the brain.

The major integrative, correlative, analytical functions of the brain are dependent upon the cerebral cortex—the convoluted outer surface of the cerebrum which has reached its greatest elaboration in the human (and some sea mammals). There are four great input channels to this analyser, and one major output. We will discount the olfactory channel in this discussion, and consider visual, auditory, and cutaneous functions (and related sensations from bones and muscles).

These three types of sensations are sensed by special organs, and information from these organs is conveyed to specific areas of the cerebral cortex where they are displayed almost as a map or image of the perceived object (Figure 3.1). Sensations coming from the body (somatosensory or somaesthetic) are projected to the central region of the cortex, with the foot being represented near the vertex and the face and hands (with a large area of representation) being located at the lower margin and adjacent to the temporal lobe (Figure 3.2).

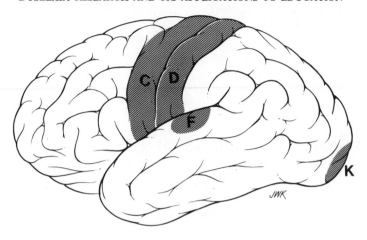

Figure 3.1. Schematic diagram of the left cerebral hemisphere showing the major sensory input areas, and the motor or major outflow area. K: Visual area. To this area in the occipital lobe (the posterior area of the cerebral cortex) is relayed visual information from the field of vision towards the opposite side of the body. F: Auditory area. To this area—the superior margin of the temporal lobe, sometimes called Heschl's gyrus, and extending into the deep central fissure (Fissure of Sylvius)—is relayed auditory information from both ears, but especially the opposite one. The extension of this area into the fissure—on the flat upper surface of the temporal lobe (Planum Temporale)—is more highly developed on the left side than on the right. D: Somaesthetic area. To this area is relayed information from the opposite side of the body. Information is displayed like a map of the body, with the face and hands represented at the lower end near area F and the feet at the top. C: Motor area. Stimulation of this area produces movement of the opposite side of the body, the areas involved matching the adjacent sensory areas

The somatosensory area also lies adjacent to the major motor outflow area from which control of body movement is also organized on a point-to-point basis. Thus, at operation, electrical stimulation of a point in the somaesthetic area will produce a sensation of tingling or numbness in the corresponding area of the body. Stimulation just anterior to that area will cause that part of the body to move.

Visual information is projected to the occipital region, a picture of what is observed being projected like an inverted map at the back of the cerebrum (Figure 3.3).

For auditory information, the point-to-point principle applies to pitch rather than to the locus of the sound. The internal ear is so designed that the interpretation of pitch depends upon selective stimulation at various points of its sense organ (called the cochlea). The cochlea contains a spiral like a seashell, and along this spiral is a row of different-sized sensitive hairs that respond to vibration. A high pitch sound stimulates one end of the spiral—a low pitch the other. This organ has a point-to-point connection with the cerebral cortex so that

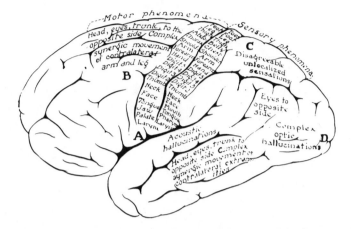

Figure 3.2. Lateral view of the left cerebral hemisphere, showing the pattern of representation of the various parts of the body as revealed by electrical stimulation. Stimulation of the anterior portion of the brain (left) including the frontal lobe (B) results in movements. Anteriorly, the effect is to produce a coordinated or synergistic movement pattern. Along the anterior margin of the central sulcus, stimulation produces discrete movements of various parts. The body is represented with the face and mouth at the lower end of this strip, and the feet at the top. Stimulation of the posterior part of the brain (right) results in sensory phenomena. Stimulation along the central sulcus produces tingling sensations in parts of the body comparable to those which move with stimulation of the adjacent motor area. Stimulation of the temporal lobe causes auditory phenomena, and of the occipital lobe (D) visual effects (results of early experiments by O. Foerster)

a chord would be displayed as a pattern on the cortex, its interpretation presumably being accomplished by analysis of the pattern of stimulation of the brain's surface (Tunturi, 1960).

In general, the connecting pathways for both sensation and movement are crossed—the left side of the brain controls the right side of the body, and receives information from that side. In respect to vision, the left side of the brain receives information from the visual field to the right of the fixation point, even though this information actually falls upon the left side of the sensory structure of the eye—the retina—the light rays having crossed within the lens of the eye (Figure 3.3). Although the preponderance of these inflow and outflow channels is crossed, there are also some ipsilateral connections. Each ear connects to both sides of the brain and cutaneous sensation is also bilaterally represented. The visual pathways are almost completely crossed. There is ipsilateral as well as contralateral control for gross motor movement.

Adjacent to each of these areas are parts of the brain where these primary impressions are subject to interpretation and analysis. Thus, injury to an area adjacent to the visual cortex, while not causing blindness, may impair pattern recognition skill. As one moves away from these input and outflow areas, the

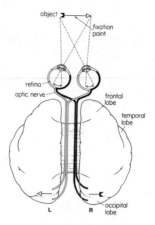

Figure 3.3. Diagram of the pathways for visual information from the eyes to the occipital cortex. Light rays from objects to the right of the fixation point cross in the lens of the eye and fall on the left side of the retina. Nerve impulses from the left side of both retinas are conveyed to the left cerebral hemisphere, and are displayed on the cortex as though on a photographic film. Information from the left of the fixation point is similarly transmitted to the right side of the brain. Because of this pattern of organization, an object displayed briefly to one side of the fixation point will be 'seen' by only one side of the brain—a principle used to test the relative abilities of the right and left hemispheres

brain functions become less specific and more integrated and intersensory in their nature. In the human brain large areas of the temporal, parietal and frontal regions are involved in interrelating and correlating somaesthetic, visual and auditory information, and the large area anterior to the motor strip—the frontal lobe—appears to be involved in planning and projecting motor activities. These large 'association' areas are essential in the performance of the various complicated intellectual functions of the brain.

For the analysis of ongoing events, the brain must be able to interrelate the information coming to the cortex through its four input channels (as well as to relate this to previous experience). This is most easily and effectively accomplished within a single hemisphere of the brain. The two hemispheres of the brain are quite separate, but connected by a rich pathway of interconnecting fibres called the corpus callosum (Figure 3.4). These connections also bear a point-to-point relation, their display on one hemisphere being a mirror image of that on the other. There is a time delay if information has to pass from one hemisphere to the other for analysis. For example, subjects being asked to recognize objects by feel will respond with greater speed and accuracy if they point with the same hand as that within which the object was felt (Gardner *et al.*, 1977). In animal experiments visual interpretations requiring association between the visual area and the temporal lobes are unimpaired if the opposite lobe from the one being

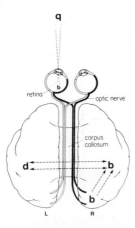

Figure 3.4. Diagram showing the location and function of the corpus callosum. This dense bundle of nerve fibres comprises the main channel of communication between the two sides of the brain (hemispheres). The connections are on a point-to-point basis, as a result of which patterns relayed from one hemisphere to the other are received as mirror images. The diagram shows how a visual pattern received at the right occipital lobe might be relayed to an association area in the occipito-temporal region, then as a mirror image to the corresponding area of the opposite side

stimulated is destroyed. However, they are seriously impaired if the ipsilateral temporal lobe is destroyed, and the association must be made between one occipital lobe and the opposite temporal lobe (Mishkin, 1962) (Figure 3.5). Possibly it is for this reason that some of the most complicated, analytical functions of the brain—those which require complex and close correlations of multisensory and motor events—become centred or lateralized to one side of the brain. Whatever the cause, one of the most important features of the human brain is that certain complex activities are lateralized (Levy, 1969).

The most complicated of all human activities is language, for its acquisition involves complex associations of somaesthetic (that is from within the body), visual and auditory data, with complex motor activity. These must in turn be associated with previous experience and ultimately with the most abstract concepts. This function is centred in the left side of the brain in over 90% of right-handed people (Figure 3.6) and in the majority of the left-handed (Branch, Milner, and Rasmussen, 1964). The degree of lateralization varies, and some adults have a significant language ability in both hemispheres (see below). This concentration of language function in the left side of the brain is reflected in significant asymmetries of brain structures—those areas of the brain within which are centred the auditory analytical processes being larger on the left than on the right (Galaburda et al., 1978; Geschwind and Levitsky, 1968) (Figure 3.7). These anatomical asymmetries are not the result of training; they

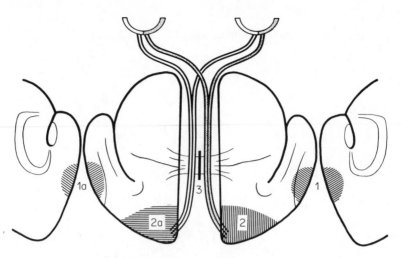

Figure 3.5. Animal experiment demonstrating that associations within a single hemi-sphere are more effective than those having to cross to the other side. Monkeys were trained to a visual discrimination task. The visual discrimination requires an interaction between the primary visual reception area of the occipital lobe (areas 2 and 2a) and an association area in the temporo-occipital region (1 and 1a). This task can be performed by either side of the brain as long as the occipital and temporal lobes are in communication. Thus, destruction of areas 1 and 2 or of areas 1a and 2a produces no deficit. In either event, the intact areas of the opposite hemisphere continue to function effectively. However, if areas 2a and 1 are destroyed, there results a serious deficit. The remaining area 2 must communicate across the corpus callosum to area 1a for the appropriate association to be established. If, subsequent to this, the corpus callosum is sectioned (area 3), the function is completely lost as there is no remaining communication between an intact occipital and temporal lobe

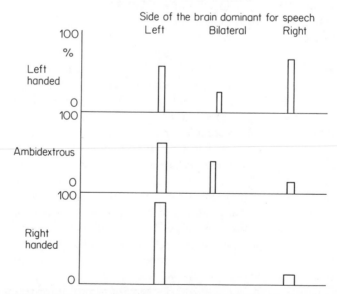

Figure 3.6. Location of the speech centre in left-handed, ambidextrous and right-handed persons as determined by putting one side of the brain to sleep by injection of sodium amytal into the artery (see Branch, Milner, and Rasmussen, 1964)

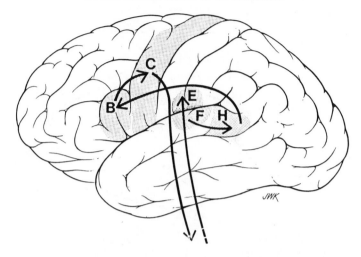

Figure 3.9. Schematic diagram of the essential components of the speech mechanism. Sounds are 'heard' in the auditory receptive area of the left temporal lobe F, and analysed in adjacent areas of the temporal lobe H. Motor patterns for the production of speech are established in Broca's area of the frontal lobe B, which controls the motor outflow to the speech mechanisms C. Proprioceptive feedback from the muscles and movements of the speech organs returns to the sensory areas of the post-central region E. The sounds of the person's speech provide further feedback. These sensorimotor activities become closely associated in a coordinated pattern of neural activity

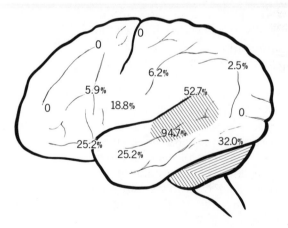

Figure 3.10. Diagram showing relative frequency of impairment of auditory recognition of phonemes subsequent to injury of various areas of the left cerebral cortex. The most critical area is the shaded pattern of the left first temporal convolution (Wernicke's area) (see Luria, 1965)

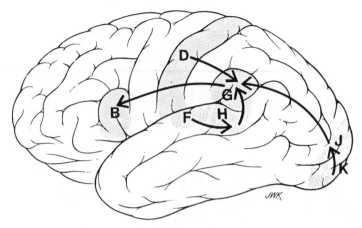

Figure 3.11. Schematic diagram of the mechanisms required for the comprehension of speech, and for speech formulation. The essential area is in the region of the supramarginal gyrus G. Within this area are established the linkages between the neural patterns of the spoken word and the various sensory experience derived through vision (K–J) and feeling (D). An association between area G and Broca's area B is required for the initiation of speech

essence of aphasia, are found in all cases of aphasia regardless of the location of the lesion in the left hemisphere.

However, certain elements of the language function can be localized to relatively discrete areas of the left cortex, and they relate to the way in which this function is performed. To talk requires first to hear, next to analyse, then to duplicate, and finally to associate with meaning.

Hearing and the analysis of sound are functions of the superior margin of the temporal lobes (Figure 3.8, area 22, and Figure 3.9). Injury to this area damages phonemic recognition (Figure 3.10). In the only reported case of early childhood aphasia studied at autopsy, this area had been completely destroyed on both sides (Landau, Goldstein, and Kleffner, 1960). In adults, damage of the left temporal lobe produces severe impairment of language comprehension. In addition, being unable to monitor his own speech the subject may speak a meaningless jargon—unaware of his own errors.

Speech is a motor skill. Word formulation for articulation depends upon the frontal lobe—that area adjacent to the motor outflow for the face, tongue, and lips (Figure 3.8, areas 44, and 45, Figure 3.9, area B) whose language function was first described by Broca. Within this region are encoded the 'rules' by which heard language is coded into articulatory form. If this area is destroyed, the ability to talk may be lost even though the individual's comprehension is preserved; often he knows the words he wishes to say, but he cannot get them out, a condition which may cause severe frustration.

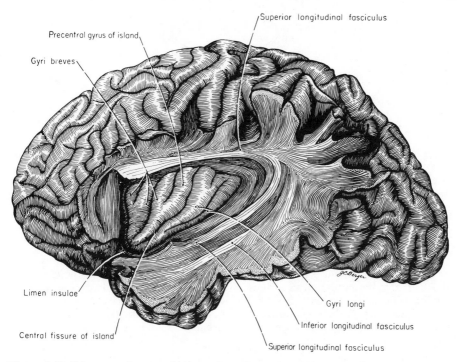

Figure 3.12. Disconnection syndromes. Drawing of a dissection of the human left cerebral hemisphere to show the rich association pathways connecting the temporal and frontal lobes and reaching out posteriorly into the association areas of the parietal and occipital lobes. Injury to these fibres at the point marked 'superior longitudinal fasciculus' interrupts the connections between the areas for speech comprehension in the temporal lobe and those for speech production in the frontal lobe. The individual can still comprehend speech, since the temporal lobe and its connections to the parietal and occipital regions are intact. However, he cannot repeat what he has heard. Injury to the fibres extending posteriorly may separate the reception and motor areas from those concerned with meaning. The individual may be able to repeat what he has heard, but without comprehension (echolalia). Crosby, Humphrey, and Lauer: *Correlative Anatomy of the Nervous System*, 1962

But for words to be associated with meaning requires that the auditory and motor patterns of word perception and production be related to the sensory experiences which they represent. This process requires the integrity of the crossroads area lying between the somaesthetic, auditory and visual areas of the cortex (Figure 3.8 area 40; Figure 3.11, area G). Damage to this area (the supramarginal gyrus) produces severe impairment of intellect and inability to comprehend.

Thus language is a highly integrated sensorimotor function. It is probable that this is the case from the initial phases of language development. The child hears

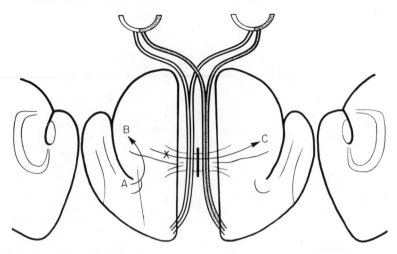

Figure 3.13. Injury producing inability to use the left hand in response to a verbal command. The command is received and interpreted in the speech area on the left (A). It is transmitted to the motor centres of the dominant hemisphere (B), and thence to the motor outflow centres of the right hemisphere C (which central the left hand). An injury at X which disconnects the motor control area of the left from the subservient outflow centre of the right leads to inability to follow the verbal command received on the left side

and analyses the sounds of speech—using the association areas of the left temporal lobe. During the babbling stage he reproduces the sounds and establishes connections between the sensory area and the motor speech centres of the frontal lobe. The process of speaking is associated with movements of the mouth, larynx, and other speech organs, and the sensations from them are fed back to the brain as are also the sounds they produce. Thus there develops a complex sensorimotor pattern of neural activity paralleling the sounds and movements of speech. Finally, at some stage these patterns become associated with meaning. (Figures 3.9 and 3.11).

In the adult, impairment of language can occur in two ways—either from injury to the sensory or motor centres for speech or by interruption of the association pathways which connect them. Thus if the language centre of the parietal lobe becomes separated from the sensorimotor speech apparatus comprehension of speech is lost. An individual may be able to hear and repeat what he has heard through intact associations between the temporal and frontal lobes, but cannot comprehend what he has heard or what he is saying (*echolalia*). If the pathways between the temporal and frontal lobe are destroyed he may be able to comprehend and to speak but cannot repeat what he has heard. Various forms of aphasia have been described depending upon which area of the brain has been injured and depending upon whether the area represents the centre for a specific subfunction of language or a pathway through which these functions are

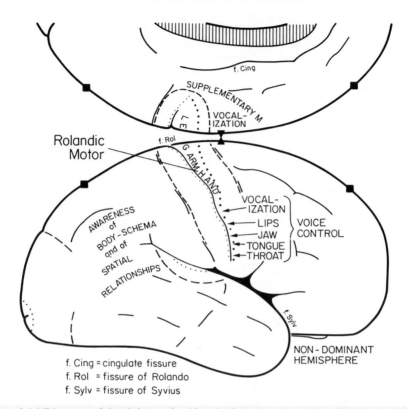

f. Cing = cingulate fissure
f. Rol = fissure of Rolando
f. Sylv = fissure of Syvius

Figure 3.14 Diagram of the right cerebral hemisphere showing centre for the recognition of body schema and spatial relationships. Destruction of the right parietal area, with disconnection from the left, leads to an unawareness of the left side of the body—sometimes even to the extent that the individual will deny that its function is impaired. Lesser injuries can cause constructional apraxia—inability to do block design and pattern recognition tasks. This latter function is also specifically impaired with removal of the right temporal lobe

integrated. These latter deficits are spoken of as *disconnection syndromes* (Figure 3.12).

In addition to its dominant role in language function, the left cerebral hemisphere shows superiority in the direction of skilled and sequential motor acts. In the majority of persons the right hand is preferred and more skilled in these activities. In addition, it is unconsciously used during gesticulation when speaking. It is probably correct to speak of the left hemisphere as 'dominant', for in certain situations it controls actions mediated through the right hemisphere, especially when executed in response to a verbal command. Thus in certain forms of brain injury where the speech centres of the left are disconnected from the right hemisphere (Figure 3.13) the person cannot carry out a purposeful act with the

Table 3.2. Shows relative superiority of right versus left hemispheres in normal right-handed persons. Figures indicate the
test score ratios of right versus left hemispheres for various
cognitive and motor tests (see Kimura, 1973)

Task	Degree of hemisphere superiority	
	Left	Right
Auditory		
Words	1.88	
Nonsense syllables	1.73	
Backward speech	1.66	
Melodic patterns		1.19
Non-speechsounds (human)		1.08
Visual		
Letters	1.23	
Words	1.47	
Two-dimensional point location		1.18
Dot and form enumeration		1.20
Matching of slanted lines		1.05
Stereoscopic depth perception		1.28
Manual		
Skilled movements	1.13	
Free movement during speech	3.10	
Tactile dot patterns (Braille)		1.20
Non-visual location		1.20
Tactile patterns recognition (callosal section)		2.05

left hand in response to a verbal command even though that hand is capable of
ordinary movement.

But the right hemisphere also has its specialized function. Injuries of the right
parietal lobe produce deficits in body image. They may be of such severity that
the individual develops a complete unawareness of the left side of the body even
to the point of denying that it is defective (Figure 3.14). Physiological studies
reveal that the right hemisphere is superior to the left in visual recognition of
faces, geometrical figures, and unfamiliar objects, and these skills are impaired
upon injury of the right temporal lobe (Milner, 1968). In tactile functions the left
hand is superior to the right in object recognition. In the auditory sphere,
whereas the right ear (left hemisphere) is superior for recognition of speech
sounds and sound frequencies, the left ear (right hemisphere) is superior for the
recognition of environmental sounds and for tonal memory and recognition of
pitch (Milner, 1962). (Note that pitch interpretation is dependent upon a spatial
array on the cerebral cortex).

In summary (Table 3.2; Kimura, 1973), the left hemisphere is superior to the
right in those functions having to do with language. There is anatomical
elaboration of that part of the left hemisphere involved in auditory analysis, and

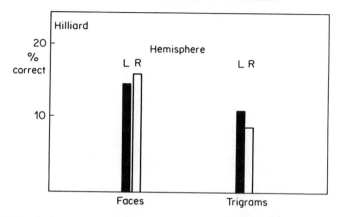

Figure 3.15. Hemisphere superiority in visual recognition of forms and words. Test objects consisted of faces and vertically displayed three-letter words (trigrams) presented tachistoscopically to each visual field. Graphs indicate superiority for unfamiliar faces in right hemisphere (left visual field) and for words in left hemisphere (see Hilliard, 1973)

its function is dominated by this skill. Important in language analysis is that it is a *sequential* event, and the left hemisphere is essential for recognition of sequences and time relationships (Efron, 1963). The right hemisphere is superior for pattern recognition and for the analysis of *parallel* events. It has been suggested that the ability of the right hemisphere to synthesize a pattern from various bits of information causes it to be the hemisphere for creativity and new concept formation.

DEVELOPMENT OF WRITTEN LANGUAGE

The acquisition of written language must ordinarily be superimposed and dependent on a pre-existing structure of spoken language. The reader must learn to recognize a visually presented pattern; then he must associate this pattern with a sound or a sequence of sounds, either a phoneme or a word; finally he must associate the pattern and the sound with its meaning. In the early stages of reading (and for long periods in some persons) the emphasis in the reading process is probably in the grapheme–phoneme relationship. However, to 'sound-out' such relationships is a slow process. In the later stages of reading, words lose their phonemic importance, and the emphasis is on rapid extraction of meaning (Ingram, Mason, and Blackburn, 1970; Luria, 1961).

In physiological terms, the initial stages of recognition of unfamiliar patterns is a function best accomplished by the right hemisphere. However, when adult readers are tested, it is found that letter and word recognition are now accomplished most efficiently by the left hemisphere. Evidently at some stage in the learning-to-read process the word recognition function is shifted to the left

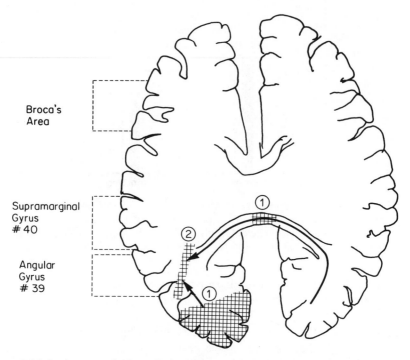

Figure 3.16. Lesions producing alexia without agraphia. Lesions which separate the angular gyrus area 39 from both occipital lobes make it impossible for the individual to associate the visually presented symbol with the language centre. This may occur in either of two conditions: (1) requires two lesions—destruction of the left occipital lobe and interruption of the fibres in the corpus callosum connecting the right visual area to the left angular gyrus; or (2) lesions undercutting the left angular gyrus

hemisphere—presumably because it is thus more closely integrated within the other language functions centred within this hemisphere (Figure 3.15; Hilliard, 1973). Bakker, (1978), suggested that there may be two stages in the learning-to-read process and that individuals vary in the ease and rapidity with which they progress from one stage to the next. In some, word processing takes place within the right hemisphere; reading is likely to be slow but accurate, the focus being on words and letter form. In others, there is a rapid shift of word recognition to the left hemisphere; the emphasis is on extraction of meaning and reading is rapid and often less accurate. That reading is in the average adult a left hemisphere function is documented by the occurrence of reading impairment after injuries of the left hemisphere, and to some extent these impairments reflect associated deficits in spoken language (Wittrock, 1978). Thus an individual with motor aphasia due to injury of the frontal lobe (see Figure 3.8, areas 44 and 45) may show parallel defects in writing. Even in the absence of actual paralysis there may

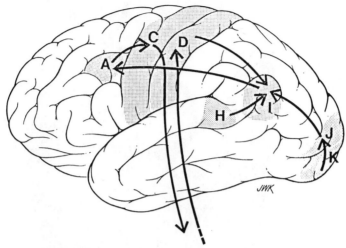

Figure 3.17 Schematic diagram of essential components of written language. The visual patterns of the written symbols are perceived in the primary visual area K and analysed in the adjacent visual association area J. In area I, they become associated with the sound of the word or letter analysed in the auditory association area H. Note also that this centre for written language is just posterior to the angular gyrus, which is the area for spoken language (see Figure 3.11). As is also the case with spoken language there is a direct outflow to the frontal lobe A which controls the movements of writing through the motor area C. Again, there is feedback to the sensory area D from the muscles and joints involved in writing. Thus within these closely integrated structures there develop the multisensory motor patterns of neural activity that underlie writing

be an apraxic type of derangement in which the individual is incapable of forming the words and letters even when he knows what he wishes to write and has the strength to make the necessary movements. Individuals with injury of the temporal lobe (Figure 3.8, area 22) exhibiting sensory aphasia may produce well-formed letters but their written productions may be incoherent and lacking in meaning; however, comprehension of written language remains intact (Heilman et al., 1979).

However, the most striking deficits of written language are those which follow injury to the areas relating to the major speech centre of the left. As noted above, it is within this area that associations are made between the stored visual and somaesthetic information which provide for object recognition and the auditory–motor–kinaesthetic patterns of written language.

It is in a region adjacent to this area—the angular gyrus (Figure 3.8, area 39)—that associations are established between the written symbol and the spoken word. For example, when the angular gyrus is destroyed, the individual loses the ability to read. In addition, without this area he cannot recall the visual memory of the words and letters and he loses the ability to write as well. Under certain other circumstances (Figure 3.16) this area may become disconnected

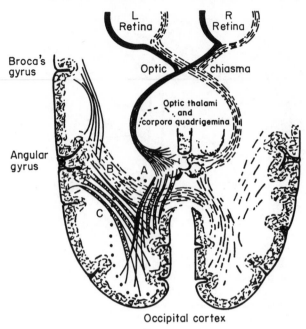

Figure 3.18. Hinshelwood's diagram (after Déjerine) in connection with a case of 'congenital word blindness'. In describing a case of congenital word blindness, Hinshelwood referred to Déjerine's previous study of alexia in adults, and postulated that a similar mechanism may be involved in the congenital case (see Hinshelwood, 1917)

from both occipital lobes either by being undermined or by severance of the connecting pathways. This causes loss of the ability to read. However, if the language centre itself remains intact, the individual retains the ability to write either to dictation or spontaneously. This condition is termed *alexia without agraphia.*

Extensive lesions of the left parietal lobe produce a combination of symptoms first described by Gerstmann (1924 and 1927). It has been suggested that the underlying deficit is an impairment of a basic physiological function involving serial ordering (Kinsbourne and Warrington, 1963). The symptoms include *dysgraphia, dyscalculia* and also right–left disorientation and *finger agnosia*—indicated by the inability to move appropriate fingers on verbal command. So there obviously exists a sensorimotor pattern for written language closely related to that previously established in the brain for spoken language (Figure 3.17). Thus, in the adult with already established spoken and written language functions, injuries of selected areas of the left cerebral hemisphere can produce specific types of deficit. These can be interpreted in terms of the location of association areas within which have been established patterns of activity that reflect spoken or written language. In other situations they are due to interruption of pathways that connect centres for somaesthetic, visual, or auditory input in the temporal, parietal and occipital lobes or those for motor output in the frontal lobes.

To what extent do these findings and results with brain damage in adults have relevance for the developmental language disorders? The disorders of function which result from the destruction of an already established structure must be very different from those which occur when functions are developed within a structure which has been abnormal or damaged throughout the developmental period. As an extreme example, the destruction of the entire left hemisphere in infancy produces minor disturbances of spoken and written language. This suggests that to produce a significant disorder of function in infancy an injury must be bilateral. As noted above the only reported case of autopsy of a child with congenital aphasia demonstrated complete bilateral destruction of the primary auditory cortical receptive areas (Landau, Goldstein, and Kleffner, 1960).

Alternatively, it is possible that partial damage or malformation of the left hemisphere which still permits the language function to be centred on that side could be more conducive to malfunction than if the entire process is shifted to the right.

When dyslexia was first described, the significance of the speech centre in the left hemisphere, and the loss of the written and spoken language associated with injury in the adult, were already recognized. Thus Morgan (1896) describing a case of 'congenital word blindness' assumed that the disorder reflected a defect of the left angular gyrus. Hinshelwood (1896 and 1917) described similar cases and also assumed a defect underlying the left angular gyrus with a disconnection of the language centre from the visual centres of the occipital lobes (Figure 3.18).

In subsequent elaborations of this concept, Hermann (1959) and Kinsbourne and Warrington (1963) showed that many children with dyslexia suffered also from dyscalculia and finger agnosia and showed disorders of right–left orientation. They equated these findings with the previously described Gerstmann syndrome observed after injuries of the left parietal lobe in the adult.

With increasing recognition of the diversity of the dyslexias and of the complexity of the language structure and function, there are now suggestions that several different types of anatomical or developmental deficits might be responsible. Mattis, French, and Rapin (1975) and Mattis (1978) described four separate dyslexia syndromes which they feel can be compared with the alexias of adult brain-injured persons, although they do not present the specific anatomical correlates of these four syndromes.

(1) The most prominent group of dyslexic children (comprising about 60%) are those with a 'language disorder'. These children exhibit anomia, poor comprehension of spoken language, disorders of imitated speech, and/or disorders of sound discrimination. Such deficits can be related to deficits of the left temporal lobe.

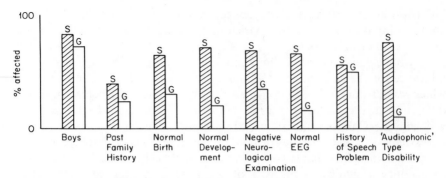

Figure 3.19. Comparison of two groups of dyslexic children. Results of a study of 82 poor readers selected to have IQ over 80, but reading attainment (Schonell) 10–14 points below Stanford–Binet IQ. The children were divided into two groups—those underachieving in reading and spelling only (specifics) and those showing in addition poor performance in arithmetic manifested by arithmetic quotient (Schonell Forms A or B) 15 or more points below IQ (generals). Both groups show frequent history of delay in language development. The 'specifics' were more likely to have a positive family history, and less likely to have history or findings suggestive of brain injury. They were also more likely to have pure 'audiophonic' difficulties (shown by difficulty in word synthesis, confusion of vowel sounds and poor phonic knowledge) uncomplicated by additional visuo-spatial difficulties. The mean IQ of the 'specifics' was 108 versus 107 for the 'generals'. The mean degree of reading disability was not statistically different in the two groups (see Ingram, Mason, and Blackburn, 1970)

(2) The second group (comprising about 10%) suffer from 'articulatory and graphomotor discoordination'. They exhibit problems in sound blending and in visuomotor skills but show normal receptive language functions. For them, one might postulate deficiencies of the motor centres of the left frontal lobe (Figures 3.8 and 3.17, A).

(3) A third group (comprising about 10%) show 'disphonemic sequencing difficulties' in which 'poor repetition scores characterized by phonemic substitutions and mis-sequencings occur despite normal naming comprehension and speech sound production'. These dysfunctions might be attributable to a deficit of the parietal area (Figure 3.18, I) comparable to that of the Gerstmann syndrome as emphasized by Hermann (1959) and Kinsbourne and Warrington (1963). However, Mattis, French, and Rapin (1975) consider the related symptoms of dyscalculia, finger agnosia and right–left disorientation to be symptoms of brain damage and not specific to dyslexia *per se*.

The finding of Mattis, French, and Rapin (1975) that dyscalculia and right–left disorientation are concomitants of brain injury derives interesting support from prior studies by Ingram, Mason and Blackburn (1970). The comparison of children with 'reading disabilities only' versus those with problems in both reading and arithmetic show that the more general group are more likely to have abnormal EEG on neurological examination and less likely to have a positive family history, suggesting the inclusion within this latter group of at least some who have brain injury (Figure 3.19).

(4) The fourth group (comprising about 5%) suffer from a 'visuospatial–perceptual disorder'. As distinct from the language disordered groups, these children show a performance score below their language score on the Weschler Adult Intelligence Scale (WAIS), and do poorly on tests of visual pattern recognition and retention. One might postulate that such deficiencies could stem from disorders of the right hemisphere parietal or temporal regions (Figure 3.14) or from disconnection of these regions from the speech centres on the left.

Mixed and unclassified account for about 15%.

The findings of Mattis, French, and Rapin represent an elaboration of previous findings (Ingram, Mason, and Blackburn 1970; Myklebust and Johnston, 1965; Boder, 1971 and 1973) that dyslexic individuals fall into two major groups—those whose problems are primarily linguistic (left hemisphere) and those with visuospatial disabilities (right hemisphere). The evidence suggests that the latter are uncommon and comprise less than 10% of the total. In a study of a small group of dyslexic children Fried (1978) demonstrated that, whereas the normal individual can differentiate words from sounds more effectively with the left hemisphere, those with the linguistic type of dyslexia did better on the right. Those with visuospatial problems showed a heightened left side superiority. These findings further support the thesis of a right-sided deficit in the visuospatial group.

Support for the 'deficit' model of dyslexia is derived from two reports of postmortem examinations of the brains of persons who had been studied during life for developmental dyslexia. The first (Drake, 1968) was a boy aged 12 years who suffered from a learning disability in arithmetic, reading and spelling and was said to display 'hyperactivity with short attention span, disturbances in auditory language integration and slowness in reading and expressing language generally'. His full scale IQ was 96—verbal 96, performance 97. His picture was complicated by episodes of mental confusion and of blackouts suggestive of complex partial epileptic seizures (commonly attributed to an epileptic process involving the temporal lobe). The family history was characterized by mixed dominance, visual and learning problems, migraine headaches, and vascular malformations. The patient died suddenly as a result of intracranial haemorrhage due to rupture of abnormal blood vessels of the cerebellum—a form of congenital malformation. In addition to this vascular abnormality of the cerebellum there were noticed 'in the cerebral hemisphere, anomalies. . . in the convolutional pattern of the parietal lobe bilaterally. The cortical pattern was disrupted by penetrating deep gyri that appeared disconnected. Related areas of the corpus callosum appeared thin.' Microscopically 'the cerebral cortex appeared more massive than normal, the laminations tended to be columnar, the

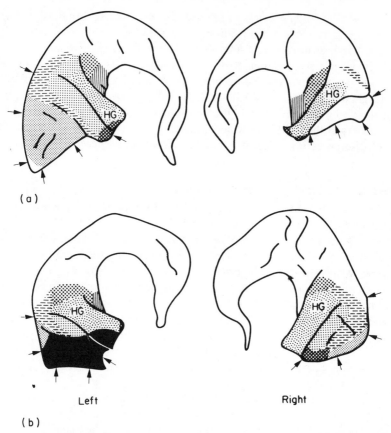

Figure 3.20. Superior temporal plane in a control brain (a) and in the brain of the patient with developmental dyslexia (b). The extent of the temporal plana are indicated by arrows; the dyslexic brain has nearly symmetrical plana. Note the location of the polymicrogyria (shown in black), primarily confined to area Tpt (Temporo-parietal integration area), posterior (but inferior in figure) to Heschl's gyrus (HG)
Guide to cytoarchitectonic auditory fields area Tpt, small closed circles; area ProA (Primitive auditory area), vertical lines; area KA (primary auditory cortex), open circles; area paAr (association cortex), large closed circles; area paAr (association cortex, crosses; area paAe (association cortex), dashed horizontal lines; and area paAcld (association cortex), cross-hatching (see Galaburda and Kemper, 1979)

nerve cells were spindle shaped, and there were numerous ectopic (displaced) neurons in the white matter that were not collected into distinct heterotopias (abnormally placed groups of cells)'.

The second case (Galaburda, 1979) was a 20-year-old left-handed man who had exhibited a severe reading disability. Birth and early development were normal but speech in full sentences was delayed until after the age of 3 years. In school he had difficulties in reading and spelling in spite of a Stanford–Binet IQ of 105. However, at age 13, the full scale WISCIQ was 88—verbal 95, performance 83. At 19, in spite of intensive remedial instruction, his reading abilities (Stanford Achievement and Gray) were at upper third grade level. His arithmetical ability at age 18 was at fourth grade level. In addition to these learning disabilities he also exhibited mild disturbances in right–left orientation and finger recognition. The general neurological examination was normal. This patient also developed seizures at age 16. His father and two brothers were slow readers, but not to the degree exhibited by the patient. Death was due to an accident. At post-mortem the brain appeared normal on gross inspection.

> The abnormalities found were confined to the left cerebral hemisphere and the most striking of these was an area of polymicrogyria. In this malformation, adjacent molecular layers of the abnormal gyri were frequently fused. . . . The polymicrogyria was confined to the posterior parts of the transverse gyrus of Heschl and the planum temporale [Figure 3.20]. In addition to this major malformation which was located in the posterior aspects of the auditory region there were many areas of mild dysplasia scattered throughout the left hemisphere where they were most frequent in the parietal, occipital and temporal lobes.

Thus, these two cases which were considered during life to be suffering from developmental dyslexia each had clearcut congenital malformation of those areas of the left cerebral hemisphere known to be essential for language in the adult.

However, in retrospect, they cannot be looked upon as 'pure' cases of dyslexia. Each also suffered from epilepsy, and, as noted above, the additional findings of dyscalculia and of right–left disorientation are considered by Mattis, French, and Rapin (1975) and Ingram, Mason, and Blackburn (1970) to be indications of brain damage apart from that related to pure dyslexia.

AN ORGANIZATIONAL MODEL

In spite of the strong evidence linking various forms of dyslexia to definable anatomical or physiological brain deficits, there are many who are reluctant to equate dyslexia with dysfunction. The two reported anatomical studies are atypical in that in both cases there was other evidence of organic brain disease. In the vast majority of cases of dyslexia there is no such evidence. Familial studies support a genetic rather than an environmental cause (although as documented above they cannot serve as proof). Possibly most difficult to explain on a basis of brain damage is the remarkable preponderance of boys who are dyslexic. Either boys are more subject to developmental or neonatal deficits, or else the organization of developmental characteristics of their brains is such as to lend greater susceptibility to impairment of language function. In this connection the

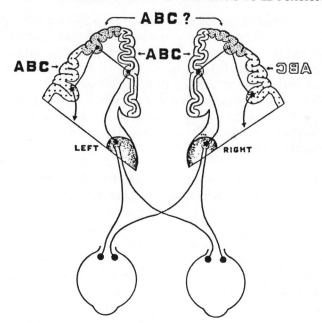

Figure 3.21. Orton's diagram to illustrate his theory of dyslexia (strephosymbolia). He postulated that in cases of poorly established dominance the responding hemisphere would be ambivalent about whether to respond to the pattern (engram) of the left hemisphere or to its mirror image derived through the corpus callosum from the right (see Orton, 1925)

findings of Stores and Hart (1976) are of particular interest. They observed an increased prevalance of specific reading retardation among children with epilepsy, but the increase was significant only among epileptic boys, and specifically those with focal epileptic discharge located in the hemisphere dominant for speech.

Orton (1925) was probably the first to suggest that the problem of dyslexia might be attributable to some peculiarity of brain organization rather than to a defect or a dysfunction of a specific structure or area of the brain. His thesis appears to have been stimulated by the study of patients in whom mirror writing was a very prominent feature and he noted that a number of patients could read as readily in a mirror or write backwards as well as forwards. However, he also noticed in some of his patients a basic and persistent inability to establish a firm association between a well-recognized visual symbol and the sound or word which it represented—a 'failure of association operating electively at the symbolic level between the strictly visual cortices and the great association area'. He further states that

> one of the most convincing observations came from a. . . little girl who on her first attempt at writing produced a definite mirrored reversal of each letter with her right hand. It seems axiomatic that the visual image

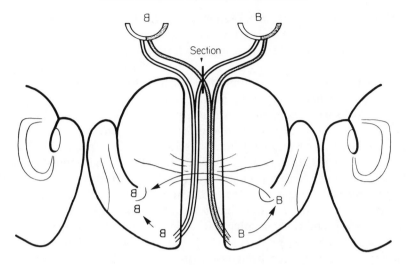

Figure 3.22. Diagram to show the principle involved in the experiments of Mello and of Noble. In each instance, one eye had input to only one hemisphere. (In the pigeon, this is because the bird does not have binocular vision, his eyes are on the side of his head and each eye connects to only one side of his brain. In the case of the monkey (Noble) the crossing fibres from each eye were cut so that each eye connected only to the same side of the brain. The animal was trained with one eye blindfolded to select an asymmetrical pattern, which would be 'seen' with only one hemisphere. However, the impression is transferred as a mirror image to the other side. When the animal is tested with the other eye blindforded, he attempts to match the direct image with the previous mirror image trace, and selects the mirror image of the previously selected test object

of the letter that was called up by its name, and which must have served as the motor pattern, existed in her brain as the mirrored reversal of that which we consider the correct form of that letter.

As a result of these observations Orton postulated that the engram (pattern) for an object perceived by one hemisphere was transferred to the other hemisphere as a mirror-image and that if the 'writing' hemisphere received its visual cue from the opposite hemisphere by transmission through the corpus callosum it would respond with the mirror-image of what was seen. There must therefore exist within the two sides of the brain competing mirror-images of any seen object (Figure 3.21): 'The process of learning to read entails the elision from the focus of attention of the confusing memory images of the non-dominant hemisphere which are in reverse form and order, and the selection of those which are correctly oriented and in correct sequence'. Orton suggests that 'those children who are neither dominantly right-handed or left-handed, or in whom clear dominance has not been well established before they begin to learn to read, probably have more trouble with reversal of letters'.

Orton's theory has been highly controversial, but there is some experimental and theoretical support from subsequent studies. Two interesting experiments support the thesis that the visual image may be transferred across the corpus callosum in mirror form. In pigeons, which do not have binocular vision, the image for each eye goes to only one hemisphere. Pigeons blindfolded in one eye were trained to select an asymmetrical object. When the opposite eye was blindfolded they then selected the mirror-image (Mello, 1966) (Figure 3.22).

Similar results were reported by Noble (1968) in monkeys whose optic chiasma had been sectioned. Under these conditions each eye also connects only to one hemisphere. Here, also, animals trained to select an asymmetrical object with one eye covered selected its mirror-image when tested with the opposite eye.

Orton's thesis was further strengthened by data regarding the dominant role of the *right* cerebral hemisphere in the processing of unfamiliar shapes and forms, and especially in the observation that in the adult familiar letters are recognized best with the *left* cerebral hemisphere (Rizzolatti, Umilta, and Barlucci, 1971). In fact, in some adults the preferred side seemed to depend upon the degree of familiarity of the letters or print being processed. The early stage of reading presents a unique problem, for it requires that there be established a stable association between an unfamiliar visual display, best processed in the right hemisphere, and a sequential auditory event or pattern previously established in the left. Difficulty in letter naming is one of the best predictors of reading disability (Denckla and Rudel, 1976a; 1976b). Evidence presented by Bakker (1978) indicates that this problem is handled differentially at different ages and by different individuals. Some appear to retain a language function in the right hemisphere, exhibiting a slow but precise letter-by-letter type of analysis. Others appear to move rapidly to a left hemisphere approach with less emphasis on letter and word patterns and more emphasis on verbal association with meaning. Studies of persons whose two hemispheres have been surgically separated by section of the corpus callosum (Zaidel, 1976; 1978) indicate that, even in the adult, the right hemisphere may retain a considerable reading skill, but one based on a non-phonetic type of pattern recognition process.

Heilman *et al.* (1979) state

> the two hemispheres in certain people may possibly process written language differently. Perhaps the left hemisphere mediates written language by reference to the auditory phonemic mode (that is the left hemisphere transcodes graphemic symbols to sonic symbols) whereas the right hemisphere uses more of the visual spatial strategy, and extracts semantic properties from iconic images without phonologic processing.

Boder (1971; 1973) describes one group of dyslexic children whose spelling represents an attempt to duplicate the phonetic characteristics of the word and another group who attempted to reproduce its visual pattern. The studies of

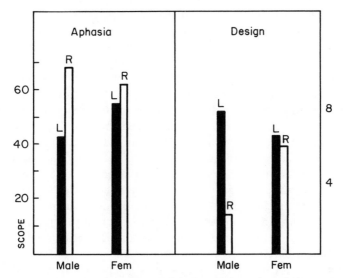

Figure 3.23. Comparison of the results of right hemisphere damage in men and women. The study is a comparison of four groups of patients- men and women with right and left cerebral lesions. 'Aphasia' refers to the test score on an aphasia battery modified from Goodglass and Kaplan (1972); a perfect score is 80. 'Design' is the score on the Block Design of the Wechsler Belleview Intelligence test; a perfect score is 12. 'L' and 'R' refer to the side of the brain damage. The bars show that in the aphasia test those with left hemisphere injury were most impaired. With the design test, those with right hemisphere injury were most impaired. The study further shows that in each test the males showed a greater degree of hemisphere specialization, with a greater difference between the two hemispheres

Fried (1978) reported above suggest that these two groups of children are using opposite hemispheres in the discrimination of words and sounds.

Thus there are a number of studies to indicate that the establishment of an association between sound and symbol is a difficult task, that symbol recognition is initially mediated by the right hemisphere, and that there are variations in the ease with which this function is selectively transferred to the left. The problem has been succinctly stated as follows (Gazzaniga, 1973).

A. . . basic and important feature of cerebral dominance seems to be the function of the dominant hemisphere as the central processing site of the brain. . . if dominance is not clearly established, there is no central point through which various cognitive acts are channelled. . . The data suggest that in language-related behaviour—in particular reading—there may be a direct and immediate need for the transfer of information between the cerebral hemispheres. One can begin to see that if this system is not operating normally obvious deficits would result in both acquiring and utilizing reading skills.

Thus, according to this theory, some forms of dyslexia might result from unusual patterns of brain organization in which cerebral dominance was not well established, or visual processing was strongly centred in the right hemisphere, or interhemispheric connections were inadequate. What evidence is there that any of these is the case in dyslexia? There are many studies revealing individual variations in information processing in humans. Variations of EEG and of response patterns in dyslexic individuals support this thesis (Duffy, Burchfiel, and Lombroso, 1979; Fried, 1978; Preston, Guthrie, and Childs, 1974).

A clue as to what these individual variations in the brain organization may be is available from the remarkable sex difference in the frequency of dyslexia. What are the established sexual differences in brain structure or cognitive function which may provide some clue as to those characteristics which predispose men to dyslexia? Because of the difficulties in distinguishing between differences of constitutional origin and differences that are culturally determined there is considerable uncertainty and controversy regarding the actual significance of the observed sexual differences in cognitive style and abilities (Wittrock, 1978). However, such differences have been consistently reported. In general (Maccoby and Jacklin, 1974) women are more proficient in the use of language and in the performance of tests which can be linguistically mediated (Cioffi and Kandel, 1979). They may also be superior in manual and manipulative skills (Denckla, 1973). Men appear to have greater mechanical abilities and are superior in such measures as Thurstone's primary abilities test of spatial relationships (McGlone and Davidson, 1974).

There is a suggestion that fine manipulative skills, such as successive finger movements, are controlled by the left hemisphere, as the two hands are about equal in skill in most children. Data suggest that in women the left hemisphere exerts a greater degree of dominance (Rudel, Denckla, and Spalten, 1974).

There are differences in the rate of maturation (Epstein, 1978; Witelson, 1976c). Girls mature more rapidly and reach the final period of physical and cognitive development at an earlier age. These observations suggest superior left hemisphere abilities in women and superior right hemisphere abilities in men. However, women also appear to have a lesser degree of hemispheric lateralization both for linguistic and spatial skills. Furthermore, hemispheric *specialization*, at least for spatial skills, is actually slower to develop in girls than in boys (Witelson, 1976c). Damage of the left hemisphere in women is less likely to produce aphasia than does similar damage in men (Lansdell, 1964) and damage of the right hemisphere is less likely to produce measurable loss of spatial skills in women (McGlone and Kertesz, 1973) (Figure 3.23).

Thus the male characteristics which might be considered to predispose to dyslexia are:

(1) less well-developed left hemisphere language functions;
(2) greater specialization of spatial skills in the right hemisphere;

(3) lesser degree of left hemisphere dominance;

(4) earlier lateralization of functions but, in general, slower maturation.

The importance of left hemisphere superiority appears especially significant. Thus, in a study of dyslexia in non-brain-damaged children of average intelligence, Symmes and Rapoport (1972) were able to find 42 boys but only one girl who met this definition. These boys showed superiority in spatial skills (note, however, that for a dyslexic child to have a normal IQ by standard tests he *has* to be superior in something). Witelson (1976c) reports similar emphasis of spatial skills in dyslexic boys. Hier *et al.* (1978) through X-ray studies (CAT) of the brain of normal and dyslexic subjects found that in the latter 42% had a right parieto-occipital area greater than the left compared with 10–12% of the general population. They postulate that among persons with developmental dyslexia there must be a subgroup with a reversal of the customary cerebral asymmetry. These findings further support the concept of a relationship between left hemisphere under-development (or right hemisphere overdevelopment) and reading disabilities. However, they still do not determine whether these characteristics are constitutional in origin or are due to malformation or injury of the left hemisphere. Anatomical–pathological studies are required to establish this point.

In considering these broad generalities of differences in cognitive functions between the sexes it is important not to overlook the extensive overlaps which exist and especially the great degree of individual variation in the specific cognitive abilities of different individuals and in the way specific tasks are handled. A variety of studies are now in progress to elucidate these variations. Newer physiological studies which include simultaneous bilateral presentation of visual, auditory, or tactile stimuli can be correlated with information about handedness to provide data regarding which part of the brain is 'dominant' for which task (Dee, 1971; McGlone and Davidson, 1974). These patterns have been shown to be different in dyslexic individuals and also to vary with handedness (Fried, 1978; Preston, Guthrie, and Childs, 1974). These physiological states can now be correlated with sophisticated methods of EEG analysis (Duffy, Burchfield, and Lombroso, 1979) with CAT studies of brain structure and with radioisotope studies to reveal which part of the brain is physiologically active during specific tasks. Over the next few years, these studies can provide information on how brain structure and function are different in the individual with a specific reading disability. Anatomic correlations involving additional post-mortem examinations, as projected by the Orton Society in the United States, will be required to ascertain the definitive causes of these diverse functional and structural patterns.

SUMMARY

In most individuals the left hemisphere of the brain is the essential structure for both spoken and written language. The right hemisphere of the brain is superior in respect to spatial abilities such as the visual or tactile recognition of unfamiliar forms or objects. However, in the adult, the recognition of letters is apparently closely tied to the language skills of the left hemisphere.

Injury of the various essential regions of the left hemisphere in the adult produces specific types of reading and writing deficits. Brain injury to these parts during the developmental period may produce specific impairments in reading and writing abilities. In addition, post-mortem studies have documented that congenital malformations of these parts can cause dyslexia, possibly even in familial forms. The possibility also exists that in some instances dyslexia may relate to unusual patterns of brain organization, especially those involving relative preponderance of spatial (right hemisphere) as opposed to verbal (left hemisphere) abilities.

REFERENCES

Bakker, D. J. (1978) A set of brains for learning to read. In K. C. Diller (ed.) *Individual Differences and Universals in Language Learning Aptitude*, Newbury House Publishers.

Boder, E. (1971) Developmental dyslexia: prevailing diagnostic concepts and a new diagnostic approach. In H. R. Myklebust (ed.) *Progress in Learning Disabilities*. New York: Grune and Stratton.

Boder, E. (1973) Developmental dyslexia: a diagnostic approach based on three atypical reading–spelling patterns. *Dev. Med. Child Neurol.*, **15**, 663–687.

Branch, C., Milner, B., and Rasmussen, T. (1964) Intracarotid sodium amytal for the lateralization of cerebral speech dominance. *J. Neurosurg.*, **21**, 399–405.

Chi, J. G., Dilling, E. C., and Gilles, G. H. (1977) Gyral development of the human brain, *Ann. Neurol.*, **1**, 86–93.

Cioffi, J. and Kandel, G. L. (1979) Laterality of stereognostic accuracy of children for words, shapes and bigrams: a sex difference for bigrams. *Science*, **204**, 1432–1433.

Dee, H. L. (1971) Auditory asymmetry and strength of manual preference, *Cortex*, **7**, 236–245.

Denckla, M. B. (1973) Development of speed in repetitive and successive finger movements in normal children, *Develop. Med. Child Neurol.*, **15**, 635–645.

Denckla, M. B. and Rudel, R. G. (1976a) Naming of object-drawings by dyslexic and other learning disabled children, *Brain and Language*, **3**, 1–15.

Denckla, M. B. and Rudel, R. G. (1976b) Rapid 'automized' naming (RAN): dyslexia differentiated from other learning disabilities, *Neuropsychologia*, **14**, 471–479.

Dennis, M. and Whitaker, H. A. (1976) Language acquisition following semi-decortication. Linguistic superiority of the left over right hemisphere. *Brain and Language*, **3**, 404–433.

Drake, W. E. Jnr. (1968) Clinical and pathological findings in a child with a developmental learning disability, *J. Learning Disabilities*, **1**, 486–502.

Duffy, F. H., Burchfiel, J. L., and Lombroso, C. T. (1979) Brain electrical activity mapping (BEAM). A method for extending the clinical utility of EEG and evoked potential data. *Ann. Neurol.*, **5** 309–321.

Efron, R. (1963) Temporal perception, aphasia and *déja vu, Brain*, **86**, 403–424.

Epstein, H. T. (1978) Growth spurts during brain development: implications for educational policy and practice. In J. S. Chall and A. F. Mirsky (eds.) *Education and the Brain*. Chicago: University of Chicago Press.

Fried, I. (1978) Classification of reading disabilities into clinical subtypes', 29th Annual Conference of Orton Society.

Galaburda, A. M. (1979) Cytoarchitectonic abnormalities in developmental dyslexia: a case study, *Ann. Neurol.*, **6**, 94–100.

Galaburda, A. M., Le May, M., Kemper, T. L., and Geschwind, N. (1978) Right–left asymmetries of the brain. *Science*, **199**, 852–856.

Gardner, E. B., English, A. G., Flannery, B. M., Hartnett, M. B., McCormick, J. K., and Wilhelmy, B. B. (1977) Shape-recognition accuracy and response latency in a bilateral tactile task. *Neuropsychologia*, **15**, 607–616.

Gazzaniga, M. S. (1973) Brain theory and minimal brain dysfuncion, *Ann. NY Acad. Med.*, **205**, 89–92.

Gerstmann, J. (1924) Fingeragnosia, eine umschreibne störing der orientierung am eigenen Körper, *Vienna Klin. Wochenschr.*, **37**, 1010–1012.

Gerstmann, J. (1927) Fingeragnosie und isolierte Agraphie—ein neues Syndrome. *Zeitschr. Ges. Neurol. u. Psychiat.*, **108**, 152–177.

Geschwind, N. and Levitsky, W. (1968) Human brain: left–right asymmetries in temporal speech region, *Science*, **161**, 186–189.

Heilman, K. M., Rothi, L., Campanella, D., and Wolfson, S. (1979) 'Wernicke's and global aphasia without alexia, *Arch. Neurol.*, **36**, 129–133.

Hermann, K. (1959) *Reading Disability: A Medical Study of Word Blindness and Related Handicaps*, Copenhagen: Munksgaard.

Hier. D. B., Le May, M., Rosenberger, P. B., and Perlo, V. P. (1978) Developmental dyslexia. Evidence for a subgroup with a reversal of cerebral asymmetry, *Arch. Neurol.*, **35**, 90–92.

Hilliard, R. D. (1973) Hemispheric laterality effects on a facial recognition task in normal subjects, *Cortex*, **9**, 246–258.

Hinshelwood, J. (1896) A case of dyslexia: a peculiar form of word blindness, *Lancet* , 1451–1454.

Hinshelwood, J. (1917) *Congenital Word Blindness*. London: H. K. Lewis.

Ingram, T. T. S., Mason, A. W., and Blackburn, I. (1970) A retrospective study of 82 children with reading disability. *Develop Med. Child Neurol.*, **40**, 1–23.

Kimura, D. (1973) The asymmetry of the human brain. *Scient. Amer.*, **228**, 70–78.

Kinsbourne, M. and Warrington, E. K. (1963) The developmental Gerstmann syndrome, *Arch. Neurol. Psychiat.*, **8**, 490–502.

Landau, W., Goldstein, R., and Kleffner, F. (1960) Congenital aphasia, *Neurology*, **10**, 915–921.

Lansdell, H. (1964) Sex differences in hemispheric asymmetries of the human brain. *Nature*, **203**, 550.

Levy, J. (1969) Possible bases for the evolution of lateral specialization of the human brain, *Nature*, **221**, 614–615.

Luria, A. R. (1961) *The Role of Speech in the Regulation of Normal and Abnormal Behaviour*. London: Pergamon.

Maccoby, E. E. and Jacklin, A. N. (1974) *The Psychology of Sex Differences*. Stanford. Calif.: Stanford University Press.

Mattis, S. (1978) Dyslexia syndromes: a working hypothesis that works. In A. L. Benton and D. Pearl (eds.) *Dyslexia*, New York: Oxford University Press.

Mattis, S., French, J. H., and Rapin, I. (1975) Dyslexia in children and young adults: three independent neuropsychological syndromes. *Develop Med. Child Nevrol.*, **17**, 150–163.

McGlone, J. and Davidson, W. (1974) The relation between cerebral speech laterality and spatial ability, with special reference to sex and hand preference. *Neuropsychologia*, **11**, 105–113.

McGlone, J. and Kertesz, A. (1973) Sex differences in cerebral processing of visuospatial tasks, *Cortex*, **9**, 313–321.

Mello, N. K. (1966) Concerning the inter-hemispheric transfer of mirror-image patterns in pigeon, *Physiol and Behav.*, **1**, 293–300.

Milner, B. (1962) Laterality effects in audition. In V. Mountcastle (ed.) *Interhemispheric Relations and Cerebral Dominance*, Baltimore: Johns Hopkins Press.

Milner, B. (1968) Visual recognition and recall after right temporal lobe excision in man, *Neuropsychologia*, **6**, 191–209.

Mishkin, M. (1962) A possible link between interhemispheric integration in monkeys and cerebral dominance in man. In V. Mountcastte (ed.) *Interhemispheric Relations and Cerebral Dominance*, pp. 107–109, Baltimore: Johns Hopkins Press.

Morgan, P. (1896) A case of congenital word blindness. *Brit. Med. J.*, **2**, 1378.

Myklebust, H. R. and Johnson, D. J. (1965) Dyslexia in childhood. In J. Hellmuth (ed.) *Learning Disorders*, Special Publication of the Seattle Sequin School Inc., Seattle, Washington.

Noble, J. (1968) Paradoxical interocular transfer of mirror-image discriminations in the optic chiasm sectioned monkey. *Brain Res.*, **10**, 127–151.

Orton, S. T. (1925) Word blindness in schoolchildren, *Arch. Neurol. Psychiat.*, **14**, 581–615.

Preston, M. S., Guthrie, J. T., and Childs, B. (1974) Visual evoked responses (VERs) in normal and disabled readers, *Psychologia*, **11**, 452–457.

Rizzolatti, G., Umilta, C., and Berlucci, G. (1971) Opposite superiorities of the right and left hemispheres in discriminative reaction time to physiognomical and alphabetical material, *Brain*, **94**, 431–442.

Rudel, R. R., Denckla, M. B., and Spalten, E. (1974) The functional asymmetry of Braille letter learning in normal sighted children, *Neurology*, **24**, 733–738.

Schuell, H., Jenkins, J. J., and Jiminez-Pabon, E. (1964) *Aphasia in Adults*, New York: Harper and Row.

Stores, G. and Hart, J. (1976) Reading skills of children with generalized or focal epilepsy attending ordinary school, *Develop. Med. Child Neurol.*, **18**, 705–716.

Symmes, J. S. and Rapoport, J. L. (1972) Unexpected reading failure. *Amer. J. Orthopsychiat.*, **42**, 82–91.

Tunturi, A. R. (1960) Anatomy and physiology of the auditory cortex, In G. L. Rasmussen and W. Windle (eds.) *Neural Mechanisms of the Auditory and Vestibular Systems*, pp. 181–200, Springfield, Illinois: Charles. C. Thomas.

Wada, J. A., Clarke, R., and Harmon, A. (1975) Cerebral hemispheric asymmetry in humans: cortical speech zones in 100 adult ad 100 infant brains, *Arch. Neurol.*, **32**, 239–246.

Witelson, S. F. (1976a) *Abnormal Right Hemisphere Specialization in Developmental Dyslexia.* Baltimore: University Park Press.

Witelson, S. F. (1976b) Developmental dyslexia: two right hemispheres and none left, *Science*, **195**, 309–311.

Witelson, S. F. (1976c) Sex and the single hemisphere: specialization of the right hemisphere for spatial processing, *Science*, **193**, 425–427.

Wittrock, M. C. (1978) Education and the cognitive processes of the brain. In J. S. Chall and A. F. Mirsky (eds.) *Education and the Brain*, pp. 61–102, Chicago: Chicago University Press.

Zaidel, E. (1978) Lexical structure in the right hemisphere. In P. Buser and A. Rougeul Buser (eds.) *Cerebral Correlates of Conscious Behaviour*. Amsterdam: Elsevier.

Zaidel, E. (1976) Auditory vocabulary of the right hemisphere following brain bisection or hemi-decortication, *Cortex*, **12**, 191–211.

Dyslexia Research and its Applications to Education
Edited by G. Th. Pavlidis and T. R. Miles
© 1981 John Wiley & Sons. Ltd.

CHAPTER 4

Alexia, Dyslexia and Normal Reading

Peter Meudell

INTRODUCTION

In the older medical literature the term alexia tended to mean a total lack of reading skills while dyslexia tended to refer to a partial lack of reading abilities; both terms, however, were meant to apply to reading difficulties occurring as a direct result of damage to the brain in previously normal individuals who could once read adequately. Since damage to the brain only occasionally produces complete loss of reading skills (and even in such cases some reading skills may still be demonstrated with suitable testing) reading difficulties consequent upon brain damage are now generally termed 'alexia' irrespective of their severity, while the term 'dyslexia' is reserved for individuals who have difficulty in *acquiring* the skills of reading during infancy and later life (Benson and Geschwind, 1969). In other words alexia is an acquired disorder of reading resulting from organic damage to the brain during adulthood, while dyslexia is a failure in the ability to learn to read during childhood. The term 'acquired dyslexia' has also been used synonymously with alexia (see Marshall and Newcombe, 1973) but in order to separate clearly what may be two quite distinct disorders of reading—one a failure of acquisition of a skill over time and the other the often sudden failure of a previously overlearned skill—two distinct terms seem advisory.

The term alexia does not, however, refer to a unitary disorder of reading since, just as there are many reasons why a child may fail to acquire reading skills, there are many possible reasons why an alexic patient is unable to read after a stroke. Thus, at a functional level of description for example, the alexic patient may be unable to read as a result of spatial, perceptual, speech or general linguistic problems or some combination of all of these. Of course, not only do alexics differ qualitatively amongst themselves they also differ quantitatively in the extent of their reading impairment. This could be assessed in much the same way that the 'reading backwardness' of the child can be assessed, but it tends not to be largely because experimental psychologists are more interested in the qualitative nature of the reading disorder rather than relating the remaining reading skills to a peer group.

Not only do alexics differ qualitatively and quantitatively amongst themselves, but the structural basis of their reading disorder also varies. In other words alexia is not caused by damage to one single part of the brain, but left temporal, parietal and even frontal lobe damage (Benson, 1977) in right-handed adults can cause alexia. There are also reports (Patterson and Zangwill, 1944; Kinsbourne and Warrington, 1962) of right hemisphere damage causing reading disorders in right-handers. The extent to which damage to many different parts of the brain can lead to alexia should not surprise us since reading is not a unitary activity but a complex set of skills requiring the integrity of many different functional systems which, accordingly, may be subserved by divergent areas within the brain (Luria, 1973). How far the different functional disorders of reading are related to damage to specific parts of the brain will be discussed in a later section.

THE CONTRIBUTION OF ALEXIA TO DYSLEXIA

What can be learned about the nature of dyslexia from the study of alexia? There appear to be at least two approaches to answering this question, one a direct approach and the other more indirect. The direct approach would simply involve comparisons of the similarities and differences in the nature of the deficits involved in the two disorders. Some of the similarities that do exist are as follows:

(1) Alexia usually occurs in the context of a more general aphasic problem although it need not do so (Benson and Geschwind, 1969) and many dyslexics are known to have delayed oral speech development (Warrington, 1967).

(2) Some alexics have colour-naming difficulties (Geschwind and Fusillo, 1966), as do some dyslexics (see Denckla, 1972).

(3) Some alexics show failures of intersensory integration or sequencing (Butters and Brody, 1968; Butters, Barton, and Brody, 1970) as do some dyslexics (Birch and Belmont, 1964).

(4) Finger agnosia is sometimes associated with alexia (Benson, 1977) and occasionally with dyslexia (Kinsbourne and Warrington, 1963).

(5) At a more structural level alexia can occur, independently of other linguistic disturbances, as a result of damage to the left parietal region (Benson and Geschwind, 1969), and EEG abnormalities (Sklar, Hanley, and Simmons, 1972) and VER abnormalities (Preston, Guthrie, and Childs, 1974; Symann-Louett et al., 1977) have been demonstrated in disabled young readers. There are, however, some obvious differences between alexia and dyslexia, the most notable being the presence in the former of hemianopias, hemipareses, loss of sensation and other 'hard' neurological signs which are clearly absent in the latter.

Direct comparisons between alexia and dyslexia make sense if, as Geschwind (1965) has argued, in some cases dyslexia is attributable to late or faulty maturation of the same structures in the child, which when damaged in the adult cause alexia. In particular Geschwind (1965) argued that the integrity of both angular gyri is necessary for normal acquisition of reading skills, and accordingly, faulty maturation of the angular gyri will lead to reading disorders. One problem with such a view is the ability of the rest of the young brain to show relatively normal functioning in the congenital absence of certain central structures (Nathan and Smith, 1950), after major surgery (Griffith and Davidson, 1966) and after missile damage (Teuber, 1977). Further, Geschwind has argued that the angular gyri are of critical importance in the acquisition and execution of reading skills since, anatomically, they could subserve cross-modal associations, but while cross-modal matching may be one aspect of reading skill it is certainly not the only one, nor may it be a necessary one since some reading can take place without the involvement of a sight-to-sound transformation (Saffran and Marin, 1977).

An important factor in any direct comparisons between alexia and dyslexia is the fact that nearly all adult brain-damaged patients show some recovery of function over time and in many cases make a marked recovery extending over several months (Reinvang, 1976); alexic patients are not an exception to this rule (Newcombe, Hiorns, and Marshall, 1976). The recovery of function shown by alexics is not uniform, however, since if the errors made in reading out loud are classified as visual errors (for example reading *p* as *q*), grapheme–morpheme errors (such as reading *phase* as *face*) or semantic errors (such as reading *symphony* as *orchestra*) the proportion of the total errors which are attributable to each of the three types of specific errors changes over time (Newcombe and Marshall, 1973). The point in the recovery curve at which an alexic patient is tested is thus an important factor in any direct comparison between alexia and dyslexia and, of course, in the interpretation of data from an alexic patient. The stage in the recovery process is also probably an important factor in determining the presence of deficits associated with alexia such as difficulties in colour naming but there is little experimental data on this issue.

A further problem with direct comparisons of acquisition failures in reading and loss of acquired reading skills may be the well-known differences in skill acquisition and skill execution. While the former requires fairly constant conscious control for success, the later requires minimal conscious involvement as skill improves—the task becomes 'automatic'. What constitutes 'automaticity' is unclear but it does seem likely that overlearned skills like reading may well involve different types of control and organizational processes than those involved in their acquisition. Exactly which stages in reading are 'conscious' and which are 'unconscious' (automatic) is uncertain but recent evidence (Patterson, 1978) from a group of patients termed 'deep alexics' suggests that when they make visual errors (such as *pivot* for *pilot*) or derivational errors (such as *contain* for *container*) in reading out loud they tend to be confident that their responses are correct; however, if they make semantic errors (such as *excavate* for *digging*) they tend to be far less confident in the accuracy of their response. This suggests, at least, that a different system may be involved in the production of visual and derivational errors to that involved in the production of semantic errors, and that conceivably the former errors are produced by a system working largely without conscious control while the latter errors are produced by a system which does require conscious monitoring. The dissociation between conscious monitoring and automatic processing is evident in other clinical situations where, for example, patients with cortical blindness can nevertheless point with some accuracy to events in the visual field but feel that they are merely guessing when they do so (Weiskrantz *et al.*, 1974), and in amnesic patients who can execute visuomotor skills but who when asked cannot remember ever having learned them (Brooks and Baddeley, 1976).

The second, indirect, contribution that the study of alexia can make to the understanding of dyslexia is through an examination of the alexic patient's reading disorders which contributes to a greater knowledge of the normal adult's reading processes. In other words, an understanding of the *failure* to learn to read would be aided by an adequate theory about how *successful* readers accomplish their task—what knowledge do adult readers possess and in what processes do they engage to enable successful reading to occur? It may well be more difficult to describe the processes involved in the acquisition of reading skills, or equally, the failure to acquire them, without exactly knowing what it is that the child is acquiring. To the extent that an understanding of normal reading is made by the study of alexic patients, then such a study contributes towards a greater understanding of dyslexia. The remainder of this chapter therefore examines what is known about reading functions after right and left hemisphere brain damage in adults.

NEUROPSYCHOLOGICAL STUDIES OF ALEXIA

Right hemisphere damage and right hemisphere function

Hécaen and Albert (1978) have briefly reviewed the general linguistic defects observable after right hemisphere damage in right-handers and it is apparent that linguistic dysfunction, if it occurs at all, is quite minimal in such patients. Reading disorders similarly are rare after right hemisphere damage and such disorders that do occur tend to be spatial (Patterson and Zangwill, 1944) or perceptual (Kinsbourne and Warrington, 1962). Thus Patterson and Zangwill showed that in two patients with right posterior damage these individuals made ill-coordinated eye movements when looking at text, frequently losing their place and found difficulties in shifting from the end of one line to the beginning of another. Spelling and writing were, however, normal in both the patients. It is important to note that this disorder was not confined to the scanning of text but manifested itself in the patients' examination of other, non-linguistic, visual inputs; the reading problem was thus a part of a more widespread visuo-spatial deficit. Kinsbourne and Warrington (1962) examined six patients all with lesions involving the right parietal cortex and found that the patients showed a tendency to report the right-hand side of words accurately, but to report inaccurately the left-hand side of words as a proper but incorrect English word (for example, on being shown *level* the patient might respond *novel* but not *bivel* not *vel*). Left-side inattention is sometimes found with large right posterior lesions and is usually associated with a left-sided hemianopia but these patients showed inaccurate reports of the left-hand side of words even when the words were presented to the intact right hemifield. The mechanisms underlying this effect are unclear but once again the disorder was not confined to the identification of words alone since the patients erroneously described incomplete geometric forms presented across the midline as being complete, a phenomenon not shown by hemianopic controls. The neglect of the left-hand side of stimuli was not therefore specific to linguistic stimuli but occurred with non-linguistic stimuli also.

Clearly damage to the right hemisphere can cause rather special difficulties in reading which are relatively peripheral, informationally speaking, in the sense that they represent inabilities to orient in space so as to process the next stimulus or to accurately extract all the information in the stimulus prior to identification and comprehension. In addition, since these disorders are also not pure disorders of reading but are part of more general spatial–perceptual deficits it makes sense to ask whether the right hemisphere is involved in any 'deeper' aspects of reading skill or whether these are exclusively a left hemisphere function, the right hemisphere contributing in a more general way to orientation and overall stimulus analysis. Much of our understanding of right hemisphere linguistic function has come from an examination of patients whose corpus callosum has been sectioned for the relief of intractable epilepsy. This work is now well known and justly famous and has suggested that the right hemisphere cannot name words out loud (Gazzaniga and Sperry, 1967), nor, since it cannot judge rhymes, can it covertly produce the sound of visually presented words (Levy and Trevarthen, 1977), has extremely limited syntactic skills (Gazzaniga and Hilliyard, 1971), and limited comprehension of speech as assessed by the Token Test (Zaidel, 1977). On the other hand the right hemisphere of corpus callosum-sectioned patients can match printed words to their pictorial counterparts (Gazzaniga and Sperry, 1967) indicating some comprehension of words which were incapable of being verbalized, and more recently Zaidel (1976) has shown that the right hemisphere can understand singly presented words of most grammatical classes. In other words the right hemisphere appears to have an extensive vocabulary of isolated words but a limited ability to cope with strings of words.

Such conclusions about linguistic functions drawn from long-standing epileptic patients who have had their corpus callosum sectioned must however, be interpreted with caution for two reasons. Firstly, the functional organization of the brains of such patients may be different from normal as a result of prolonged susceptibility to seizures, and secondly, because of the plasticity of even the adult brain (Teuber, 1977) there may well be progressive changes over time after, and as a result of, surgery. For example, it has recently been reported (LeDoux *et al.*, 1978) in confirmation of earlier reports (Butler and Norssell, 1968) that while shortly after surgery only the left hemisphere of a commissurotomized patient could speak, some 2 to 3 years after the operation, his right hemisphere was acquiring the capacity to utter speech. In other words, not only may there be changes in the functional organization of the brain of epileptics as a result of the epilepsy itself, but there may well be changes in right (or left) hemisphere function as a result of the surgery designed to alleviate the condition. These problems have been pointed out before but they are worth reiterating in view of recent suggestions (Coltheart, 1977) that the remaining reading skills after lesions to the *left* hemisphere which lead to a particular form of alexia are in fact not remaining left hemisphere function but represent the residual intact right hemisphere function. If the functional organization of the hemispheres are changed as a result of seizure disorders or as a result of surgery designed to alleviate them, then exactly what can be learned about hemisphere function from these patients is unclear. Gardner (1978) has succinctly summarized the contribution of split brain patients to our knowledge of hemisphere function: 'All in all, the study of such patients may tell us only how the human brain under extreme duress can be reorganized; what it reveals about the brains of normal individuals is far from clear'.

Another possible way of examining isolated right hemisphere function is in cases where the left hemisphere has been removed because of the presence of large infiltrative tumours (see Gott, 1973). This operation is rarely, if ever, carried out in adults since it would render them globally aphasic with poor prognosis for recovery. In children, however, prognosis after left hemispherectomy can be very good (Basser, 1962), because the plasticity of the young brain enables the right hemisphere to take over linguistic skills normally carried out by the right hemisphere. This plasticity, however, means that it is as difficult to draw meaningful conclusions about normal right hemisphere function from such patients as it is from commissurotomized patients since the residual right hemisphere function will be partly what was present originally and what has been 'released' or relearned after the operation. Further, the presence of a longstanding congenital tumour will of itself tend to cause a different pattern of functional organization throughout the brain compared to that of a normal individual.

In summary, the role of the right hemisphere in syntactic or semantic aspects of reading remains rather unclear but since there appear to be no reports of disorders of these 'deeper' aspects of reading after right hemisphere damage, either the right hemisphere makes no contribution to processing these deeper aspects or it simply duplicates some of the left hemisphere functions.

Left hemisphere damage and left hemisphere function

There are many classifications of reading disorders after damage to the left, dominant hemisphere (Benson, 1977), but a classification based upon the types of error made by alexic patients is currently influential (Marshall and Newcombe, 1973). Marshall and Newcombe have classified the errors made by alexic patients in reading into three types: visual errors, grapheme–morpheme transformation errors, and semantic errors. These errors are shown to a greater or lesser extent by all alexic patients and the preponderance of one type of error over another varies over time (Newcombe and Marshall, 1973) but Marshall and Newcombe believe that patients with reading difficulties eventually resolve into those who make primarily 'sounding' errors and those who make primarily semantic errors in their reading out loud. Further, they argue that the types of errors that patients make are not random but reflect selective breakdown in different stages of the reading process: thus while visual errors might occur early in the analysis of words or letters, errors of meaning might occur at a later or deeper stage of analysis after adequate perceptual processing has occurred.

Recently patients who show a significant proportion of semantic errors in reading out loud have become the subject of detailed experimental investigation because of their contribution to an understanding of some aspects of normal reading processes and these patients have been termed 'deep' (Marshall and Newcombe, 1973) or 'phonemic' alexics (Shallice and Warrington, 1975). What essentially characterizes these patients' remaining reading skills is a relatively intact ability to read single words silently for comprehension but a relatively impaired ability to read single words out loud—many of the commission errors being semantically related to the target word. Reading out loud is not completely impossible for these patients, however, and the words that they can read out loud are not randomly determined but tend to be words of high compared to low frequency of occurrence, or of high imageability rather than abstract words; nouns are read better than other grammatical classes, function words in particular causing much difficulty (Shallice and Warrington, 1975). When frequency and imageability are controlled word length appears not to be a significant factor in determining whether a word can or cannot be read out loud (Shallice and Warrington, 1975).

While many of the errors that the patients make in reading out loud are errors of omission (no overt response) a major characteristic of their commission errors is the presence of a large proportion of errors which bear a semantic relationship to the presented word (Saffran, Schwartz, and Marin, 1976). These errors are important in that they suggest that the visually presented word can gain access to the appropriate areas of the patient's semantic system without him being able to produce the exact phonology associated with the word. The semantic relationship between the uttered erroneous word and the presented word varies, sometimes being category related (such as *robin* for *bird*, sometimes synonymously related (such as *merry* for *happy*), and sometimes associatively related (such as *holly* for *Christmas*); there is thus no simple relationship between the nature of the semantic error and the target words (Saffran, Schwartz, and Marin, 1976), except that there is a tendency for nouns to be produced in response to words of all parts of speech (Marshall and Newcombe, 1973) and that the errors produced are in some ways similar to the types of free associations that normal individuals produce to words (Rinnert and Whitaker, 1973). Shallice and Warrington's (1975) patient also showed a significant proportion of visual in addition to semantic errors, but one of the patients reported by Patterson and Marcel (1977) did not show a significant proportion of visual errors; whether the latter are a factor in the syndrome of deep alexia is therefore unclear.

It has also been shown (Patterson and Marcel, 1977; Saffran and Marin, 1977) that these patients are unable to read out loud pronounceable nonsense words (*dube*, for example) which, nevertheless, could be repeated out loud if heard. (In the nonsense reading conditions the patients were on the whole unwilling to make overt responses to the words, but when encouraged to make some response the errors that they made tended to show visual relationships to the presented word (Patterson and Marcel, 1977)—this is to be expected, of course, since semantic errors cannot be made in response to nonsense words.) Clearly the ability to repeat a proper word or nonsense word out loud when the word is heard but not seen excludes any general disability associated with speech production; rather the deficit is associated only with the spoken equivalent of *visually* presented words. Can the patients *covertly* produce the sound corresponding to a word even though they cannot overtly produce it? In other words do the patients have internal speech that can be matched to words even though they cannot produce external speech to the same word? The answer to this question appears to be negative since although the patients can judge whether two words rhyme with each other when they are visually similar (for example *rain–chain*) they cannot accurately make this judgement when the pairs are visually dissimilar (for example, *laugh–staff*) and where the rhyming judgement must be based upon some comparison of the sounds of the two words (Saffran and Marin, 1977). Further, in contrast to normal readers the patients show no extra difficulty (in terms of reaction time) in deciding whether a homophone (such as *blud*) is not a true English word compared to pronounceable non-homophones (such as *dake*). In normal subjects (Rubenstein, Lewis, and Rubenstein, 1971) it has been argued that covert pronunciation of pronounceable nonsense words leads to conflicting evidence in the case of homophones since the orthography of the word does not represent an English word while its phonological characterization does; in the absence of putative covert pro-nunciation the patients do not suffer from these conflicting pieces of evidence and accordingly show no extra difficulty with homophones compared to non-homophones.

Whether the inability to read nonsense words out loud simply reflects a special case of the difficulty that the patients have with low frequency, low imageability words, or whether it represents a more general loss of the ability to make grapheme—morpheme transformations is unclear, but it is apparent that for unknown reasons the information about the way in which a visually presented word is pronounced is more closely tied to familiar, concrete words than it is to less familiar, abstract words.

That the patients have some comprehension of words that cannot accurately be overtly or covertly read is, of course, evident from the semantic errors they make in reading out loud; but comprehension of individual words seems to be quite extensive since Saffran and Marin (1977) have shown that their patient had an above normal score on a written version of the Peabody picture vocabulary test (a test requiring the matching of words to one of four pictures of objects or actions) where no spoken response was required. Whether the comprehension of individual words is entirely normal in these patients remains, however, an open issue since, for example, the ability to match a word to its pictorial representation is only a demonstration that *one* aspect of the words meaning is intact (namely what the object that the word represents looks like). Comprehension of individual words does seem remarkable, however, in the face of the patient's relatively poor ability to read out loud or to covertly produce the sound of a word, and this must imply that words need not be covertly pronounced before they are at least partially understood and that, accordingly, comprehension of the written word can occur directly from its visual characteristics. Since covert speech activity always seems to accompany normal silent reading (McGuigan, 1970) it might be inferred that such activity may simply be a concomitant of reading skill that plays no causal role in comprehension of words, but, since the deep alexic patients tend to find silent reading of texts (as opposed to individual words) difficult—the patient of Albert *et al.* (1973) could not respond to written commands for example—it is also possible that covert speech does play a significant role in comprehension, perhaps by acting as a check on the outcome of other more direct routes to word comprehension based upon visual form (Klieman, 1975).

Since the inability to repeat words is confined to visual presentation and is not present with auditory presentation, the syndrome of deep alexia is thus a relatively pure disorder of reading; nevertheless, it does not occur in the absence of other linguistic deficits (that is, it appears to occur within the context of an aphasia). Table 4.1 shows some of the other deficits that tend to occur with the specific features of deep alexia. It can be seen that there is no obvious relationship with the length of time since the brain damage occurred, but follow-up studies on

Table 4.1 Characteristics of patients showing good comprehension of visually presented words who find concrete words easier to read out loud than abstract words. 1 = point of entry, 2 = determined at operation, 3 = determined from EMI-scan, 4 = determined from technetium scan 5 = reported as Broca's aphasics. Mild, moderate and severe refer to reported degree of impairment.
CVA = cerebovascular accident. ? = not reported. T, P, O refer to the temporal, parietal and occipital lobes respectively

Study	Patient	Aetiology	Lesion site	Approximate time since damage	SPEECH				Writing	Spelling
					Production	Comprehension	Repetition	Object-naming		
Newcombe and Marshall, 1973	GR	Missile	T–P[1]	26 yrs	Telegrammatic	Mild	Moderate	Mild	Severe	Severe
	KU	Missile	P–O[1]	26 yrs	Telegrammatic	Mild	?	Mild	Moderate	Moderate
Shallice and Warrington, 1975	KF	Accident	P[2]	3 yrs	'Halting, non-paraphasic'	Mild	Severe	Mild	?	Severe
Saffran, Schwartz and Marin, 1976	V	CVA	?	3–4 yrs	Telegrammatic[5]	———	Not reported		↑	↑
	H	CVA	?	3–4 yrs	Telegrammatic[5]	———	Not reported		↑	↑
Saffran and Marin, 1977	VS	CVA	T–O[3]	3 yrs	Telegrammatic[5]	Mild	?	?	Mild	?
Patterson and Marcel, 1977	DE	Accident	?	5 yrs	Telegrammatic[5]	Mild	?	Mild	?	Severe
	PW	CVA	?	10 yrs	Telegrammatic[5]	Moderate	?	Mild	?	Severe
Andrewsky and Seron, 1975	MD	CVA	P–T[2]	7 yrs	Agrammatic	Mild	?	Mild	?	?
Albert et al. 1973.	JH	Tumour	T–P–O[2,4]	1yr	Fluent, paraphasic	Mild	Normal	Moderate	Severe	Mild

individual patients may well prove informative. Table 4.1 shows too that in all cases where they were reported, spelling and writing were also impaired in addition to the reading impairment. Object-naming and auditory comprehension were also usually mildly impaired (when reported) and eight of the ten cases had spontaneous speech which could be described as 'telegrammatic' or 'agrammatic', in other words their spontaneous speech consisted mostly of content words, few function words, and short phrase length with simple syntactic structure. These are all the characteristic features of Broca's aphasia which was how the patients were described in five out of the eight cases. Usually Broca's aphasia is associated with anterior lesions (Kertesz, Lesk, and McCabe, 1977), but the only clear localization data on a deep alexic patient described as a Broca's aphasic (VS) had an EMI-scan showing a posterior lesion. While both Marshall and Newcombe's (1973) patients may also have been Broca's aphasics, localization of the lesion is difficult because of the missile nature of their brain damage. In short the parts of the left hemisphere of the brain damaged in deep alexia are essentially unknown.

At first sight Table 4.1 shows an apparent association between deep alexia and the presence of the telegrammatic speech characteristics of Broca's aphasia. There are, however, two clear exceptions to this generalization—JH (Albert *et al.* 1973) and KF (Shallice and Warrington, 1975), who has in fact been described as a conduction aphasic—and what characterises both Broca's and conduction aphasics is not their spontaneous speech, which is quite different (Goodglass and Geschwind, 1976), but the presence of only mild or moderate impairment of auditory comprehension. It may therefore be that it is the presence of mild comprehension deficits which are related to deep alexia rather than some characteristic of speech output. This view receives some support from recent evidence (Gardner and Zurif, 1976) that left hemisphere lesion site did not affect the pattern of performance on tests of reading comprehension, but the degree of general auditory language comprehension deficit (as assessed by the Boston Diagnostic Aphasia Examination) did affect the pattern of performance on the reading comprehension tests. In particular, patients with significant comprehension deficits were relatively poor at matching written nouns to their pictorial equivalent while those with mild comprehension deficits were relatively good at this task. Further Gardner and Zurif (1975) have shown that all aphasics of whatever clinical type show a tendency to find concrete nouns easier to read out loud than abstract nouns, and all find nouns easier to read out loud than other grammatical classes. Taken together the results of Gardner and Zurif (1975; 1976) suggest that any aphasic with mild comprehension deficits might show some of the major features of the syndrome of deep alexia and Table 4.1 shows that all the reported patients have mild or moderate degrees of auditory comprehension impairment.

Marshall and Newcombe (1973) have argued for the essential normality of the errors made in reading by brain-damaged patients, that is, these patients make errors which are qualitatively similar to errors made by normal individuals under difficult conditions. Thus in some conditions of backward masking, for example, Allport (1977) has shown that normal individuals cannot read a word out loud yet are able to extract some aspects of a word's meaning; normal individuals find it easier to report words of high as opposed to low frequency of occurrence in the language when presented tachistoscopically (Howes and Solomon, 1951) and normal individuals find concrete words easier to report than abstract words with brief presentation (Riegal and Riegal, 1961)—although there are negative reports on this issue (Paivio and O'Neill, 1970). It may be therefore that brain damage which leads to, or resolves through recovery of function to, a mild auditory comprehension deficit does not necessarily produce a disconnection or disruption of one route to comprehension of a word's meaning but produces a reduction in cognitive abilities which is similar in its effect to that induced by testing normal individuals under less than optimum conditions. If this is the case than it should be possible to simulate systematically the patterns of reading deficit found in brain-damaged individuals by testing reading in normal individuals under difficult conditions. Simulation studies could in principle, of course, be carried out on normal children in an attempt to understand developmental reading disorders.

Finally it should be pointed out in the context of aphasic alexia that all aphasics have object-naming difficulties to a greater or lesser extent, and while mild object-naming problems have been noted in deep alexics (Table 4.1) the implication is usually that their difficulties in naming objects is small in comparison to their difficulties in naming words (that is, reading out loud) and that, accordingly, the difficulty in word-naming is a specific problem and not part of a more general naming problem. Unfortunately, while this may well be correct the condition under which object-naming is tested is typically with highly familiar objects capable of pictorial representation (that is, concrete objects). But the names of such objects are typically those which the deep alexic can read out loud, so simple naming tests do not control for the presence of a more widespread non-specific naming disorder. Fortunately it appears unlikely that such a non-specific disorder is necessarily responsible for all the data on deep alexics since Andrewsky and Seron (1975) have shown that a word presented in one linguistic context as a noun could be read out loud, while exactly the same word presented in another linguistic context as a function word could not be read out loud. Such context effects argue against non-specific naming disorders and imply, rather paradoxically in view of the preponderance of noun reponses to written words of all grammatical classes (Marshall and Newcombe, 1973), that these patients can also detect the grammatical class of a word even though they cannot say it.

Specific alexia

One issue which has been of concern to developmental psychologists and educationalists interested in the acquisition of reading skills has been whether children can show a selective disorder in learning to read, in other words whether a learning disorder specific to visually presented linguistic information can occur and such specificity of reading disorders has also been an issue in reading problems associated with neurologically impaired individuals.

It is apparent that the dissociation between reading out loud and reading for comprehension seen in adult deep alexics occurs against the background of more general linguistic deficits such as telegrammatic speech and mild comprehension deficits, but other forms of alexia occur (alexia with and without agraphia) in which there is minimal linguistic impairment (Goodglass and Geschwind, 1976). Thus while reading deficits can occur in the context of aphasia they need not necessarily do so.

A more general problem is whether acquired reading disorders are just one manifestation of a more widespread cognitive failure, the most obvious possibility being that the reading problem in brain-damaged individuals occurs against a background of general intellectual loss, that is, dementia. Certainly reading problems may well occur with dementing illnesses but none of the patients described here would be classified as demented—neurologically all had focal rather than diffuse damage to the brain, and behaviourally the non-aphasic individuals would have had WAIS intelligence quotients in the normal range, or at least perform normally on specific subtests of the WAIS (McFie, 1975). Intellectual status is often difficult to access in aphasia but it is likely that many of the performance subtests of the WAIS would be adequately performed by these patients. The reading disorder is therefore not part of a general cognitive impairment and to that extent it reflects a relatively pure, isolated disorder.

If acquired reading disorders can occur in the absence of global intellectual loss or extensive linguistic impairment, to what extent are difficulties in naming or understanding visually presented words specific to words, and to what extent are the difficulties manifest with all types of visually presented material? In other words although alexia may not simply be a manifestation of dementia or one manifestation of aphasia it may well be one manifestation of difficulties in the interpretation of *any* type of visual material; in other words, the disorder is specific in the sense that it is confined to visually presented information but it is not specific in the sense that it is confined to any one class of visual material. At some early level within the visual system of course there must be, and are, common systems responsible for the processing of all types of visually presented material; the issue is, therefore, whether at a later or deeper stage of visual analysis there are specific systems responsible for the processing of material of different types (one of which is responsible for the analysis of print) or whether even at a late stage of visual information processing the same system is responsible for categorization of all types of material.

Common systems for the processing of types of visual stimuli have been shown in a patient reported by Benson and Greenberg (1966)—an 'apperceptive agnosic' patient who had normal elementary visual function (visual fields, acuity, colour vision and brightness discrimination were all within normal limits) but who was quite unable to name, demonstrate comprehension of, or copy either visually presented words or objects. The inability to copy visually presented stimuli suggests that the disorder occurred at a relatively low level of visual analysis, and that the visual information the patient received was scrambled in such a way to make interpretation and naming impossible. Rubens and Benson (1971) have reported another patient (whose disorder was termed 'associative agnosia') who was unable to name or interpret print or objects or faces, but who could copy what he saw with remarkable accuracy. Since the patient could copy so well this suggests a high level of intact visual analysis (in other words he received unscrambled high level sensory data) but he was unable to attach meaning to what he saw and this difficulty manifested itself across objects, faces and words. In both apperceptive and associative agnosia the patients were able to name and comprehend objects if palpated or heard, so the disorders are specific to visual processing but not specific to any particular class of stimuli (or at least not to words, objects or faces).

Such reports of fairly extensive agnosia would tend to argue against the notion of specific systems responsible for the analysis of different types of visual material whether at a relatively low level (manifested by poor copying) or at a relatively high level (manifested by good copying) of visual analysis, were it not for the fact that there are other reports of patients who do show a dissociation between naming and comprehension of one class of visual stimuli and an inability to name or comprehend other classes. In other words widespread, high level impairment of visual processing *may* occur, but so may more specific impairments. Thus Albert, Reches, and Silverberg (1975) report a patient who was unable to name or comprehend drawings of objects in the face of an intact ability to copy (associative agnosia) but who could read out loud and for comprehension. In other words, the patient was relatively *able* to name and classify *words* but was relatively *unable* to name and classify *objects*. This dissociation between verbal and non-verbal performance may reflect the fact that different systems are involved in the processing of words and objects with visual presentation, and that brain damage has selectively impaired one of them; but on the other hand it is also possible that a common system is involved in the processing of both types of visual material, and that even for normal individuals naming and classifying words is somehow easier than naming and classifying objects and under conditions of neurological impairment these differences tend to be heightened. In other words the brain-damaged patient may simply show an exacerbation of the normal patterns of performance rather than qualitatively different patterns. The normal literature shows that words can be read faster than objects can be named, while objects tend to be classified as belonging to a specified category slightly faster than their verbal equivalents (Potter and Faulconer, 1974). Thus if latency is indicative of difficulty the pattern of performance observed by Albert, Reches, and Silverberg (1975) in their patient does not entirely reflect exacerbated normal performance. On the other hand if normal performance were examined under other conditions (with backward masking for example), where accuracy rather than latency was the dependent variable, other patterns of performance may occur, but unfortunately there appear to be no data on accuracy of name and classification tasks with words and objects as stimuli under difficult perceptual conditions; accordingly the normal patterns of performance under such conditions remain unknown.

One obvious type of solution to the above problem is to seek for double dissociation of function. In other words, if a patient could be identified who had difficulties in reading but not in identifying objects, the opposite of Albert, Reches, and Silverberg's (1975) case, then clearly *both* patterns of performance cannot reflect exacerbated normal behaviour and accordingly distinct processing systems may be responsible for the observed double dissociation. Patients diagnosed as alexics with agraphia do not normally have problems in object-comprehension (although they do with object-naming) and could therefore be described as demonstrating a reading difficulty in the absence of a difficulty in object comprehension. However, finer analysis of an alexic with agraphia patient showed that his difficulty was with word-naming rather than word-comprehension—in other words, the patient had difficulties in naming both words and objects but also had relative preservation of comprehension of both words and objects (Albert *et al.*, 1973). The alexic with agraphia patient therefore shows a dissociation between word-naming and word-comprehension but not between word-comprehension and object-comprehension, and if this patient is typical, patients having alexia with agraphia do not provide evidence for a dissociation between word-naming and comprehension on the one hand, and object-naming and comprehension on the other. Recently, however, Heilman, Tucker, and Valenstein (1976) have reported a case of transcortical motor aphasia in which the patient was able to name visually presented objects and words and, while he was also able to demonstrate some comprehension of objects in a task requiring pointing to one of four objects which was related to a fifth in some way, he was quite unable to comprehend print since he was never able to execute printed commands such as 'point to the ceiling'. Relative preservation of object comprehension in the face of relatively impaired reading comprehension, together with the results from Albert, Reches, and Silverberg's (1975) patient, appears to provide the necessary evidence for a double dissociation between verbal and non-verbal processing systems, but unfortunately Heilman, Tucker, and Valenstein's (1976) comprehension tests are clearly not comparable in the case of objects and words. In the case of words, to carry out the task the patient must be able to comprehend verbs, prepositions and nouns and their relationships within a sentence; in the case of objects the patient simply had to decide which of four objects belonged to the same category as a target object. It is simply not possible, therefore, to evaluate differential performance in word and object-comprehension in this study.

It is apparent, therefore, that, although there is some evidence which is suggestive of a specific system involved in the categorization of visually presented words which may be impaired or disconnected after brain damage, the issue is still an open one.

CONCLUSIONS

It was argued earlier that one contribution the study of alexia could make to an understanding of developmental reading difficulties is an indirect one, through alexia providing a greater insight into normal reading processes in adults, and this knowledge in turn providing a context for the evaluation of reading failure in children. Experimental psychologists have in fact only relatively recently become interested in the systematic investigation of cognitive breakdown after focal brain damage, and accordingly the contribution that the study of such patients can in fact make to an understanding of normal processes in general and reading processes in particular is as yet difficult to evaluate. The approach is not without its critics, however—most recently Oatley (1978)—most of whom argue that the pattern of breakdown even after focal damage to the brain is fairly non-specific and thus has little of use to tell us about specific aspects of normal functioning. While it is true that pure disorders of one aspect of cognition, and only one aspect, are rarely if ever observed after brain damage, it would in fact be very surprising that 'pure' disorders would be observed, not simply because lesions may spread across several regions of the brain and thus involve many functional system, but because it would imply that we already knew enough of cognitive function and organization to anticipate the way in which cognition *should* break down after brain damage; in other words, it implies that we know in advance what 'pure' cases should be like. No cognitive theory is that advanced, nor is such a theory on the scientific horizon.

The constellation of symptoms that reliably occur together after brain damage may tell us something of significance about cognitive organization *especially* if the constellation conflicts with *a priori* expectations about what aspects of cognitive functioning should or should not be related. The Gerstmann syndrome is a case in point. Although the reliability of the cluster of symptoms associated with this syndrome is sometimes disputed (Gardner, 1977), it illustrates the case in that it forces a consideration about what the elements of the Gerstmann syndrome (finger agnosia, agraphia, acalculia and left—right disorientation) have in common—a question that might well otherwise have not been asked about cognition. Neuropsychologically, therefore, it is precisely *because* some disorders are 'impure' that they may be particularly interesting.

REFERENCES

Albert, M. L., Reches, A., and Silverberg, R. (1975) Associative visual agnosia without alexia. *Neurology*, **25**, 322–326.

Albert, M. L., Yamadori, A., Gardner, H., and Howes, D. (1973) Comprehension in alexia. *Brain*, **96**, 317–328.

Allport, D. A. (1977) On knowing the meaning of words we are unable to report: the effects of visual masking. In S. Dornic (ed.), *Attention and Performance*, Vol. VI, London: Academic Press.

Andrewsky, E. and Seron, X. (1975) Implicit processing of grammatical rules in a classical case of agrammatism. *Cortex*, **11**, 379–390.

Basser, L. S. (1962) Hemiplegia of early onset and the faculty of speech with special reference to the effects of hemispherectomy. *Brain*, **85**, 427–460.

Benson, D. F. (1977) The third alexia. *Arch. Neurol.*, **34**, 327–331.

Benson, D. F. and Geschwind, N. (1969) The alexias. In P. J. Vinken and G. W. Bruyn (eds.) Handbook of Clinical Neurology. Amsterdam: North Holland.

Benson, D. F. and Greenberg, J. P. (1969) Visual form agnosia: a specific defect in visual discrimination. *Arch. Neurol.*, **20**, 82–89.

Birch, H. G. and Belmont, L. (1964) Auditory–visual integration in normal and retarded readers. *Amer. J. Orthopsychiat.*, **35**, 852–861.

Brooks, D. N. and Baddeley, A. D. (1976) What can amnesic patients learn? *Neuropsychologia*, **14**, 111–122.

Butler, S. R. and Norrsell, U. (1968) Vocalisation possibly initiated by the minor hemisphere. *Nature*, **220**, 793–794.

Butters, N. and Brody, B. A. (1968) The role of the left parietal cortex in the mediation of intra and cross-modal associations. *Cortex*, **4**, 328–343.

Butters, N., Barton, M., and Brody, B. A. (1970) Role of the right parietal lobe in the mediation of cross-modal associations and reversible operations in space. *Cortex*, **6**, 174–190.

Coltheart, M. (1977) Phonemic dyslexia: some comments on its interpretation and its implications for the study of normal reading. *Paper presented to the International Neuropsychology Society,* Oxford.

Denckla, M. B. (1972) Color naming defects in dyslexic boys. *Cortex*, **8**, 164–176.

Gardner, H. (1977) *The Shattered Mind.* London: Routledge and Kegan Paul.

Gardner, H. (1978) What we know (and don't know) about the two halves of the brain. *Bull. Inter. Neuropsychol. Soc.*, **3**, 27–31.

Gardner, H. and Zurif, E. (1975) Bee but not be: oral reading of single words in aphasia and alexia. *Neuropsychologia*, **13**, 181–190.

Gardner, H. and Zurif, E. (1976) Critical reading of words and phrases in aphasia. *Brain and Language*, **3**, 173–190.

Gazzaniga, M. S. and Hillyard, S. A. (1971) Language and speech capacity of the right hemisphere. *Neuropsychologia*, **9**, 273–280.

Gazzaniga, M. S. and Sperry, R. W. (1967) Language after section of the cerebral commissures. *Brain*, **90**, 131–148.

Geschwind, N. (1965) Disconnection syndromes in animals and man. *Brain*, **88**, 237–294, 585–644.

Geschwind, N. and Fusillo, M. (1966) Color-naming defects in association with alexia. *A.M.A. Arch. Neurol.*, **15**, 137–146.

Goodglass, H., and Geschwind, N. (1976) Language disorders (aphasia). In E. C. Carterette and M. P. Friedman (eds.) *Handbook of Perception, Vol. VII, Language and Speech.* London: Academic Press.

Gott, P. S. (1973) Language after dominant hemispherectomy. *J. Neurol., Neurosurg. Psychiat.*, **36**, 1082–1088.

Griffith, H. and Davidson, M. (1966) Long-term changes in intellect and behaviour after hemispherectomy. *J. Neurol., Neurosurg. Psychiat.*, **29**, 571–576.

Hécaen, H. and Albert, M. L. (1978) *Human Neuropsychology*, New York: Wiley.

Heilman, K. M., Tucker, D. M., and Valenstein, E. (1976) A case of mixed transcortical aphasia with intact naming. *Brain*, **99**, 415–426.

Howes, D. H. and Solomon, R. L. (1951) Visual duration threshold as a function of word-probability. *J. Exper. Psychol.*, **41**, 401–410.

Kertesz, A., Lesk, D., and McCabe, P. (1977) Isotope localisation of infarcts in aphasia. *Arch. Neurol.*, **34**, 590–601.

Kinsbourne, M. and Warrington, E. K. (1962) A variety of reading disability associated with right hemisphere lesions. *J. Neurol. Neurosurg. and Psychiat.*, **25**, 339–344.

Kinsbourne, M. and Warrington, E. K. (1963) The developmental Gerstmann syndrome. *Arch. Neurol.*, **8**, 490–501.

Klieman, G. M. (1975) Speech recoding in reading. *J. Verbal Learning and Verbal Behav.*, **14**, 323–339.

LeDoux, J. E., Volpe, B. T., Smylie, C. S. and Gazzaniga, M. S. (1978) Plasticity in brain organisation of speech following callosotomy. *Bull. Inter. Neuropsycholog. Soc.*, **3**, 13–14.

Levy, J. and Trevarthen, C. (1977) Perceptual, semantic and phonetic aspects of elementary language processes in split-brain patients. *Brain*, **100**, 105–118.

Luria, A. R. (1973) *The Working Brain*. Harmondsworth: Penguin.

Marshall, J. C. and Newcombe, F. (1973) Patterns of paralexia: a psycholinguistic approach. *J. Psycholinguistic Res.*, **2**, 175–199.

McFie, J. (1975) *Assessment of Organic Intellectual Impairment*. London: Academic Press.

McGuigan, F. J. (1970) Covert oral behaviour during the silent performance of language tasks. *Psycholog. Bull.*, **74**, 309–326.

Nathan, P. W. and Smith, M. C. (1950) Normal mentality associated with a maldeveloped 'rhinencephalon'. *J. Neurol. Neurosurg. Psychiat.*, **13**, 191–197.

Newcombe, F., Hiorns, R. W., and Marshall, J. C. (1976) Acquired dyslexia: recovery and retraining. In Y. Lebrun and R. Hoops (eds.). *Neurolinguistics 4, Recovery in Aphasics*. Amsterdam: Swets and Zeitlinger B. V.

Newcombe, F. and Marshall, J. C. (1973) Stages in recovery from dyslexia following a left cerebral abscess. *Cortex*, **9**, 329–332.

Oatley, K. (1978) *Perceptions and Representations*. London: Methuen.

Paivio, A. and O'Neill, B. J. (1970) Visual recognition thresholds and dimensions of word meaning. *Perception and Psychophys.* **8**, 273–275.

Patterson, A. and Zangwill, O. L. (1944) Disorders of visual space perception associated with lesions of the right cerebral hemisphere, *Brain*, **67**, 331–358.

Patterson, K. E. (1978) Reading impairment in aphasia: errors of meaning and the meaning of errors. *Paper read to the Experimental Psychology Society*.

Patterson, K. E. and Marcel, A. J. (1977) Aphasia, dyslexia and the phonological coding of written words. *Q. J. Exper. Psychol.*, **29**, 307–318.

Potter, M. C. and Faulconer, B.A. (1974) Time to understand pictures and words. *Nature*, **253**, 437–438.

Preston, M.S., Guthrie, J. T. and Childs, B. (1974) Visual evoked responses (VERs) in normal and disabled readers. *Psychophysiology*, **11**, 452–457.

Reinvang, I. (1976) Sentence production in recovery from aphasia. In Y. Lebrun and R. Hoops (eds.) *Neurolinguistics 4, Recovery in Aphasics*. Amsterdam: Swets and Zeitlinger B. V.

Riegal, K. F. and Riegal, R. M. (1961) Prediction of word recognition thresholds on the basis of stimulus parameters. *Language and Speech*, **4**, 157–170.

Rinnert, C. and Whitaker, H. A. (1973) Semantic confusions by aphasic patients. *Cortex*, **9**, 56–81.

Rubens, A. B. and Benson, D. F. (1971) Associative visual agnosia. *Arch. Neurol.*, **24**, 305–316.

Rubenstein, H., Lewis, S. S. and Rubenstein, M. A. (1971) Evidence for phonemic recoding in visual word recognition. *J. Verbal Learning and Verbal Behav.*, **10**, 645–657.

Saffran, E. M. and Marin, O. S. M. (1977) Reading without phonology: evidence from aphasia. *Q. J. Exper. Psychol.*, **29**, 515–525.

Saffran, E. M., Schwartz, M. F., and Marin, O. S. M. (1976) Semantic mechanisms in paralexia. *Brain and Language*, **3**, 255–265.

Shallice, T. and Warrington, E. K. (1975) Word recognition in a phonemic dyslexic patient. *Q. J. Exper. Psychol.*, **27**, 187–199.

Sklar, B., Hanley, J., and Simmons, W. W. (1972) An EEG experiment aimed toward identifying dyslexic children. *Nature*, **240**, 414–416.

Symann-Louett, N., Gascon, G. G., Matsumiya, Y., and Lombroso, C. T. (1977) Wave form difference in visual evoked responses between normal and reading disabled children. *Neurology*, **27**, 156–159.

Teuber, H-L. (1977). Recovery of function after brain injury in man. In: *Outcome of Severe Damage to the Central Nervous System. (CIBA Foundation Symposium 34)*. Amsterdam: Elsevier.

Warrington, E. K. (1967) The incidence of verbal disability associated with reading retardation. *Neuropsychologia*, **5**, 175–179.

Weiskrantz, L., Warrington, E. K., Sanders, M. D., and Marshall, J. (1974) Visual capacity in the hemianopic field following a restricted occipital ablation, *Brain*, **97**, 709–728.

Zaidel, E. (1976) Auditory vocabulary of the right hemisphere after brain bisection or hemidecortication, *Cortex*, **12**, 191–211.

Zaidel, E. (1977) Unilateral auditory language comprehension on the Token Test following cerebral commissurotomy and hemispherectomy. *Neuropsychologia*, **15**, 1–13.

Dyslexia Research and its Applications to Education
Edited by G. Th. Pavlidis and T. R. Miles
© 1981 John Wiley & Sons Ltd.

CHAPTER 5

Temporal Order in Normal and Disturbed Reading

DIRK J. BAKKER AND HANS J. F. SCHROOTS

TEMPORAL ORDER PERCEPTION (TOP): A DETERMINANT OF READING (DIS)ABILITY

Antecedent studies

Birch and Belmont's work on sensory integration is well known, as is their test of visual–auditory matching of tapped-out patterns (Birch and Belmont, 1964; 1965). In this test rhythmic patterns are tapped out which the subject has to match with visual dot configurations; thus auditory–temporal patterns have to be matched with visual–spatial ones.

Birch and Belmont as well as other investigators (Muehl and Kremenak, 1966; Sterrit and Rudnick, 1966; Van de Voort, Senf, and Benton, 1972) have shown that intersensory integration measured this way not only differentiates normal and specific reading disturbed children, but also correlates with reading ability in general. This finding is understandable since reading requires the integration of visual–spatial and auditory–temporal patterns. Printed letters and words are ordered in space from left to right while speech sounds are ordered in time. In considering such experiments one may wonder where the difficulties arise for reading disabled children. Are they in the auditory–visual, in the temporal–spatial or in both forms of integration? Marion Blank and her associates (Blank and Bridger, 1966; Blank, Weider and Bridger, 1968) set up a task requiring temporal–spatial but not auditory–visual integration. This task also proved more difficult for the reading-disabled than for the normal readers. But more was evident. Merely perceiving and remembering temporal patterns was already problematic for reading-disturbed subjects, at least under certain conditions. This became apparent when Blank and Bridger (1966) had their subjects reproduce tapped-out temporal patterns. In one assignment the pattern had to be retapped, in another it had to be imitated verbally. In the latter case, after the pattern . . . had been presented the subject would react with 'one–two–three–four'. It was only when the patterns had to be imitated verbally that difficulties arose for the dyslexics. This was an important finding which led to the conclusion that some reading-disabled persons have difficulty in perceiving and/or remembering temporal patterns only when a verbal medium is used.

Temporal order defined

In the investigations of Blank and Bridger (1966) and Blank, Weider, and Bridger (1968) tapped-out patterns had to be repeated by the subject, either manually or verbally. These tasks respectively require non-verbal and verbal imitation of temporal sequences (Bakker, 1972). Another example of a verbally imitated temporal sequence is the subject's repetition of digits as tested in the Digit Span subtest of the Wechsler Intelligence Scale for Children (WISC). If one requires the subject to indicate explicitly the serial position of a digit in a series, one could speak of the explication of a temporal order. When, for example, the series 7, 5, 9, 6, 4 is presented one may ask which serial position is taken by 5 (2nd), 6 (4th), etc. Non-verbal series can be explicated as well; one may show meaningless figures, one at a time, and after presentation expose these figures again and ask the subject the position of an item in the original series. Temporal sequences, in summary, can be imitated and explicated, in both cases either verbally or non-verbally. Temporal order is confounded with spatial order in some tasks. The Knox Cubes Test, for instance, provides for a number of cubes which are arrayed in front of the subject. The examiner taps the cubes in a certain order and the subject responds by tapping the cubes in the same sequence. It will be clear that this test provides the subject with both temporal and spatial information about the serial position of the various cubes.

Amsterdam studies

In these investigations (Bakker, 1967; 1972; Groenendaal and Bakker, 1971) the temporal sequences presented had to be explicated by the subject; after presentation of a series he had to indicate which item was shown first, which next, and so on. The ordering tasks were otherwise varied in many ways. Thus, temporal sequences of letters, digits, colours, meaningful figures and meaningless figures were presented. The presentations were under different sensory conditions, mostly visual, but also auditory and haptic. Interval and presentation times varied from relatively short units (75 msec) to rather long (4000 msec). With one exception, the findings all pointed to a relationship between TOP and reading proficiency. The one exception involved the perception of temporally ordered *meaningless* figures. However, the perception and retention of verbal as well as verbally codifiable stimuli like meaningful figures and colours appeared to be related to reading performance and to differentiate between good and poor

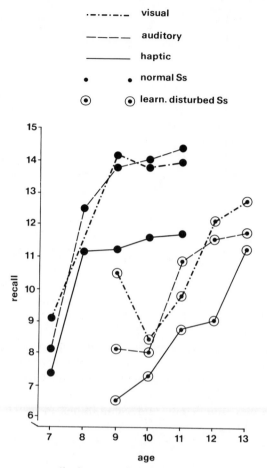

Figure 5.1. Mean correct recall of temporal sequences by modality and age for normal children (across sexes) and for learning disturbed boys (Bakker, 1972). Reproduced by permission of Swets Publishing Service

readers. Moreover, the TOP–reading relationship was found for the number, as well as for the nature, of the errors made. Thus it was shown that children with relatively little ability to perceive and retain temporal sequences made proportionally more errors in letter ordering in reading and writing. Furthermore, TOP was shown to develop with age and to be related to sex. A TOP–age relationship was evident for both 7–11-year-old normal children and for 9–13-year-old disturbed readers, although the slopes indicated a slower rate of development for the disturbed readers (Figure 5.1). Girls showed a faster rate of development than boys up to the ages 7–8; this lag was no longer evident, however, by age 9 (Figure 5.2). The fact that TOP development in boys is slower

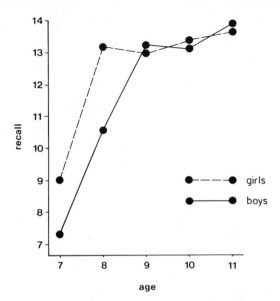

Figure 5.2. Mean correct recall of temporal sequences across modalities by sex and age for normal children (Bakker, 1972). Reproduced by permission of Swets Publishing Service

than in girls during the period of reading acquisition may partly account for the higher proportion of male children in disabled-reading populations. The Amsterdam studies, in summary, clearly showed that the perception and retention of temporal order is related to the learning-to-read process. However, the relationship was found only under conditions in which TOP is verbally mediated.

Recent studies

The Amsterdam investigations have partly been replicated in Brussels by Pierre (1974). Children showing above and below average reading proficiency were presented with an auditory TOP test adapted from Bakker (1972).

The subjects listened to a number of series of three letters each. After presentation of a series the child had to indicate the serial position of two of the letters mentioned by the examiner; 9 and 10-year-old above average readers showed significantly better TOP performance than below average readers of the same ages. Between-group differences could not be shown for 11-year-olds, however. While in the Pierre study verbal stimuli were administered, non-verbal information was presented in an investigation by Doehring and Libman (1974). The subjects, being normal and disturbed readers 7 years of age and older, listened to three-item series of pure tones, the serial position of one of which had to be indicated. No between-group differences could be demonstrated on this non-verbal TOP test. Imitation of temporal order is realized when strings of digits or words have to be recalled in order of presentation. Digit Span is a subtest of the WISC and provides much information on the TOP–reading relationship any time the WISC is used for between reading-group comparisons. Digit series have been used more explicitly in some other investigations. Corkin (1974), in examining serial-ordering deficits in inferior readers, presented strings of digits, ranging in length from 3 to 9, to average and deficient readers aged 6–11 years, and found both age and between reading-group effects.

Torgesen, Bowen, and Ivey (1978), on the other hand, while comparing 9–10-year-old good and poor readers, found these groups non-significantly differing in the vocal and written recall of visually and auditorily presented digit series. Aaron (1978) found digit span performance related to type of reading disability. Contrasting dysphonetic and dyseidetic dyslexics (Boder, 1971), Aaron showed that the former were less able to recall digit series than the latter. Kim (1976) found such temporal sequencing tasks primarily mediated by the left hemisphere. The difficulty of dysphonetic dyslexics in recalling series of digits may thus be due to abnormal functioning of the left cerebral hemisphere. One of the larger studies on the perceptual and linguistic antecedents of reading proficiency has recently been carried out at the Netherlands Institute for Preventive Medicine in collaboration with the Free University Department of Developmental Psychology (Schroots and Van Alphen de Veer, 1976; Schroots et al., 1975). The part of that study which deals with temporal perception and reading will be discussed in the next section.

TEMPORAL ORDER PERCEPTION (TOP): A PREDICTOR OF READING (DIS)ABILITY

Subjects

The study drew on a sample of 411 children, sampled by age, sex and socioeconomic status from 19 nursery schools in 's Hertogenbosch and Rosmalen. Socioeconomic status was assessed by paternal occupation and/or education (Van Westerlaak, Krapman, and Collaris, 1975). If paternal information were not available, maternal occupation and/or education served as a substitute. Table 5.1 presents the sample characteristics.

Predictive measures

Knox Cubes

This is an abbreviated version of the Revised Knox Cube Test (Arthur, 1947). After two practice trials (two cubes), thirteen trials of respectively two (series 1), three (series 2–5), four (series 6–9), and five (series 10–13) cubes are presented.

Table 5.1 Sample by age, socioeconomic status and sex*($n = 411$)

Age	SES-I			SES-II			SES-III			Total		
	b	g	t	b	g	t	b	g	t	b	g	t
5,05–5,10	31	19	50	27	36	63	59	52	111	117	107	224
5,11–6,04	22	22	44	27	22	49	43	51	94	92	95	187
Total	53	41	94	54	58	112	102	103	205	209	202	411

*Age in years and months; SES = socioeconomic status (SES-I = high, SES-II = middle, SES-III = low); b = boys, g = girls; t = total

The cubes are tapped by the examiner and it is the child's task to tap them in the same order. The score (maximum 13 points) is the number of series correctly tapped.

Wordspan

This is based on Bakker's (1972) Temporal Order Auditory–Visual Test (TOAV), modified and ameliorated in several ways. Most important is the division into two separate tests: Wordspan and Picture Matching. As to Wordspan, the subject has to repeat a series of nouns spoken by the examiner. After two practice trials (two words), twelve trials of respectively two (series 1), three (series 2–5), four (series 6–9) and five (series 10–12) words are presented. The score (maximum 12 points) is the number of series recalled in correct order.

Picture matching

Immediately following the recall of a Wordspan series of nouns the subject is required to match the just recalled words with pictures, randomly arranged on a card. Besides the word matches each card shows one additional picture without a match. Matching has to be done in correct order. The score (maximum 12 points) is the number of correctly matched series.

Sentence imitation

This is a ten-sentence story test about a mother who is shopping with her child. Subsequent to reading the story at length each sentence, again being read, has to be recalled by the subject. The score is the summed number of words in each sentence correctly recalled, irrespective of the serial position of these words. Although Sentence Imitation is not a typical temporal ordering task, the test does have some interesting characteristics from a comparative point of view.

Knox Cubes, Wordspan, Picture Matching and Sentence Imitation are subtests of a standardized battery called Leyden Diagnostic Test (Schroots and Van Alphen de Veer, 1976).

Criteria measures

Reading achievement was assessed by two tests and teacher ratings at the end of the first grade of the primary school.

Comprehensive reading

This group-administered test (Van Calcar, Telligen and Van Soest, 1974), requires the child to read words and sentences and to subsequently answer questions about the test.

Technical reading

This individually administered test (Brus and Voeten, 1973) requires the child to read as many words as possible within one minute.

Teacher ratings

These rate the child's reading ability on a five-point scale, varying from very weak (1) to excellent (5) performance as compared with his classmates.

Procedure

Nursery school testing, lasting 3–4 hours approximately, was done in the schools by experienced graduate students in psychology. Primary school testing was done some 15 months later by psychological assistants of local School Advisory Centres. Due to change of address, non-admittance to the primary school, and illness, only 327 children of the original 411 could be tested at the end of the first grade. A small 'restriction-of-range' effect seems likely as 25 dropouts were not admitted to the first grade in view of their insufficient intelligence.

Results

Reliability

Mean, standard deviation and two types of reliability coefficients of the predictive measures are presented in Table 5.2. All four tests have a satisfying split-half reliability, and as expected a somewhat lower homogeneity (coefficient α).

Table 5.2 Mean (M), standard deviation (s), split-half reliability co-efficient (r_{11})* and coefficient α (r_{kk}) of four predictive measures

	M	s	r_{11}*	r_{kk}
Knox Cubes	5.94	2.52	0.83	0.73
Wordspan	6.99	2.04	0.80	0.75
Picture Matching	4.44	2.34	0.81	0.75
Sentence Imitation	44.39	8.79	0.87	0.85

*Split-half reliability coefficients are odd–even correlations corrected by the Spearman–Brown formula

Table 5.3 Three-way analysis of variance on the predictive measures with age, sex and socioeconomic status as factors

Source	df	F ratios*			
		Knox Cubes	Wordspan	Picture Matching	Sentence Imitation
A :age	1	*17.08*	1.31	*10.77*	1.41
B :sex	1	0.01	1.40	2.90	3.69
C :socioeconomic status	2	*11.89*	*6.84*	*7.72*	*20.62*
A × B	1	2.33	1.22	0.81	0.22
A × C	2	1.81	0.12	1.09	1.50
B × C	2	1.33	3.59	2.87	0.24
A × B × C	2	0.64	0.09	1.54	0.24

*F ratios in italics are significant at 1% level ($p < 0.01$)

Relations to age, sex and socioeconomic status

Multivariate factorial analysis was applied to the predictive measures as dependent and age (5:05–5:10 versus 5:11–6:04-year-olds), sex (boys versus girls) and socioeconomic status (SES I versus SES II versus SES III) as independent variables. If the multivariate level of significance is fixed at the 5% level then the univariate F-levels of significance become 1%. The results of the statistical analysis are shown in Table 5.3. Age is significant for Knox Cubes and Picture Matching only: older children perform better on these tests than younger children. Sex affects none, but socioeconomic status all of the test performances. Interactions appear to be non-significant. *A posteriori* analysis of the socioeconomic status effects showed that all tests differentiated significantly between SES II and SES III as well as between SES I and SES III, and only Knox Cubes and Sentence Imitation differentiated between SES I and SES II. High SES children, as expected, showed better test performance than lower SES children.

Table 5.4. Correlations (product moment)* between predictive and criterion measures

Tests	1	2	3	4	5	6	7
1. Knox Cubes							
2. Wordspan	0.35						
3. Picture Matching	0.45	0.63					
4. Sentence Imitation	0.39	0.55	0.55				
5. Comprehensive reading	0.45	0.38	0.45	0.49			
6. Technical reading	0.35	0.32	0.44	0.40	0.71		
7. Teacher ratings	0.32	0.31	0.42	0.40	0.69	0.71	

* All correlations are significant at 1% level ($p < 0.01$)

Table 5.5 Cumulative multiple correlations (cum.R)* between predictive and criterion measures

Comprehensive reading cum.R		Technical reading cum.R		Teacher ratings cum.R	
Sentence Imitation	0.49	Picture Matching	0.44	Picture Matching	0.42
Knox Cubes	0.59	Sentence Imitation	0.49	Sentence Imitation	0.47
Picture Matching	0.61	Knox Cubes	0.52	Knox Cubes	0.49

* Only those predictive measures are rendered, which contributed to a significant increment of cum.R at 1% level ($p < 0.01$)

Relations to reading ability

Correlations between predictive and criterion measures are presented in Table 5.4. As expected all correlations between the three criteria measures for reading ability are high. That this is also true for the correlation between Wordspan and Picture Matching may be due to the fact that performance on the latter task is dependent on performance on the first one; if the child fails on Wordspan, he has little chance to make a correct response on Picture Matching. From all predictive measures Sentence Imitation and Picture Matching show the highest correlations with reading ability, followed by Knox Cubes and Wordspan. Table 5.5 shows the results of a stepwise regression analysis (forward solution). While Wordspan does not contribute significantly to the multiple correlations with the criterion measures, the other predictors do. Sentence Imitation, Knox Cubes and Picture Matching are particularly effective in predicting reading comprehension.

General discussion

The results of the present investigation agree substantially with those of a former study by Bakker (1972) in that TOP tests, especially those requiring intermodal matching (Picture Matching) and 'temporal meaningfulness' (Sentence Imitation) account for a significant amount of the variance in the reading performance of first-grade elementary school children. TOP, moreover, appears to be related to age and socioeconomic status. Sentence Imitation, a culturally determined test, not surprisingly differentiates best between socioeconomic groups.

TOP was investigated in nursery school children, both in Bakker's and the present study. The correlations found between TOP at prereading ages and subsequent reading proficiency in the elementary school thus suggest that poor temporal order perception causes poor reading, rather than vice versa.

However, since the TOP–reading relations, although significant, are after all not markedly high, one could conclude that other factors have a greater impact on the learning-to-read process than just the perception of temporal order. Moreover, one could refer to evidence (Liberman *et al.*, 1971) that sequencing errors constitute less than 10% of all mistakes made in reading, thus suggesting that ordering ability is of limited importance in learning to read. However, no *firm* conclusion as to the importance of a factor can be based on relationships found in a cross-sectional study. What would one conclude about the importance of piles under a house, given an observed correlation of, say, 0.50 between the size of the piles and the size of the house, and the volume of the piles constituting less than 10% of the volume of the whole building? Such figures do not tell that piles are so crucial that cutting them would destroy the walls and that consequently the roof and ceiling would come down, destroying the furniture. A building is a complex construction requiring the integrity of numerous, hierarchically structured components. Reading is a complex process presuming the adequacy of a number of functions, one of which is temporal ordering, which possibly show a hierarchical structure with a cumulative effect on learning to read. Poor temporal order perception could affect the processes which depend on TOP. Weakened secondary functions could ultimately affect reading proficiency.

The question is, of course, how basic is temporal order perception to reading in the hierarchical constellation of functions? The impact of TOP on reading has recently been questioned by those (Shankweiler and Liberman, 1978; Vellutino, 1977) who believe that linguistic rather than temporal ordering deficits underlie reading difficulties. Shankweiler and Liberman presented sequences of rhyming and non-rhyming letters to normal and reading-impaired children. The latter made more errors than the normals only in recalling the non-confusing series; the confusing (rhyming) series were equally difficult for both groups. The between-group difference for non-confusable letters was found for both a visual and an auditory input. The authors conclude that impaired readers are relatively little influenced by the phonetic characteristics of letters, whereas normal readers *are* affected by that variable. However, since ordered recall was required in all conditions the results do not warrant a clearcut inference as to the question whether a phonetic or a temporal perception deficit is basic to a reading difficulty. More pertinent seem the results of another investigation referred to by

Shankweiler and Liberman. These results are said to show that good readers are more adversely affected by rhyming letters than poor readers in an experiment that avoids the requirements of ordered recall. The authors finally conclude (1978, p. 121) that 'there is ample reason to suppose that phonetic coding processes and not merely length of memory span or temporal order perception must be taken into account in order to find the causes of reading backwardness . . . poor serial recall is a symptom of difficulties in phonetic coding, not an independent deficit'. Thus phonetic coding is hierarchically first, and ordering ability second in the aetiology of reading backwardness.

It is interesting to note in this context that another step backward is taken by Tallal (1976) who holds that phonetic coding difficulties are secondary to inferior discrimination of sound qualities. She argues that at least some reading-impaired children may have basic problems in responding to acoustic inform-ation that is presented rapidly. Tallal found that such children have great difficulty in reading nonsense words, presumably because this task relies heavily on phonetic analysis, which may in turn be built upon adequate processing of acoustic information.

Thus one is left with the question of what might be the basic problem for a reading-disturbed child, given that there is just one basic problem. Is it a temporal ordering or a linguistic problem, or perhaps a difficulty in handling linguistic information in a time-scheme (Bakker, 1972)? Or is it basically a difficulty in acoustical information processing? The outcomes of our own studies do not warrant a clear-cut answer to these questions since temporal order perception was essential in all experiments. A conclusion which *is* warranted, however, is that the temporal processing of verbal and verbally codifiable information is a predictive and an explanatory factor in reading (in)ability. Whether this factor is either primary or secondary to other functions like linguistic and acoustical analysis has still to be settled.

ACKNOWLEDGEMENTS

We would like to thank Dr Steve Apter who was willing to read the text, the Free University Audio-Visual Centre where the figures were designed, staffs and pupils of schools who participated in the investigation, and Teddy Slit who typed the manuscript.

REFERENCES

Aaron, P. G. (1978) Dyslexia, an imbalance in cerebral information-processing strategies. *Percept. Motor Skills*, **47**, 699–706.
Arthur, G. (1947) *A point Scale of Performance Tests; Rev. Form II; Manual for Administering and Scoring the Tests*. New York: Psychological Corporation.
Bakker, D. J. (1967) Temporal order, meaningfulness and reading ability, *Percept. Motor Skills*, **24**, 1027–1030.
Bakker, D. J. (1972) *Temporal Order in Disturbed Reading*, Lisse: Swets and Zeitlinger.

Birch, H. G. and Belmont, L. (1964) Auditory–visual integration in normal and retarded readers, *Amer. J. Orthopsychiat.*, **34**, 852–861.

Birch, H. G. and Belmont, L. (1965) Auditory–visual integration, intelligence and reading ability in school children. *Percept. Motor Skills*, **20**, 295–305.

Blank, M. and Bridger, W. H. (1966) Deficiencies in verbal labeling in retarded readers, *Amer. J. Orthopsychiat.*, **36**, 840–847.

Blank, M., Weider, S., and Bridger, W. H. (1968) Verbal deficiencies in abstract thinking in early reading retardation. *Amer. J. Orthopsychiat.*, **38**, 823–834.

Boder, E. (1971) Developmental dyslexia: prevailing diagnostic concepts and a new diagnostic approach. In H. R. Myklebust (ed.) *Progress in Learning Disabilities, Vol. 2*, pp. 293–312, New York: Grune and Stratton.

Brus, B. Th. and Voeten, M. J. M. (1973) *Een-Minuut-Test (Vorm-B)*. Nijmegen: Berkhout.

Corkin, S. Serial ordering deficits in inferior readers, *Neuropsychologia*, **12**, 347–354.

Doehring, D. G. and Libman, R. A. (1974) Signal detection analysis of auditory sequence discrimination by children. *Percept. Motor Skills*, **38**, 163–169.

Groenendaal, J. H. A. and Bakker, D. J. (1971) The part played by mediation processes in the retention of temporal sequences by two reading groups. *Hum. Devel*, **14**, 62–70.

Kim, Y. C. (1976) Deficits in temporal sequencing of verbal material: the effect of laterality of lesion. *Brain and Language*, **3**, 507–515.

Liberman, I. Y., Shankweiler, D., Orlando, C., Harris, K. S., and Bell Berti, F. (1971) Letter confusions and reversal of sequence in the beginning reader: implications for Orton's theory of developmental dyslexia, *Cortex*, **7**, 127–142.

Muehl, S. and Kremenak, S. (1966) Ability to match information within and between auditory and visual sense modalities and subsequent reading achievement, *J. Educ. Psychol.*, **57**, 230–239.

Pierre, C. (1974) *Analyse de la Comprehension de la Lecture chez des Garçons de l'Enseignement Primaire Normal Ages de 9 à 12 Ans*. Brussels: Institut Libre Marie Haps.

Shankweiler, D. and Liberman, I. Y. (1978) Reading behavior in dyslexia: is there a distinctive pattern? *Bull. Orton Soc.*, **28**, 114–123.

Schroots, H. J., Bakker, D. J., Van Alphen de Veer, R. J., and Groenendaal, J. H. A. (1975) Temporele orde en het lees-leerproces, *Ned. Tijdschr. Psychol.*, **30**, 337–361.

Schroots, H. J. and Van Alphen de Veer, R. J. (1976) *Leidse Diagnostische Test (LDT); Deel I, Handleiding*. Lisse: Swets en Zeitlinger.

Sterrit, G. M. and Rudnick, M. (1966) Auditory and visual rhythm perception in relation to reading ability in fourth grade boys, *Percept. Motor Skills*, **22**, 859–869.

Tallal, P. (1976) Auditory perceptual factors in language and learning disabilities. In R. M. Knights and D. J. Bakker (eds.) *The Neuropsychology of Learning Disorders*, pp. 315–323, Baltimore: University Park Press.

Torgesen, J. K., Bowen, C., and Ivey, C. (1978) Task structure versus modality of presentation: a study of the construct validity of the visual–aural digit span test. *J. Educ. Psychol.*, **70**, 451–456.

Van Calcar, C., Tellegen, B., and Van Soest, W. (1974) *Handleiding voor de Toets Begrijpend Lezen I*. Arnhem: Cito.

Van de Voort, L., Senf, G. M., and Benton, A. L. (1972) Development of audiovisual integration in normal and retarded readers, *Child Devel.*, **43**, 1260–1272.

Van Westerlaak, J. M., Kropman, J. A., and Collaris, J. W. M. (1975) *Beroepenklapper*. Nijmegen: Inst. v. Toegep. Sociologie.

Vellutino, F. (1977) Alternative conceptualizations of dyslexia: evidence in support of a verbal deficit hypothesis. *Harvard Educ. Rev.*, **47**, 334–354.

Dyslexia Research and its Application to Education
Edited by G. Th. Pavlidis and T. R. Miles
© 1981 John Wiley & Sons Ltd.

CHAPTER 6

Sequencing, Eye Movements and the Early Objective Diagnosis of Dyslexia

GEORGE TH. PAVLIDIS

Does dyslexia exist? Are dyslexics qualitatively different from backward readers of the same chronological and reading ages? Can we objectively diagnose dyslexics and differentiate them from backward readers on the basis of objective measures in non-reading but 'reading-related' tasks?

Are the dyslexics' erratic eye movements (EM) a reflection of their bad reading habits or of the difficulties they have with the reading material or do they reflect a 'constitutional' deficit which is completely independent of the reading process? If the latter is true then what causes dyslexia? How can we successfully treat dyslexics?

The purpose of the studies reported in this chapter has been to provide the data which will enable us to answer some of the above questions. It has also shown conclusively, for the first time ever, that dyslexics are qualitatively different from backward readers of the same chronological and reading ages.

The results of our reported studies suggest the possibility of developing an international objective test for the diagnosis of dyslexia. The author's potential test, as it does not depend on reading, can lead to early diagnosis of dyslexia, even before reading age; but how early can it be applied? All the above questions are discussed and a theoretical framework explaining the dyslexics' symptoms is provided below.

Dyslexia is one of the most controversial topics of psychology, medicine, and education. Its significance is drawn from the millions of people it affects world wide, and its controversy from some scientists and educationalists who still remain sceptical about its existence.

The ability to read constitutes the milestone of education, communication and success in life. Unfortunately, in some people the reading and writing skills are considerably limited; dyslexics form part of this group. Before discussing

```
Lost Child    Name Alistair Slinn
Last seen     Last seen  _ _ _ _ _ _   Appleton.
Age 7 years. Fair hair. green eyes.
Medium height.  If seen bring to a policeman.
```

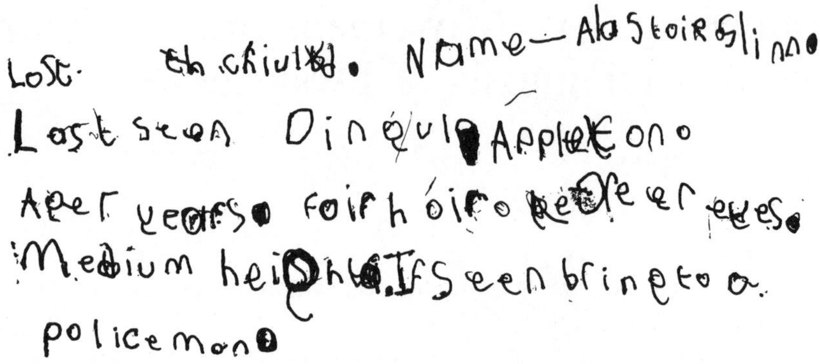

Figure 6.1. Hand writing of a dyslexic boy of 8 years 8 months old, IQ: 104. His frequent reversal, illegible writing, and bizarre spelling are most striking

dyslexia, it is worth while briefly examining the reading process and trying to understand some of the difficulties encountered.

Poor or backward readers are deficient in one or more factors known to determine reading success or failure, such as intelligence, motivation, emotional stability, physical health, socioeconomic background, educational opportunities, language spoken at home, parents' education, teacher's quality and culture (Vernon, 1971). Their backwardness can be attributed to one or a combination of such adverse factors.

Since so many factors influence reading success or failure, why are dyslexics not considered to be the victims of some of the above factors, as are backward readers? What is the objective scientific evidence which allows us to differentiate dyslexics from normal and especially backward readers?

As existing scientific evidence can be interpreted in more than one way, this has made dyslexia a controversial issue in education, medicine and psychology. Those who do not accept the concept of dyslexia argue that within the existing scientific knowledge there is not enough convincing evidence to prove that different causes exist for backwardness in reading and dyslexia. They claim that the dyslexic's symptoms can be attributed to the same negative psychosociocultural factors which are at work in backward readers. They consider dyslexia to be a 'middle-class syndrome', a convenient label used by wealthy parents in preference to the socially unacceptable category of backwardness. Consequently, the 'anti-dyslexia' faction feels that by recognizing dyslexia an extra advantage (via educational concessions), will be given to already socially privileged middle-class children. The issue is also economic, because official acceptance of dyslexia would require appropriate funds to cope with it. Another practical argument used by educationalists against dyslexia is that since we neither know the causes of dyslexia nor have any special treatment for dyslexics, why should we differentiate dyslexics from backward readers?

Matters are complicated even further by the lack of a widely acceptable definition of dyslexia, though it is hoped that the present investigation, among others, will contribute to the finding of a positive definition of dyslexia.

The 'pro-dyslexia' faction argues that lack of knowledge about the causes of dyslexia does not necessarily mean that the problem does not exist. On the contrary, if a reader is advantaged in terms of all the psychosocio-intellectual factors and has no known physical handicap (such as brain injury and/or tumour), he is expected to do well in reading. All other factors being even, the brighter one is, the better reader one should be (Rutter and Yule, 1975). However, it is an incontrovertible fact that a number of individuals, though advantaged in all the above respects, are nevertheless severely retarded in their reading, their writing is almost illegible and their spelling is bizarre! (Figure 6.1).

Since no known psychosocio-intellectual factor can account for their disability it is reasonable, therefore, to seek another aetiology to account for this category of reading disability (dyslexia).

If dyslexia cannot be attributed to environmental causes (Critchley, 1970, 1981; Miles, 1970) then constitutional factors such as sequencing disability and maturational lag (Bender, 1975; Critchley, 1970; Kinsbourne and Warrington, 1963a), must be considered. Dyslexia, therefore should occur in all socioeconomic backgrounds and levels of intelligence. Of course, environmental factors can increase or decrease the severity of dyslexia, but they cannot *cause* it. If environmental factors could cause dyslexia then the concept would be super-fluous; it would be describing a population adequately covered by the concept of reading backwardness.

SYMPTOMS OF DYSLEXIA

The symptomatology of dyslexia is not uniform. Dyslexics, however, may show some of the following signs: difficulty in performing accurately even the simplest sequential tasks such as reciting in order the days of the week, the months of the year, the letters of the alphabet, a maths table, or drawing a clock etc. Often they also find it extremely difficult to perform the above tasks in the reverse order. It is known from clinical observations that dyslexics have sequential behavioural problems (Hornsby, 1980; Pavlidis, 1980a). I know from my interviews with dyslexics and their families that the sequential problems are present not only under test conditions but also in everyday activities. If asked which is the right order of doing a particular task they will probably give the correct order, but when performing it 'automatically', and especially under stress, they frequently reverse or alter the order. (For example, one dyslexic I know, when in a hurry almost invariably dresses first and shaves afterwards!)

A few dyslexics, especially severe cases, have problems in distinguishing left from right and are bilateral. They sometimes show a delay in language development and their speech is not perfect. Some have not crawled as children, are clumsy and have difficulties in rhythmic dancing, playing ballgames, and musical instruments. Some dyslexics are also accident-prone, hyperactive, easily distractable, with a low level of tolerance, and very poor concentration. Dyslexia usually runs in families (Critchley, 1970; Hallgren, 1950; Hermann, 1959; Mattis, French, and Rapin, 1975; Owens, 1978). Hallgren (1950) examined the family background of 276 children with a long history of reading disability. He found that in 88 per cent of the cases there was evidence of a reading disability in the immediate family of each child. Mattis, French, and Rapin (1975) found that 79 per cent of the developmental dyslexics had a family history of reading disability. The heritability of dyslexia is strongly supported by Owens (1978) and by the results of our work. The most convincing results come from Hermann's (1959) study of monozygotic and fraternal twins. He found that twelve out of twelve monozygotic twins had dyslexia, while only eleven pairs were both dyslexic, out of 33 fraternal pairs in which one of the two was dyslexic. All the known evidence strongly supports the heredity element in the transmission of dyslexia.

Dyslexia is more common in boys than in girls, with a ratio of about three or four boys to one girl (Critchley, 1970, 1981; Doehring, 1968; Naidoo, 1972; Owens, 1978; Pavlidis, 1980a; Zangwill, 1981). It is noteworthy that children can have some of the above characteristics and have no reading or spelling problems. But a child with the majority of the above signs is likely to have severe reading–spelling problems. The dyslexic's worst performance is in spelling, followed by reading, and for no apparent reason they usually do better in maths and science subjects. A further findings is that they have difficulty in reading other people's handwriting and rarely read for pleasure.

PROBLEMS OF DEFINITION

The term 'dyslexia' has been interchangeably used with many other terms like 'wordblindness', 'specific developmental dyslexia', 'developmental dyslexia', 'strephosymbolia', 'reading disability', 'reading difficulty', 'primary reading retardation', 'learning disability', 'poor reading', 'inferior reading', 'inadequate reading', ect. The symptomatology and populations described by the above terms are variable but they all share one main factor, the severe reading problem which cannot be explained by the same factors which cause reading backwardness.

The best picture of the chaotic state of the terminology concerning dyslexia is given by Cruickshank (1968) who commented that

> if the child diagnosed as dyslexic in Philadelphia moved to Bucks County, ten miles north, he would be called a child with language disorder. In Montgomery County, Maryland, a few miles south, he would be called a child with special or specific language problems. In Michigan, he would be called a child with perceptual disturbances. In California he would be called either a child with educational handicaps or a neurologically handicapped child. In Florida and New York State, he would be called a brain-injured child. In Colorado the child would be classified as having minimal brain dysfunction.

The same confusion also exists in England and Europe. In this chapter the term dyslexia will be used instead of and in place of any of the above-mentioned alternative terms.

The word dyslexia is of Greek origin and means, loosely translated, 'difficulty with words' (*dys* = difficulty with, *lexis* = word). It was first coined by Berlin (1887), but it was 'introduced' into literature by Orton (1937), and has since been adopted instead of the term 'wordblind' first described by Morgan (1896), but generally attributed to Hinshelwood (1917), who also used it at about the same time as Morgan.

Unfortunately, there is no single definition of dyslexia which is universally acceptable. However, the most frequent quoted is the following adopted in 1968 by the World Federation of Neurology: Specific Developmental Dyslexia: 'A disorder manifested by difficulty in learning to read despite conventional instruction, adequate intelligence, and socio-cultural opportunity. It is dependent upon fundamental cognitive disabilities which are frequently of constitutional origin' (Critchley, 1970). A new definition has been provided by Critchley in 1978:

> Specific Developmental Dyslexia is learning disability which initially shows itself by a difficulty in learning to read, and later by erratic spelling and by lack of facility in manipulating written, as opposed to spoken, words. The condition is cognitive in essence, and usually genetically determined. It is not due to intellectual inadequacy or to lack of socio-cultural opportunity or to failure in the technique of teaching, or to emotional factors, or to any known structural brain lesion. It probably represents a specific maturational defect which tends to lessen as the child grows older and is capable of considerable improvement, especially when appropriate remedial help is offered at the earliest opportunity.

Sometimes the term 'specific' is used in order to emphasize that dyslexia is not due to intellectual inadequacy or to lack of educational opportunities, but is 'specific' to reading. However, the use of this term is inappropriate because if dyslexia is not due to environmental factors, then it should be caused by central factors. In such a case it is logically inconceivable for the same parts of the brain to perform inadequately only during reading, while performing adequately in all other tasks which require similar processing to reading. So, as constitutional causality of dyslexia, and being 'specific' to reading, are two mutually exclusive, concepts the term 'specific', therefore, should not be used.

Each definition reflects the emphasis that is given in the symptomatology and aetiology of dyslexia. Orton (1925) who considered reversals, directional confusion and difficulties with orientation as the essence of dyslexia, narrowly defined it as follows: 'The hallmark of specific reading disability or strephosymbolia is a failure in recognition of a printed word even after it has been encountered many times'.

Hinshelwood's (1917) 'hard' neurological explanation of dyslexia is clearly reflected in his definition: 'A congenital defect occurring in children with otherwise normal and undamaged brains, characterized by a disability in learning to read so great that it is manifestly due to a pathological condition and where the attempts to teach the child by ordinary methods have completely failed'.

To date, dyslexia is defined by exclusion. It would be most desirable and very helpful for the concept of dyslexia if it was possible to deficit it in a positive way. Such a definition presupposes that common, essential and identifiable factors are shared by dyslexics, and that such factors can differentiate dyslexics from backward readers. The lack of a universally accepted definition also has negative implications for the evaluation of dyslexic research (Wheeler and Watkins, 1978). For example, different populations are often described by the same terms, so findings are not directly comparable. Some studies have included children of pre-reading ages or with 6 months or less reading retardation in dyslexic groups.

In general, different investigators use different criteria, which are often too general and subjective. Only rarely are the criteria very similar (Pavlidis, 1980a; Vellutino and Scanlon, 1980). The issue of dyslexia becomes even more controversial when its aetiology is sought.

In all our studies the criteria used for identifying dyslexics have been fairly strict and as 'quantitative' as possible. The children had to fulfil all the following criteria in order to be included in our studies. These were:

1. Performance or verbal IQ of more than 90.*
2. At least 2 years retarded in reading if more than 10 years of age; and 18 months retarded if less than 10 years of age.
3. Normal vision and hearing.
4. From a middle-class socioeconomic background (English-speaking).*

---

* Since the cause of dyslexia is attributed to constitutional factors it should be encountered in all levels of intelligence and in all sociocultural backgrounds. However, low intelligence level and adverse sociocultural background have been excluded from this study in order to rule them out as primary causal factors of the reading problem.

5. Adequate motivation to read.

6. No lack of educational opportunities.

7. No more than two school changes (excluding normal transfer from nursery to primary to secondary schools).

8. Not been absent for more than 2 weeks per term.

9. No overt physical handicaps (that is, brain injury and/or tumour).

10. No overt emotional problems prior to commencing reading.

Our criteria were finally set after long consultations with educational psychologists and careful critical search through the dyslexia literature. The main aim of the criteria is to distinguish dyslexics from backward readers, and for dyslexics to be at least as retarded in reading as backward readers. Another aim has been the quantification of as many qualitative factors as possible, that is, educational opportunities.

The limitations put by almost all current definitions of dyslexia mean that a child has first to fail in learning to read and only subsequently may be diagnosed as dyslexic. But by that time it is very likely that the child would have developed an aversion for school, and probably have some psychosocial problems.

Schiffman's (1968) (cited by Goldberg, 1968) findings clearly emphasize the significance of early diagnosis. After having studied 10 000 children he found that

if diagnosis of dyslexia is made within the first 2 grades of school, nearly 82% of dyslexic children can be brought back to normal grade classwork. When diagnosis is not made until the 3rd grade, salvage drops to 46%. By the 4th grade, it is down to 42%. If these children are not diagnosed by the 5th, 6th or 7th grades, regardless of the teacher or technique used, only 10 or 15% can be brought to a normal grade level.

The current definitions and diagnostic tests of dyslexia not only lead to delayed identification of dyslexics, but also to exclusion of children whose reading problems could be attributed to psychosocial factors; so children from adverse socio-economic background and/or without adequate educational opportunities, or of low intelligence or emotionally disturbed, cannot be unequivocally diagnosed as dyslexics by any existing diagnostic test. However, in all the above cases it is possible for a child to have some or all of the adverse psychosocial conditions, but to be dyslexic as well.

Since the causes of dyslexia do not appear to be due to environmental, psychosocial or intellectual factors, the only remaining causes can be constitutional (Critchley, 1970, 1981; Miles, 1970; Morgan, 1896; Naidoo, 1972; Orton, 1937). If the latter is true then dyslexics should also show 'dyslexic' symptoms in non-reading, but reading-related, tasks, which require similar skills to reading and exert similar demands on the same parts of the brain as reading. Only tests based on non-reading tasks and free of the influence of all the environmental and psychological factors involved in reading could serve as objective diagnostic tests of dyslexia. Such test(s), since they do not depend on reading, could make the diagnosis of dyslexia possible at much younger ages, across all socio-economic backgrounds, cultures and languages, for most levels of intelligence and independent of the level of motivational and emotional adjustment.

The development of such test(s) would make research on dyslexia more coherent, its extent known, results comparable, and would probably lead to the development of appropriate methods for treating dyslexics, or at least it would suggest what methods of treatment should be avoided. Every diagnostic test is founded on a number of assumptions about the nature and causality of the skill or disability it sets out to test. Many theories of the causes of dyslexia have been put forward over the years (Bakker, 1972; Bender, 1975; Birch and Belmont, 1964; Boder, 1971; Corkin, 1974; Critchley, 1970; Doehring, 1968; Griffin, Walton, and Ives, 1974; Hinshelwood,1917; Ingram, 1960, 1964; Johnson and Myklebust, 1967; Jorm, 1979; Kinsbourne and Warrington, 1963a and b; Miles and Ellis, 1981; Naidoo, 1972; Orton, 1925; 1937; Pavlidis, 1981a; Vellutino, 1977; Vernon, 1971).

EYE MOVEMENTS AND READING

The eyes are the most sensitive and reliable sensory organs. They enable us to interpret accurately the physical and 'emotional' properties of the environment. The effectiveness of vision and visual perception mainly relies on the proper functioning of eye movements whose main function is to bring the retinal image of the fixated item onto the most sensitive part of the retina, the fovea.

The retinal image moves continuously relative to the retina. It is clearly demonstrated in retinal stabilization experiments that, if a strictly stationary and unchanging retinal image is artificially created, after 1 to 3 seconds, all visual contours disappear, to be replaced by a field described as 'blacker than night' (Yarbus, 1967).

The significance of human eye movements is so great that infallible nature has devoted to them almost three out of twelve cranial nerves (oculomotor, III; trochlear IV; and abducens VI). The generous allocation of cranial nerves to eye movements can be appreciated even further if one takes into account that vision—which is our most precious sense—is given just one cranial nerve (optic II). Each of our other senses has been allocated far less than one cranial nerve!

Some of the functions of eye movements still remain mysterious and enigmatic. Why, for instance, do we move our eyes during the paradoxical part of sleep, when neither visual stimulation nor voluntary action exists? Also, why do people blind from birth have eye movements? It is almost certain that at least in the last condition, the eye movements have nothing to do with vision.

What then is their functional role besides serving vision? The author has undertaken an extensive study to try to find some answers to these important questions.

It is surprising how little we know about the behaviour of the most mobile part of the body, the eyes. Eye movements form an integral part of the reading process. Reading is one of the most complex skills and like all skills it develops gradually, improving in precision and speed. The development of the reading skill is clearly reflected in the patterns and characteristics of the reader's eye movements. There are different categories of eye movements the main ones being as follows.

1. *Saccadic:* the fastest and most frequently movements of the eye, conjugately shifting eyes from one fixation point to another (such as during reading, picture scanning, visual search, etc.). They are mainly voluntary movements whose aim is to keep the retinal image on the fovea by matching the eye and target position. These are some of their characteristics: amplitude $\geq 0.1°$ to $50°$ of are, velocity $100°-900°$sec, simple reaction time: $120-280$ msec.

   The size and direction of the saccades depends not so much on how the cortex is stimulated (above threshold), as where it is stimulated. Stimulation of different subdivisions of the frontal eye field produces saccades which range from $2°$ and $60°$ amplitude, depending only on stimulus location (Robinson, 1968a). Saccades are represented cortically in the frontal eye field located in the posterior end of the middle frontal gyrus (Pirozzolo and Rayner, 1978). Some evidence has been presented by Barlow and Ciganek (1969) suggesting that neurones in area 8 fire about $150-200$ msec before the commencing of a saccade. Bizzi's (1968) data suggests that neurones of the frontal area fire only during the saccade. The functional significance of area 8 seems to be the mediation of coordinated saccades (Luria, 1966).

   Particularly interesting for the study of the relationship between eye movements and dyslexia is the finding that a small number of cells in area 7 of the parietal lobe appear to be saccade neurones (Lynch *et al.*, 1977).

   The pathway connecting area 7 with the brain stem oculomotor mechanisms has not been conclusively established. However, it has been suggested that the abundant cortico-cortical fibres between the inferior parietal lobule and the frontal eye field carry efferent information before it is projected to the brain stem (Pirozzolo and Rayner, 1978). Inferior parietal lobule malfunction has been implicated in dyslexia (Jorm, 1979).

   The role of the cerebellum is of vital importance for the precision of saccades. The cerebellum computes the target position and integrates visual and vestibular information (Kornhuber, 1973). Saccades may also be produced in monkeys by stimulating the median zone of the pontive reticular formation (Robinson, 1968b).

2. *Smooth pursuit:* 'automatic' conjugate movements. They aim at keeping the retinal image on the fovea by matching the eye and target velocity (for

example, when following a moving object in a stationary environment). Their effective velocity ranges from $< 1°$ to $> 30°$/sec, and their reaction time is from 120–140 msec.

3. *Vergence (convergence–divergence)*: disjunctive automatic movements which deal with depth perception and binocular vision (for example, when following an object coming towards our nose (convergence) or going away from it (divergence). Their velocity ranges from 7° to 25°/sec, and their reaction time is from 150–200 msec.

4. *Miniature eye movements*: minute involuntary movements which have been observed to occur during fixation. They prevent the formation of an 'empty field'; although their entire function is not yet clear, they are considered to be related to visual acuity. The following are the three kinds of micro-movements:

(a) Flicks: Rapid saccadic-like involuntary movements, occurring irregularly at intervals between 30 msec and 4 sec. Amplitude from 2 to 50 minutes of arc. Maximum velocity $> 10°$/sec, depending on the amplitude.

(b) Drift: The tendency of the eye to move slowly away from the fixation point in a random direction or opposite to that of saccades. Characteristics: Amplitude 0.8–6 minutes of arc, duration 200–300 msec, velocity range 0.1–30 min/sec (average 5–6 min/sec).

(c) Tremor: Rapid oscillations of the eye, with frequency ranging between 30 and 200 Hz, and amplitude 5–45 seconds of arc, maximum velocity about 20 min/sec.

5. *Nystagmus*: consists of rhythmic eye movements of an oscillatory or unstable nature. Nystagmus can be involuntary (for example, congenital, which is binocular and appears at or around birth; latent, which is present when only one eye is occluded), or voluntary, which is binocular and is characterized by high frequency wobble voluntarily produced by some individuals. All kinds of nystagmus reduce visual resolution.

6. *Compensatory movements*: involuntary smooth movements which compensate for head or body movements. Effective velocity range is 1°–30°/sec, latency 10–100 msec.

7. *Rapid eye movements* (REMs): involuntary movements which occur during the paradoxical phase of sleep. They can sometimes be related to dreaming.

8. *Torsional or rolling eye movements*: these are involuntary movements around the visual axis which partially compensate for the displacement of the visual vertical.

9. *Intraocular movements*: pupillary reflex actions which result from changes in illumination and emotional state.

Saccadic, pursuit, vergence, and compensatory movements are in constant interaction during reading.

The position, magnitude, velocity, acceleration, frequency and latency of the various types of eye movements can be recorded by a number of different methods. The eye movements can be sensed subjectively by direct observation or by the after-image method, and objectively by direct photography of the eye, corneal reflection, contact lens, electromagnetic, photoelectric method, and electro-oculography. The most popular and versatile methods are: the photo-electric, corneal reflection and electro-oculography. To date no method has been found to be perfect, so the final choice of method is a compromise, as the kind and the purpose of eye movements under study, and the degree of accuracy required will more or less determine the method to be chosen (Young and Sheena, 1975).

Emile Javal (1879) was the first to observe and report that during reading the eyes do not move continuously from left to right along the line, but proceed by a succession of short fast jumps (saccades) and pauses (fixations).

The different saccadic eye movements parameters which occur during reading will be reviewed so that the reader can grasp better the significance of the results of our studies. They are: duration of fixation, perceptual span, and regressions. The relevant studies on eye movements and dyslexia will also be reviewed below.

Duration of fixation

The two alternating phases of eye behaviour are: fixations (pauses), and eye movements. Visual acuity is so drastically reduced during an eye movements that very little, if any, visual perception and information intake takes place just before, during, and just after it (Matin, 1974; Volkmann, 1976).

So, almost all information during reading is perceived during fixation. In the course of reading the eyes have been reported to be in a state of fixation for about 90 to 95 per cent of the total reading time (Rayner, 1978; Tinker, 1958). There is a great variability in the duration of the fixation (100–800 msec). It is influenced by age, text difficulty, comprehension requirements and purpose of reading. The duration of fixation is directly affected by cognitive processes occurring during the fixation (Abrams and Zuber, 1972; Just and Carpenter, 1978; O'Regan, 1979; Rayner, 1975; 1978; Scinto, 1978).

The average duration of fixation has been found to be between 200–250 msec for adults, although considerable variation between the within subjects has been reported to exist (Andriessen and De Voogh, 1973; Hawley, Stern, and Chen, 1974; Just and Carpenter, 1978; Tinker, 1958).

Its variability increases with increased text difficulty, and comprehension requirements for good and poor readers (Anderson, 1937; Judd and Buswell, 1922; Tinker, 1958; Walker, 1933). Griffin, Walton, and Ives (1974), and Rubino and Minden (1973) have found no significant difference in fixation duration between normal disabled readers. The above findings are not surprising since duration of fixation alone has poor validity as a measure of reading proficiency (Tinker, 1958).

The average duration of fixation is about 220 msec for easy prose, 236 msec for scientific prose, and 270 and 324 msec for reading objective test items (Tinker, (1958). Arnold and Tinker (1939) found an average pause duration of 172 msec in fixating each of a horizontal array of dots. Since the above task requires similar eye movements scanning to reading, and its duration of fixation was shorter, it was concluded that fixation duration reflects processing time rather than oculomotor limitations. Supporting evidence for the above finding comes from the fact that processing demands such as difficulty, purpose and comprehension requirements affect the duration of fixation.

Tinker (1958) attributed the longer fixations during reading to (1) oculomotor adjustments of the eyes (convergence–divergence), and (2) comprehension processes. He concluded that 'pause duration includes perception time plus thinking time'. He further justified his conclusion by his finding that 'in reading without attention to meaning, pause durations are brief and constant while for reading algebraic problems they are long and variable'. The oculomotor and information processing components of fixations during reading have recently been 'separated' (Pavlidis, 1981b).

The variability of the duration of fixation and its relation to grade level will be better understood if seen developmentally.

The development of the reading skills are more clearly reflected in the number of fixations than in the duration of fixation (Carmichael and Dearborn, 1948). However, the duration of fixation has been found to drop from about 330 msec at 6 years of age to about 240 msec at college level (Taylor, Franckenpohl, and Pette 1960) (Table 6:1). It is noteworthy that two-thirds of the 90 msec differences found between first graders and college students is eliminated by the 9th year of age (3rd grade).

The above developmental trend is not unique to reading. It is also found in developmental studies of eye movement behaviour during picture viewing and pattern recognition. Their comparison has shown that eye movements clearly reflect the different developmental stages. Younger children have longer fixations (Lloyd and Pavlidis, 1977, 1978; Mackworth and Bruner, 1970; Spragins, Lefton and Fisher 1976; Zaporozhets, 1965) and shorter saccades than adults (Mackworth and Bruner, 1970). Their visual search is not goal directed and younger children do not show systematic search strategies, unlike older children and adults (Olson, 1970; Pecheux, 1976; Vurpillot, 1968, 1976; Vurpillot and Taranne, 1974). Studies of Piagetian conservation tasks have also revealed the same kind of differences in the eye movement patterns and search strategies between younger (non-conservers) and older children (conservers) (Boersma *et al.*, 1969; Boersma, O'Bryan, and Ryan 1970; Boersma and Wilton, 1974).

The emerging developmental trend clearly suggests that both during visual search and reading an inverse relationship exists between age and duration of fixation at least until about the tenth year.

Table 6.1 Eye movement characteristics as a function of grade level and age (slightly adapted from Taylor, Franckenpohl, and Pette, 1960)

Grade level	1	2	3	4	5	6	7	8	9	10	11	12
Ages (years)	6	7	8	9	10	11	12	13	14	15	16	17
Average duration of fixation (in sec)	0.33	0.30	0.28	0.27	0.27	0.27	0.27	0.27	0.27	0.26	0.26	0.25
Regressions per 100 words	42	40	35	31	28	25	23	21	20	19	18	17
Fixations (not including regressions) per 100 words	183	134	120	108	101	95	91	88	85	82	78	77
Number of words per fixation	0.55	0.75	0.83	0.93	0.99	1.05	1.10	1.14	1.18	1.22	1.28	1.30
Rate with comprehension in words per min	80	115	138	158	173	185	195	204	214	224	237	250

This could partly be attributed to faster information processing and assimilation of the searched or read material. However, it would be reasonable to assume that part of the longer durations of the younger readers might be due to oculomotor control limitations. These are reflected in the longer saccadic latencies found for younger children. Saccadic latency has also been found to be inversely related to age at least for the first few years of schooling (Lesevre, 1964; Miller, 1969; Piaget and Vinh-Bang, 1961) Vurpillot (1976) has attributed the relative slowness and lack of precision of the sensorimotor activities of young children to 'a certain immaturity of the nervous system'.

Unfortunately there is not a single study on saccadic latency for children younger than 6 years of age. The evolution of saccadic latency has not been given the attention it deserves. Knowledge of its development will help us to understand and explain its share in the development of the duration of fixation during reading and visual scanning.

On the basis of existing knowledge, it is very difficult to assess how much of the decrease in the duration of fixation during reading and visual search is due to the maturation of the oculomotor control system, and how much it is due to more effective information-processing ability reinforced by experience. The developmental significance of the duration of eye fixation in cognition will be better understood only if we first understand the development of the saccadic latency, which is its major component. Studies on the above questions are very much needed in this area.

Perceptual span

Perceptual span refers to the size of the area from which the reader is able to perceive and organize information during a single fixation. It varies a lot between readers, and even within individuals, although not to the same extent. Usually the faster the reader the wider his perceptual span, poor readers have a very narrow perceptual span. A wide span contributes to a wide 'eye–voice span' for oral reading and a wide 'eye–memory span' for silent reading (Buswell, 1920; Taylor, 1957).

Patberg and Yonas (1978) found that 'perceptual span may increase as reading skill develops but does not change under the influence of momentary task variables' (for example, text difficulty).

During reading perception is achieved through foveal, parafoveal and peripheral vision. Such a division is functionally determined. The fovea covers 3 square degrees out of the roughly 10 000 square degrees of the visual field (Bouma, 1976). The foveal area covers about $1–2°$ of arc around the point of fixation (Ditchburn, 1973). Visual acuity drops off sharply towards the periphery, and is not limited by the optical quality of the retinal image (Millodot et al., 1975), but rather by interference and central processing factors. Taylor (1957) has estimated the falloff of visual acuity for the normal eye reading a line of text as follows; at 1° 28′ visual acuity is estimated at 75 per cent; at 2° 45′ per cent; and 6° 30′ 25 per cent.

The parafoveal region borders on the foveal area and extends to about 15° around the fixation point, while peripheral vision includes all regions beyond the parafoveal area.

Javal (cited in Huey, 1908) found that there was a pause about every ten letters, and thought that this was about the amount that could be seen clearly at one fixation. Javal's findings were fairly accurate, because it is now established that the number of character positions perceived varies from two to twenty with an average of seven to eight characters per fixation (Huey, 1908; Andriessen and de Voogh, 1973; McConkie and Rayner, 1973). If the above figures are expressed in terms of visual angle, then the range will be from 0.5° to 5° with an average of about 2° of arc which coincides with the size of the foveal region. The number of words read per fixation increases with reading grade and ranges from about 0.5 of a word for first graders to 1.33 at college level (Taylor, Franckenpohl, and Pette, 1960) (Table 6.1).

Foveal vision has maximal acuity and minimum lateral interference which might extend slightly into the right visual field (Bouma, 1976). He further suggested that the functional visual field in reading is limited by interference effects, that initial and final letters of words benefit from the adjacent blank space, and also that the smaller interference effects in the right visual field may be one cause of the extended right functional visual field. O'Regan (1979) found that central vision permits unambiguous identification of two to three letters to the right and left of the fixation point irrespective of viewing distance. Ahlen (1974), and McConkie and Rayner (1975) presented a text on a visual display unit. They made the text presentation contingent upon the reader's eye position. They controlled the size of the visual field available to the reader by allowing the reader to see the text through a window. By varying the size of the window the role of parafoveal and peripheral vision in reading was investigated. Duration of fixation was used as the criterion of the relative contributions of parafoveal and peripheral vision. They found that

> first the Ss acquired specific letter information not more than 10 to 11 character positions (2.5°) from the point of central vision, and second, general word shape information is not acquired any further into the periphery than this either. Thus, word shape patterns other than word-length characteristics, appear to be acquired no further into the periphery than is specific visual information needed to identify letters.

Word-length can be acquired up to 15 character positions into the periphery. Schiepers (1976) also obtained similar results. He found that fairly good information about word-length is available up to 21 letters around the fixation point.

McConkie and Rayner (1973) found that visual information obtained on one fixation from parafoveal vision can influence the time required to name a word presented in the fovea at the next fixation. Their data also indicated that 'the making of a saccade was in some way related to the region of the visual field from which visual information was acquired prior to the saccade'. Dodge (1907), Levy-Schoen (1980), O'Regan (1975), and Rayner (1975) and have also found that foveal identification of a word is speeded up when the same word is seen in the peripheral vision during the preceding fixation. The time saved has been estimated to be between 50 and 100 msec (Levy-Schoen, 1980).

Fisher (1974) filled the spaces between words and altered the type-face. He found that both reading and visual search slowed down to one-third of their normal value. Similar results were obtained by McConkie and Rayner (1975) when they filled the spaces between words with x's.

The reduction of peripheral visual cues has stronger negative effects on good readers than on poor readers (Walker, 1933).

Dyslexics have been found to have a significantly smaller perceptual span (Griffin, Walton, and Ives, 1974; Pavlidis, 1978b). Patberg and Yonas (1978) found that 'by removing peripheral information by wide spacing (13 letter space) improved comprehension for low-ability 8 graders, but did not affect their overall reading efficiency'.

Fisher (1980) has put a great emphasis on the role of peripheral vision in dyslexia. He claimed that 'for the disabled reader the competition between foveal and peripheral input, because of the tense array of text, leads to the attenuation of all peripheral input and hence poor reading performance results. This is not to be interpreted as a visual deficit but a visual dysfunction which may be susceptible to compensatory training or reacquainting with text.'

Perceptual span, like the duration of fixation, develops over time not only for reading but also for visual search. Mackworth and Bruner (1970), Nodine and Steurle (1973), Rayner (1978), and Spragins, Lefton, and Fisher (1976) have noted that there are marked developmental differences in the use of the parafoveal and peripheral vision. Their general conclusions are: (1) younger children do not have cognitive control over their eye movements to the extent that older children do; (2) they do not use peripheral vision to the extent that older children do; and (3) readers of English have asymmetric peripheral vision and more useful information is obtained from the right of the fixation than from the left.

The data of the existing studies leave many questions unanswered. For instance, are there constitutional factors responsible for the perceptual span and saccadic size differences between younger and older children, or do the older ones make better use of the same physical structure? Why do dyslexics have an extremely narrow perceptual span? Is it due to defective or 'immature' functioning of the peripheral vision, or to their unsystematic and erratic scanning, or both? Is this 'dyslexic' disability restricted to reading or is it evident in other visual tasks, such as scanning? Well-controlled studies are needed to answer the above questions. Such studies should eliminate in their experimental design, as much as possible, the information-processing requirements, and if any differences should be found then they could be attributed to more general non-foveal visual deficits.

Regressions

Regressions are the right-to-left eye movements made during reading. However, the large saccades which return the eye from the end of the line to the beginning of another are called return sweeps.

Regressions are considered to be necessary components of the reading process and aid comprehension (Bayle, 1942; Tinker, 1958, 1965). According to Tinker (1965) regressions are not the cause of the difficulty in reading, but rather they reflect the difficulty the reader has with textual material.

The number of regressions is fairly high at 6 years (first grade) and gradually decreases with age (Table 6.1). Their number drops almost proportionally, over the years, in relation to the number of forward movements during reading. From the first grade to college level the number of forward movements is reduced by 60 per cent, while the number of regressions drops by 64 per cent (Taylor, Franckenpohl, and Pette, 1960). Similar results were obtained by Gilbert (1953), who also found that most of the gain is obtained in the lower grades. Advanced, normal and backward readers make about 10 to 25 per cent regressions, while dyslexics can reach 30 to 82 per cent of the total number of eye movements during reading. Is the drop in the number of regressions over the years due to more efficient information processing or to oculomotor control limitations?

Bayle (1942) concluded that regressions were due to processing requirements which in turn are dependent on word order, word grouping, unexpected positional arrangements of certain words, lack of clarifying punctuation, changes in the word meaning from sentence to sentence and position of key words. She further divided the regressions into six categories:

1. Initial regressions, which are the corrective movements following in-accurate return sweep.

2. Corrective regressions are internal regressions which serve to tie up fields of vision when the forward movement of the eyes in reading has over-reached the span of recognition (Pavlidis, 1981c, 1981d).

3. Reference regressions are infrequent brief re-examinations of a textual element and serve the purpose of verification or of recall.

4. Word analysis patterns of regressions are limited to re-examination of a single word.

5. Phrase analysis patterns of regressions are adaptations to difficulty in apprehending the meaning of a combination of words and serve to review several

words in sequence. These are the most frequent patterns of regressions for skilled readers.

6. Line analysis patterns of regressions are characterized by re-examination of the whole line.

Bayle (1942) commented that any one of the three analysis patterns—word, phrase, or line—may arise from failure to interpret. The first two patterns of regressions—initial and corrective—are likely to appear in all kinds of reading and may be more frequent for skilled than unskilled readers. The last four patterns of regressions are not likely to appear as often in single assimilative reading as they are in reading that requires thoughtful interpretation. She suggested that 'they may appear even in easy material for readers whose habits of attack upon textual materials are immature'. The relative frequency of regressions increases after large forward saccades (Anderson, 1937; Andriessen and De Voogh, 1973). These kinds of saccades would correspond to Bayle's 'corrective regressions'. Just and Carpenter (1978) have considered regressions to be particularly susceptible to semantic control, and thought of them as being corollaries of certain semantic processes such as inference-making. Geyer (1968) has hypothesized that at least in oral reading, regressions are a means of maintaining a temporal balance between input and output.

ERRATIC EYE MOVEMENTS AND DYSLEXIA

A considerable amount of systematic research has been devoted to the relationship between eye movements and reading (Gilbert, 1953; Huey, 1908, 1968; O'Regan, 1979; Rayner, 1978; Scinto, 1978; Tinker, 1946, 1958, 1965; Woodworth and Schlosberg, 1954). The above and many other studies have investigated almost all eye movement parameters in normal readers. However, very few studies have dealt with the role of eye movements in reading disabilities and particularly dyslexia. The scarcity of such studies becomes even more pronounced by the fact that there are not enough systematic comparisons with the eye movements of dyslexics and other readers eye movements. The existing studies are either case reports (Ciuffreda et al., 1976; Elterman et al., 1980; Pavlidis, 1978; Pirozzolo and Rayner, 1978; Zangwill and Blakemore, 1972) or have looked at specific eye movement characteristics alone, without paying attention to eye movements patterns and general characteristics (Dossetor and Papaioannou, 1975). Only in five studies have the eye movement of dyslexics and normal readers been compared and statistically analysed Griffin, Walton, and Ives, 1974; Heiman and Ross, 1974; Lefton, Lahey and Stags, 1978; Pavlidis, 1980c); Rubino and Minden, 1973). However, even in those studies only a few eye movement parameters have been considered and actually only two of them (Griffin, Walton and Ives 1974; Pavlidis 1979b) have looked at a dyslexic's eye movement patterns during reading.

Clinical evidence suggests that 'patients afflicted with eye movement disorders have problems in reading' (Pirozzolo and Rayner, 1978). The frequent complaint of patients with eye movement disorders are reading difficulties, low comprehension of reading material, difficulties in maintaining fixation; they quickly get fatigued, have headaches and have difficulties in sequentially fixating words or lines of text. Erratic eye movement in disabled readers have been noticed in the first quarter of this century by Freeman (1920, cited in Gilbert, 1953) who was the first to report that certain children with reading disability had irregular and wandering eye movements. He attributed them to extensive phonetic drill, which had forced the pupil to read words from the sounds of individual letters and letter groups, without any attempt to synthesize them into meaningful units. In one particular case the eye movements were so irregular and uncoordinated that it was almost impossible to tell where one line started or ended.

Similar records were obtained by Gray (1921, cited in Gilbert, 1953) from a child with no apparent defect in his visual memory, who, however, exhibited irregular and wandering eye movements. Gray thought that the erratic* eye movements derived from a tendency to read in small units, without proper attention to meaning. Mosse and Daniels (1959, cited in Critchley, 1970) described a particular defect in the return sweep of dyslexics, which was broken down into many movements. They named the condition 'linear dyslexia', and considered it responsible for difficulties in comprehension. A similar case has been reported by Pavlidis (1978), and Pirozzolo and Rayner (1978) who associated the return sweep abnormalities with spatial orientation disorders and suggested that the visual disorientation is caused by a congenital parietal lobe dysfunction.

Lesevre (1964) tested 22 dyslexics and an equal number of controls in reading and non-reading tasks. She found that dyslexics exhibit more ocular instability, a greater number of short and long fixations than the controls, and irregular eye movement patterns. Lesevre thought that reading habits, bad teaching and social reasons could not account for the dyslexics' irregular eye movements.

The performance of the oculomotor control system of the dyslexics has been studied by Dossetor and Papaionnou (1975). They have compared the saccadic latency of dyslexic children with normal children and a group of normal adults. The mean latency of the dyslexic group was significantly longer (494 msec, SD = 54) than the other two groups (children 394 msec, SD = 40; adults 410 msec, SD = 30 msec). Dyslexics had shorter latencies to the right, while the other two groups had then to the left. Dossetor and Papaionnou (1975) did not

---

* The main characteristics of erratic eye movements are the excessive number of eye movements and particularly of regressions, which often occur two or more in succession. The sum of amplitudes or individual amplitudes of regressions can be larger than the preceeding forward saccade, unlike those of advanced, normal and backward readers. Other characteristics of erratic eye movement include a great variability in the size and duration of regressions and forward eye movements. The overall impression given by an erratic eye movement pattern is its irregularity and lack of a consistent repetitive 'staircase' pattern line after line.

describe the diagnostic criteria used for the identification of the dyslexics, some of which were 6 years old! Their reported latencies are much too long and can be explained only if they include the latency and duration of any corrective movements that were used in order to finally fixate the 40 degrees of arc apart targets. They suggested, as a possible explanation of the longer latencies found in 'dyslexics', the malfunction of the cortical 'centres' initiating voluntary eye movements.

Other studies that compared the reaction times of dyslexic children with normal children have also found that dyslexics have longer latencies (Lesevre, 1964, 1968). However, she failed to find any lateral asymmetries in the reaction time of the dyslexics, while the normal had shorter latencies to the right, which is confirmed by Rayner's (1978) findings. Comprehensive developmental studies will be useful in this area, because the existing data are controversial and inconclusive.

Case studies of dyslexics have been popular; for example Ciuffreda et al. (1976) reported five case studies. However, one of them was a dyslexic, a 24-year-old male college student who complained of headaches after short periods of reading. Reading difficulties were of familial nature. He had reduced accommodative amplitude and velocity, and increased latency. His saccadic and pursuit movements were normal, but he could not sustain fixation for long because of the many interfering microsaccades. He showed the erratic right-to-left eye movement patterns, similar to ones found by Gruber (1962), Zangwill and Blakemore (1972) and Pavlidis (1978). Gruber (1962) attributed the 'reverse-staircase' eye movement pattern to lack of control in performing the return sweep saccades. Ciuffreda et al. (1976) attributed the dyslexic's erratic eye movements during reading to 'higher level motor control or information-processing difficulties'.

Pirozzolo and Rayner (1978) reported two cases, one male and one female dyslexic. The male was a 22-year-old right-handed student. He had superior visual–spatial abilities and verbal skills at his age level, but his comprehension was very low (equivalent to a 10-year-old). He showed eye movement patterns associated with slow readers.

The 21-year-old female student, on the other hand was diagnosed as having 'developmental Gerstmann syndrome' with average verbal abilities and lower spatial ones. She performed different tasks with different hands. She had 'erratic' eye movement patterns and she broke down her return sweep into many small saccades. However, when she read a text rotated by 180° her eye movements and reading became as normal. Pirozzolo and Rayner (1978) suggested that her disordered visual orientation might have been responsible for the persistent reading disability. They finally suggested that dyslexics with auditory–linguistic deficits have slow readers' eye movement patterns, while those with visual–spatial deficits have erratic eye movements and inaccurate return sweeps. Unfortunately, Pirozzolo and Rayner (1978) did not mention either the criteria used for classifying their subjects as dyslexics or the degree of their reading backwardness (apart from the comprehension scores). So, it is difficult to know the severity of 'dyslexia' in the cases reported. However, it is interesting that they also found erratic eye movements in one of the two selected dyslexics.

Elterman *et al.* (1980) recorded the horizontal and vertical eye movement of five dyslexics and two normal readers, who were given a variety of reading and non-reading tasks. In the reading task they were given three texts to read: at their reading age and one year below and one year above it. The non-reading task involved the fixation of 25 *x*s. Each line had five *x*s, spaced $5\frac{5}{8}°$ degrees apart, while the lines were spaced 7.5 degrees apart (vertically).

It is most unfortunate that they did *not* attempt a quantitative analysis of fixations, regressions and pauses; instead they only identified gross eye movement reading patterns and selectively reported some of them.

From the five 'dyslexic' cases they reported *none* would fulfil either the criteria for dyslexia used in the studies reported here or even the standard criteria used for reading backwardness (they should have been at least $1\frac{1}{2}$ years backward in reading) (Vernon, 1971). All their subjects were just 7 years old and were able to read, so they could have been in the worst cases, less than a year retarded in reading. Since neither the criteria for dyslexia nor their reading age were given it is impossible to assess if they were dyslexics or not. To the above must be added that three out of five 'dyslexics' were on medication. It is possible that some of them might prove to be dyslexics later on. However, it is noteworthy that four out of five (80 per cent) of their 'dyslexics' showed some kind of sequencing oculomotor problem and erratic eye movements. One had normal eye movement patterns while sequentially fixating the *x*s, and showed some erratic eye movement during reading, but only when he read the difficult text. One boy made a reverse-staircase return sweep during one of five lines of symbols, but never during reading. However, two of them exhibited erratic eye movements both during reading and sequentially fixating the dots.

It is noteworthy that the sequential skills of the only girl of the study, were so impaired that 'she was unable to move her eyes along the pattern of symbols, although they were pointed out to her sequentially while she was urged to look at the designated target. Even with this prompting she was unable to generate a good EM pattern'. Elterman *et al.* (1980) stressed the importance of simultaneous horizontal and vertical eye movement recording. They concluded '. . . that a primary EM abnormality may play a contributing role in some cases of developmental dyslexia'. However, it must be remembered that none of their subjects fulfilled the conventional criteria of dyslexia.

The best-known case study of a dyslexic has been presented by Zangwill and Blakemore (1972). They recorded the eye movements of a 23-year-old dyslexic student as he tried to read. He performed different tasks with different hands, but he was left-eyed and left-footed. His mother and a maternal cousin were left-handed. He also found it exceptionally difficult to distinguish between right and left. His oral reading was slow and it was marked by occasional self-corrected misreadings and verbal transpositions. His spelling was bizarre and included omissions of individual letters and homophones (such as *fore* for *for*). When he was younger he often reversed words. However, his saccadic and vergence eye movements were normal when he fixated between two points.

His reading eye movements were most interesting, being erratic, with a strikingly large number of regressive movements. Sometimes, 'he started from the right side of the line and made a perfect, fast series of flicks along the line from right to left without a single "regressive" movement in the correct direction'. Zangwill and Blakemore (1972) thought that he had an 'irrepressible tendency to move his eyes from right to left rather than left to right'. They explained his reversals and transposition in terms of his erratic eye movements. Since he perceived them the wrong way round he also reproduced them in this way. The fact that their dyslexic could perceive with normal accuracy words presented tachistoscopically, led Zangwill and Blakemore to the conclusion that 'the amount of verbal material he could take in at a single fixation was by no means below average'. So they suggested that erratic eye movements 'may not be a primary symptom in all dyslexic patients, but it may be in some, particularly those who show mixed laterality'. They also went on to suggest that 'if the problem is a relatively peripheral one, it might even be possible to improve their reading skills, by simple course of training to scan from left to right'.

A more extensive study has been reported by Rubino and Minden (1973) who recorded the eye movements of 23 children with learning disabilities (average age 11.1 years, SD 1.52 years) and of 23 normal readers (average age 11 years, SD 1.46 years) while reading a passage appropriate for their reading age. Six eye movement measures were analysed: fixations, regressions, span of recognition, duration of fixation, words read per minute and directional attack. No subject was included in their study whose comprehension was less than 60 per cent. The criteria for their learning-disabled children were insufficient. Their only criteria were: no visual problems, at least 1 grade reading retardation in relation to their chronological age and a teachers' report on their reading disability.

Rubino and Minden (1973) found significant differences in favour of the control group for number of fixations, regressions, span of recognition and number of words read per minute, while there were no differences in their duration of fixation and directional attack.

Rubino and Minden's (1973) results should not be taken at face value because they excluded anyone with less than 60 per cent comprehension scores, and because their retarded readers had a moderate degree of reading retardation of unknown origin. So their children with reading disabilities could equally well have been just backward readers and/or dyslexics. Therefore, the main interesting conclusion which can be drawn from this study will be a confirmation of previous findings (Anderson, 1937; Tinker, 1958; Walker, 1933) that 'poor readers' make more forward and regressive eye movements than normal readers.

Adler-Grinberg and Stark (1978) have studied the oculomotor performance of

25 'dyslexics' and 19 normal children matched for chronological age ($\bar{x}$ 10.5 years and 10.4 years respectively). The 'dyslexics' had very mild reading difficulties, being on average only 1.5 years backward in reading; of course a number of them would have not been backward enough in reading to have been classed as dyslexics. Their subjects were tested in a number of tasks. They found no significant differences between the two groups when they fixated a meaningless target or during a pictorial task not related to reading. Adler-Grinberg and Stark (1978) found that 'dyslexics' and normal controls had similar peak saccadic velocities and reaction times. On the contrary, 'dyslexics' showed more abnormal smooth pursuit eye movements that the normal controls. The 'dyslexics' had significantly longer fixations and shorter perceptual span than the normal controls during reading. Adler-Grinberg and Stark (1978) concluded that 'the dyslexics' difficulty lies beyond visual perception, perhaps in the language area itself. The dyslexics characteristic deficit seems to involve the integration of visual input into the language-acquisition function. However, it should be kept in mind that the reading retardation of many of their 'dyslexics' was not enough even to class them as backward readers (Vernon, 1971).

Griffin, Walton, and Ives (1974) recorded the eye movements of thirteen male inadequate readers (average age 10.5 years) and thirteen normal controls (average age 10.5 years) who were reading at or above grade level, while the inadequate readers were a very heterogeneous group with reading age ranging from 1 to 5 years below their chronological age. Both groups were given reading and non-reading tasks. The reading material ranged in difficulty from primary to junior high school. Ten comprehension questions accompanied each reading section. The subjects were instructed to read silently for comprehension. The following eye movement parameters were analysed: total fixations per line, forward fixations, regressions and duration per line, span of recognition, reading rate and comprehension.

Griffin and his colleagues chose to analyse their data according to the performance on each line which was not the best way to communicate their results. Only on some eye movement parameters were the inadequate readers significantly different from normal readers (total number of fixations per line, span of recognition, and number of words read per minute). They attributed the lack of clearcut statistical results to the heterogeneity of the inadequate reader group. Indeed, looking at the speed of reading scores of the two groups, one can see that the fastest inadequate reader was three times faster than the slowest inadequate reader, while the fastest inadequate reader was twice as fast as the slowest normal reader! As in most of the previous studies, the selection criteria for inadequate readers were neither fully reported, nor did the ones that were seem satisfactory. However, Griffin, Walton and Ives (1974) concluded that 'inadequate readers seem to have less efficient EMs regardless of the type of material used'. They attributed the disordered saccadic eye movements to 'a problem of microsequencing'.

It is clear from the preceding review of the literature that there are no studies which have compared the eye movements of dyslexics and matched backward readers. Studies comparing the eye movement patterns and characteristics of both non-dyslexic readers and dyslexics are desperately needed in this area. Such studies should use definite criteria for the selection of their subjects, especially for the dyslexics, since, todate, in most studies either the criteria were inadequate or they were not reported. The present study has been designed in order to systematically compare the eye movements of dyslexic and other readers, using well-defined and educationally accepted criteria for selecting the subjects.

In the remaining part of this chapter the results of our four studies into the relationship between eye movements and dyslexia will be reported. Two of them (one being a preliminary experiment) deal with eye movements during reading, while the other two, (one being a preliminary experiment) deal with eye movements in non-reading sequential tasks. In all reported studies the selection criteria of dyslexics have been the same as those previously reported.

DYSLEXICS' ERRATIC EYE MOVEMENTS DURING READING

In our case studies (Pavlidis, 1978) it has been found that dyslexics exhibited erratic eye movements, while a backward and a normal reader did not. In another study (Pavlidis, 1981c) the eye movements of nine dyslexics (average age 12 years 5 months), and nine matched normal readers (average age 12 years 3 months) were recorded while they read silently at their reading age for comprehension.

Highly significant differences were found between dyslexic and matched normal readers in some eye movement characteristics (Table 6.2); the dyslexics were significantly worse than the normal readers in most of their eye movement characteristics. Those taken together with their overall eye movement patterns suggest that dyslexics eye movements are erratic during reading, while normal readers exhibit a systematic and consistent eye movement pattern (Figure 6.2). The differences between the two groups seem to be not only quantitative but also qualitative (for example, dyslexics, unlike normal readers appeared to exhibit erratic eye movement patterns and clusters* of regressions); the most striking difference was in the number, size and position of regressions. For instance normal readers' regressions are almost invariably smaller in size (Figure 6.3) than the preceding forward saccade which is in agreement with similar data reported in the literature (O'Regan, 1979). On the contrary the regressions of the dyslexics vary in size and are sometimes bigger than the preceding forward saccade; unlike normal readers regressions occur in clusters of two or more in succession. This means that dyslexics in these instances scan the text from right to left. In both groups it was found that the bigger the saccade the more the chances for a

---

* Cluster refers to two or more regressions occurring in succession (except during return sweep).

Table 6.2   Results of one-way ANOVA: dyslexics' and normal readers eye movements while reading at their reading age

EM variable	$\bar{X}$	SD	F	DF	Level of sig-nificance
Number of forward eye move-ments/100 words					
Dyslexics	134	45	14.1	(1, 16)	0.002
Normals	74	16			
Number of regressions/100 words					
Dyslexics	77	29	31.0	(1, 16)	0.0000
Normals	20	11			
Total number of eye movements/100 words					
Dyslexics	211	68	23.6	(1, 16)	0.0002
Normals	95	23			
Average duration of forward fixations					
Dyslexics	315	52	0.6	(1, 15)	0.449
Normals	296	50			
$\bar{X}$ duration of regressive fixations					
Dyslexics	296	54	4.3	(1, 15)	0.056
Normals	252	27			
$\bar{X}$ duration of all fixations					
Dyslexics	307	53	1.3	(1, 16)	0.267
Normals	282	41			
$\bar{X}$ number of words per fixation					
Dyslexics	0.51	0.13	24.1	(1, 16)	0.0002
Normals	1.1	0.36			
$\bar{X}$ size of regressive movements					
Dyslexics	3.0	0.3	49	(1, 2)	0.02
Normals	1.0	0.0			
$\bar{X}$ size of forward movements					
Dyslexics	4.4	0.4	8.8	(1, 10)	0.01
Normals	2.3	1.2			
Number of regressive fixations as per cent of total					
Dyslexics	36.5	7.3	21	(1, 16)	0.0003
Normals	19.3	8.6			
Number of forward fixations as per cent of total					
Dyslexics	63.5	7.3	21	(1, 16)	0.0003
Normals	80.7	8.6			

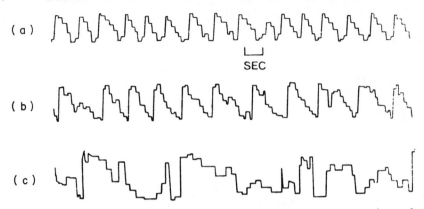

Figure 6.2. Illustrative eye movement records of a normal and a slow reader and of a dyslexic while they read. (a) Eye movements record of a normal reader during reading. It consists of successive similar eye movements and fixations which form a repetitive staircase pattern. The regressions are rare and they are invariably smaller in amplitude than the preceding forward saccade. The horizontal lines represent fixations. The vertical lines represent eye movements. (b) Slow reader's eye movement record during reading. It is noteworthy that they make more forward and regressive movements than normal readers, but the amplitude of their regressions is also smaller than the preceding forward saccades. His eye movements form a prolonged staircase pattern. (c) Dyslexic's 'erratic' eye movement record. Every line has its own idiomorphic shape, unlike normal and backward readers' patterns which are consistent throughout. It is often difficult to distinguish the end of one line from the beginning of the next. Their regressions are not only very frequent but also often occur in clusters of two or more. Their amplitude is frequently bigger than that of the preceding forward saccade. These eye movement characteristics are unique to dyslexics.

regression to occur. This finding confirms Andriessen and de Voogh's (1973) similar findings.

Dyslexics were unable to move their eyes accurately from the end of a line to the beginning of the next with one saccade. Instead they broke the return sweep into little saccades, some giving the impression that they were scanning the text from right to left. The overall impression was that most of the dyslexics exhibited erratic eye movement while none of the normal readers did. The data show that the eye movement patterns and characteristics of dyslexics and matched normal controls are quantitatively and qualitatively different (Figure 6.4), but what causes the dyslexics' erratic eye movements? Is it a malfunctioning oculomotor control system that often causes the erratic eye movements and dyslexia (Griffin, Walton and Ives, 1974; Hildreth, 1963; Lesevre, 1964, 1968; Stockwell, Sherard and Schuler 1976; Zangwill and Blakemore, 1972); or are erratic eye movements nothing else but a reflection of the problems dyslexics and other readers have with the reading material (Ellis and Miles, 1981; Goldberg and Arnott, 1970; Tinker, 1958). If erratic eye movements are the reflection of the difficulty the reader has with the text, then the backward readers with the same chronological

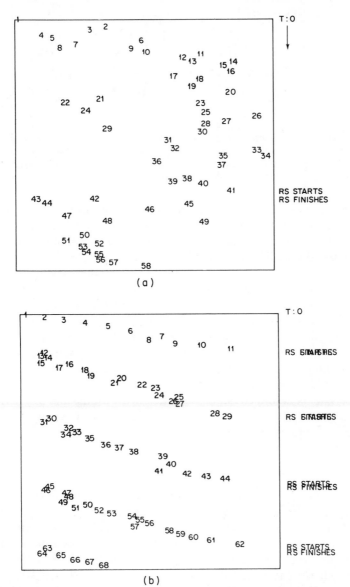

Figure 6.3. (a) Computer produced eye-movement record of a dyslexic child. His eye movements are erratic with R to L scanning in evidence. He is unable to move his eyes with one eye movement from the end to the beginning of the next line. Computer print-out of eye-movement positions in relation to the line of print. The consecutive numbers represent the order in which the fixations were made (RS = return sweep). The time runs from top to bottom. (b) Computer-produced eye-movement record of a normal reader. The regular L to R scanning can be clearly seen

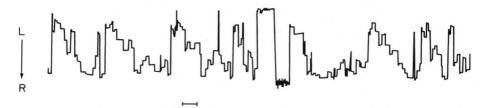

SECOND

Figure 6.4. Erratic eye movements record of a dyslexic boy (chronological age = 12 years 6 months, reading age = 9 years 7 months). Beginnings and ends of lines are very difficult to distinguish. Very large regressions as well as clusters of regressions are the rule rather than the exception

and reading ages as the dyslexics should show similar eye movements, but do they? Another possibility is that erratic eye movements and dyslexia are, for most dyslexics, the symptoms of another central deficit, namely sequential order disability (Pavlidis, 1980a and 1981a).

The data of the present study cannot give answers to the above questions. Only a well-controlled study comparing dyslexics and other readers and especially backward readers of the same chronological and reading ages could answer the above questions. It would be also interesting to compare dyslexics and other readers to see what happens to the eye movements when subjects read texts whose difficulty varies from too easy to too difficult, because only such an experimental design can show if the dyslexics' erratic eye movements are caused by the difficulty they have with the reading material.

The experiments described below were designed with the aim of providing the necessary data in order to test the above-mentioned hypotheses and contribute to a better understanding of the causes of dyslexia.

Text difficulty does *not* cause the dyslexics' erratic eye movements

In the previous study it has been found that many dyslexics exhibit erratic eye movements during reading while none of the normal readers do. But the question remains: do the dyslexics' erratic eye movements reflect the problem they have with the reading material or are such erratic eye movements a manifestation of another central malfunction? Another fundamental and most controversial question is whether dyslexics' eye movements are any different from those of backward readers matched for both chronological and reading ages. The concept of dyslexia itself depends on the results of studies with such a subject matching.

It is most surprising that such an obvious matching has never been employed to date.

The purpose of the present study was to compare dyslexics with backward readers matched for chronological and reading ages and also with normal and advanced readers matched for chronological age.

In order to make available the data which might provide the answers to the previously mentioned questions, the four groups of readers (dyslexics, backward, normal and advanced) were given texts to read ranging from too easy to too difficult for them. The hypothesis being that if the dyslexics' erratic eye movements are the manifestation of the difficulty they have with the text, then when they read material too easy for them their eye movements should become 'regular'. Backward readers of the same chronological and reading ages should have similar eye movements to dyslexics. However, the other readers' eye movements must be expected to become 'irregular' when they read a text too difficult for them. Dyslexics have been referred to us from many sources including educational and clinical psychologists, general practitioners, remedial teachers, Dyslexia Associations and Cheshire and North Wales Dyslexia Association. Most of the children referred to us were already diagnosed as dyslexic in different establishments.

Unfortunately, the diagnostic criteria of dyslexia vary so much from one diagnostic centre to the next that out of the 49 children referred to us and diagnosed as dyslexic somewhere else only fourteen (about one-third of the total referred to us) fulfilled all of our criteria for dyslexia which have been more clearly defined and probably more strict than those usually applied by others.

Fifty-eight children (41 boys and 17 girls whose ages ranged from 7 years 9 months to 13 years 6 months) took part in this study. They were divided into four groups (advanced, normal, backward readers and dyslexics) according to their reading ability, based on their scores on the reading tests and on the rest of the criteria previously reported. The four groups of readers represent almost the whole spectrum of reading ability. The relevant information for each group is given below (also in Pavlidis, 1981d).

Dyslexics

There were fourteen children (thirteen boys and one girl) whose ages ranged from 8 years 3 months to 13 years 6 months, with an average age of 10 years 1 months (sd 2 years 1 month).

Backward readers

Seventeen children (fifteen boys and two girls) from 8 years 1 month to 11 years 7 months, with an average age of 10 years 2 months (sd 1 year 1 month), were included in this group. The criteria for their selection were the following:

1. They must be at least 2 years retarded in reading if more than 10 years old, and 18 months retarded if less than 10 years old. Backward readers were of the same chronological age and were equally retarded in reading as the dyslexics of this study, so, they were matched for both chronological and reading ages.

Criteria 1, 2, and 3 were identical with those of dyslexics.

2.   They must have normal vision and hearing.

3.   They must have no overt physical handicap (such as brain injury and/or tumour).

4.   Their backwardness should be attributable to overt low intellectual abilities or disadvantaged socioeconomic background or lack of educational opportunities or generally to adverse environmental factors. They were referred to us by the child guidance clinic of Salford and were drawn from either psycho-socially disadvantaged or educationally indifferent homes. The reading backwardness of every single case could be accounted for by one or more of the above-mentioned factors. However, for the reasons explained in the criteria for dyslexics, we cannot rule out the possibility that some of the backward readers of this or of any other study could be dyslexics as well. Of course this factor could influence the results in the opposite direction to that predicted by my hypothesis, that dyslexics should have different eye movements from backward readers matched for both chronological and reading ages.

Normal readers

There were sixteen children (eight boys, eight girls) between 7 years 10 months and 10 years 6 months, with an average age of 9 years 3 months and sd of 10 months. As in our previous study (Pavlidis, 1980a) they were matched with the dyslexics on the basis of their chronological age, and socioeconomic background while almost all other criteria used for the selection of dyslexics were also applied to the selection of normal readers, apart from criterion (2). Instead, there should be no more than 3 months' difference between their reading and chronological ages.

Advanced readers

There were twelve children (eight boys, four girls) whose ages ranged between 7 years 9 months and 11 years 6 months, with an average age of 9 years 7 months (sd 1 years 2 months). They all came from a middle class socio-economic background. The criteria for their selection were:

1.   They must be at least 2 years advanced in reading if more than 10 years old, and 18 months advanced if less than 10 years old.

2.   They must have normal vision and hearing.

3.   They must have no overt physical handicaps (such as brain injury and/or tumour).

4.   They must be from an advantaged socioeconomic background.

Criterion (1) was the reverse of the one used for the selection of dyslexics and backward readers, while criteria (2), (3), and (4) were identical to those of dyslexics.

In all our studies the horizontal and vertical eye movements of the children were recorded using the photoelectric technique modified by the author to suit our experimental requirements. For more information above projection equipment, laboratory calibration, recording and experimental procedure see Pavlidis (1981a); (1981d). The laterality of dyslexics, backward and normal readers has been tested.

The children read, for comprehension, Neale's reading test. Some children were given to read four different texts, which were:

1. One year below their reading age.
2. At their reading age.
3. One year above their reading age. All three texts were read for comprehension.
4. At their reading age, but without any comprehension requirements ('fun' slide). Each child was given to read an easy 'trial' slide.

The trial slide was followed by the 'fun' slide. The children were asked to read it as they read a story at home for pleasure. It was emphasized that no questions would be asked when they finished reading it, but they were reminded that they should read the whole text only once. Every test slide was preceded and followed by a blank slide to eliminate interference. All data analysis was done blind by my assistants using computers.

The SPSS computer package (version 7.0, 27 June 1977) was used for the statistical analysis of eye movement data.

A number of statistical tests have been employed for the data analysis. The analysis of variance (ANOVA) was used to find out if the relative dispersion of scores was significantly different between the four groups of readers. Two separate analyses were performed: one between groups, and the other within groups in order to establish if the text difficulty had any effect on the childrens' eye movements.

Data on laterality were collected from all groups, except the advanced readers. The differences in laterality were not significant between any groups, in fact they were very similar indeed.

This study produced a colossal amount of data. Their computerized statistical analysis alone runs to well over 2000 pages of computer output! For clarity, however only a small portion of it will be included in this chapter. But a summary (Table 6.3) of the analysis of the results is presented here (for a full report of the results see Pavlidis, 1981d).

The findings of the previous studies, that most dyslexics have erratic eye movements during reading while normal readers do not, was replicated using different subjects (both dyslexics and control readers). Again the overall

Table 6.3   Mean and sd of eye movement and other measures of dyslexics (D), backward (B), normal (N), and advanced (A) readers while reading text at RA (at their reading age with comprehension). The DF and level of significance of one-way ANOVA are also given in this table

Measures		Dyslexics	Backward	Normal	Advanced	Significance
Number of regressive fixations per 100 words	$\bar{X}$	91.1	48.7	28.8	22.6	D–B, DF = 1, 30 ($p < 0.01$); D–N, DF = 1, 25 ($p < 0.0004$); D–A, DF = 1, 22 ($p < 0.0006$); B–N, DF = 1, 31 ($p < 0.06$); B–A, DF = 1, 28 ($p < 0.03$).
	SD	54.6	34.5	16.8	15.2	
Number of regressive fixations as percentage of total number of Fixations	$\bar{X}$	34.0	22.9	20.8	18.0	D–B, DF = 1, 30 ($p < 0.0008$); D–N, DF = 1, 25 ($p < 0.0001$); D–A, DF = 1, 22 ($p < 0.0001$); B–N, DF = 1, 31 ($p < 0.4$); B–A, DF = 1, 28 ($p < 0.1$).
	SD	8.0	8.3	6.8	8.4	
Number of forward fixations per 100 words	$\bar{X}$	163.2	148.4	99.8	88.6	D–B, DF = 1, 30 ($p < 0.3$); D–N, DF = 1, 25 ($p < 0.0001$); D–A, DF = 1, 22 ($p < 0.0000$); B–N, DF = 1, 31 ($p < 0.0001$); B–A, DF = 1, 28 ($p < 0.0000$).
	SD	44.0	32.0	26.7	20.9	
Number of forward fixations as percentage of total number of fixations	$\bar{X}$	66.0	77.1	79.2	82.0	D–B, DF = 1, 30 ($p < 0.0008$); D–N, DF = 1, 25 ($p < 0.0001$); D–A, DF = 1, 22 ($p < 0.0001$); B–N, DF = 1, 31 ($p < 0.4$); B–A, DF = 1, 28 ($p < 0.1$).
	SD	8.0	8.3	6.8	8.4	
Total number of fixations per 100 words	$\bar{X}$	254.3	197.1	128.6	111.2	D–B, DF = 1, 30 ($p < 0.04$); D–N, DF = 1, 25 ($p < 0.0001$); D–A, DF = 1, 22 ($p < 0.0001$); B–N, DF = 1, 31 ($p < 0.001$); B–A, DF = 1, 28 ($p < 0.0002$).
	SD	92.4	61.8	41.9	35.2	
Average number of words read per fixation	$\bar{X}$	0.4	0.5	0.8	0.9	D–B, DF = 1, 30 ($p < 0.04$); D–N, DF = 1, 25 ($p < 0.04$); D–A, DF = 1, 22 ($p < 0.0001$); D–B, DF = 1, 30 ($p < 0.0006$); D–A, DF = 1, 22 ($p < 0.0001$);
	SD	0.1	0.1	0.4	0.4	

Measure						Significance
Average duration of ALL fixations	$\bar{X}$	417.0	328.0	291.5	258.7	B–N, DF = 1, 31 ($p < 0.001$); B–A, DF = 1, 28 ($p < 0.0001$).
	SD	124.7	49.8	58.6	26.6	
Average duration of forward fixations	X	420.1	321.9	294.9	264.9	D–B, DF = 1, 30 ($p < 0.009$); D–N, DF = 1, 25 ($p < 0.002$); D–A, DF = 1, 22 ($p < 0.0005$); B–N, DF = 1, 31 ($p < 0.06$), B–A, DF = 1, 28 ($p < 0.0002$).
	SD	151.2	49.2	53.3	27.2	
Average duration of regressive fixations	$\bar{X}$	416.2	353.8	278.6	226.5	D–B, DF = 1, 30 ($p < 0.01$); D–N, DF = 1, 25 ($p < 0.008$); D–A, DF = 1, 22 ($p < 0.003$); B–N, DF = 1, 31 ($p < 0.1$); B–A, DF = 1, 28 ($p < 0.002$).
	SD	102.3	92.4	79.4	37.7	
Average size of forward eye movements	X	2.2	1.8	2.1	2.6	D–B, DF = 1, 30 ($p < 0.08$); D–N, DF = 1, 25 ($p < 0.0006$); D–A, DF = 1, 22 ($p < 0.0000$); B–N, DF = 1, 31 ($p < 0.02$); B–A, DF = 1, 28 ($p < 0.0002$).
	SD	0.5	0.4	0.4	1.3	
Average size of regressive eye movements	$\bar{X}$	2.0	1.3	1.4	1.5	D–B, DF = 1, 30 ($p < 0.03$); D–N, DF = 1, 25 ($p < 0.6$); D–A, DF = 1, 22 ($p < 0.4$); B–N, DF = 1, 31 ($p < 0.06$); B–A, DF = 1, 28 ($p < 0.03$).
	SD	0.8	0.5	0.6	1.1	
Comprehension scores (correct answers out of 8 questions)	$\bar{X}$	4.3	4.5	3.5	—	D–B, DF = 1, 30 ($p < 0.006$); D–N, DF = 1, 25 ($p < 0.03$); D–A, DF = 1, 22 ($p < 0.2$); B–N, DF = 1, 31 ($p < 0.6$); B–A, DF = 1, 28 ($p < 0.5$). D–B, DF = 1, 30 ($p < 0.9$); D–N, DF = 1, 25 ($p < 0.3$); B–N, DF = 1, 31 ($p < 0.2$).
	SD	2.2	1.7	2.1	—	

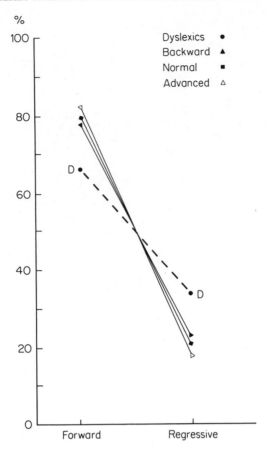

Figure 6.5. Percentages of forward and regressive eye movements of dyslexics, backward, normal, and advanced readers while reading a text at their reading age. Please note the striking similarity with Figure 6.9 (where the same Ss were following the sequentially illuminated LEDs)

impression was that most of our dyslexics showed erratic eye movements, characterized by an excessive number of regressions, which frequently occurred two or more in succession (Figure 6.5). The dyslexics who did not exhibit erratic eye movement patterns had an excessive number of regressions.

In this study, for the first time ever, dyslexics' eye movements have been compared with those of backward readers matched for both chronological and reading ages. So, if the dyslexics' erratic eye movements were caused by bad reading habits, or bad teaching, or by the difficulty they had with the reading material then:

1. Dyslexics and their matched backward readers, since they have the same

reading problems, should have shown similar erratic eye movements, or at least they should not, statistically, have had significantly different eye movements i.e., percentage of number of forward and regressive eye movements.

2. When dyslexics read 1 year below their reading age (and sometimes almost up to 5 years below their chronological age) or for 'fun' their eye movements should have been converted to regular staircase patterns, because the difficulty they had with the text was minimized.

3. Normal readers should have had their eye movements converted to erratic, or should have made an excessive number of regressions when they read a difficult text (their comprehension scores and their statement to me afterwards confirmed that they found the text a year above their age difficult).

4. The within-group analysis of dyslexics' data should have produced significant differences in eye movement characteristics when reading both easy and difficult texts.

However, *none* of the above hypotheses were confirmed by the results of our study. On the contrary, it has been shown that although text difficulty and comprehension requirements can negatively affect the dyslexics' eye movements patterns and characteristics they *can not* cause their erratic eye movements during reading.

It is a most important finding that dyslexics and the matched (for both chronological and reading ages) backward readers have significantly different eye movement patterns and characteristics during reading. (Table 6.3). These differences are both quantitative and qualitative (Figure 6.6). The fact that eye movements are a centrally controlled function beyond 'conscious' control during reading make the above findings even more significant. However, if dyslexia, unlike reading backwardness, is not caused by environmental factors but by a central malfunction, then such a malfunction should show itself not only during reading but also during other tasks which depend on skills which are also fundamental to reading. So, the findings of this chapter would become more conclusive, and dyslexics become an identifiable category of readers if they were found to be also significantly different from other readers (and especially backward readers) in non-reading tasks, which should test skills fundamental for the reading process. The skill consistently found to be involved in almost all stages of reading is that of sequential order (Bakker, 1972; Doehring, 1968; Naidoo, 1972; Vernon, 1977).

The results of every reading experiment could almost invariably be partly attributed to teaching strategies and other enviromental factors involved in reading. Any theory about the causes of dyslexia should be shown to be correct by both reading and non-reading experiments. Such experiments should be carefully designed to exclude the possible effects of any environmental, intellectual, emotional, memory, psychological, and linguistic influences (includ-

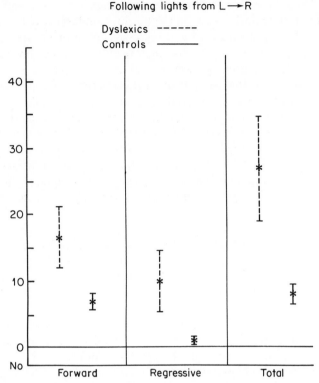

Figure 6.6. Average and sd of the number of eye movements made while the children followed the LEDs from left to right. Note that no overlap exists between the two groups

ing labelling). Only such experiments comparing dyslexics and all other readers could establish dyslexia (or not) as a distinct category separate from reading backwardness.

The experiments described below have been designed with all the above-mentioned points in mind and are aimed at providing the vital data which would test the theory that dyslexics' erratic eye movements are not a mere reflection of the difficulty dyslexics have with the reading material. Furthermore, such an experiment might lead to a better understanding of the causes of dyslexia, which could in turn lead to the discovery of an appropriate remedial method.

DYSLEXIS' ERRATIC EYE MOVEMENTS IN NON-READING SEQUENTIAL TASKS

In our previously reported studies the relationship between eye movements during reading and dyslexia was investigated. It was found that many dyslexics exhibit erratic eye movements during reading, while the other readers do not. It was further found that the dyslexics' erratic eye movements were *not* caused by the difficulty they had with the reading material, while at the same time the non-dyslexic readers' eye movement patterns were *not* converted to erratic by giving them a difficult text to read which was 1 year above their reading age. Thus, the results of the two previously mentioned studies have shown that the dyslexics' erratic eye movements found during reading are *not* caused by the problems they have with the reading material (at least for text difficulty, level 1 year above their reading age). This later view draws further support from the fact that matched for chronological and reading ages backward readers who had equally severe problems with the reading material as did dyslexics should also have shown equally erratic eye movements, but they did not. Hence, the dyslexics' erratic eye movements during reading could be caused by some other deficiencies, non-specific to reading. It is possible that such deficiencies could be caused by non-environmental factors (because if they were caused by such factors then they should also have been present in backward readers). Adverse psychosocial conditions and increased information-processing requirements make dyslexics' eye movements during reading even more erratic, but they do *not* cause them.

The results of any study on dyslexia based only on reading experiments cannot be safely attributed to any particular factor, because too many processes are involved in reading (Vernon, 1971).

If the causes of dyslexia reside in the brain and not in the environment (Critchley, 1970), then whatever causes dyslexia should manifest itself not only in reading but also in other tasks which exert similar demands on the same parts of the brain as reading.

We shall only be able to discover what causes the dyslexics' erratic eye movements and possibly the cause(s) of dyslexia itself if we can design such experiments as to exclude all environmental, psychological and intellectual factors known to be involved in the reading process, for example, memory, linguistic factors (including naming), intelligence, socioeconomic background, emotional stability, quality of the teacher and educational opportunities, etc. The task chosen should be a non-reading one, but at the same time it should be directly testing a constituent component of the reading process. The most vital process involved in reading is that of sequential order which has been consistently found by clinicians (Hornsby, 1980; Naidoo, 1972; Welchman, 1980) and researchers (Corkin, 1974; Fisher, 1980; Gilbert, 1953; Griffin, Walton, and Ives 1974; Katz and Deutch, 1964; Kinsbourne and Warrington, 1963a, 1963b; Lesevre, 1964, 1968; Mattis, French and Rapin, 1975; Naidoo, 1971; Pavlidis, 1979b, 1980a; Zurif and Carson, 1970) to be one of the most fundamental deficiencies in dyslexia. Sequential ordering constitutes an essential prerequisite for almost all stages of the reading process from visual perception to sound blending (Naidoo, 1972; Vernon, 1977). What is here referred to as 'sequential order' or 'sequencing' is encountered in many forms during reading, such as when putting letters in the right order to form a word, or words in the correct order to make a meaningful sentence (syntax), moving the eyes in a properly timed correct sequential order from left to right in order to correctly transform the spatially arrayed visual sequences to temporally ordered language equivalents. However, one should be careful to exclude from the present enumeration any sequential activity not directly involved in reading such as speech or any logical sequential performance which does not require 'automated' sequencing, for example, sequence of thoughts followed in order to solve a problem. Lashley (1951) placed great significance on order and temporally integrated actions, considering it to be ' . . . one aspect of the most complex type of behaviour that I know; the logical and orderly arrangements of thought and action'; adding that

> . . . the problem of temporal integration . . . seems to me to be both the most important and the most neglected problem of cerebral physiology. Temporally integrated actions do occur even among insects, but they do not reach any degree of complexity until the appearance of the cerebral cortex. They are especially characteristic of human behaviour and contribute as much as does any single factor to the superiority of human intelligence.

Sequential skills as any other develop over the years. Gesell, Thompson, and Amatruda (1934) found that a child of 4 weeks old is able to fixate points in succession. However, sequential order skills do not become accurate until at least the age of 7 (Gilbert, 1953; Kinsbourne and Warrington, 1963a; Lesevre, 1964, 1968; Vurpillot, 1976).

Studies of the development of sequential skills have been carried out by both Gilbert (1953) and Lesevre (1964). Gilbert (1953) tested 486 children from 6 to 14 years old. They were asked to read prose and to sequentially fixate horizontally arrayed digits. Their eye movements were recorded while reading and fixating the digits. He found that children before beginning reading showed marked individual differences and considerably less maturity that those who were about 6 months older and had 6 months' experience in reading. He stressed that 'exceptional pre-readers may surpass readers of many years experience in the excellence of their oculomotor behaviour'. He also found that their ability to sequentially fixate the digits improved with age, the most striking improvement taking place between the 6th and 7th year and for any 2 years the greatest progress took place during the first 2 years of school (6 to 8 years). Even more important, Gilbert (1953) found that 'from the (second half) of the first grade on, growth curves for the various EM measures in reading prose resemble in general contour the growth curves in the corresponding measures in reading the simple digit cards'.

Similar results to Gilbert (1953) have been obtained by Lesevre (1964) who tested children between 5 and 12 years old. She asked them to fixate successively, as quickly and as accurately as possible, 48 St Andrew's crosses set out in seven lines each containing a different number of crosses spaced irregularly. The 5-year-olds were not able to do the task, they tried at the beginning, then explored the field randomly, and finally gave up. Most of the 6-year-olds had showed a marked improvement, but they were still unable to perform the task accurately. There was rapid improvement until the 7th year, but after that it slowed down considerably. As in Gilbert's study all subjects exceeded the minimum number of eye movements needed to fixate every single cross. The functionally important movements (corrective, verification, regressive, etc.) became less and less frequent with age. However, the redundant movements also decreased rapidly with age, particularly between 6 and 8 years. Between 6 and 7 years the total number of eye movements was reduced by 8 per cent, between 6 and 8 by 20 per cent, between 6 and 9 by 26 per cent, between 6 and 10 by 32 per cent, between 6 and 11 by 36 per cent, between 6 and 12 by 40 per cent, between 6 and adulthood by 47 per cent. It is noteworthy that the number of irrelevant (non-functional) movements were the first to disappear. Their number decreased rapidly between 6 and 9 years by 44 per cent, between 6 and 12 by over 90 per cent and between 6 and adulthood by 100 per cent. A third of the 7-year-old fixated every single cross and this proportion remained unchanged in adults. This may suggest that maturation of the parts of the brain responsible for the sequential control of the saccadic or any other system might constitute a prerequisite for the accurate execution of any sequential task, such as reading. Clifton-Everest (1976) wrote that 'the ability to attend in a systematic way to sequential order appears at about the time the child starts school and it is possible that in some dyslexics there is a lag in the development of certain critical processes governing this ability.

According to Kinsbourne and Warrington (1963a) the essential ingredient of the writing difficulty relates to the order of letters within the word; and Stengel (1944) found that the difficulty in calculating the rank of the numbers as determined by their relative position lies with sequential ordering. They attribute both the above problems to a difficulty with sequential ordering.

Kinsbourne and Warrington (1963b) found that 'the ability to recall and manipulate sequences (at least in relation to the fingers) is not as a rule developed much before the age of 6 years nor even much later in some instances and is impaired by damage to the dominant parietal lobe in some adults'. Kinsbourne and Warrington (1962) concluded that 'the young child, the older child with the developmental Gerstmann syndrome and the adult with the acquired Gerstmann syndrome, all lack the same basic ability, each in a quite different setting and with somewhat different consequences'.

In another study Kinsbourne and Warrington (1963a) tested children with Gerstmann syndrome (finger agnosia, right–left disorientation, dysgraphia, dyscalculia). This has long been recognized as indicative of a disease of the parietal lobe of the dominant hemisphere and is apparently due to impairment of a basic physiological function involving sequential ordering. However,

Kinsbourne and Warrington (1963b) replaced the tests of finger agnosia (in children) with that of 'finger differentiation and order', failure at which was highly correlated with failure on the conventional tests of finger agnosia. Three of these tests were then standardized on a group of normal children, and it was shown that by the age of $7\frac{1}{2}$ years the criterion was met by 95 per cent of the children. They concluded that 'unlike finger naming the test of finger differentiation and order are suitable for use with children and that failure to reach criterion on these tests at above the age of 8 years is of pathological significance and indicates the presence of finger agnosia'. Kinsbourne and Warrington (1963b) concluded from their study that 'correct order is essential (for reading); where there is ordering difficulty as in the present cases, some reading retardation is to be expected'.

The sequential order skill constitutes an essential component of almost all stages of the reading process. For instance, Vernon (1977) argued that the following four (possibly overlapping) main deficiencies may be instrumental in preventing children from learning to read:

1. The analysis of sequential visual and/or auditory linguistic structures.
2. The linking of visual and auditory linguistic structures.
3. An inability to establish regularities in variable grapheme–phoneme correspondence.
4. An inability to automatize grapheme–phoneme correspondence.

She suggested that sequential order is vital not only for the first of the above four deficiencies but also for the second and third. Since these three deficiencies can account for the greatest majority of dyslexics, it is reasonable to assume that sequential order deficits and dyslexia are strongly linked.

One of the most essential skills required for sound blending is the ability to remember the sequence of the perceived letters and to reproduce them in the correct order (Naidoo, 1972). The same view was held by Orton (1937) who considered that the major source of interference with the process of recognizing or recalling a word stemmed from a failure to reproduce the exact order of its constituent letters.

It is now a well-established fact that a strong relationship exists between sequential ability and reading disability (Bakker, 1972; Corkin, 1974; Doehring, 1968; Fisher, 1980; Pavlidis, 1979b, 1981a; Zurif and Carson, 1970). Sequential (visual memory) skills have even been found to be good predictors of initial reading ability (Lunzer, 1978). He found that the ability of pre-readers to reproduce a visual sequence was a good predictor of initial reading achievement. The sequential order deficit found in dyslexics is not modality specific. It manifests itself in both visual and auditory tasks. Doehring (1968) found that 'tests requiring visual and verbal sequential processing were highly correlated with the reading factor for retarded readers'. He also added that 'the reading disability of retarded readers was most highly correlated with visual and verbal tasks that require the sequential processing of related material'. He further concluded that

> as a final step in the interpretation of the present results it has been proposed that the reading disability of retarded readers was closely associated with a difficulty in the processing of certain visual, verbal, and visual–verbal sequences, and that this selective disturbance could be associated with chronic dysfunction somewhere near the conjunction of the temporal, parietal and occipital areas in the left cerebral hemisphere.

Doehring's (1968) findings were supported by Corkin (1974) who tested three groups of children (average, inferior and pre-readers) on two tasks (visual and verbal) that required them to remember the correct serial position of visual and auditory stimuli. In the visual tasks the subjects were asked to tap cubes in the same sequence as the examiner. In the auditory task the subjects were presented orally with digit strings, one per second, and were asked to repeat as many digits as possible in the same order as they had been given. In another two conditions the children were required to perform the above tasks, but after a 2 second interval between the presentation of the task by the examiner and its performance by the child.

Corkin (1974) hypothesized that it was 'possible that marked reading disorders in children might be attributable to a more general deficit in organising items sequentially independent of the symbolic nature of the reading process'. She found significant differences in performance among the four age groups (4–5, 6–7, 8–9, 10–11 years old) on the above-mentioned visual and auditory tasks. The inferior readers consistently scored below the average readers ($p < 0.01$). The performance of the inferior readers broke down even more when they had to keep the items in mind for slightly longer periods of time.

Since her task had at least two constituent components, namely sequencing and short-term memory, it led Corkin (1974) to the logical conclusion that her findings did not indicate whether it was the ordering or the mnemonic aspects of these tasks that caused the lower scores among inferior readers. Her comment also applies to all other studies testing sequential memory (Vellutino, 1977). Therefore, studies testing different factors (memory and sequencing) independently and in interaction are needed in this area, in order to establish whether the breakdown is due to memory and/or sequential order malfunction.

In two studies the eye movements of dyslexics and normal controls in non-reading scanning tasks were recorded. Heiman and Ross (1974) compared the eye movements of thirteen males and one female (age 7–12, median 9 years) who were at least 6 months retarded in reading, with fourteen children matched with the inadequate readers for age and sex. Their reading age was at or slightly above their chronological age. The criteria for selecting the inadequate readers (especially those with only 6 months reading retardation) makes the results of this study not directly comparable with ours.

The children were presented with slides of scenes, objects and pairs of four or five letters words for 10 seconds, and they were asked to look at them carefully. All subjects were tested twice at 7-monthly intervals. The inadequate readers participated in a remedial reading programme with individual tutoring; their performance improved in 7 months by 1.2 years. The normal readers were not contacted between the pre-testing and the post-testing sessions. The measure taken was the number of eye movements per second.

The scorable eye movements were $2°$ or more. Heiman and Ross (1974) found that in the pre-test session normal readers emitted more eye movements than inadequate readers. After 7 months training the inadequate readers increased significantly their eye movements frequency from pre-test to post-test, while no significant increase was found in the normal readers.

Heiman and Ross (1974) considered eye movements to be modifiable through learning and to serve an information-gathering function which varies with the nature of the stimulus presented. They finally concluded that 'it could be that children with an initially higher saccadic rate have an easier time becoming proficient in reading than those whose rate is lower'.

Lefton, Lahey, and Stagg (1978) compared the eye movements strategies used by adults, normal and dyslexic children while they tried to choose from one of four five-letter alternatives that matched a sample. They were free to look back and forth between sample and alternatives as much as they wanted. Accuracy was very important.

Lefton and his colleagues found that when attention had to be maintained for more than 5 seconds the eye movement search patterns of dyslexics became erratic, and error rates rose steeply. They finally concluded that the children's inaccuracies in this task were due to 'their failure to use a positive systematic sequential examination under sustained attention'.

Zurif and Carson (1970) compared dyslexics and normal readers on a number of perceptual tasks, such as auditory and visual temporal processing. The subjects had to judge whether two rhythmic patterns tapped out in quick succession were the same or different. They had to make the same judgement of two sets of flashes with varying intervals.

In an auditory–visual integration task the subjects had to choose the one visual dot pattern from amongst three which corresponded to a previously delivered auditory pattern. Zurif and Carson (1970) found that dyslexics were significantly inferior in dealing with the temporal aspects of non-verbal auditory and visual information. They further found that the measures of reading skill, temporal analysis and cross-modal matching were significantly related to each other.

Bryden (1972) required from matched good and poor readers to make the same–different judgements for various combinations of auditory sequential, visual sequential and visual spatial patterns. He found a high correlation between reading ability and matching performance in the poor reading group, but only a small correlation in the good readers; he also found that matching performance is a good predictor of reading ability only in poor readers—once a certain level of matching ability has been acquired, it no longer serves to predict reading performance.

Bryden's (1972) results should not be taken at face value, because the poor readers were on average $1\frac{1}{2}$ years retarded in reading, which means that a number of them should have been retarded in reading appreciably less than this amount. Also no other information about the rest of the criteria has been reported, so, as in other studies, it is questionable whether the poor readers were actually dyslexic.

Dyslexics' sequential deficits are not only present in auditory, visual or auditory–visual sequential tasks, but also in any other task where sequential order (of the kind involved in reading) is involved. Eye movements have been recorded by Gilbert (1953), who attempted to distinguish between intellectual and motor factors in reading by isolating the motor factors in an activity closely resembling reading, but without any comprehension requirements. He recorded the eye movements of 528 subjects, of whom 486 were pupils from 6 years to 14 years old, and the rest (42) were college students. The children constituted a normal sampling, as indicated by intelligence, reading test scores and by teachers' judgements. The subjects' eye movements were photographed while they (a) read two prose cards, and (b) fixated three digit cards, with the digits substituting for words.

The subjects were asked to read the digits from left to right along each line. They were asked to look at each number just once before passing to the next. The prose cards were read for comprehension. Like in Lesevre's (1964, 1968) experiments all Gilbert's (1953) subjects used an excessive number of eye movements. An inverse relationship was found between age and number of eye movements needed to fixate the digits. The first-graders approximated two pauses per digit, the ninth-graders one and a third pauses. Regression proved to be the most sensitive index of motor efficiency of the eyes. The coefficients of correlation in frequency of regressions during reading prose and sequentially fixating digits were found to be 'positive, substantial, and somewhat closer than the relationship in fixation frequency'.

Another important finding was that

> there was no instance of a pupil who was very superior in reading prose and yet proved very inferior in fixation frequency in reading digits. Rather the data are consistent in pointing out the fact that individuals whose EM behaviour is most efficient in one type of reading show

superiority in the other type also; and very inferior performance in either activity is generally predictive of inferior performance in other type.

Gilbert's (1953) conclusions could be summarized as follows: the eye movement control 'is not the pure product of experience in reading'. A substantial relationship was shown to exist 'in the eye movements during reading and sequentially fixating digits'. A gross correspondence exists between chronological age and development of eye movements, but at any given grade the relationships are negligible. The results of the genetic study of eye movements, reaffirms the findings secured from cross-section samplings of the different grade levels'. The experimental evidence points to the possibility that unequal oculomotor endowment is present before the age of six, while eye movement control is virtually completed by the time a pupil reaches the upper grades in the elementary school. He also added that 'it seems clear that a small percentage of readers are substantially handicapped by sluggish or inaccurate oculomotor coordination'. The non-reading task was a sequential task, hence from Gilbert's (1953) results it cannot be concluded if it was an oculomotor control problem, or/and a sequencing problem, and/or a feedback problem between the two functions. However, the findings of Gilbert (1953), Lesevre (1964) and Griffin, Walton, and Ives (1974) are in agreement that non-reading sequential oculomotor deficiency is highly correlated with severe reading disability, while those with highly efficient oculomotor control are very likely to be very good readers. However, that correlation is not high for the non-extreme cases of reading ability.

Gilbert's (1953) study addressed itself to testing the eye movements in reading and non-reading sequential task, while reference to severely disabled readers was only symptomatic and was done for illustrative purposes. On the contrary, Griffin, Walton, and Ives's (1974) study concentrated on inadequate readers. They compared thirteen male inadequate readers (average age 10 years 5 months, ranging from 9 years 11 months to 11 years 10 months), with thirteen male adequate readers. The reading retardation of the inadequate readers was very variable, ranging from 1 to 5 years, while the adequate readers were reading at or above grade level.

Griffin and his colleagues tested their subjects on reading and non-reading tasks. The non-reading tasks were free of comprehension requirements and were composed of four cards. The first card consisted of 25 black ink animal drawings each subtending $1.6°$ of arc and equally spaced ($4°$) five across in five rows. The second was a dot card similar in format to the picture card, with dots of $0.53°$ of arc replacing the animal drawings. The third card had two words separated by $15°$ visual angle measured from the middle of the words. The fourth was a five-word card with five words to a row spaced $4°$ apart. No size was given for the length of the word used in this experiment except that they were three-letter words taken from the Dolch Lists. The subjects were instructed 'to merely look at each configuration as in a reading situation'. On the reading card they were asked to read silently for comprehension.

Griffin, Walton, and Ives (1974) found that inadequate readers performed worse than the adequate readers, both in reading and non-reading sequential tasks. The main difference between the two groups was in the number of regressions they made. They stressed that the heterogeneity of their subjects (1–5 years reading retardation) was possibly the reason for the lack of clear-cut statistical results.

Griffin and his colleagues concluded that: 'Inadequate readers seem to have less efficient saccadic EMs regardless of the type of material used. While the inadequate readers were a heterogeneous group, two distinguishable categories at either end of the range of performance emerged. The first group sequenced saccadic EMs too rapidly, skipping and omitting material. The second group sequenced saccades too slowly, resulting in overfixation'. Their final conclusion was that 'a disorder of saccadic EMs is a problem of microsequencing'.

The problem of eye movement sequencing has also been noted by Fisher (1980) who stated that disabled readers 'show atypical sequencing showing more regressions, short intersaccadic distances and longer fixations than 250 msec average exhibited by normal readers'. He thought that 'EMs cannot be the cause of the disability as they are led by the cognitive process rather than vice versa, but it is essential that cognitive, perceptual and oculomotor systems are co-ordinated'.

To summarize, all the above studies have consistently found that the performance of 'inferior readers' (dyslexics) is significantly worse than that of normal readers in any task that involves sequential or temporal order. The above findings apply equally well to visual stimuli (Birch and Belmont, 1964; Bryden, 1972; Corkin, 1974; Doehring, 1968; Zurif and Carson, 1970), verbal stimuli (Corkin, 1974; Doehring, 1968), non-verbal stimuli (Corkin, 1974; Doehring, 1968; Zurif and Carson, 1970), and cross-modal stimuli (Bakker, 1972; Doehring, 1968; Zurif and Carson, 1970). The results of eye movements during sequencing (Gilbert, 1953; Griffin, Walton, and Ives, 1974; Lesevre, 1964, 1968) are in full agreement with those obtained in *all* studies which had been testing for sequential order.

The results of all the above studies clearly point to the existence of a general sequential ordering problem in dyslexics. The evidence is overwhelming, and suggests that dyslexics may have a superordinate sequential order deficit which is independent of stimulus modality.

However, as Corkin (1974) has pointed out, in most of the above studies it is impossible to attribute the dyslexics' inferior performance to either sequential disability or defective memory. Vellutino (1977) has even argued that in most of the above studies the dyslexics' inferior performance can be attributed to inadequate language skills and specifically to 'labelling' skills, but the findings of our studies, reported below, completely refute the above theory.

Different explanations have been offered (Corkin, 1974; Ellis and Miles, 1981;

Griffin, Walton, and Ives 1974; Vellutino, 1977) for the consistent finding that dyslexics perform inadequately in sequential tasks. However, for a critical test the only way to establish the cause of dyslexics' inferior performance in any sequential task would be to design experiments which would test reading-related sequential skills, but the task employed should be non-reading and free of all environmental and psycho-physiological factors known to be involved in reading such as memory, intelligence, emotional stability, culture, socioeconomic background, and language factors including naming and labelling.

The experiments described below were designed specifically with the aim of trying to establish whether sequential disability and/or oculomotor disability free of all the above-mentioned factors, could cause the dyslexics' erratic eye movements. If dyslexics were found to still exhibit erratic eye movements in such 'pure' tasks then those data would refute the theories which claim that dyslexia is caused by 'problems in the area of language alone'. On the positive side, they would provide support to the theory that behind dyslexics' difficulties lie their oculomotor/sequential problems.

Dyslexics' erratic eye movements in non-reading oculomotor/sequential tasks

The first of the two experiments was meant to be a preliminary study to establish whether a longer study along the same lines was justified. Since these two

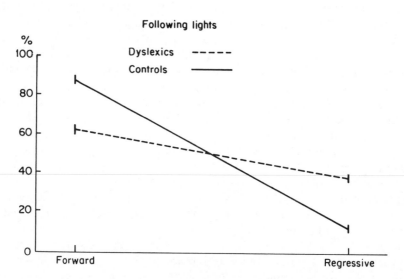

Figure 6.7. Percentage of forward and regressive movements made by dyslexics and normal readers while tracking sequentially illuminated LEDs from left to right. There is a clear qualitative difference between the two groups, with the dyslexics having an excessive percentage of regressions

experiments were addressing themselves to the same problem (oculomotor and/or sequential deficit) their results will be discussed together. In the first experiment we tested twelve dyslexics whose ages ranged from 10 to 16 years old, with an average age of 12 years 3 months, (Pavlidis, 1981a). The controls were twelve normal readers from 10 to 16 years old, with an average age of 12 years 1 month.

The children's eye movements were recorded with the same photoelectric technique as in our previous studies. At the end of the experimental session each child was asked if the task was difficult and if they thought that they performed it accurately. The answer was the same: the task was very easy and they were sure that they did it accurately.

Highly significant differences were found between the two groups for all eye movement parameters (Pavlidis, 1981a).

The children sat about 90 cm away from the light-emitter diodes (LEDs), the extreme left and right ones being 16° apart.

The stimuli were five red light-emitter diodes of 5 minutes of arc in diameter of matched luminance (2.0° log units above foveal threshold), and spaced equidistantly (4°) in a horizontal array. They sequentially flashed one at a time and each stayed on for a second, apart from the two extreme LEDs which each stayed on for 2 seconds. They started on the extreme left and each lit up in turn until the extreme right light was lit up, then the reverse sequence was completed. The lights were lit up three times in each direction to make sure that one 'legible' record would always be available for analysis.

Lights were chosen because they constitute a universal cross-cultural stimulus. The task itself satisfies both the previously mentioned criteria, because eye movements and sequencing are constituent components of reading and the task itself excludes the main factors involved in reading like memory, high-level information processing, cultural and language factors (including naming of the stimuli), socioeconomic background, emotion and intelligence. The task is completely free of all environmental and intellectual factors, and eye movements are a centrally controlled function beyond the awareness of the children; so if dyslexics were to be found significantly different from the matched non-dyslexic readers, it could be taken as direct evidence that dyslexics, unlike non-dyslexic readers, have a handicap of central origin, for example, sequential order disability, and/or oculomotor control problems and/or a faulty feedback between the two.

The children were asked to 'hold your eyes on the light which is on. Wait for it to move and then move your eyes to the new light as quickly and as accurately as you can. Although you might know where the light is going to move next, please do *not* move your eyes before the light moves.'

In left-to-right tracking the normal readers made seven forward (sd = 3) one regressive (sd = 1.25) and a total of eight movements (sd = 3.1) (Figure 6.6). The differences between the groups were statistically significant ($p < 0.001$), for forward, regressive and total number of movements. Both groups had a similar performance for left-to-right and right-to-left tracking.

The directional differences were not significant. The qualitative differences found during reading, between dyslexics and all other readers, were also found while they followed sequentially illuminated LEDs. When their percentages were compared instead of the absolute number of forward and regressive fixations, it was found that dyslexic made a significantly higher percentage of regressions (Figure 6.7) than the normal controls.

The results of this study were most encouraging and surprising both for the children themselves and for us. So it seemed worthwhile to design another study to establish whether the erratic eye movements with their excessive number of regressions exhibited by dyslexics had anything to do with bad teaching or bad reading habits, or with the difficulty they experienced with the text. In such cases the erratic eye movements should be a characteristic shared also by the backward readers who had similar difficulties with reading. The next experiment was designed to test the above hypothesis.

The eye movements of dyslexics are different from those of matched backward readers of the same chronological and reading ages

This study is of vital importance because if dyslexics were found to be significantly different from backward readers of the same chronological and reading ages, then it would suggest that dyslexics, unlike backward readers, have a central malfunction, namely sequential and/or oculomotor malfunction and/or in the feedback between the two.

The same children (dyslexics, backward, normal and advanced readers) participated in this experiment as those of the experiment described above (page 127). The same photoelectric method, stimuli and experimental procedure, and data analysis were employed here as those described above and in (Pavlidis, 1981c). The data were analysed using one-way ANOVA for comparing the number of forward, regressive and total number of eye movements between groups. The Student t test was used to compare whether any differences existed for the same eye movement variables and group for both left-right and right-to-left tracking.

Finally, discriminant analysis was used to reclassify the subjects as dyslexics, backwards, normals and advanced readers on the basis of their performance in terms of eye movements in the sequentially illuminated light-emitter diodes.

All data were analysed 'blind' (by Mrs E. Baker), and their significance computed. The results of this study fully confirmed those of our preliminary experiment. The dyslexics were again unable to follow accurately the sequentially illuminating lights while *all* other readers, including the backward readers, were able to perform this simple task very accurately.

As during reading, the most striking differences between dyslexics and all other

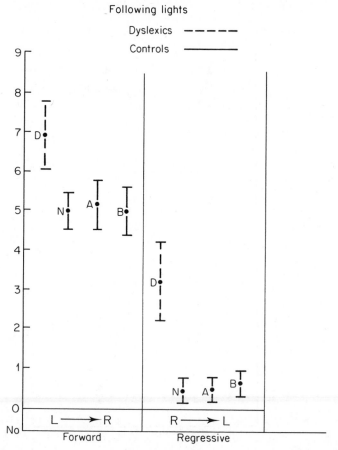

Figure 6.8. Average and sd of the number of eye movements made while children followed the lights from left to right. Note that no overlap exists between dyslexics and all other readers. (D = dyslexics, N = Normal, A = advanced, and B = backward), while all non-dyslexics' performance was very similar indeed

readers were found in the number of their regressions (Figure 6.8). Dyslexics and backward readers had highly significant differences in almost all eye movement variables, while the performance of backward readers was not significantly different from normal and advanced readers (Table 6.4). As can be seen in (Figure 6.8) there is very little overlap between dyslexics and all other readers in the number of their regressions. However, one could also ask: do dyslexics or backward reader have more regressions than other readers because they make more eye movements in general? This question can be answered by comparing the percentages of both forward and regressive fixations. Such a comparison yields qualitative results.

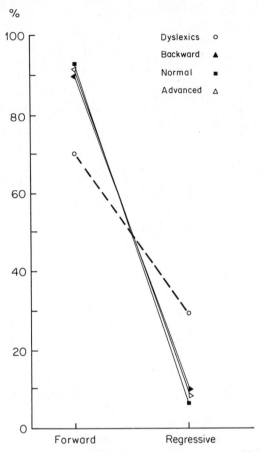

Figure 6.9. Percentages of forward and regressive eye movements of dyslexics, backward, normal, and advanced readers while followed sequentially illuminated LEDs. Please note the striking similarity, (for dyslexics) with Figure 6.5 (where the same children read text at their reading age)

The qualitative differences found during reading between dyslexics and all other readers were also found while they followed sequentially illuminated LEDs. When instead of the absolute number of forward and regressive fixations their percentages were compared, it was found that dyslexics made a significantly higher percentage of regressions (29.9 per cent) (Figure 6.9) than each of the other groups ($p < 0.0000$, for all groups), while there were *no* significant differences between backward and normal ($p < 0.4$), or advanced readers ($p < 0.7$), or between normal and advanced readers ($p < 0.7$). It is particularly noteworthy that dyslexics made almost the same percentage of regressions during reading (at their reading age − 1 year, 30.5 per cent; at their reading age, 34 per cent; for 'fun', 33.5 per cent) as they did during following the sequentially

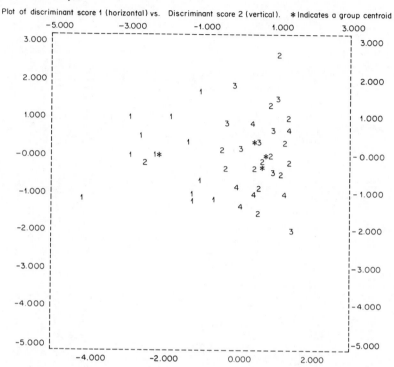

Figure 6.10. Computer-produced diagram of discriminant analysis. On the basis of their eye-movement data the children were differentiated into the four groups (1 = dyslexics, 2 = backward, 3 = normal, and 4 = advanced). Please note that dyslexics are mainly on the left side, while all other readers are mixed with each other. Note also that one 'backward' reader has been put in the dyslexics' space. The computer's classification was in agreement with our initial classification in 93.2 per cent of the cases, while there was 100 per cent correct classification when only dyslexics, normal, and advanced readers were taken into account

illuminated LEDs (29.9 per cent). On the other hand, the percentage of regressions for backward, normal and advanced readers during reading dropped respectively from 21.8, 21.5, and 18.4 per cent in the 'fun' slide to 9.8, 6.8 and 8.4 per cent respectively during following the sequentially illuminated LEDs!

The discriminant analysis showed that dyslexics can be differentiated from all other groups of readers on the basis of their eye movement scores while following the sequentially illuminated lights (Figure 6.10). Such a finding suggests the possibility of developing a diagnostic test of dyslexia from the test employed in this experiment. The classification of the computer (discriminant analysis) was in agreement in 93.2 per cent of the cases, with our original classification of the children as dyslexics, backwards, normals and advanced readers according to the

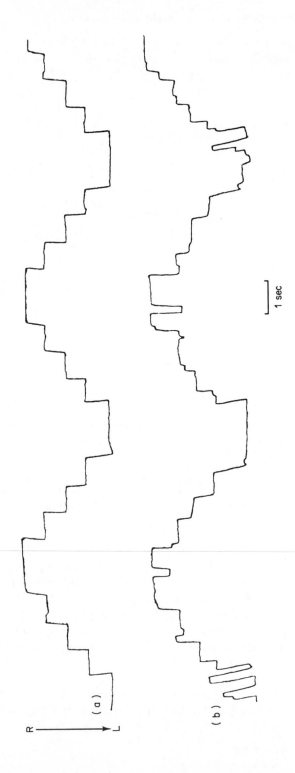

Figure 6.11. Eye-movement record of a normal reader (a) and a dyslexic (b) while following the sequentially illuminated LEDs. (a) Eye-movement record of a normal reader 12 years 6 months old, with average IQ while he follows sequentially illuminated LEDs as they proceed from left to right and right to left. (b) Eye-movement record of a severely dyslexic boy 12 years 6 months old with IQ 120, while he follows the sequentially illuminated LEDs as they proceed from left to right and vice versa. He makes many regressions and forward movements. It is noteworthy that this child's performance is better from right to left than from left to right. His erratic eye movements are 'similar' to those he made while reading

Table 6.4 Mean and sd of eye movement measures of dyslexics (D), backward (B), normal (N), and advanced (A) readers while they follow sequentially illuminated LEDs. The DF and level of significance of one-way ANOVA are also included in this table

Measures		Dyslexics	Backward	Normal	Advanced	Significance
Number of regressions left to right	$\bar{X}$	3.2	0.6	0.4	0.5	D–B, DF = 1,29 ($p < 0.0000$); D–N, DF = 1,28 ($p < 0.0000$); D–A, DF = 1,24 ($p < 0.0001$); B–N, DF = 1,31 ($p < 0.4$); B–A, DF = 1,27 ($p < 0.6$); N–A, DF = 1,26 ($p < 0.8$).
	SD	2.0	0.7	0.6	0.7	
Number of forward movements left to right	$\bar{X}$	6.9	5.1	5.0	5.2	D–B, DF = 1,29 ($p < 0.002$); D–N, DF = 1,28 ($p < 0.0005$); D–A, DF = 1,24 ($p < 0.008$); B–N, DF = 1,31 ($p < 0.9$); B–A, DF = 1,27 ($p < 0.8$); N–A, DF = 1,26 ($p < 0.7$).
	SD	1.7	1.2	0.9	1.3	
Number of forward movements and number of regressions left to right	$\bar{X}$	10.1	5.7	5.4	5.7	D–B, DF = 1,29 ($p < 0.0001$); D–N, DF = 1,28 ($p < 0.0000$); D–A, DF = 1,24 ($p < 0.0003$); B–N, DF = 1,31 ($p < 0.009$); B–A, DF = 1,27 ($p < 0.9$); N–A, DF = 1,26 ($p < 0.6$).
	SD	3.5	1.6	1.2	1.2	
Percentage of regressive movements left to right	$\bar{X}$	29.9	9.8	6.8	8.4	D–B, DF = 1,29 ($p < 0.0000$); D–N, DF = 1,28 ($p < 0.0000$); D–A, DF = 1,24 ($p < 0.0000$); B–N, DF = 1,31 ($p < 0.4$); B–A, DF = 1,27 ($p < 0.7$); N–A DF = 1,26 ($p < 0.7$).
	SD	8.1	10.0	9.4	11.4	
Percentage of forward movements left to right	$\bar{X}$	70.1	90.2	93.2	91.6	D–B, DF = 1,29 ($p < 0.0000$); D–N, DF = 1,28 ($p < 0.0000$); D–A, DF = 1,24 ($p < 0.0000$); B–N, DF = 1,31 ($p < 0.4$); B–A, DF = 1,27 ($p < 0.7$); N–A, DF = 1,26 ($p < 0.7$).
	SD	8.1	10.0	9.4	11.4	

previously mentioned criteria. However, two dyslexics were classified by the discriminant analysis as non-dyslexics, while two backward readers were classified as dyslexics.

The results of both previous experiments have clearly shown that dyslexics are unable to track accurately sequentially illuminated LEDs, while all other readers, including backward readers matched for both chronological and reading ages are able to perform accurately the same task (Figure 6.11). Even when the subjects in the second experiment were requested to track sequentially, as quickly and accurately as they could, equidistant horizontally spaced digits, dyslexics were still significantly worse in that task than backward and normal readers (Pavlidis, 1979a ; 1981f).

Similar results were obtained by Gilbert (1953) and by Griffin, Walton, and Ives (1974) who found that their 'inadequate readers' made significantly more regressions than their controls on following dots or five words on a card. They also found that although the majority of their pupils were left-to-right oriented, some children were not left-to-right oriented and reached percentages of regressions as high as 82 per cent!

It is intuitively acceptable that some regressions during reading are caused by comprehension requirements and reflect the difficulty the reader has with the textual material (Bayle, 1942; Tinker, 1965). However, the striking similarity in the number of regressions during reading on one hand (Table 6.3) and following dots, crosses, numbers (Gilbert, 1953; Griffin, Walton and Ives, 1974; Lesevre, 1964, 1968; Pavlidis, 1979a) or while following sequential illuminated LEDs (Table 6.4) on the other hand, suggests that in dyslexics other reasons beyond reading habits and comprehension are responsible for those regressions and the erratic eye movements.

In both studies it has been observed that dyslexics found it extremely difficult to maintain fixation for a few seconds or more. The dyslexics' inability to concentrate was observed in both experiments when they tried to fixate the LEDs during calibration. The eyes of a number of dyslexics simply wandered around the fixation point.

Previous studies have also found that it is very difficult to maintain strict fixation on a particular point for more than a second or so (Lloyd and Pavlidis, 1977; Vurpillot, 1976). The level of this difficulty appears to be even more pronounced in children below 7 years of age. Piaget and Vinh-Bang (1961), and Lesevre (1964, 1968) found a significant improvement in steady fixation between the 6th and 7th year of age. Piaget and Vinh-Bang (1961) also found that if the 6-year-olds fixated for 2 seconds the fixation point spread to about 14° of arc, while for the same period the fixation area was reduced to 6° for 7-year-olds and to 3° for adults. Lesevre (1964, 1968) found that 6 to 7-year-olds, as well as younger children, find it difficult to fixate continuously on a target and that they exhibited small oscillatory movements around the fixation target. She mentioned, however, that the above phenomenon was limited to only a few subjects.

Similar results were also obtained by Lefton, Lahey, and Stagg (1978) who found that dyslexics' eye movements, unlike those of the control readers, became disorganized when they had to hold their attention for more than 5 seconds. Their task, unlike ours, was a cognitive one involving memory and search for the correct answer. So the 5 seconds 'attention span' cannot be directly applied to our findings.

The dyslexics' inability to concentrate for long periods of time has also been noticed by clinicians (Hornsby, 1980). However, the eye movement records analysed in our experiments were of the first 12 seconds. So it is unlikely that any serious concentration problems were involved in our study.

The possibility that the dyslexics' erratic eye movements might be caused by maturational lag was explored by comparing the oldest dyslexics (mean age 11 years 10 months (sd 1 year 3 months), range 10 years to 13 years 6 months) with the 3 years and 4 months younger normal readers (mean age 8 years 6 months (sd 6 months), range 7 years 10 months to 9 years 3 months). The dyslexics' performance was still significantly worse than that of the youngest normal readers (for example, for number of regressions, df 1, 14; $p < 0.002$). So a maturational lag of at least 3 years and 4 months cannot account for the dyslexics' sequential/oculomotor disability (Pavlidis, 1981e).

Zangwill and Blakemore (1972) reported that their dyslexic subject could accurately fixate two points $20°$ apart. However, he exhibited erratic eye movements and sometimes scanned the text from right to left. Erratic eye movements, therefore, can exist during reading even in the absence of oculo-motor fixational problems.

The results of the above-mentioned studies show that the dyslexics' erratic eye movements are present not only during reading but also in non-reading sequential tasks as in trying to follow sequentially illuminated light sources. The dyslexics' inability to perform accurately in such a simple sequential task indicates that there is a 'constitutional' disability involved in dyslexia. The dyslexics' oculomotor sequential disability found in this study could be attributed to a malfunctioning oculomotor control system and/or to a more general sequencing problem, or even to a faulty feedback between them, but on the basis of our findings it can not be attributed to any one factor in particular.

A series of systematic experiments testing oculomotor control, with and without sequential requirements, should be carried out in order to obtain more precise information about the cause of the dyslexics' inability to follow accurately the sequentially illuminated LEDs. Their results might reveal whether oculomotor control or sequential order alone can cause the dyslexics' erratic eye movements, or whether they are present only in tasks where both the above factors are involved. Such experiments are at present being carried out by the author.

The sequential order disability, as the previously reviewed studies have shown, manifests itself in varying degrees not only in visual, but also in verbal, non-verbal and cross-modal sequential stimuli, as well as in the everyday behaviour of dyslexics. All the above lead to the existence of a 'general' sequential problem which is independent of stimulus modality. Hence the dyslexics' erratic eye movements could also be attributed to such a central sequential disability, and this could sometimes be exaggerated by the presence also of the directional confusion known to exist in some severe cases of dyslexia (Zangwill and Blakemore, 1972; Pavlidis, 1978, 1981a). Such a combination of disabilities should explain the excessively erratic eye movements and great number of regressions found both when dyslexics read and when they follow sequentially illuminated lights, or even when they are asked to sequentially fixate synchronously presented, equally spaced numbers (Gillbert, 1953; Pavlidis, 1979a; 1981f). However, it is irrelevant, at least for the diagnosis of dyslexia, whether erratic eye movements are caused by a malfunctioning oculomotor control system and/or a sequential order disability; for, if the deficit lies with the oculomotor control system, erratic eye movements could be the cause of dyslexia; but if the unsystematic scanning of the text during reading, the inability to accurately follow the sequentially illuminated LEDs, and the resulting erratic eye movements are one of the several manifestations of the more general sequencing disability of dyslexics, then the erratic eye movements will have the same cause as dyslexia. In both cases, although in a different way, the erratic eye movements will be linked to dyslexia. However, it must be emphasized that the knowledge of the relationship between eye movements and dyslexia can lead not only to the objective diagnosis, but it could also offer a basis for discovering the appropriate method of treatment. Such a method is currently being tested in our laboratory.

The impressive finding that sequential eye movement disability is unique to dyslexics suggests the possibility of the 'lights test' becoming an objective diagnostic test for dyslexia. Since it is not dependent on reading it offers the possibility of early diagnosis, even before reading age. The author is currently standardizing such a test.

Maturational lag of at least 3 years 4 months must also be ruled out as a major cause of dyslexia because when the eye movements of the older dyslexics' (mean 11 years 10 months) were compared with those of normal readers 3 years and 4 months younger (mean 8 years 6 months), the dyslexics' performance was still significantly worse than that of the younger normal readers. Our data rather supports the maturational deficit model.

Since no memory requirements were involved in the author's test, it can be concluded that dyslexics can have sequential eye movement control difficulties independent of memory. Of course, it is possible for them to have memory problems on top of the above problems. The fact that the sequential eye movements are centrally controlled suggests that dyslexics, unlike all other readers, have a deficit of central origin. It can be attributed to sequential order and/or oculomotor malfunction and/or a faulty feedback between them.

The dyslexics' extremely narrow perceptual span is the consequence of their erratic eye movements. The alternative hypothesis (i.e. 'defective' peripheral vision being the cause of the dyslexics' narrow perceptual span) is not supported by our data; because, if the above hypothesis was correct then dyslexics should have had their forward and regressive eye-movement sizes similar to those of matched backward readers. They should also be smaller than those of normal and advanced readers. However, as can be seen in Tables 6.2 and 6.3 none of the above hypotheses was supported by our data. On the contrary dyslexics not only had exceptionally large eye movements but they also had their regressions occurring in clusters of two or more.

All the aforementioned data suggest that the dyslexics' exceptionally narrow perceptual span is the product of their erratic eye movements and excessive number of regressions. However, it is possible for them sometimes to have a 'defective peripheral vision' independently of their erratic eye movements.

A sequential order deficit could be at the heart of the dyslexics' problems. Such a deficit would explain the sequential behaviour problems of dyslexics. It would also be consistent with the findings that dyslexics cannot accurately perform any non-reading but reading-related, sequential tasks.

The verbal-deficit hypothesis (Vellutino, 1977) must be rejected as the single cause of dyslexia, because it fails to explain the dyslexics' sequential problems, especially in non-reading sequential tasks where no memory, naming, or any other language factors are involved. On the contrary, the 'language' problems can be also expected and explained by the sequential order deficit, because language is the skill most dependent on accurate sequential order (Lashley, 1951). However, it is possible for some dyslexics to have a language deficit as well as their sequential order deficit.

The sequential order hypothesis is also consistent with the fact that in Japan there are far fewer dyslexics than in the English-speaking countries (Critchley, 1978), because in both Japanese languages, the syllabic Kana and the idiographic Kanji, the sequential order requirements at all levels are much less than those of our language. The dyslexics' difficulties in learning foreign languages can also be explained by the sequential order deficit hypothesis because, apart from all other factors, each language has its own word order structure (Lashley, 1951). It is noteworthy, that the 'sequential order deficit' hypothesis is the only one which explains the behavioural sequential problems of dyslexics.

Recent neurological evidence (Galaburda and Kemper, 1979) could be taken as supporting the sequential order deficit in dyslexics. They examined the brain of a 20-year-old male dyslexic who died suddenly after falling from a great height. He had severe reading problems, and his two brothers and father also had reading problems. His isotope brain scan was normal; also at autopsy his brain showed no evidence of trauma or other gross abnormalities. However, they found a consistently wider left cerebral hemisphere, an area of polymicrogyria in the left temporal speech region and wild cortical dysplasias in limbic, primary, and association cortices of the left hemisphere. They also found that 'on microscopic examination, there was remarkable cortical dysplasia with polymicrogyria involving predominantly cytoarchitectonic area Tpt on the left planum temporale, and mild cortical dysplasias throughout the left hemisphere. The right cerebral hemisphere and remainder of the brain appeared normal'. Galaburda and Kemper (1979) speculated that 'it is possible that the increased amount of white matter in our patient's left hemisphere reflect the formation of abnormal fibres, which in turn relate to the abnormal behaviour...'.

Norman Geschwind (1980) called the abnormality found by Galaburda and Kemper (1979) as 'a miswiring of the actual basic structure of the brain which would not have been caused by a mechnical injury, internal bleeding, or a cut-off of the blood supply occurring after birth. It had to occur during the formation of the brain tissue in the womb.'

Of course, one cannot generalize from the results of a case study. It is most encouraging, however, that the results of this study and especially Geschwind's (1980) interpretation that there was a 'miswiring of the actual basic structure of the brain. . . ' supports and explains our findings and hypothesis that sequential order disability is the main cause of dyslexia; for, 'miswiring' can lead to the disruption of sequential order.

The results of our studies have shown that dyslexics cannot accurately follow the sequentially illuminated LEDs; so their erratic eye movements can be attributed to oculomotor control problems and/or sequential order deficit or faulty feedback between the two. However, they do not indicate whether it is an oculomotor or sequential problem. Only well-designed experiments, testing the oculomotor control of dyslexics in tasks with and without the existence of sequential order, could help us to pinpoint the cause of the erratic eye movements. Such experiments are under way in our laboratory.

The results of the non-reading tasks have been fascinating. The discriminant analysis revealed that dyslexics can be clearly differentiated from *all* other readers, including backward readers of the same chronological and reading ages, on the basis of their eye movements results while following the sequentially illuminated LEDs. This finding suggests that the author's test could become an objective test of dyslexia. Since such a test would be independent of socio-economic, psychological, and intellectual factors, unlike any existing test of dyslexia, it should be possible, for the first time ever, to have the possibility of diagnosing as dyslexics children from disadvantaged socio-economic backgrounds, emotionally disturbed children, and/or children of relatively low intelligence. Since it is also independent of language and culture and is objective, it could be used internationally.

The results of our completed studies in conjunction with those of our current experiments will clarify even further the issue of causality of dyslexia. The above information and our knowledge of the symptomatology of dyslexia, could become instrumental in guiding us to *a positive definition of dyslexia*, which is most desirable for both the research and the applied aspects of dyslexia.

A correct diagnosis is one of the prerequisites for the discovery of an appropriate remedy. The possible prognostic capabilities of a diagnostic method enhances its usefulness. The early diagnosis of dyslexia is useful for more than one reason. On the one hand, the earlier we diagnose it the greater the possibilities to ensure maximum advantage of the plasticity of the brain by either energizing its 'dormant' circuits or forming new ones (as happens to young children who suffer brain injury in accidents—the function of the damaged parts of the brain is very often taken over by other unaffected parts of the brain). On the other hand, the possible early diagnosis will also increase the chances of ameliorating the consequent negative educational and psychosocial effects of dyslexia.

The author's potential test is independent of reading skills, so it could be used even for pre-readers. The limits of its earliest possible diagnosis could be determined by the outcome of a developmental investigation into the development of oculomotor/sequential skills. Such a study is under way in our laboratory. I feel that a word of caution is necessary here. It is important that the recognition of the handicap of dyslexia should become neither a convenient excuse for the lazy child and the incompetent teacher, nor the socially acceptable label for the 'pushy' parents of the 'slow' child.

However, the early objective diagnosis of dyslexia will benefit the family atmosphere, the child's emotional stability, and the teacher–child relationship if it leads to both an adjustment of teaching strategies and to a more sympathetic attitude towards the child. These changes are likely to result, apart from the aforementioned benefits, in raising the educational standards of dyslexics, and eventually to contribute to their happiness.

ACKNOWLEDGEMENTS

Studies of the size of those reported in this chapter cannot be carried out successfully by one person without the dedicated cooperation of others. I am grateful to my assistants Mrs E. Baker, Mrs. L. Dawson, Mrs J. Gruber, Mrs P. Harris, and Mrs I. Michaelson for their most valuable help during the different stages of my research. I am also grateful to Mr G. Bookbinder and Mr P. Pumfrey for their constructive suggestions in the use of reading tests, and to Mr G. Noland for spending incalculable hours, day and night, in order to finish the computerized data analysis.

To the children who participated in our experiments I am particularly grateful for their warm cooperation, and for giving me the opportunity to play and feel like one of them again.

SSRC (U.K.) research grants HR 8 pp 31 and HR 6057 to George Th. Pavlidis are acknowledged.

BIBLIOGRAPHY

Abrams, S. G. and Zuber, B. L. (1972). Some characteristics of information processing during reading, *Read. Res. Q.*, **8**, 40–51.

Adler-Grinberg, D. and Stark, L. (1978). Eye movements, scanpaths and dyslexia, *Amer. J. Optom. and Physiol. Optics*, **55**, 557–570.

Ahlen, J. (1974). Spatial and temporal aspects of visual information processing during reading. Unpublished doctoral dissertation, University of Illinois Medical Centre.

Anderson, I. H. (1937). Studies in the eye movements of good and poor readers, *Psychol. Monogr*, **48**, 1–35.

Andriessen, J. J. and DeVoogd, A. H. (1973). Analysis of eye movement patterns in silent reading, *IPO Ann. Prog. Rep.*, **8**, 30–35.

Arnold, D. C. and Tinker, M. A. (1939). The fixational pause of the eyes, *J. Exp. Psychol.*, **25**, 271–280.

Bakker, D. J. (1972). Temporal order and disturbed reading, Rotterdam: Rotterdam University Press.

Barlow, J. S. and Ciganek, L. (1969). Lambda responses in relation to visual evoked responses in man, *Electroenceph. Clin. Neurophysiol.*, **26**, 183–192.

Bayle, E. (1942). The nature of causes of regressive movements in reading, *J. Exp. Educ.*, **11**, 16–36.

Bender, L. (1975). A fifty-year review of experiences with dyslexia, *Bull. Orton Soc.*, 5–23.

Berlin, R. (1887). *Eine besondere Art der Wort blindheit (Dyslexia)*. Wiesbaden.

Birch, H. G. (1962). Dyslexia and the maturation of visual function reading disability. Progress and research needs in dyslexia. In: J. Money (ed.) Baltimore: John Hopkins Press.

Birch, H. G. and Belmont, L. (1964). Auditory-visual integration in normal and retarded readers, *Amer. J. Orthopsychiat.*, **34**, 852–861.

Birch, H. G. and Belmont, L. (1965). Lateral dominance, right–left awareness, and reading disability, *Child Develop.*, **36**, 257.

Bizzi, E. (1968). Discharge of frontal eye field neurons during saccadic and following eye movement in anaesthetized monkeys. *Exp. Brain Res.*, **6**, 69, 80.

Bizzi, E. (1974). The co-ordination of eye-head movement, *Sci. Amer.*, **231**, 100–106.

Boder, E. (1971). Developmental dyslexia: prevailing diagnostic concepts and a new diagnostic approach. In: H. R. Myklebust (ed.) *Progress in Learning Disabilities, 2*, pp. 293–321, New York: Grune and Stratton.

Boersma, F. J., Muir, W., Wilton, K., Barham, R. (1969). Eye movements during embedded figure tasks, *Percep. and Motor Skills*, **28**, 271–274.

Boersma, F. J., O'Bryan, K. G. Ryan, B. A. (1970). Eye movements and horizontal decolage: some preliminary findings, *Percep. and Motor Skills*, **30**, 886.

Boersma, F. J. and Wilton, K. M. (1974). Eye movements and conservation acceleration, *J. Exp. Child Psychol.*, **17**, 49–60.

Bookbinder, G. (1976). *Manual for the Salford Sentence Reading Test*. London: Hodder & Stoughton Educational.

Bookbinder, G. (1978). Personal communication.

Bouma, H. (1976). Visual search and reading: eye movements and functional visual field. Paper presented at 17th International Symposium on attention and performance, Senanque, 1–8 August.

Bryden, M. P. (1972). Auditory, visual and sequential-spatial matching in relation to reading ability, *Child. Develop.*, **43**, 824–832.

Buswell, G. T. (1920). An experimental study of the eye–voice span in reading, *Suppl. Educ. Monogr.*, **17**.

Carmichael, L. and Dearborn, W. F. (1948). *Reading and Visual Fatigue*, London: Harrap.

Ciuffreda, K. J. Bahill, A. T., Kenyon, R. V. and Stark, L. (1976). Eye movements during reading: case reports, *Amer. J. Optom. Physiol. Opt.*, **53**, 389–395.

Clifton-Everest, I. M. (1976). Dyslexia: is there a disorder of visual perception? *Neuropsychol.*, **14**, 491–494.

Corkin, S. (1974). Serial-ordering deficits in inferior readers, *Neuropsychol.*, **12**, 347–354.

Critchley, M. (1970). *The Dyslexic Child*, London: Heinemann.

Critchley, M. (1978). Neurological aspects of dyslexia. Paper presented at the Symposium on dyslexia: its diagnosis and treatment, Manchester, 15–17th February.

Critchley, M. (1981). Dyslexia: an overview. In: Pavlidis, G. Th., and Miles, T. R. (eds.), *Dyslexia Research and its Applications to Education*, London: J. Wiley & Sons (this volume).

Cruickshank, W. M. (1968). The problems of delayed recognition and its correction. In: Keeney, A. H. and Keeney, V. T. (eds), *Dyslexia; Diagnosis and Treatment of Reading Disorders*, St Louis: C. V. Mosby.

Ditchburn, R. W. (1973). *Eye Movements and Visual Perception*, Oxford: Oxford University Press.

Dodge, R. (1907). An experimental study of visual fixation, *Physiol. Monogr.*, **8**, 1–95.

Doehring, D. G. (1968). Patterns of Impairment in Specific Reading Disability, Bloomington, Ind.: Indiana University Press.

Dossetor, D. R. and Papaioannou, J. (1975). Dyslexia and eye movements, *Language and Speech*, **18**, 312–317.

Ellis, N. and Miles, T. R. (1981). A lexical encoding deficiency 1: experimental evidence. In: Pavlidis, G. Th. and Miles, T. R. (eds.) *Dyslexia Research and its Applications to Education*, London: J. Wiley & Sons (this volume).

Elterman, R. D., Abel, L. A., Daroff, R. B., Dell'Osso, L. F. and Bornstein, J. L. (1980). Eye movement patterns in dyslexic children, *J. Learn. Disabil.*, **13**, 16–21.

Fisher, D. F. (1974). Reading as visual search: a look at processes. *Dissertation Abstracts Int.*, **35**, 1–13, 539.

Fisher, D. F. (1980). Research in reading: the compensatory reading program, *Yearbook of National Reading Conference*.

Galaburda, A. M. and Kemper, T. L. (1979). Cytoarchitectonic abnormalities in developmental dyslexia; a case study, *Ann. Neurol.*, **6**, (2), 94–100.

Geschwind, N. (1980). Brain 'Miswired' in dyslexics? *Medical News*, March 6.

Gesell, A., Thompson, H. and Amatruda, C. S. (1934). *Infant Behaviour: Its Genesis and Growth*, New York: McGraw-Hill.

Gilbert, L. C. (1953). Functional motor efficiency of the eyes and its relation to reading, *Univ. Calif. Publ. in Educ.*, **11**, 159–231.

Goldberg, H. K. (1968). Vision, perception and related facts in dyslexia. In: Keeney, A. H. and Keeney, V. T., (eds.) *Dyslexia*, St Louis: C. V. Mosby Co.

Goldberg, H. K. and Arnott, W. (1970). Ocular motility in learning disabilities, *J. Learn. Disabil.*, **3(3)**, 160–162.

Griffin, D. C., Walton, H. N. and Ives, V. (1974). Saccades as related to reading disorders, *J. Learn. Disabil.*, **7**, 310–316.

Gruber, E. (1962). Reading ability, binocular co-ordination and the ophthalmograph, *Arch. Ophthalmol.*, **67**, 280–288.

Hallgren, B. (1950). Specific dyslexia, *Acta Psychiat. Neurol.*, **65**, 1–287.

Hawley, T. T., Stern, J. A. and Chen, S. C. (1974). Computer analysis of eye movements during reading, *Read. World*, **13**, 307–317.

Heiman, J. R. and Ross, A. O. (1974). Saccadic eye movements and reading difficulties, *J. Abnorm. Child Psychol.*, **2**, 53–61.

Hermann, K. (1959). *Reading Disability*, Copenhagen, Munkgaard.

Hildreth, G. H. (1963). Early writing as an aid to reading, *Elem. Eng.*, **40**, 15–20.

Hinshelwood, J. (1917). *Congenital Word-blindness*, London: Lewis.

Hornsby, B. (1980). How can dyslexics be taught to read, write and spell? Paper presented at the International Symposium on: dyslexia research and its educational applications, Manchester, 20–22 February.

Huey, E. B. (1908). The psychology and pedagogy of reading, New York: Macmillan.

Huey, E. B. (1968). The psychology and pedagogy of reading, Cambridge, Mass: MIT.

Ingram, T. T. S. (1960). Pediatric aspects of developmental dysphasia, dyslexia and dysgraphia, *Cerebral Palsy Bull.*, **2**, 254–277.

Ingram, T. T. S. (1964). The dyslexic child. *The Practitioner*, **192**, 503–516.

Javal, L. E. (1879). Essai sur la physiologie de la lecture, *Anales d' Occulistique*, **82**, 242–253.

Johnson, D. and Myklebust, H. (1967). *Learning Disabilities: Educational Principles and Practices*, New York: Grune and Stratton.

Jorm, A. F. (1979). The cognitive and neurological basis of developmental dyslexia: a theoretical framework and review, *Cognition*, **7**, 19–33.

Judd, G. H. and Buswell, G. T. (1922). Silent reading: a study of the various types, *Suppl. Educ. Monogr.*, **23**.

Just, M. A. and Carpenter, P. A. (1978). Inference processes during reading: reflections from eye fixations, In: Senders, J. W., Fisher, D. F. and Monty, R. A. (eds). *Eye Movements and the Higher Psychological Functions*, Hillsdale, NJ: Lawrence Erlbaum Assoc.

Katz, P. A. and Deutch, M. (1964). Modality of stimulus presentation in serial learning for retarded and normal readers, *Percep. Motor Skills*, **19**, 627–633.

Kinsbourne, M. and Warrington, E. K. (1962). A study of finger agnosia, *Brain*, **85**, 47–66.

Kinsbourne, M. and Warrington, E. K. (1963a). Development factors in reading and writing backwardness, *Brit. J. Psychol.*, **54**, 145–156.

Kinsbourne, M. and Warrington, E. K. (1963b). The developmental Gerstmann Syndrome. *Arch. Neurol.*, **8**, 40–51.

Kornhuber, H. H. (1973). Cerebellar control of eye movements, *Adv. Otorhinolaryngol*, **19**, 241–253.

Lashley, K. S. (1951). The problems of serial order in behaviour. In: Jeffress, L. A. (ed.), *Cerebral Mechanisms in Behaviour,* New York: J. Wiley & Sons.

Lefton, L. A., Lahey, B. B., Stagg, D. I. (1978). Eye movements in reading disabled and normal children: a study of systems and strategies, *J. Learn. Disabil.*, **1**, 22–31.

Lesevre, N. (1964). Les Mouvements oculaires d'exploration: étude électro-oculagraphique comparée d'enfants normaux et dyslexiques. Thèse de 3 cycle (ronée).

Lesevre, N. (1968). L'organisation du regard chez des enfants d'age scolaire, lecteurs normaux et dyslexiques, *Rev. de Neuropsychiat. Infant.*, **16**, 323–349.

Levy-Schoen, A. (1980). Flexible and/or rigid control of oculomotor scanning behaviour. Paper presented at the Last Whole Earth EM Conference, St Petersburg, Florida, 10–13 February.

Lloyd, P. and Pavlidis, G. Th. (1977). Child language and eye movements. The relative effects of sentence and situation on comprehension in young children. Paper presented at the British Psychological Society Conference, London, 19 December, and *Bull. Brit. Psychol. Soc.* (1978), **31**, 70–71 (abstract).

Lloyd, P. and Pavlidis, G. Th. (1978). The relationship between child language and eye movements; a developmental study. *Neuroscience Letters Suppl.*, **1**, 248. (Abstracts of the 2nd European Neuroscience meeting, Florence, Italy, 4–9 September).

Lunzer, E. A. (1978). Short term memory and reading, Stage 1. In: Gruneberg, M. M., Morris, P. E., and Sykes, R. N. (eds.), *Practical Aspects of Memory*, London: Academic Press.

Luria, A. R. (1966). *Higher Cortical Functions in Man*, New York: Basic Books.

Lynch, J. C., Mountcastle, V. B., Talbot, W. H. and Yin, T. C. T. (1977). Parietal lobe mechanisms for directed visual attention, *J. Neurophysiol.* **40**, 362–389.

Mackworth, N. H. and Bruner, J. (1970). How adults and children search and recognize pictures, *Hum. Develop.*, **13**, 149–177.

Matin, E. (1974). Saccadic suppression: a review and an analysis, *Psychol. Bull.*, **81**, 899–917.

Mattis, S., French, J. H., Rapin, I. (1975). Dyslexia in children and young adults: three independent neuropsychological syndromes, *Dev. Med. Child Neurol.*, **17**, 150.

McConkie, G. W. and Rayner, K. (1973). An on-line computer technique for studying reading: identifying the perceptual span, In; Nacke, P. O. (ed.). *Diversity in Mature Reading: Theory and Research. Twenty-second Yearbook*, Nat. Read. Conf., 119–130.

McConkie, G. W. and Rayner, K. (1975). The span of the effective stimulus during a fixation in reading, *Percep. and Psychophysiol.*, **17**, 578–586.

Millodot, M., Johnson, C. A., Lamont, A., Leibowitz, H. W. (1975). Effects of dioptrics on peripheral visual acuity, *Vis. Res.*, **15**, 1357–1362.

Miles, T. R. (1970). *On Helping the Dyslexic Child*, London: Methuen.

Miles, T. R. and Ellis, N. C. (1981). A lexical encoding deficiency: clinical observations. In: Pavlidis, G. Th., and Miles, T. R. (eds.), *Dyslexia Research and its Applications to Education*, London: J. Wiley & Sons (this volume).

Miller, L. M. (1969). Eye movement latency as a function of age, stimulus, uncertainty and position in the visual field, *Percep. Motor Skills*, **28**, 631–636.

Morgan, W. P. (1896). A case of congenital word blindness. *Brit. Med. J.*, **2**, 1378.

Naidoo, S. (1971). Symposium on reading disability, *Brit. J. Educ. Psychol.*, **41**, 19–22.

Naidoo, S. (1972). *Specific Dyslexia*, London: Pitman.

Nodine, C. F. and Steurle, N. L. (1973). Development of perceptual and cognitive strategies for differentiating graphemes, *J. Exp. Psychol.*, **97**, 158–166.

Olson, D. R. (1970). *Cognitive Development: The Child's Acquisition of Diagonality*, New York: Academic Press.

O'Regan, J. K. (1975). Structural and contextual constraints on eye movements in reading, Unpublished doctoral dissertation, University of Cambridge.

O'Regan, J. K. (1979). Moment to moment control of eye saccades as a function of textual parameters in reading. In: Kolers, P. A. Wrolstad, M. and Bouma, H. (eds.), *Processing of Visible Language*, New York: Plenum Press.

Orton, S. T. (1925). Word-blindness in school children, *Arch. Neurol. and Psychiat.*, **14**, 581–614.

Orton, S. T. (1928). An impediment in learning to read: a neurological explanation of the reading disability, *School and Soc.*, 286–290.

Orton, S. T. (1937). *Reading, Writing and Speech Problems in Children*, London: Chapman and Hall.

Owens, F. W. (1978). Dyslexia: genetic aspects. In: Benton, A. L. and Pearl, D. (eds.). *Dyslexia: An Appraisal of Current Knowledge*, New York: Oxford University Press.

Patberg, J. P. and Yonas, A. (1978). The effects of the reader's skill and the difficulty of the text on the perceptual span in reading, *J. Exp. Psychol. Hum. Percep. and Perf.*, **4**, 545–552.

Pavlidis, G. Th. (1978) The dyslexic's erratic eye movements; case studies, *Dyslex. Rev.*, **1**, 22–28.

Pavlidis, G. Th. (1979a). Eye movements and the objective diagnosis of dyslexia. Paper presented at the Symposium on Dyslexia, the New Approach, Manchester University, 14–16 February.

Pavlidis, G. Th. (1979b). How can dyslexia be objectively diagnosed? *Reading*, 13 (3), 3–15.

Pavlidis, G. Th. (1980a). Sequential deficit: the main cause of dyslexia. Paper presented at the British Psychological Society, Cognitive Section's Conference on Reading, Exeter, 22–23 March.

Pavlidis, G. Th. (1981a). Do eye movements hold the key to dyslexia? *Neuropsychologia,* **19**, 57–64.

Pavlidis, G. Th. (1980b). Diagnosing dyslexia by abnormal eye movements. Paper presented at the Annual Conference of the British Psychological Society, Aberdeen, 27–31 March. Also in: *Bull. Brit. Psychol. Soc.,* **33**, 203 (Abstract).

Pavlidis, G. Th. (1981b). How much of a fixation time is due to oculomotor and how much to information processing requirements? To be submitted for publication.

Pavlidis, G. Th. (1981c). Eye movement differences between normal readers and dyslexics during reading. To be submitted for publication.

Pavlidis, G. Th. (1981d). The effects of text difficulty on the eye movement characteristics of backward, normal, advanced readers and dyslexics during reading. To be submitted for publication.

Pavlidis, G. Th. (1981e). Dyslexics have erratic eye movements in non-reading sequential tasks while matched backward, normal and advanced readers do not. To be submitted for publication.

Pavlidis, G. Th. (1981f).'The Dyslexics' erratic eye movements during looking at digits'. To be submitted for publication.

Pecheux, M. (1976). Localisation spatiale et activite oculomotrice: une étude génétique, *Année Psychol.,* **76**, 7–24.

Piaget, J. and Vinh-Bang, I. (1961). L'enregistrement des mouvements oculaires en jeu chez l'adulte dans la comparaison de verticules, horizontales ou obliques et dans les perceptions de la figure en équerre, *Arch. Psychol. (Geneva),* **38**, 167–200.

Pirozzolo, F. J. and Rayner, K. (1978). The neural control of EMs in acquired and developmental reading disorder. In: Avakian-Whitaker, H. and Whitaker, H. A. (eds). Advances in Neurolinguistics and Psycholinguistics. New York; Academic Press.

Rayner, K. (1975). The perceptual span and peripheral cues in reading, *Cogn. Psychol.,* **7**, 65–81.

Rayner, K. (1978). EMs in reading and information processing, *Psychol. Bull.,* **85**, 618–660.

Rayner, K. and McConkie, G. W. (1976). What guides a reader's eye movements, *Vis. Res.,* **16**, 837–839.

Robinson, D. A. (1968a). Eye movement control in primates, *Science,* **161**, 1219–1224.

Robinson, D. A. (1968b). The oculomotor control system: a review, IEEE, **56**, 1032–1049.

Rubino, C. A. and Minden, H. A. (1973). An analysis of eye-movements in children with a reading disability, *Cortex,* **9**, 217–220.

Rutter, M. and Yule, W. (1975). The concept of specific reading retardation, *J. Child Psychol. Psychiat.,* **16**, 181–197.

Schiepers, C. W. J. (1976). Global attributes in visual word recognition: the contribution of word length, *Vis. Res.,* **16**, 1445–1454.

Schiffman, G. [Cited in: Goldberg, H. K. (1968)] Visual perception and related facts in dyslexia. In: Keeney, A. H. and Keeney, V. T. (eds.), *Dyslexia, Diagnosis and Treatment of Reading Disorders,* St Louis: C. V. Mosby Co.

Scinto, L. F. (1978). Relation of eye fixations to old–new information of texts. In: Senders, J. W., Fisher, D. F., and Monty, R. A. (eds.). *Eye Movements and the Higher Psychological Functions,* Hillsdale, NJ: Lawrence Erlbaum Associates.

Spragins, A. B., Lefton, L. A. and Fisher, D. F. (1976). Eye movements while reading spatially transformed text: a developmental study, *Mem. Cognit.* **4**, 36–42.

Stengel, E. (1944). Loss of spatial orientation, constructional apraxia and Gerstmann's syndrome, *J. Ment. Sci.*, **90**, 753–760.

Stockwell, C. W., Sherard, E. S., Schuler, J. V. (1976). EOG findings in dyslexic children, *Trans. Amer. Acad. Ophthalmol. Otolol.*, **82**, 239–243.

Taylor, E. A. (1957). The spans: perception, apprehension, recognition, *Amer. J. Ophthalmol.*, **44**, 501–507.

Taylor, S. E., Franckenpohl, H. and Pette, J. L. (1960). Grade level norms for components of the fundamental reading skill, *EDL. Inf. Res. Bull.* **3.**, Huntington, New York: Educ. Devel. Labs.

Tinker, M. A. (1946). The study of eye movements in reading, *Psychol. Bull.*, **43**, 93–120.

Tinker, M. A. (1958). Recent studies of eye movements in reading, *Psychol. Bull.*, **55**, 215–231.

Tinker, M. A. (1965). *Bases for Effective Reading*, Minneapolis; University of Minnesota Press.

Vellutino, F. R. (1977). Alternative conceptualizations of dyslexia: evidence in support of a verbal deficit hypothesis, *Harvard Educ. Rev.*, **47**, 334–354.

Vellutino, F. R. and Scanlon, D. (1980). Free recall of concrete versus abstract words in poor and normal readers. Paper presented at the British Psychological Society Conference on Reading, Exeter, 22–23 March.

Vernon, M. D. (1971). *Reading and its Difficulties*, Cambridge: Cambridge University Press.

Vernon, M. D. (1977). Varieties in deficiency in the reading process, *Harvard Educ. Rev.*, **47**, 396–410.

Vernon, M. D. (1979). Variability in reading retardation, *Brit. J. Psychol.*, **70**, 7–16.

Volkmann, F. C. (1976). Saccadic suppression; a brief review. In: Monty, R. A. and Senders, J. A. (eds.), *Eye Movements and Psychological Processes*, Hillsdale, NJ: Lawrence Erblaum Associates.

Vurpillot, E. (1968). The development of scanning strategies and their relation to visual differentiation, *J. Exp. Child Psychol.*, **6**, 632–650.

Vurpillot, C. (1976). The visual world of the child, London: George, Allen and Unwin Ltd.

Vurpillot, E. and Taranne, P. (1974). Jugement d'identile ou de non-identile entre dessins et exploration oculomotrice chez des enfants de 5 et 7 ans, *Année Psychol.*, **74**, 79–100.

Walker, R. Y. (1933). The eye movements of good readers, *Psychol. Monogr.*, **44**, 95–117.

Welchman, M. (1980). Social and education implications of dyslexia. Paper presented at International Symposium on dyslexia research and its educational applications, Manchester, 20–22 February.

Wheeler, T. J. and Watkins, E. J. (1978). Dyslexia: the problem of definition, *Dyslex. Rev.*, **1**, 13–15.

Woodworth, R. S. and Schlosberg, H. (1954). *Experimental Psychology*, London: Methuen.

Yarbus, A. L. (1967). *Eye Movements and Vision*, New York: Plenum Press.

Young, L. R. and Sheena, D. (1975). Survey of eye movement recording methods, *Behav. Res. Meth. and Instrum.*, **7**, 397–429.

Zangwill, O. L. (1981). Foreword. In: Pavlidis, G. Th. and Miles, T. R. (eds.), *Dyslexia Research and its Applications to Education*, London: J. Wiley & Sons (this volume).

Zangwill, O. L. and Blakemore, C. (1972). Dyslexia: reversal of EM during reading, *Neuropsychol.*, **10**, 371–373.

Zaporozhets, A. V. (1965). The development of perception in the preschool child. In: Mussen, P. H. (ed.) European research in child development, *Monogr. of Soc. for Res. in Child Develop.*, **30**, 82–101.

Zurif, E. B. and Carson, G. (1970). Dyslexia in relation to cerebral dominance and temporal analysis, *Neuropsychol.*, **8**, 351–361.

Dyslexia Research and its Applications to Education
Edited by G. Th. Pavlidis and T. R. Miles
© 1981 John Wiley & Sons Ltd.

CHAPTER 7

Visual Recognition Experiments in Dyslexia

Ch. P. Legein and H. Bouma

SUMMARY

In this chapter a review is presented of our experiments with dyslexics and normally reading children as to their reading processes. We come to the conclusion that the underlying cause of dyslexia is most likely a specific recoding deficiency.

INTRODUCTION

In fluent reading, three basic visual processes have to function in a close time relationship. These processes are:

(1) eye movements–in reading; these are saccadic in nature; during the eye-jumps from one fixation point to the next there is no useful perception, so that all information has to be gathered during the eye-fixation pause;

(2) the recognition of text; this takes place during the eye-pause, and is limited to an area around the point of fixation called the visual reading field;

(3) an integration process, that is, a process in which the information from successive eye-pauses is integrated.

Research on visual processes involved in ordinary reading has been in progress in our Institute for a number of years. We have concentrated on adult readers and have investigated such processes as the control of eye saccades (Andriessen and De Voogd, 1973; Bouma and De Voogd, 1974); recognition of isolated letters (Bouma, 1971), and recognition of embedded letters and of words (Bouma, 1970; 1973). In the recognition experiments, we have particularly studied parafoveal vision since the saccadic nature of eye movements keeps part of the text outside the centre of foveal vision. We soon found that parafoveal text recognition is not limited by decreased visual acuity, but by strong interference effects between adjacent letters. Thus, it is far more difficult to recognize embedded letters than isolated letters. The precise nature of this interference is as yet unknown.

We decided to extend the investigation to include beginners in reading, and in particular to the 5% or so of children, mostly boys, who experience difficulties in reading. Development of visual reading functions is an interesting subject in itself, and malfunctions might profitably be described in terms of deviations from undisturbed reading processes.

There is an overwhelming mass of useful literature on dyslexics (Jorm, 1979; Valtin, 1978, 1979; Vernon 1971), but facts about the way they read and about their reading processes are scarce.

We have focused our attention on the recognition process during the eye-fixation pauses in both dyslexics and in normally reading children. We started with tachistoscopic recognition experiments in foveal and parafoveal vision (Bouma and Legein, 1977). Later on we measured response latencies, and we changed the way of presenting long words that are normally poorly recognized by dyslexics in such a way that they were now better recognized. On the grounds of these and other experiments, some of which are not mentioned in this paper, we propose a simple sequential processing scheme which can explain the results. According to this scheme the main source of difficulties for dyslexics is the translation from visual items into speech code. A more detailed description can be found in Bouma and Legein (1980).

EXPERIMENTAL DATA

Twenty dyslexic children (two of whom were girls) were selected by the staff of a remedial teaching school as to specific reading difficulties in the absence of emotional and intellectual deficits. According to the school's files, WISC (Wechsler Intelligence Scale for Children) IQ values were between 92 and 135, with an average of 105, and the children were between 10–15 years at the time of testing. All of them underwent a complete ophthalmological examination.

The control group of twenty children of about the same age (nine of whom were girls) were selected by their teachers as to average reading level from grades 4, 5 and 6 of an ordinary primary school.

Finally, five experienced adult subjects (25–40 years old) from the staff of our Institute also took the battery of tests, for an estimate of the 'maximum' value obtainable.

Figure 7.1 gives the reading classification of all 40 children according to the Tanghe test. The area between the two oblique lines is taken to be the 'normal' area. The average reading level of the dyslexics turned out to be 3 years below normal; the grades conform to the class level of the elementary school.

Foveal and parafoveal recognition was tested by means of a two-channel tachistoscope. Experiments were done with isolated letters, embedded letters (a letter between two other letters), and with words up to a length of five letters. The presentation time was 100 msec, which is brief enough to exclude eye movements. In the parafoveal experiments the eccentricity was one degree from fixation

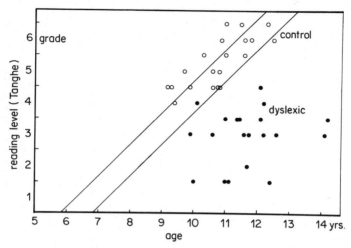

Figure 7.1. Classification of reading quality levels of all subjects versus age levels according to grades of elementary school. Normal level between oblique lines. One subject from the dyslexic group appeared to have a 'normal' score on the reading test, although his way of reading sounded peculiar. In order not to bias our results by a *posthoc* selection of subjects, we retained him as one of the dyslexic group

point, corresponding to four letter positions. Parafoveal recognition was tested right and left of the eye fixation point. In word recognition the letter closest to the fixation point was always at one degree eccentricity.

Figure 7.2 shows the results of these experiments for isolated letters /a/; letters between two other letters (embedded letters) /xax/; and for words of lengths of 3, 4 and 5 letters /wrd/. The figure shows the averaged correct recognition score for each group of children, together with the results of a group of five adult readers.

As regards foveal and parafoveal recognition of isolated letters, there is no difference between the two groups of children. This implies that dyslexics have a normal knowledge of letters. However, especially in parafoveal recognition, but also in foveal recognition, there is a great difference between the two groups in the embedded letter and word experiments. This indicates that masking effects between adjacent letters play a considerable role in these experiments. The gap between normally reading children and adults suggests a maturation process. It is striking to see that dyslexics frequently fail to recognize foveally a very simple word with a maximum length of five letters. In addition a difference is observed in the recognition scores in parafoveal vision, which favours the right visual field.

As word lengths are increased, the recognition score in foveal vision drops progressively in dyslexics, whereas in normally reading children long words have a 100% score (Figure 7.3). Follow up experiments one year later showed that there was an improvement in the results of all children; not only was the reading level higher but the tachistoscopic results were better as well. We also looked for

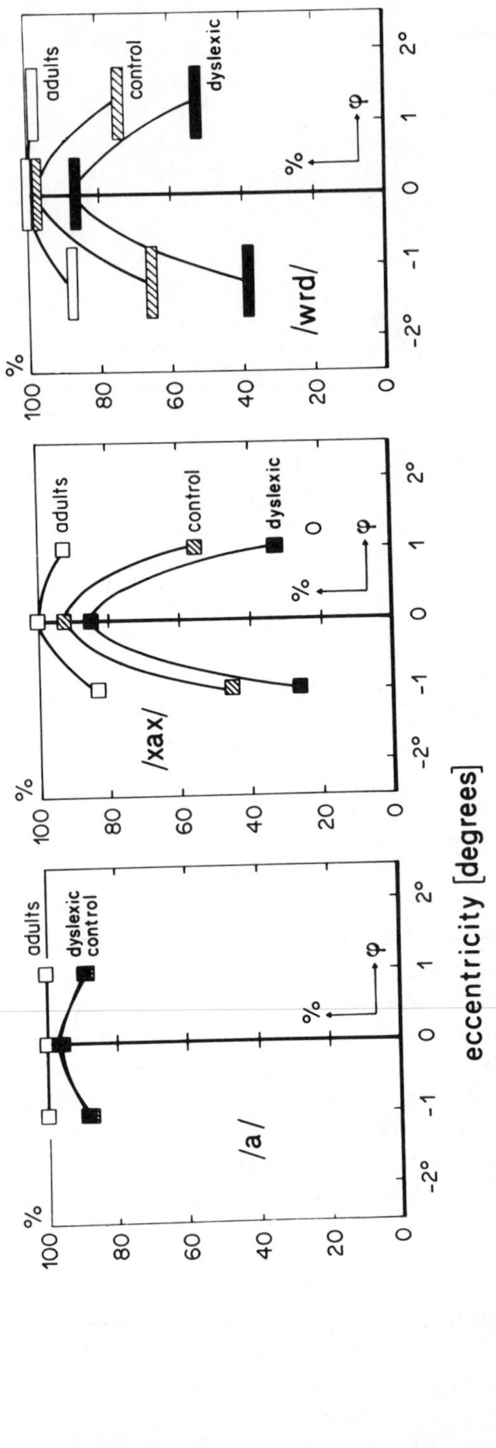

Figure 7.2. Average correct recognition scores in tachistoscopic presentations ($t = 100$ msec) of single letters /a/, embedded letters /xax/ and of words /wrd/ in foveal and parafoveal presentations. Word scores are averaged for different lengths ($l = 3, 4$ and 5)

	dysl.	contr.
l = 3	96	98
l = 4	87	98
l = 5	75	98
l = 6	42	100
l = 7	38	100
l = 8	33	96

Figure 7.3. Foveal word recognition of different word lengths for both groups of children. Data for $l = 3,4,5$ concern twenty subjects, for $l = 6,7,8$ four subjects. Note that dyslexics have decreasing scores with increasing word length

	Score (%)			latency (ms)		
	Dysl.	Contr.	Diff.	Dysl.	Contr.	Diff.
Foveal words	88	98	-10	900	680	220
Parafoveal words	58	77	-19	940	730	210

Figure 7.4. Foveal and parafoveal word recognition scores and response latencies of correct responses averaged over all subjects ($n = 400-800$). Note the constant latency difference of about 220 msec between dyslexics and normally reading children in foveal and parafoveal recognition experiments. (These experiments have been carried out a year later than those of Figures 7.2. and 7.3)

the influence of lateral dominance on the recognition scores. Children with a crossed lateral dominance (eye versus hand—50% of all dyslexics) were not distinguishable from those with a unilateral dominance.

Since in fluent reading the three basic processes should function in close time relationships, we wanted to measure latency times in recognition experiments. For this purpose we designed an experimental arrangement in which an electronic counter was started at the onset of the stimulus and stopped by a voice switch reacting to the initial vocalization of the response.

Figure 7.4 shows the results for foveal and parafoveal word recognition. Although there is a considerable difference in recognition scores between the two groups of children foveally and parafoveally, it is striking to see that there is a constant latency difference of 200 msec between the two groups. This means that dyslexics are slow responders compared with the normally reading children.

From earlier experiments (Bouma, Legein, and Van Rens, 1975), we know that tachistoscopic (100 msec) recognition of long words (length $\geq$ six letters), presented foveally, is nearly perfect in children reading normally, whereas dyslexic children have a very low score. Such a big difference is not observed in shorter words. We had indications that recognition scores would improve if the presentation time were prolonged.

When listening to dyslexic children reading aloud one of the most remarkable characteristics observed—apart from a rigid intonation pattern—is the way they deal with longer words. As they cannot recognize and pronounce longer words at once, they analyse them one part after another, whispering the already recognized first part or parts repeatedly while spelling others. In this way the child sometimes ultimately succeeds in composing and pronouncing the complete word correctly. Usually it fails, and a wrong word or non-word which resembles the printed word is pronounced, or further reading may be blocked altogether.

Their slow recognition could be the reason why they fail to recognize long words both in tachistoscopic experiments and in ordinary reading. After one part of a long word is recognized, the time spent for the other part is too long for them to retain the first part for making a correct integration. Apart from time factors, masking effects may play a role.

We therefore planned a tachistoscopic experiment in which only words of eight letters were used. All these words consisted of two words of four letters each, such as 'headline'. As we knew, the constituent parts are recognized rather well when presented separately, but the combination is seldom recognized. The purpose of the experiment was how to present an eight-letter word so as to get a better recognition score. The problem for the dyslexic in dealing with an eight-letter word is possibly in splitting or separation. Perhaps the subject cannot distinguish between the different parts. Several mechanisms might play a role. Firstly, the strong interference effects between adjacent letters could reduce the recognition score on longer words considerably in dyslexic children. If this were the case, spatial separation of the word halves could be of help.

Another factor could be the recognition latency time. We have found that when dyslexic children recognize four-letter words correctly, the latency time is nevertheless about 200 msec longer than for normal readers. So in 100 msec presentations of eight-letter words the second word part may already have vanished the moment the first part is recognized. Prolonged presentation or temporal separation would then be of help in increasing recognition scores. The stimulus time was therefore prolonged from 100 to 500 msec, and in the temporal separation experiment the two word-halves were presented in their proper places one after another with a 200 msec pause in between.

Figure 7.5 shows the results of these experiments. As can be seen, both temporal separation and prolonged stimulation favour the recognition score. The recognition of the component word halves ($l = 4$) separately is given in Figure 7.6. The first part was presented just left of fixation and the second part just right of fixation, in correspondence with their proper positions in the $l = 8$ word. From a comparison of these results with those obtained in the temporal

	normal $l=8$ 100 ms	spatial $l=4\#l=4$ $\quad$ $l=4$ 100 ms		temporal $l=4$ Δt $l=4$	prolonged $l=8$ 500 ms	
Dyslexics	21	18	19	36	33	%
Controls	85	79	71	88	88	%

Figure 7.5. Recognition scores of eight-letter words. Foveal presentation in different modes. Temporal separation favours recognition in dyslexics, as do longer presentation times (12 subjects, $n = 240$)

	first part	second part	
Dyslexics	67	54	%
Controls	96	94	%

Figure 7.6. Correct scores for the component word-halves separately (see Figure 7.5) ($n = 240$; $t = 100$ msec)

separation experiment ($l = 4\Delta tl = 4$) of Figure 7.5, it is suggested that in the temporal separation mode the processing of the two halves could be independent.

The improved recognition scores obtained with prolonged and with temporally separated stimulation indicate difficulties in simultaneous processing in dyslexics. This lends support to the view that dyslexics read a long word by segmenting it into parts and processing the parts in succession. When the first part has been recognized it has to be retained by rehearsal while the second part is being read.

INTERPRETATION

What are the implications of the present results for a better understanding of dyslexia as a specific reading weakness? We shall first interpret the findings in terms of a simple scheme of information processing in overt word recognition (Figure 7.7). Results to be incorporated are response latencies fairly characteristic of individual subjects are generally longer in dyslexics than in control subjects. The latency difference depends on the type of stimulus to be recognized (for example, letters versus words) but not on the way they are presented (foveal versus parafoveal). Response latencies increase with increasing difficulty of recognition. Moreover, we have found that incorrect responses take longer than correct ones and that long latencies and low correct scores tend to go together.

We propose the following explanation: the visual quality of the stimulus influences the time needed for *visual analysis*. Thus, if visual information is decreased by parafoveal presentation or by letter embedding (increased lateral

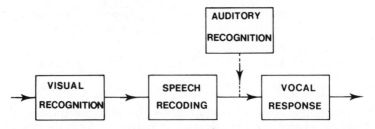

Figure 7.7. Block diagram of assumed serial stages in the oral reading of letters and words

interference), a longer latency will result before the visual recognition units are triggered.

Time differences between correct and incorrect recognitions are attributed to the *decision* phase, where one item is selected for response out of a number of alternatives. In the case of correct recognition, activation of the corresponding item will usually have surpassed activation of alternative candidates. Thus, the decision is relatively easy and straightforward. In the case of incorrect recognition, a decision between the activated incorrect unit and at least one other unit (that is the correct unit) is required. The latency differences between correct and incorrect recognitions are thus attributed to the extra time necessary for the difficult decision.

The *speech recoding phase* is the most likely candidate to account for the differences between dyslexic and control subjects. Thus, the idea is that dyslexic subjects need somewhat more time for recoding a visually recognized letter into its letter-name than the controls, and even more time for recoding a visual word into its sound (name). The primary reason for attributing this difference to the phonological recoding process is that the latency difference does depend on the item to be recognized but not on recognition difficulty. If the time difference were attributed to the visual activation phase, the latency difference would be expected to increase with recognition difficulty.

Finally, it is postulated that the *articulation phase* is equally developed in dyslexics and controls. The basic evidence for this is that dyslexic children are normal speakers and listeners. In a pilot experiment in which both dyslexic and control children repeated spoken words, which included long and difficult ones, there were no obvious extra delays for the dyslexic subjects. This is in strong contrast to the reading of long words, which dyslexics find particularly difficult (Bouma and Legein, 1977; Bouma, Legein, and Van Rens, 1975). This makes it unlikely that slow articulation is the source of the long latencies in visual letter and word recognition. On the same grounds, a general slowness of dyslexic children in all kinds of recognition seems unsuitable for explaining the specific delays observed in the experiments.

Summarizing this part of the discussion, we propose that dyslexic children's visual information processing and articulation are just as efficient as those of control children, but their phonological recoding is deficient.

Why, then, should their recognition scores be lower? The explanation proposed here takes a lead from the finding that low recognition scores and long latencies tend to go together. Also it is of interest to note that latencies are often as long as 1–2 sec. During this period, the information should reside somewhere in the visual or the response system. On the assumption that storage of the response is possible only after that response has become available internally, the preceding phases of the recognition process should have their own storage facilities. If we take the first storage facility after the retina to retain rather unprocessed visual information for some 0.25 sec, we clearly need other forms of visual storage before the information can be carried to a more lasting response form. These storage facilities are assumed to be volatile, such that each extra delay automatically leads to decreased performance (lower probability of correct response).

There can be little doubt that the picture as sketched above is a simplistic one. However, it has the advantage of clearly assigning experimental results to assumed processing stages and thus lends itself to further experimental tests. Such an approach has recently be advocated by a number of researchers in the field (Frederiksen, 1978; Valtin, 1978).

Before discussing how a number of findings, reported in the literature, relate to the above scheme, it seems relevant to consider briefly the relation between word recognition and letter recognition. Longer latencies for embedded letters as compared with those for words suggest that word recognition occurs earlier than recognition of the constituent letters and thus cannot be based on the latter. We think that this conclusion is premature. During actual word recognition, neither an explicit decision between alternative letters nor a phonemic recoding of individual letters into their names is necessary. Thus, in our view, word recognition can be based on the activation of a number of the word's constituent letters. For a quantitative theory on how precisely the relation between word recognition and letter recognition may be envisaged, the reader is referred to Bouwhuis and Bouma (1979).

As regards word recognition and reading, correlations between word recognition scores and reading level turned out generally to be positive though small, and correlations between word recognition latency and reading level were negative though small. This indicates that the reading level of the children cannot be deduced from their word recognition in any simple way. On the other hand, in our data a low foveal word score implies a low reading level and a quick foveal word response excludes a low reading level. It seems then that other components of the reading process sometimes make up for shortcomings in word recognition, for example a good eye movement strategy, better concentration, or a better utilization of context. Frederiksen (1978) has given a useful survey of component skills in reading. It can be maintained, therefore, that word recognition skills are necessary for adequate reading, besides other skills. Perhaps it should be added that a simple reading test, such as the one we used, was not designed to reflect the intricacies of the component skills; as our insight advances, the need for more sophisticated reading tests increases.

By way of illustration, the above discussion has been based on group averages. We wish to stress that the distribution of results of dyslexic subjects and control subjects overlap and in particular there are marked differences between individual dyslexic subjects. Therefore, the group averages are closely dependent on the selected subjects. The framework sketched above is clearly suited for individual results as well.

Recently, a number of investigators have advocated a view somewhat similar to ours, although the primary deficiency is hypothesized in somewhat different processes. There is now rather strong evidence that dyslexics have hardly any deficiency in visual processing tasks, provided that no overt or silent speech recoding is necessary (Vellutino et al., 1975; Vellutino, 1977). If letter and word recognition is involved, response latencies are clearly longer in dyslexics (Perfetti and Hogaboam, 1975). Both Vellutino, and Perfetti and Hogaboam think of the phonological recoding as the primary source of difficulty, just as we do. Vellutino (1977) also leaves open the option of a more general language deficiency. Jorm (1979) thinks rather in terms of a primary (auditory) short-term memory deficiency. Valtin (1978) has remarked that certain auditory difficulties may well be secondary to spelling difficulties.

In conclusion, a number of specific hypotheses has been advanced and the main task at hand seems to be to get a clearer view on the relation between primary and secondary deficiencies. Specific theories should be of help particularly in making specific predictions and our present position puts the primary deficiency in visual word to speech recoding and vice versa.

ACKNOWLEDGEMENT

Thanks are due to Mr A. L. M. van Rens for his enthusiastic assistance throughout the investigation and to Mr A. van Vroenhoven and Mr J. Hupperetz, directors of the schools involved, as well as to their staffs, for their interest and consistent cooperation.

REFERENCES

Andriessen, J. J. and De Voogd, A. H. (1973) Analysis of eye movement patterns in silent reading, *IPO Annual Progress Report*, **8**, 29–34.
Bouma, H. (1970) Interaction effects in parafoveal letter recognition. *Nature (London)*, **226**, 177–178.
Bouma, H. (1971) Visual recognition of isolated lower-case letters. *Vision Res.*, **11**, 459–474.

Bouma, H. (1973) Visual interference in the parafoveal recognition of initial and final letters of words. *Vision Res., 13,* 767–782.

Bouma, H. and De Voogd, A. H. (1974) On the control of eye saccades in reading. *Vision Res.,* **14,** 273–284.

Bouma, H., Legein, Ch. P., and van Rens A. L. M (1975) Visual recognition by dyslectic children. Further exploration of letter, word and number recognition in 4 weak and 4 normal readers. *IPO Annual Progress Report,* **10,** 72–78.

Bouma, H. and Legein, Ch. P. (1977) Foveal and parafoveal recognition of letters and words by dyslexics and by average readers. *Neuropsychologia,* **15,** 69–80.

Bouma, H. and Legein, Ch. P. (1980) Dyslexia: a specific recoding deficit? Analysis of response latencies for letters and words in dyslectics and in average readers. *Neuropsychologia,* **18,** 285–298.

Bouwhuis, D. G. and Bouma, H. (1979) Visual recognition of three-letter words as derived from the recognition of the constituent letters, *Perception and Psychophys.,* **25,** 12–22.

Frederiksen, J. R. (1978) A chronometric study of component skills in reading, Bolt, Beranek and Newman, Report 3757.

Jorm, A. F. (1979) The cognitive and neurological basis of developmental dyslexia: a theoretical framework and review. *Cognition,* **7,** 19–33.

Perfetti, C. A. and Hogaboam, T. (1975) The relationship between simple word decoding and reading comprehension skill, *J. Educ. Psychol.,* **67,** 461–469.

Tanghe, M. (1971) *De B. V. L. Individuele Leestests* Tessenderloo: Broeders van Liefde.

Torgeson, J. K. (1978/1979) Reading performance of disabled children on serial memory tasks: a selective review of recent research. *Reading Res. Q.,* **14,** 57–87.

Valtin, R. (1978/1979) Dyslexia: deficit in reading or deficit in research? *Reading Res. Q.,* **14,** 201–221.

Vellutino, F. R., Steger, J. A., Desetto, L., and Phillips, F. (1975) Immediate and delayed recognition of visual stimuli in poor and normal readers. *J. Exper. Child Psychol.,* **19,** 223–232.

Vellutino, F. R. (1977) Alternative conceptualizations of dyslexia. Evidence in support of a verbal deficit hypothesis. *Harvard Educ. Rev.,* **47,** 334–354.

Vernon, M. D. (1971) *Reading and Its Difficulties,* London: Cambridge University Press.

Vernon, M. D. (1977) Varieties of deficiency in the reading process. *Harvard Educ. Rev.,* **47,** 369–410.

Dyslexia Research and its Applications to Education
Edited by G. Th. Pavlidis and T. R. Miles
© 1981 John Wiley & Sons Ltd.

CHAPTER 8

A Lexical Encoding Deficiency I: Experimental Evidence

N. C. ELLIS AND T. R. MILES

INTRODUCTION

The thesis of this chapter and Chapter 9 is that the difficulties commonly observed in dyslexic children and adults are the result of a deficiency at the level of *lexical encoding*. In the present chapter the experimental evidence for this thesis will be reviewed.

The methods of investigation and reasoning to be used will be those of cognitive psychology. This approach involves the assumption that when an organism receives stimulation from the outside world or from within its own body there are mechanisms for transforming, reducing, elaborating, storing and retrieving particular characteristics of the original stimulus, the generic term for such operations being 'information processing' (Neisser, 1967). The neurological structures of the mechanisms in question are not open to immediate investigation but their functions can be inferred from suitably controlled experimental studies. Cognitive psychology thus primarily concerns itself with functions rather than structures.

If, for example, the investigation addresses the functions involved in the processing of visually presented verbal material (that is, reading), it might initially be supposed that a word is represented in terms of (i) its visual features: how it looks; (ii) its phonological features: how it sounds; (iii) its semantic features: what it means; or (iv) its articulatory features: how it is said. Given that a visually presented word is both understood and spoken by the reader, we can thus ask (a) which of these possible representations are used, (b) what functions are involved in their creation, and (c) if the stages of processing occur serially, what is their order? If the answers to these questions were known for the normal reader, the 'flowchart' of functions involved in reading could then form the starting point for research into the reading of dyslexic subjects. For example, if a model of reading were to include a pattern recognition stage where the visual pattern is analysed for its features, one might in that case ask whether their reading difficulties were wholly or partly the result of a failure of the functions concerned in pattern recognition.

Unfortunately it is far from being the case that the functions involved in reading are totally understood, and thus we cannot directly apply 'handbook' knowledge to the poor reader as does a mechanic to the poorly car. Indeed the handbook often grows as a result of investigations into reading failure (see, for example, Coltheart, Patterson and Marshall, 1979; Marshall and Newcombe, 1973). Some rudimentary principles have been formulated, however, and these will be discussed below.

For the greater part of this chapter, when we use the words 'dyslexia' and 'dyslexic', it should be understood that we are talking about *developmental* dyslexia—the group of difficulties described by Hinshelwood (1917), Orton (1937), Hermann (1959), Critchley (1970) and many others. (For a discussion of the unity and diversity of these difficulties see Chapter 9.) In Section IV, however, we refer to the literature on various forms of *acquired* dyslexia (phonemic dyslexia, surface dyslexia etc.), and to avoid ambiguity we shall either add the qualifying adjective 'developmental' or indicate the type of acquired dyslexia being discussed.

Although difficulty with reading is not necessarily the most important feature in the total dyslexic handicap—and certainly not the only feature worth investigation—the study of reading and reading failure turned out to be a valuable starting point for our research. A link was possible with the ideas of those psychologists who had been concerned with visual information processing and short-term memory, and the resultant descriptions of the functions involved in reading (see Model A, below) constituted the 'handbook' which guided our experiments.

Although not all the authors whose work we cite describe their subjects as 'dyslexic' and 'non-dyslexic'—some of them using simply the terms 'good reader' and 'poor reader'—we found no major differences in selection procedures whichever pair of terms was used, and these selection procedures typically included the most important criterion of subjects being of average or above average intelligence. Thus it is likely that many of those classed as 'poor readers' were in fact dyslexic or at least were responding in relevant respects like the typical dyslexic person. We have therefore not hesitated to regard studies of 'poor readers', providing they were of at least average intelligence, as relevant to dyslexia, though in what follows, for the sake of accuracy, we shall make use of the expression 'poor reader' whenever the original author did so.

The study of the specific functions involved in reading often necessitates that the experimental task appears far removed from reading in its normal forms. Artificial 'reading' tasks are created, for example by requiring the subject to find the letter *b* hidden among a page of *a's* or by requiring him to say which of the following letter-strings are words: *zmpt, carrot, coff, forg, pea*. The time taken by different subjects to carry out such tasks and the types of error which they make can with suitably designed experiments throw light on the underlying mechanisms; for example, the first task is relevant to the study of mechanisms for pattern recognition and the second to the study of mechanisms for the storage and retrieval of words. This artificiality might lead to the objection that the approach lacks 'ecological validity': in other words it is too remote from everyday reading to be meaningful (see Neisser, 1976; Newell, 1973; and replies by Underwood, 1978; Underwood and Holt, 1979). The eventual aim of the research, however, is practical: it is to understand the dyslexic child's very real problems with a view to providing more efficient remedial help. To fulfil this aim it is necessary to use the experimental control available in apparently artificial tasks, since this is the only way in which the different functions involved in reading can be studied few at a time or, indeed, singly.

The starting point for a serial process of investigation into reading difficulties must of course be a consideration of the peripheral visual structures, the eyes. Now although it can be taken as established that dyslexic subjects are no different from anyone else as far as optical factors in the visual system are concerned (see Critchley, 1970), one cannot *a priori* exclude the possibility of other ophthalmological disorders; and, in particular, slow or inefficient eye movements could be the source of the dyslexic person's difficulties in reading and other tasks. It is indeed established that dyslexic children do have unusual eye movements in reading (Lesèvre, 1964; Pavlidis, 1978). However, there is good reason to believe that these abnormalities are not the origin of the dyslexic difficulties. It appears to be the case that training in making appropriate eye movements does not necessarily result in improved comprehension (Goldberg, 1968; De Leeuw and De Leeuw, 1969). In addition, the dyslexic child's information-processing deficiency is evident in situations where no eye movements are involved; for example, Ellis and Miles (1977; 1978b) have shown that when arrays of digits are presented at brief exposure times dyslexic subjects are able to report fewer digits correctly in the time available than are controls; this is the case even at exposure times of less than 150 msec when eye movements are impossible. It seems likely, therefore, that the uncertainty associated with inefficient eye movements is itself the result of some more basic deficiency at information processing rather than an early stage in a causal chain.

Once ophthalmological disorders are eliminated as primary causal factors, more central visual information processing functions need to be investigated. It is at this stage of investigation that it becomes necessary to develop a conceptual model of these functions. The body of evidence and reasoning which underlies the belief in the proposed conceptualization is too large and detailed to allow its justified exposition here. Only the essentials will be discussed, and the reader is referred to the work of others for elaboration.

Section I contains a presentation and discussion of Model A. This model, though undoubtedly an oversimplification, was a useful guide in the early stages of the research, and Section II involves a description of the performance of dyslexic and control children in terms of it. The conclusion is drawn that it is *linguistic* material which appears to be the source of many of the dyslexic person's difficulties. Such a conclusion, however, is both incomplete and unoriginal; and since it is clearly necessary to consider not just language, *simpliciter*, but the interaction of spoken, heard, and read language, a further model (Model B) is presented in Section III which takes these other aspects of language into account. Section IV contains a description of the performance of dyslexic and control children in terms of this second model, while Section V contains some general remarks relating to the chapter as whole.

To conclude this section it may be of help of refer to three technical terms which will be used in later discussion: *grapheme*, *phoneme*, and *morpheme*. The *grapheme* is the smallest unit of visual representation of language (usually a single letter of the alphabet), and the *phoneme* is the smallest unit of auditory language capable of indicating contrasts in meaning; thus in the word *pit* there are three phonemes, /p/, /i/, /t/, each of which differs from phonemes in other words, such as *bit*, *pet*, and *pin*. Finally, the *morpheme* is the smallest meaningful language unit, the basic 'building block' of meaning, as it were. A 'free' morpheme is a unit which can stand alone, *hop* or *hope*, for example, while a 'bound' morpheme is one which cannot occur except in conjunction with other morphemes; thus the suffix *-ing*, representing the present participle, cannot occur on its own but can occur, for example, in the words *hopping* and *hoping* where it is described as a 'grammatical morpheme'.

I DEVELOPMENT OF MODEL A

The evidence of Sperling (1963; 1967) has shown that if visual material is presented for short exposure times and is then removed potential information remains available in what is called the 'visual information store' (VIS) or 'iconic store' (Neisser, 1967) for up to 250 msec. This store is said to be 'precategorical'; in other words sensory traces are held there before categorization operations select certain features to produce a 'code', that is, a coded representation of particular characteristics of the original stimulus. It is believed to have a large storage capacity and the potential information so stored is believed to be subject to fast passive decay; that is to say there are no mechanisms for its active maintenance. The visual traces, which represent certain physical characteristics of the original stimulus, for example location, size, shape and colour (Coltheart, 1972; Haber, 1973; Sperling, 1963) can be categorized in such a way that selection for further processing is possible.

The nature of this further processing has been a subject of considerable debate. It is generally agreed (Baddeley, 1966; Baddeley and Hitch, 1974; Conrad, 1964; Morton; 1970) that, at least in situations where the eventual response is spoken, there is the involvement of a mechanism for 'articulatory encoding', that is, a mechanism by which an internal speech code is generated. Since, however, the rate of implicit speech has been reckoned to be about 150 msec per monosyllabic item (Landauer, 1962), one must assume that the rate of articulatory encoding is relatively slow; and since the initial rate of information acquisition from the VIS for verbal material is considerably faster than this (Sperling, 1963; 1967), it has been necessary to postulate some kind of 'buffer store' between the VIS and the articulatory encoding mechanism. (The notion of a 'buffer' implies that the input comes in quickly but that the output is much slower.) Sperling (1967) has argued that the information in the VIS, after being rapidly scanned, is converted into a 'program of motor instructions' for later articulation, these motor instructions being stored in a limited capacity 'recognition buffer'. There is, however, evidence of a short-term visual information coding store which differs from the VIS in that the information so stored is not affected by backwards masking and the visual code trace, which requires active processing for maintenance, can be held for as long as 11 sec (Phillips, 1974; Phillips and Christie, 1977; Posner, 1969). ('Backwards masking' refers to the presentation of a masking stimulus immediately after offset of the original stimulus; such masking has been found seriously to affect the amount of information which can be processed from the VIS; see Section II.) Following this notion Coltheart (1972) has argued for a visual code buffer, and similarly Mitchell (1976) proposes that short-term visual memory may act as the buffer store between VIS and articulatory code.

The evidence for the existence of a short-term visual code is incontrovertible. However, there are many demonstrations that the rate of readout from the VIS is primarily determined not by the number of visual or graphemic features to be encoded (as the visual code buffer hypothesis would predict), but rather by the number of linguistic units that the visual features represent. For example, Allport (1973) has shown that the rate of readout from the VIS is essentially the same for single unrelated consonants as it is for arrays of unrelated common words of three to six letters in length (see also Allport, 1968, 1973, 1978a; Ellis, 1980; Mackworth, 1963). Allport therefore concludes that the rate of information acquisition from the VIS reflects rate of non-visual linguistic or 'lexical' encoding. This is in effect to say that after the visual properties of a verbal stimulus have been represented in the VIS they activate a mechanism which generates words or symbols. A mechanism conceived along similar lines had earlier been postulated by Morton (1969), who describes it as a 'logogen', that is, a pattern-recognizer for words. In addition it has been proposed by Treisman (1960) that we should think of each individual as equipped with an internal lexicon or dictionary containing word-representations against which incoming stimuli can be compared, and it is suggested that as a result of access to this lexicon the linguistic representation appropriate to the visual stimulus is created (for further discussion see Section III). Sperling's idea of a program of motor instructions, a non-articulatory linguistic representation, is in some ways similar to the notion of a lexical code but is less well specified. In this chapter we shall

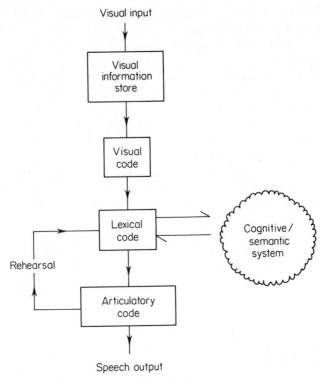

Figure 8.1. Model A: a simple flow chart of the processes involved in reading, naming and immediate memory

therefore follow Allport in speaking of a 'lexical code', and the processing stage by which stimulus traces (from whatever sense they originate) are converted into a lexical code we shall refer to as *lexical encoding*.

It is certain that information processing from the VIS does not immediately involve articulatory encoding: (i) Ellis (1980) has shown it to be unaffected by articulatory suppression (a technique designed to prevent articulatory encoding, see p. 190); and (ii) its rate is some ten times faster than that of implicit speech. It is similarly certain, however, that an articulatory representation is eventually created for output or short-term rehearsal (Baddeley, 1966, 1968; Baddeley and Hitch, 1974; Morton, 1970).

There is thus evidence implicating the following stimulus representations in reading aloud: the VIS and the visual, lexical and articulatory codes. Although there is debate as to whether the processes involved in the creation of the post-VIS representations occur serially or in parallel, for present purpose a serial arrangement, as in Figure 8.1, will be assumed.

The reading process is thus conceived of as follows. When a person looks at a written or printed word a representation of that word is stored temporarily in the VIS. The stimulus traces in the VIS are thereafter analysed so as to form a 'code' in which the stimulus pattern is represented conceptually, that is irrespective of handwriting, typescript, case etc. This code is 'graphemic' in the sense that it represents the graphemes or basic units of writing; and, as a result of the activation of a pattern recognition unit, items in the lexicon are accessed (or made available for use) and the entry in the lexicon (that is, the 'lexical code') corresponding to the stimulus pattern is retrieved.

It is also necessary to postulate a 'semantic system' which makes possible recognition of meaning. It is not known in detail how such a system might work, but one must assume that it comes into operation at this stage, with access to it occurring as a result of activation of the appropriate pattern recognition unit in the lexicon (compare Section III). Finally, if the word is to be read aloud it is necessary for the lexical code to activate a mechanism for articulatory encoding, in other words, for providing a set of instructions to the speech muscles as a result of which there can be the appropriate speech output.

Model A is of course a gross oversimplification of what, after all, must be processes of quite astonishing complexity. It is reasonable to assume, however, that the above are some of the functions involved in reading aloud; and it therefore follows that experiments can be designed which test the abilities of dyslexic and control children at each function in turn. It should perhaps be added at this point that Model A is concerned to account only for the reading of words within the subject's whole-word reading vocabulary. Reading by means of the generation of grapheme–phoneme correspondences will be considered when Model B is discussed below.

II DYSLEXIC CHILDREN'S PERFORMANCE AT TASKS INVOLVING THOSE FUNCTIONS SHOWN IN MODEL A

1. Experiments involving the VIS

There are two ways in which VIS abnormalities might be implicated in poor reading: the decay of information might either be unusually rapid, in which case there would be insufficient availability of the 'raw material' for further processing, or it might be unusually slow, in which case further processing would be impaired as a result of masking.

The former is self-explanatory. With regard to the latter, it is, of course, well known that when a person watches the display produced by a film the impression of temporal continuity is an illusion, since there are in fact 'blank' periods, usually occurring about 24 times per sec, when the projector shutter is closed. The overwriting of frame 2 information upon frame 1 information is called 'backwards masking' and that of residual frame 1 information upon frame 2 information is called 'forwards masking'. Now if the successive frames are similar the visual information merges and there is no disadvantage; if, however, successive inputs to the VIS are different, as they are in the case of reading (since they occur as the result of successive saccades, or eye movements, across the page), there is the possibility of interference; in the case of forwards masking there is interference with the information of fixation 2 by the already processed but residual information of fixation 1, while in the case of backwards masking there is interference with the information of fixation 1 as a result of the superimposed information from fixation 2. It follows that if the information in the VIS decays abnormally slowly there would be the disadvantage of a masking effect, with the previous fixation's trace merging with that of the to-be-processed present fixation. The foundation sensory information of the present fixation would thus be relatively impure.

To test whether VIS abnormalities are an important feature in dyslexia it is therefore necessary to investigate VIS duration in both dyslexic and control children. This has been done by Stanley and Hall (1973) and by Ellis and Miles (1978a). Both investigations took as an operational definition of VIS duration the longest inter-stimulus-interval at which a subject judges two temporally discrete visual stimuli to be a composite percept. This is analogous to slowing down the rate of projection of a film and seeing at what inter-frame-interval the audience notices temporal discontinuity of picture. The findings of both studies, however, were inconclusive; if anything, it is possible that the VIS holds information for a marginally longer duration in the case of dyslexic subjects. This difference was small, however, and, since there are large differences between dyslexic and control children at single fixation processing under backwards masking conditions which effectively prevent any use of post-fixation VIS information (see page 189 below), it must be concluded that there is insufficient evidence that a disorder at the level of the VIS could account for the large differences between dyslexic and control children in other respects.

2. Experiments involving the visual code

Coltheart (1972) and Mitchell (1976) argue that short-term visual memory is important in the naming of visual stimuli on the grounds that the creation of a visual code which outlives the VIS representation would, theoretically at least, provide the articulatory encoding mechanism with a database on which to operate. If this view is correct, it follows that the visual encoding function is one of the suspects as the source of the deficiency in dyslexia. In that case there appear to be three possibilities: (a) the rate of visual encoding may be abnormally slow; (b) the visual code store may be of a smaller capacity, or (c) the information in the visual code store may be subject to unusually rapid decay. A deficiency in respect of either (a), (b), or (c), whether singly or in any conjunction, would be sufficient to impede or delay eventual naming. These possibilities must therefore be considered in turn.

With regard to the rate of visual encoding (a), that is the speed at which visual representations are created, it has been found that when two letters of the same case are presented simultaneously and the subject has to report whether they are the same (OO) or different (OB), dyslexic and control children do not differ either in the speed or in the accuracy with which they can perform this task (Ellis and Miles, 1978b). Nor are the dyslexic children poor readers slower when the letters, though different, are visually confusable (OQ, RP, EF, CG) (Ellis and Miles, 1978b; Supramanian and Audley, 1976). This task can be assumed to involve a post-VIS level of processing, and performance is typically interpreted to reflect the speed of creation and comparison of visual codes for the letters (Posner, 1969). It seems unlikely, therefore, that dyslexic children have difficulty in dealing with the visual characteristics of letters as such.

With regard to (b) and (c), that is, the capacity of the visual code store and the rate of decay of information from it, Ellis and Miles (1978b) tested dyslexic and control children using a procedure devised by Phillips and Baddeley (1971) and Phillips (1974). This involved a 1 sec presentation of a 'random chessboard' where half the cells were filled at random; after a variable interval, which was filled with a masking stimulus so as to prevent VIS storage, a second matrix was presented and the child had to report whether the two matrices were the same or different. In these conditions there is insufficient time for the subjects to count the squares and it must be assumed that they were relying on the visual (not the nameable) features of the patterns presented. There were no significant group performance differences at any of the inter-stimulus-intervals used.

Bakker (1967, 1972) has shown that, when good and poor readers were presented with temporal sequences of meaningless figures, meaningful figures, letters, and digits, the good readers were better than the poor readers at remembering the meaningful figures and letters but that the two groups did not differ when the stimuli were non-verbal meaningless figures. In a similar study Done and Miles (1978) presented dyslexic subjects and age-matched controls with arrays of five, six, and seven digits and afterwards made the correct digits available and asked the subjects to place them in the original order. At this task, where the stimuli are nameable, the dyslexic subjects scored considerably lower than the controls, but when non-verbal nonsense shapes were used as stimuli in place of digits the difference was minimal. Finally, when both groups had been given a Paired Associate Learning task where names were learned for the nonsense shapes, the performance of the controls again became significantly superior. Thus it appears that dyslexic children do not differ from control children in immediate memory for visual material which cannot readily be named, but that they perform less accurately when naming is required.

It must be concluded that there are no essential differences between dyslexic and control children in respect of speed of visual coding, visual code capacity or rate of decay of visual code.

3. Experiments involving both lexical and articulatory codes

In terms of Model A the naming of a visual stimulus is an end product of iconic, visual, lexical and articulatory encoding operations. From this it follows that a subject's difficulty at naming or reading aloud might reflect a functional deficiency at any of these four stages. In subsections 1 and 2 above, however, we have presented evidence which suggests that the dyslexic child's problems at reading aloud are not attributable to functional deficiencies at either iconic or visual code levels. Their exclusion leaves only the lexical and articulatory encoding mechanisms of Model A as possible sources of deficiency.

Model A does not restrict itself to the naming of words, but in its present from concerns the naming of any visual stimulus for which there is a pattern recognition unit. It is therefore necessary to test the generality of any naming deficiency in dyslexic children: for example, if the subjects were slow or inaccurate at naming the word *dog* but not at naming a picture of a dog, the deficiency must be pre-lexical (since the lexical codes for both stimuli are the same) and must reside at the levels of graphemic analysis or pattern recognition units for words; if, in contrast, they had equal difficulty in naming both the word and the picture, while it is possible that there is a deficiency in all the pattern-recognition units for words and pictures (and any other stimuli which they found difficult to name), the simplest explanation would be that there is a deficiency in the accessing of the items in the lexicon and in the retrieving of the appropriate lexical code.

We shall start by showing that there is a general naming deficiency associated with dyslexia. This of itself supports the view that in some way lexical or articulatory functions are deficient as opposed to pattern-recognition units. Moreover it is a matter of common experience that when one has to hold in mind a new telephone number, having looked it up or having been told it, continual rehearsal by means of implicit speech is necessary; and it is commonly said that in these circumstances articulatory codes are both generated from lexical representations and reactivate these representations (compare Baddeley and Hitch, 1974; Ellis, 1979; Morton, 1970). We shall therefore review briefly the evidence for impairments in dyslexic subjects of short-term memory for verbal material. Such evidence will be found to give further support to the idea that an important feature in dyslexia is some kind of language-processing deficiency, even if at this stage of the argument it is unresolved whether the deficiency is to be found at the level of lexical or of articulatory encoding.

With regard to experiments on naming, Jansky and de Hirsch (1973) have suggested that the two best predictors of 'reading readiness' are object naming and alphabet-letter naming. N. C. Ellis (1980) has shown that dyslexic children, who at 10–14 years of age have had much exposure to the letters of the alphabet, are reliably slower than age-matched controls at naming visually presented single letters of the alphabet. Denckla and Rudel (1974), Audley (1976), and Spring and Capps (1974) have also demonstrated poor readers dyslexic children to be slow at letter naming. Now, on the basis of Model A, such slowness could imply a deficiency either in processing the visual properties of letters or in accessing their name representations. The evidence cited in subsection 2, however, shows that dyslexic subjects perform no differently from controls in responding to the visual properties of letters; the alternative is therefore a deficiency at either lexical or articulatory encoding levels.

There is also evidence (Audley, 1976; Denckla, 1972; Denckla and Rudel, 1974, 1976; Spring and Capps, 1974; Spring, 1976); that poor readers/dyslexic children are slow at naming objects, pictures and colours. Moreover the less frequent the name of the pictured object the greater the difference in the naming-time between dyslexic and control subjects (compare Oldfield and Wingfield, 1965) and the less the likelihood that the former will find the correct name at all (N. C. Ellis, 1980). A study by Mackworth and Mackworth (1974) shows that these results (like those of the letter-naming experiments) can not be due to a visual encoding problem. They found that while poor readers made more errors than good readers in letter naming and in recognizing homophones (such as *sew* and *so*) there was no relation between reading ability and performance in a non-verbal pictorial task where the children had to compare a picture with another picture which they had previously seen. Similarly Spring and Capps (1974) showed that, as stimuli became more nameable in the progression from pictures to colours to digits, so the dyslexic subjects named these items relatively more slowly than the controls. They suggest (p. 782) that 'the interaction is congruent with the common clinical observation that dyslexic children are specifically impaired on tasks requiring perception of verbal material, while they evidence no dramatic inability to function in an environment of concrete stimuli'. They account for their results in terms of slow speech–motor encoding (name coding of an articulatory nature) in dyslexic subjects and suggest that this slow speech encoding of verbal material may limit rehearsal in short-term memory and so underlie the reduced immediate memory span of dyslexic children.

N. C. Ellis (1980) has shown that dyslexic children, aged 10–14, were slower than control children at reading common and frequent words even though these words were within their reading vocabulary and presented them with no difficulty in oral speech.

There is also considerable evidence (Baddeley *et al.*, 1981; Firth, 1972; Seymour and Porpodas, 1979; Snowling, 1980) that dyslexic children are both slower and more error prone than chronological-age and reading-age matched controls at naming orthographically regular non-words.

It seems, therefore, that dyslexic children are slow, in relation to controls, at naming a broad range of visual stimuli (letters, digits, colours, words, non-words, pictures, objects) and the generality of this naming impairment suggests that the processing limitation occurs after the pattern recognition stage where the visual features of the stimuli are analysed. The deficiency is rather to be found at the level of access to the internal lexicon where lexical codes are generated or at the next stage which involves articulatory encoding.

With regard to the evidence relating to short-term memory for verbal material, it is conclusively established that dyslexic children are weak at recall of auditorily presented digits. Since this is an item in the Wechsler Intelligence Scale for Children (1949) there is no shortage of evidence. Both the dyslexic groups studied by Naidoo (1972) were considerably weaker than the controls at this task; and there is confirmatory evidence based on extensive reviews by Spache (1976), and Rugel (1974).

In addition there are similar differences between dyslexic and control children when verbal material (letters and digits) are presented visually (Ellis and Miles 1978b; Ellis *et al.*, in preparation; Miles and Wheeler, 1977; Stanley and Hall, 1973).

If non-nameable material is used, however, the position is very different. Dyslexic and control children do not differ in their immediate memory for nonsense material, as has been shown for the visual input modality in subsection 2 above; and there is corresponding evidence with the auditory input modality. Thus in a well-known experiment Birch and Belmont (1965) found that poor readers were less efficient than controls at a task which involved matching auditorily presented taps with visual marks. It was later suggested by Blank and Bridger (1966) that this might be the result of difficulty by the poor readers in verbally labelling the rhythms so as to mediate and facilitate memorization. They provided evidence for this conclusion by showing that poor readers (a) had difficulty in applying verbal labels to sequences of flashes of light, (b) had difficulty at matching temporal stimuli to spatial stimuli within the same visual modality, and (c) had no difficulty in imitating rhythmic patterns non-verbally despite having difficulty in imitating them verbally (Blank, Weider, and Bridger, 1968). In an interesting follow-up study Cashdan (1977) reports a similar finding: when subjects were given the Birch and Belmont task but were shown how verbal labelling might be a useful strategy, the differences between poor readers and controls were much reduced. Torgeson and Goldman (1977) similarly demonstrate that inferior performance by poor readers on verbal memory span tasks was associated with less verbal rehearsal (as indexed by lip movements) in the retention interval, and that when verbalization was encouraged both the amount of rehearsal and the amount of material retained by the two groups became more nearly equal.

All these studies support the view that dyslexic subjects do not differ from controls in immediate memory for visual or auditory material which cannot readily be named but perform more slowly or less accurately in tasks where immediate naming is required. In terms of Model A, it must therefore be concluded that there is a functional deficiency in dyslexic children at the level (s) of either lexical and/or articulatory encoding. In subsections 4 and 5 below experiments will be reviewed which differentiate between these possibilities.

4. Experiments involving lexical encoding

Two groups of experiments will be considered in this section: (a) those involving backwards masking and (b) those involving letter matching according to name features.

(a) If arrays of letters or digits are presented at short exposure times and are followed immediately by a pattern mask consisting of a jumble of overlapping digit parts, and if the number of items correctly reported is plotted against the exposure times, the resultant function is two-limbed (Coltheart, 1972; Sperling, 1967). The first limb increases from the origin to a dogleg point of about four items at 100 msec exposure time in adults. Ellis and Miles (1978a and b) have shown that this initial rate of stimulus acquisition in dyslexic children is significantly less than that of chronological-age matched controls; indeed there appears to be a general correlation between reading ability and first limb slope (Ellis and Miles, in preparation). Since first limb slope also increases as one moves from nonsense, non-verbal stimuli to easily named stimuli (Allport, 1968, 1973; N. C. Ellis, 1980), it was argued in the exposition of Model A that first limb slope reflects the rate of lexical encoding. The underlying function certainly cannot be articulatory encoding since it operates much faster than internal speech and is unaffected by articulatory suppression (N. C. Ellis, 1980).

If the evidence that first limb slope reflects the rate of lexical encoding is combined with the evidence that this slope is less steep in dyslexic subjects than in controls, it becomes difficult to resist the conclusion that dyslexic subjects have a limitation at the level of lexical encoding; it is a conclusion which follows from the interlocking of two originally independent sources of evidence.

(b) In subsection 2 it was reported that dyslexic children perform no worse than do controls at adjudging same case letters to be the same or different on the basis of visual features. In contrast, when two letters of different case have to be adjudged same (*Gg*) or different (*Gw, Gd*) on the basis of name characteristics, the dyslexic children were found to be reliably slower and more error prone than age-matched controls (Ellis and Miles, 1978b; compare also Supramanian and Audley, 1976). It thus appears that dyslexic children have no extra difficulty in dealing with the visual characteristics of letters as such but that, when the task demands letter analysis for name features, they demonstrate their information-processing weakness. This 'matching according to name features' might be a result of matching either lexical or articulatory codes. Since, however, N. C. Ellis (1980) has demonstrated this task to be unaffected by articulatory suppression, it must be concluded that it occurs by means of the comparison of lexical representations. As dyslexic children are slow and inaccurate at this task, the lexical code is again implicated.

5. Experiments investigating articulatory encoding

Spring and Capps (1974) (see Section II, 3) account for their experimental findings in terms of slow speech motor encoding (articulatory name encoding) in dyslexic children, while Baddeley (1979; Baddeley and Hitch, 1978) has raised the question of whether they are defective in their utilization of the *articulatory loop*. This concept is one devised by Baddeley and Hitch (1974) to account for the close association between memory span and speech coding. The loop is assumed to be one component of a composite short-term or working memory system. It is a subsystem whereby the limited capacity central component of working memory may supplement its storage capacity by subvocalization. The articulatory loop is assumed to be responsible for the phonemic similarity effect (poorer memory span for stimuli that are phonemically similar), the word length effect (poorer span for longer words) and the effect of articulatory suppression (poorer span when the subject is prevented from rehearsing by the need to articulate some irrelevant item). Further evidence for the concept of the articulatory loop comes from the observation that, with visually presented material, the prevention of the subject from using the articulatory loop by suppression abolishes both the phonemic similarity and word length effects. Baddeley (1979) has suggested that the articulatory loop is an important component in the mechanisms involved in reading since it allows the temporary storage of phonemic information during the reading process.

Now if dyslexic children do not use the articulatory loop, then preempting the loop by articulatory suppression would not be expected to affect their memory span. Similarly they would show no evidence of either phonemic similarity or word length effects. When these points were tested, (Ellis *et al.*, in preparation), it was found that the memory span of the dyslexic children was less than that of control children matched for age and similar to that of younger children matched for reading ability. In addition it was demonstrated that dyslexic children are affected by articulatory suppression, phonemic similarity and word length as much as their controls. Although the immediate memory span of dyslexic children is smaller than that of chronological-age-matched control children, the contribution to the overall span made by articulatory encoding is in similar proportion in the two groups. In other words, these findings are clearly incompatible with the thesis of an articulatory name encoding deficiency in dyslexic children.

Further evidence for this conclusion is as follows. In the first place, Cohen and Netley (1977) compared two groups of reading disabled children and a control group on a modified running memory test which used long lists of auditory digits presented at high rates. Both reading disabled groups performed significantly worse than their controls at this task where the effective use of an articulatory rehearsal strategy is, if not impossible, extremely difficult. Secondly, Ellis and Miles (in preparation) found no difference between dyslexic and control children in the speed at which they could articulatorily encode single high frequency words presented auditorily. Thirdly, the naming deficiency in dyslexic children is evident in the slope of the first limb in backward masking experiments and in experiments involving letter matching by name features. As was argued in sub-section 4 above, these tasks are thought to involve lexical rather than articulatory functions.

It must therefore be concluded that, at least in the case of dyslexic subjects in the age-range investigated, the linguistic deficiency is not one of articulatory encoding but is rather at the 'lexical' level, that is, it affects those functions which involve access to the lexicon and the retrieval of appropriate lexical codes. The experiments on naming and on immediate memory for verbal material which suggested either a lexical and/or an articulatory encoding impairment (sub-section 3 above) should be interpreted accordingly.

The reference to age range is important, since there is some evidence that younger poor readers (age 8) may be less efficient than controls at short-term memory tasks which involve articulatory encoding (Liberman *et al.*, 1977; Torgesen and Goldman, 1977), and longitudinal studies are needed for the investigation of changes which occur from age 8 upwards.

In Sections I and II of this chapter we have developed a model for the understanding of the mechanisms involved in reading aloud, and we have used it to interpret the differences in performance between dyslexic and control children. Our conclusion is that *dyslexic children show a deficiency at the level of lexical encoding.*

It is interesting to note that several investigators have independently reached similar conclusions. Thus Perfetti and Hogaboam (1975), Vellutino (1977; 1978; 1979), Legein and Bouma (chapter 7 of this volume) and Jorm (1979) are alike in suggesting that there is no deficiency in dyslexic children in the processing of the visual features of the stimulus. Jorm (1979) holds the view that they have difficulty in accessing items in the lexicon via a phonological encoding route. While we agree with this, we believe that these children have a more general deficiency in lexical encoding of written words. This will be discussed in further detail in the following sections. Vellutino (1978), in his extensive review, also finds evidence for general semantic and syntactic deficiencies in dyslexic subjects on top of those difficulties (phonemic segmen-tation, blending, rhyming, and reading by application of grapheme–phoneme correspondences) which are typically explained by the hypothesis of a phonologi-cal reading deficiency. Like us, he therefore concludes that there is a general verbal processing deficiency in dyslexia. Finally, we fully endorse the views of Legein and Bouma that 'the main source of difficulties for dyslexics is the translation from visual items into speech code' (this volume, p. 166) and that the difficulty occurs prior to articulatory encoding. The functional deficiency which is regularly found in dyslexia is at the level of access to the lexicon and retrieval of internal lexical representations.

In Sections III and IV below we attempt to specify further the characteristics of the lexical encoding system so as to make our thesis more specific and comprehensive. We shall also have occasion to consider further the spoken language of dyslexic children as well as their written language, and we shall again draw on the work of those cognitive psychologists who have made a study of the functions involved.

III DEVELOPMENT OF MODEL B

We begin this section by examining further the concept of an internal lexicon or dictionary (see Treisman, 1960). It can fairly be said that the precursor of this idea was Head's (1920) doctrine of the schema, which was later developed by Bartlett (1932), and further refined by Oldfield and Zangwill (1942; 1943) and by Oldfield (1954). Head's original suggestion, based primarily on the observation that some brain-damaged patients were unable, without visual cues, to appreciate changes in their own bodily posture, was that we build up some kind of mechanism (which he called a 'schema') by which we appreciate the space occupied by our own bodies. In taking over this idea Bartlett suggested, in effect, that it is possible to build up schemata for all kinds of 'stock' situations, such as the typical adventure story, and remember later material accordingly. (One of his experiments shows how a very quaint eastern tale becomes transmuted into such an adventure story in the hands of subjects with a typically western background.) Now, it could similarly be argued that we build up schemata for the identification of letters and words; and the fact that we can carry out such identification despite variations in typeface and handwriting and between upper and lower case has its analogy in the suggestion, implicit in the work of Bartlett (1932) and made explicit by Oldfield (1954), that once schemata have been built up the same schema can be activated despite differences in the physical characteristics of the incoming stimulus.

It then becomes an easy step to pass from the concept of the schema to the models developed by Morton (1964; 1969; 1970; 1978; 1979). These models were primarily designed to explain the growing body of evidence relating to word recognition. Thus it is known that a word can be more easily recognized in a context than in isolation and that high frequency words have a lower recognition threshold (in terms of the intensity of the stimulus and the duration over which it is available) than do low frequency words. To explain these facts Morton put forward the concept of a *logogen* system. A logogen, as we saw above (Section I), is in effect a pattern-recognizer for words. It is assumed to function by collecting 'evidence' that a particular word is present as a stimulus, appropriate as a response, or both. Besides the logogen system it was necessary in addition to postulate a 'semantic' (or 'cognitive') system (Morton, 1970). This system interacts with the logogen system bidirectionally. As a result of activation of a logogen unit the semantic system is accessed and the stimulus word is understood. In return, the semantic system is thought to influence the logogen system by passing information about what word is the most likely or probable one in a given context.

According to this view, the visual recognition of a word is assumed to involve the combined operation of a whole word visual pattern recognition unit, the internal lexicon, and the semantic system. Thus when a person is presented with a written word which he recognizes, it is supposed that there are mechanisms which analyse the visual features of the stimulus and pass the appropriate information to the logogen system, while at the same time this system receives information from the semantic system as to what word is most likely in the context. For example, if the subject has been made aware, by whatever sense modality, of the words 'Once upon a . . .', the word *time* has a high probability and the word *ball* a low probability. These two sources of information—the pattern-recognizer and the semantic system—interact in determining the availability of word responses for saying aloud. If for 'lexicon' in Figure 8.1 one reads 'logogen system', then Model A is essentially the bare bones of the model suggested by Morton (1970). Thus, as an account of reading, one can say, using this model, that it is only after a logogen unit is activated that the semantic system can be accessed and the appropriate lexical code made available for articulatory encoding and spoken output; and access to the semantic system is a necessary condition if the word is to be understood. To account for evidence that fluent readers can analyse words for meaning when they are presented at short exposure times under backward pattern masking, while at the same exposure times they cannot produce any articulatory representation of the words (see, for example, Marcel, 1976; in preparation), Morton has suggested that access to the semantic system can occur at a lower level of activation of a logogen unit than that required for the logogen unit to access the mechanism responsible for articulation.

As we believe that dyslexic subjects are deficient in making available the language (lexical) equivalents of visual stimuli, and as the development of the logogen model directly addresses the question of how in general lexical codes become available, it makes good sense to look at this body of research in greater depth.

In the Morton (1970) formalization there was a single logogen system. Morton (1969) showed that if a person had seen or used a word recently he could recognize it more easily in conditions of brief display, and Murrell and Morton (1974) have shown that this priming effect operates at a morphemic level: while *boring* and *born* show similar degrees of visual and acoustic similarity to the word *bored*, experience of the word *born* was found to have no facilitative effect upon subsequent recognition of the word *bored* although recognition of the word *bored* was primed by the morphologically related word *boring*. Similarly Morton has used the evidence of Neisser (1954), where the recognition of *phrase* was facilitated by previous experience of *phrase* but not by previous experience of *frays*, to argue that the logogen is not simply a mechanism which produces an articulatory code for output (otherwise the results for *phrase* and *frays* would be

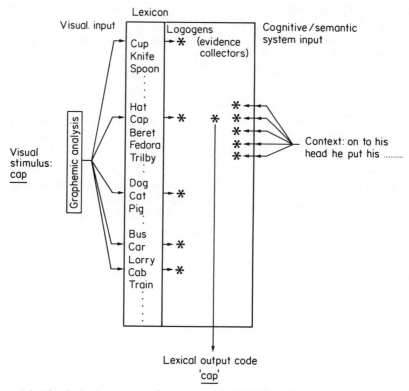

Figure 8.2. The lexical output code *cap* made available; this logogen unit activation
represents combined information from visual analysis and cognitive system inputs

the same) but one which functions as the interface between visual, auditory, and
semantic codes. The basic theme of the logogen model thus evolved to be that
each free morpheme in a subject's lexicon is represented by an independent
detector (a logogen unit) whose function in reading is to collect evidence for the
occurrence of that morpheme. Such evidence is derived from two sources: (a)
contextual information from the semantic system and (b) evidence from pattern
analysers. In reading, for example, the result of visual analysis of the word *cap*
might activate several logogen units, those corresponding to the lexical entries of
cat, cap, cup, cab, car, etc.; the result of information from the semantic system
given a previously read context of 'on to his head he placed his . . . . .' might
activate the logogens corresponding to the lexical entries of *hat, beret, fedora,
cap,* etc. The logogen activation from both these sources will be summated so as
to result in most activation for the logogen unit associated with the lexical entry
cap, and it is thus that this particular lexical entry becomes available. This
process is shown diagrammatically in Figure 8.2.

As was noted above, Morton (1970) initially supposed that there was just one system of logogens, with each logogen collecting auditory and visual sensory evidence and evidence from the cognitive system. This idea, in combination with the evidence of long-term (frequency) and short-term (priming and context) effects led to a central theme of the logogen concept being that any use of a logogen unit will give rise to subsequent facilitation of its use. Thus, just as visual experience of a word facilitates its subsequent visual recognition, so it was predicted that auditory experience of a word would also facilitate its subsequent visual recognition and vice versa. The results of studies by Winnick and Daniel (1970) and Morton (1978) do not confirm this, however. Whereas auditory experience facilitates subsequent auditory recognition and visual experience facilitates subsequent visual recognition, cross-modality facilitation does not occur. It thus became necessary to expand the model in such a way that two input logogen systems were postulated, namely a visual input logogen system (VIL) which collected evidence of a word from visual and semantic sources, and an auditory input logogen system (AIL) which collected evidence of a word from auditory and semantic sources. It was also discovered that even within the same modality, vision, whereas visual experience of a word facilitated later visual word recognition and experience of a picture primed later picture recognition, experience of a word did not prime subsequent recognition of a picture which shared the same lexical reference, nor did picture experience facilitate later word recognition (Morton, 1978; Seymour, 1973; Winnick and Daniel, 1970). Within the visual modality, therefore, it was necessary to postulate both recognition units for words—VILs fed by both graphemic and semantic information—and separate recognition units for pictures—the *pictogen* system, fed by both visual and semantic information. Thus excitation of the VIL for the word *dog*, with the resultant retrieval of the appropriate lexical entry, does not facilitate the retrieval of the same lexical entry when subsequently the pictogen for *dog* is activated.

Similarly it was argued that, if there were but one logogen system which was responsible both for access to the semantic system and for the production of an articulatory response, an independent variable which affects naming would also affect access to the semantic system. However, Marcel and Patterson (1978) demonstrated that although the rated imageability (I) of a word has an effect on word naming (with high I words such as *drama* being named at lower thresholds than low I words, *excuse*, for example), it does not have an effect upon semantic access as demonstrated by associative priming effects in a lexical decision task. For this reason Marcel and Patterson (1978) expanded the model to include functionally distinct input and output logogens, with imageability having its effect at the level of the semantic system, after input logogen activation but prior to output logogen activation.

If these ideas are amalgamated, it must be concluded that, at least in adult subjects, there is no single logogen system whose function is to produce a lexical code when information from sensory sources and the semantic system have sufficiently activated a logogen unit. Rather there are independent logogen

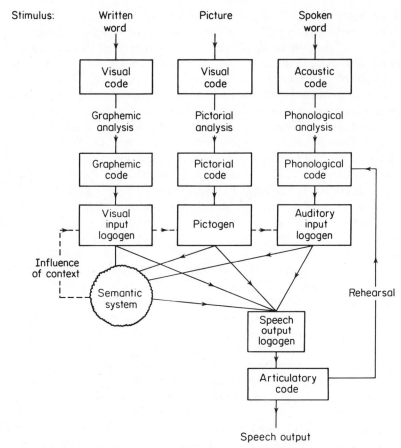

Figure 8.3. The revised logogen model (Model B), with functionally distinct input and output logogens, and modality-specific input logogens

systems responsible for the production of entries in the lexicon corresponding to visual written stimuli, pictures, or auditory spoken stimuli. There is in addition a functionally distinct output logogen (OL) system which is responsible for the production of articulatory output (compare Allport, 1978; Marcel and Patterson, 1978; Morton, 1978;). In what follows we shall therefore speak of the 'VIL vocabulary', that is, the store of words available to be activated by VIL input, and similarly one may speak of the 'pictogen vocabulary', the 'AIL vocabulary', and the 'OL vocabulary'. These notions are represented diagrammatically in Figure 8.3. In brief we are postulating VILs as pattern-recognizers for the linguistic representation of visual material, pictogens as pattern-recognizers for pictorial material, AILs as pattern-recognizers for the linguistic representations of auditory material, and OLs as mechanisms for the production of an articulatory code.

Now, although in the normal adult these separate internal logogen systems have come to serve independent functions, it is unlikely that they develop independently of each other. Indeed, there is good reason for supposing that there is considerable overlap between our spoken, heard, and written vocabularies; most words which we can understand we can also write, and most words which we can both understand and write we can also say. This is perhaps obvious from introspection, but it has also been demonstrated experimentally by Mittler and Ward (1970), who gave the Illinois Test of Psycholinguistic Abilities (ITPA) (McCarthy and Kirk, 1961) to 4-year-old children. Since some of the subtests involve the understanding of spoken words and pictures, the ability to express oneself verbally and the ability to associate words with pictures, Mittler and Ward were in effect testing input and output logogen systems independently; yet they claim that a large part of the variance in test scores was attributable to a single general factor of linguistic ability. Additional confirmation comes from the fact that, should the development of one of these vocabularies be hindered early in ontogeny, the development of the others is often limited *pari passu*. Thus the restricted AIL development in the prelingually deaf child severely retards the development of spoken and reading vocabularies (OL and VIL systems), as is discussed on p. 209. It can speculatively be concluded, therefore, that the development of VIL and OL systems depends very heavily on the availability of a substantial AIL (heard) vocabulary. This is of course not surprising since, for everyone apart from the prelingually deaf, a knowledge of language is initially acquired from auditory sources. Indeed, the first year of life has been called the period of 'readiness to listen' (Fry and Whetnall, 1954), the next 6 months being the period of 'readiness to speak' (Stinchfield and Young, 1938), whereas it is not until he is aged 4 or 5, by which time he has had considerable familiarity with oral language, that the child is 'ready to read' (Savin, 1972). Moreover Wilkinson (1971) has argued that the ability to read is largely dependent on ability to speak and that the major skills required for reading are therefore already present once children have learned to talk.

Now whereas an intact AIL system aids the development of the VIL system, the reverse is not necessarily the case, since prelingual blind subjects and illiterates develop apparently normal levels of AIL and OL vocabularies. The relationship between the AIL and OL systems thus appears much closer than either that between the VIL and AIL or that between the VIL and OL systems.

Now, on the assumption that the word to be read is within the subject's VIL vocabulary, a description of reading in terms of Figure 8.3 would be as follows. The written stimulus word is analysed visually. Since visual priming occurs with experience of words written in handwriting different from that used at recognition testing (Morton, 1978), it is assumed that the visual analysis results in a graphemic code where the word is represented visually but conceptually, that is, irrespective of typescript, handwriting, upper/lower case, etc. (compare Marcel, 1979; Patterson, 1978). This graphemic code accesses the visual input logogen system where the individual logogen units collect the visual evidence. That logogen unit which receives the most evidence (in terms of visual stimulation and stimulation from the semantic system as a result of context) will reach the output threshold necessary to activate the corresponding lexical entry. This, in turn, allows access to the semantic system, just as looking up a word in the dictionary allows access to its meaning. The process so far results in the word having been read and understood.

If the word is to be spoken aloud, however, there are further complications since it is necessary to consider how output logogens come to be activated. At this point it is necessary to consider evidence from the field of acquired dyslexia. It is known that patients suffering from 'deep dyslexia' (Marshall and Newcombe, 1973) or 'phonemic dyslexia' (Patterson, 1978; Shallice and Warrington, 1975) make paralexic errors in reading (that is, say a complete word but the wrong one) and that these errors sometimes show a semantic rather than a physical similarity to the target word. Thus *little* might be read aloud as *small* and *projector* as *camera* (Patterson, 1978). In these cases one can say that the activation of the output logogen is semantically determined; in other words the route involved is that of input logogen—semantic system—output logogen, and it would seem that a direct input–output logogen route (which precludes semantic paralexic errors in the normal reader) is impaired in these patients (compare Patterson and Marcel, 1977). It is therefore likely that the same two routes are involved in normal reading. It is obvious that normal readers, when they read aloud, are quite well able to make the correct sound in response to homographs (*lead, bow* for example), and this would clearly be impossible without the involvement of the semantic system. Moreover since the degree of imageability of a word affects the recognition threshold (see above) and determination of imageability must involve semantic processing, this is further evidence for the involvement of the semantic system in normal reading aloud.

In the case of the recognition of words presented auditorily it is assumed that the sensory input is analysed so as to form a 'phonological code'. This code cannot directly reflect the physical properties of the auditory stimulus, since priming effects are found when, after initial recognition of a word, the subjects are presented with the same word from a different speaker (Morton, 1978). It is therefore necessary to postulate some representation at the conceptual level. Such a code can be assumed to access the auditory input logogen system where, as in the visual system, the input logogen receiving the most information from sensory and cognitive sources activates the appropriate lexical code. Input logogen activation also allows access to the semantic system, which is a necessary condition if the word is to be understood. Finally, if the word is to be repeated aloud, an output logogen must be activated so as to produce an articulatory representation, and once again it is thought that this may be achieved by two routes: (a) input logogen–semantic system–output logogen; (b) input–output logogen. There is also the possibility of a third route to naming in the auditory system, that of a direct link between phonological code and articulatory code. That this possibility exists is demonstrated by the fact that a normal subject has no difficulty in repeating an auditorily presented nonsense word.

In the section which follows we shall try to show how some of the typical behaviour of dyslexic children can be interpreted in terms of Model B.

IV DYSLEXIC CHILDREN'S PERFORMANCE INTERPRETED IN TERMS OF MODEL B

The revised model of functions. Model B, which has just been described, loses some of the benefits of Model A, the most notable of these being simplicity. This loss is justified, however, by its greater explanatory power. Similar conceptualizations have in fact proved very valuable in providing descriptions both of normal reading and of phonemic and surface dyslexia (see Allport, 1978b; Marcel and Patterson, 1978; Marcel, 1979; Marshall and Newcombe, 1973; Shallice and Warrington, 1975), and in addition it is characteristic of all such conceptualizations that they distinguish language-receptive mechanisms from speech-production mechanisms, a distinction which is central to our understanding of the expressive, conductive and receptive aphasias (Geschwind, 1974; Osgood and Miron, 1963).

We concluded the interpretation of dyslexic children's visual information processing in terms of Model A with the hypothesis that dyslexic children are deficient at lexical encoding. It has been demonstrated, however, in Section III that there are several separate logogen systems concerned with lexical encoding. These need to be considered separately. In particular such examination may throw light on the question as to whether the deficiency is generalized or whether it is specific to one or more sense modalities.

1. The output logogen system

The output logogen system is responsible for setting up articulatory encoding and speech output. It has been shown (Section II, 5) that the dyslexic child's lexical encoding deficiency is apparent in tasks which do not involve articulatory encoding, from which it follows that any demonstration of an output logogen/articulatory encoding impairment in dyslexic children could not explain all of their information-processing deficiency. It was also shown in this section that dyslexic children are quite capable of using articulatory encoding strategies in short-term memory tasks. However, the tests of articulatory encoding ability did not stretch the vocabulary of the output logogen system to its limits and more sensitive tests of speech output vocabulary and speed of OL access are needed.

There is considerable evidence in the literature which suggests late development and later deficiencies of oral language in dyslexic children (see for example Naidoo, 1972; Vernon, 1971, pp. 70–4; Warrington, 1967). It is difficult to determine whether disorders of expressive language occur on their own or whether they are invariably the result of a concomitant receptive (AIL) deficiency, as appears to be the case in deaf children (see Section V).

Ellis *et al* (in preparation) tested the operation of the output logogen system in 12-year-old dyslexic children. The experimental task was one in which the subjects were required to produce as many items from a given category as they could within a 1 min interval. This task has been studied extensively, typically with the use of taxonomic categories such as birds or colours (see Bousfield and Sedgewick, 1944; Indow and Togano, 1970). It probably involves at least two components, one being a semantic search of long-term memory for instances, the other being access to the appropriate lexical code. In an attempt to separate these, three types of category were used: one was the conventional procedure of asking for items from taxonomic categories (for example, birds); in a second the category was defined phonologically (for example, words rhyming with *dog*), and in a third the category was visually defined (for example, green things). Any difference between these three types of category would have implications for the nature of the deficit.

The pattern of results suggested that dyslexic children were less fluent at category generation than normal readers of the same age. Their level of performance appears to be roughly what one would expect of younger children with similar reading ability. How should this be interpreted? A possible suggestion is that it reflects an impoverished semantic memory in dyslexic children. Although this explanation cannot be decisively ruled out, it seems to be inconsistent with teachers' reports of their relatively normal vocabulary and might furthermore be expected to lead to a much more general pattern of decrement in performance. An alternative explanation is to attribute the slow performance of the dyslexic children to impairment in the generation or utilization of lexical codes. One feature of all the category generation tasks, whether based on semantic, phonological or colour criteria, is that ultimately the subject must generate a word. If this process is in some way defective, then it would be expected that the performance would be impaired. Furthermore, since the hypothetical defect involves a final common path shared by all the generating tasks, a clear difference between impairment on semantic, phonological and visual tasks would not be expected; such an explanation is therefore consistent both with the positive differences between dyslexic subjects and their chronological age controls and with the absence of a systematic relationship between types of item generated and amount of impairment.

Such a deficiency, however, though it may explain some of the information processing problems found in dyslexia, cannot explain all of them, since the evidence of Section II, 5 shows that dyslexic children are sometimes deficient in tasks which do not involve either the OL or the articulatory encoding systems.

2. The auditory input logogen system

Slow or incomplete development of the AIL system would manifest itself as an impairment in understanding spoken speech.

The parallels between dyslexia and aphasias have often been stressed. For example, MacMeeken (1939), after discussing difficulties that would now be regared as typically dyslexic, says: 'There can be no doubt whatever that we are in touch with a pattern of difficulty aphasic in type'. Similarly Rabinovitch *et al.* (1954) found receptive, expressive and nominal types of language difficulty such as occur in adult aphasics to be present in some of the dyslexic cases whom they studied, while De Hirsch, Jansky, and Langford (1966) found auditory perceptual and oral language deficiencies in all their sample of children who subsequently failed at reading.

This point, however, appears to be in conflict with the anecdotal reports made by teachers who often say of a dyslexic child that he is one of the brightest in the form except when it comes to dealing with written material. Similarly there are many experimental studies which have failed to establish a relationship between impairment in the understanding of spoken speech and impairment at reading. In reviewing thirteen studies which compared good and poor readers on the subtests of the Illinois Test of Psycholinguistic Abilities, Spache (1976) found that there were group performance differences on the auditory digit span test, the memory for shapes test, the grammatic closure test (sentence completion according to actions specified in pictures) and the auditory–vocal association test (completion of incomplete analogies). In contrast the auditory decoding task (where simple sentences have to be answered 'yes' or 'no') failed to differentiate between the groups in eleven of the thirteen studies. Silver (1968) similarly failed to find backward readers deficient in the understanding of word meanings as measured by ability to match pictures to spoken words. Vernon (1971) in reviewing studies of the relationship between linguistic impairment and reading disability concludes that the findings depend on both the sample tested and the degree of backwardness, and such a relationship will not appear in all cases of reading disability.

One aspect of comprehension which often does appear to be defective in dyslexic children is the ability to obey complex commands involving right–left discriminations. For example, dyslexic children often appear to make errors or at least hesitate in obeying an instruction such as 'Point to my left ear with your right hand' (Miles, 1978; Miles and Ellis, Chapter 9 of this volume). This is typically attributed to problems of lateralization, but could also be attributed to a more general defect in comprehension, possibly based on reduced memory span. Patients with reduced memory span, such as the patient KF described by Shallice and Warrington (1975), also show an impairment in comprehension when this is measured by means of the Token Test. This test, originally developed by De Renzi and Vignolo (1962), involves presenting the subject with an array of shapes varying in size and colour and instructing him to perform various operations. These range in complexity from simple commands such as 'Point to the green circle' to much more complex instructions such as 'Touch the large red circle with the small green triangle'. While this is typically regarded as a test of 'comprehension', patients such as KF may be grossly defective on this test and yet show no evidence of comprehension failure in either conversation or in processing normal prose. The most parsimonious suggestion would seem to be that the Token Test is dependent on short-term memory as well as on comprehension. It in fact involves a very rapid input of information which must be interpreted very precisely; and, whereas normal prose tends to be largely predictable and redundant, the sentence in a Token Test may need to be stored in short-term memory while its semantic features are being processed.

What might be expected of dyslexic subjects in a Token Test? If it is assumed that they are suffering primarily from a comprehension deficit, then one might expect a dramatic impairment. On the other hand, if it is assumed that any deficit in comprehension is a result of their somewhat impaired memory span, then a much smaller decrement would be predicted. Finally, if one attributes the difficulties over tasks such as 'Point to my left ear with your right hand' to left–right confusion resulting from inadequate lateralization, then a test which involves no left–right discrimination might be expected to produce no decrement in performance. Ellis *et al.* (in preparation) therefore compared the performance of dyslexic children with that of both chronological-age-matched and reading-age-matched controls, using the shortened form of the Token Test (Warrington, Logue, and Pratt, 1971). The result was a small but significant difference between the performance of the dyslexic subjects and the age-matched controls. The mean difference in performance, however, was only in the order of two questions correctly answered out of fifteen; and on a test which was originally designed to be a 'sensitive tool to reveal *slight* disturbances in the understanding of speech' (our italics) (De Renzi and Vignolo, 1962, p. 667), this hardly suggests a major comprehension difficulty. A more plausible interpretation is offered by the limitation in short-term memory hypothesis, and this is supported by the fact that the dyslexic groups performed at the same level as the reading-age controls who in fact had an equivalent memory span for visually presented verbal material.

Interpreted in terms of Model B, the ability to reproduce digits after auditory presentation involves the interactive operation of phonological and articulatory codes and the AIL and OL systems, and the weakness of dyslexic subjects at this tast could *prima facie* be due to a limitation at any of these four levels (compare Ellis, 1979).

From the evidence of Section II, however, a deficiency at the level of phonological encoding or in the AIL or OL systems seems more likely, and there are several further studies which appear to support this view. In the first place, it is likely that the blending of auditorily presented word parts is difficult for dyslexic children. This, at any rate, is the natural inference from the work of Newton and Thomson (1976), who found that a sound-blending test, in which discrete phonemes were spoken to the child who then had to say the word which these phonemes constituted, was a better predictor of later reading performance than were tasks involving the sequencing of visually and auditorily presented material. Secondly, there is evidence that the segmenting of words into phonemes or syllables is relatively more difficult for poor readers (Gibson and Levin, 1975; Gleitman and Rozin, 1977; Liberman *et al.*, 1977). Finally, Bradley and Bryant (1978) have shown that when four words are auditorily presented, three of them sharing a sound in common which the fourth did not share (such as, *nod, red, fed, bed*), backward readers were less efficient than younger normal readers, matched for reading ability, at saying which was the 'odd one out'.

It is arguable, however, that impairments to the AIL system are less severe and are more likely to disappear with age than are impairments to the systems involved in the lexical encoding of visual stimuli; and it is these systems that we will now consider.

3. The pictogen system

It was pointed out in Section II that dyslexic children, while no different from controls in their ability to remember and compare pictures according to their visual features, are often incapable of finding the right name when pictures with low frequency names are presented and that, even when successful, they are likely to respond more slowly than chronological-age-matched controls.

It must therefore be concluded that the system which links the pictogens and their lexical referents (the P-to-L system) contains fewer entries and operates more slowly in dyslexic children.

4. The visual input logogen system

The evidence presented in Section II also shows that there is no deficiency in dyslexic subjects in tasks which involve responding simply to the visual characteristics of symbols and do not require any kind of naming. In contrast, where lexical encoding is involved, for instance in letter-matching in situations where letters of different case have to be compared and in the initial acquisition of information from alphanumeric arrays in conditions of backwards pattern masking, their deficiency immediately shows itself. In terms of Model B one can say that all the latter tasks involve the VIL system but not the OL system.

It is at this point that it is necessary to consider one of the most obvious facts about the dyslexic child: that the number of words which be can read falls far short of the number of words which he can say. This fact, however, calls for special care in its interpretation. While it could simply reflect a VIL limitation, the situation may well be more complex: VIL units are by definition pattern-recognizers for whole words or morphemes, and, in addition to his whole-word reading problem, the dyslexic child often fails to recognize correctly word parts.

It is generally agreed that there are two available strategies for reading aloud: (a) a whole-word pattern-recognition strategy where the word is represented by a VIL, and (b) an orthographic strategy which allows the reading of words which are not represented by a VIL. 'In the orthographic mechanism the effective units for accessing pronunciation are letters or letter groups; in the lexical mechanism the units are whole words or morphemes' (Baron and Strawson, 1976). The orthographic strategy makes use of general relations between letters or letter groups and their sounds (these being termed grapheme–phoneme correspondences) and thus allows naming by synthesis. That this option must exist is demonstrated by people's ability to read orthographically regular non-words (for example, *nate*) which cannot be represented by a VIL since they have never been seen before.

Now if the reader has a VIL for the word in front of him he can understand and name that word directly, as indicated in the explanation of Model B. In contrast, if a visually presented word fails to activate a visual input logogen, the only available strategy to the word's meaning is by means of synthesis via a phonemic route. Known grapheme–phoneme correspondences are applied to different word parts and the resultant phonemic representations concatenated. It has been suggested that this concatenation occurs in an implicit speech form, resultant from the cyclical interaction between working memory and the articulatory loop (see Baddeley and Hitch, 1974; Baddeley, 1979). Should the result of this process approximate to the correct word pronunciation and should the word be within the reader's heard (AIL) vocabulary, an auditory input logogen unit will be activated and the word understood. The understanding of a word which is not represented in the visual input logogen system is therefore indirect, and it may be mediated by an articulatory representation.

Now, these orthographic reading strategies can readily be redescribed in terms of the logogen model. Just as we learn the typical pronunciations of words-as-a-whole, so also we learn the typical pronunciations of common and regular spelling patterns, examples of these being digraph names (for example, *ch*), 'rules' (for example, *a–e*), or syllables (for example-*ing*). Just as we develop a system for the production of articulatory representations of visual words (the VIL and OL systems in combined operation), so also we must be assumed to develop a mechanism for the production of articulatory representations of word parts. For the purposes of this discussion the postulated system of 'cognitive demons' (Selfridge, 1959) for word parts will be termed visual information lower level-logogens (VILLLs). This term does not specify the units of analysis (compare higher order translation units for Vocalic Centre Groups (VCGs), Smith and Spoehr, 1974) since the system may perhaps deal with the range of visual stimulation between letters and morphemes. In the case of children who are learning to read, the units of analysis must in part be determined by whether the reading tuition given is primarily 'look and say', syllabic (see Rozin and Gleitman (1977), or phoneme by phoneme, as in the familiar *ker-ah-ter*, *cat* method.

Evidence that the same system deals with the naming both of words and of word parts is to be found in a number of sources. Glushko (1978) has argued that if this were not so it would not be possible to make sense of our ability to read phonically irregular words. Thus (to adapt an example which he himself uses in another context), even if one had the rule that words ending-*ave* (like *wave*) were pronounced with a long *a*, there would still be no way of knowing that *have* is pronounced with a short *a*. If, however, the rules are modified so as to be sensitive to features in the context (see Venezky, 1970) the resultant complexity would make them largely arbitrary (for example '-*ave* is always long except when preceded by the letter *h*'). Glushko also demonstrates that non-words like *tave*, which share orthographic features with phonologically inconsistent words such as *have*, take longer to pronounce than non-words like *taze* whose graphemes have a consistent pronunciation in all the words (for example, *haze*) in which they occur. If non-words or words for which there is no VIL were pronounced by means of a separate system which operates not by the recognition of whole words but by the application of abstract spelling-to-sound rules this would not occur. To account for this and similar evidence Glushko suggests that non-words (or words not represented in the VIL) are pronounced by the activation of words in the VIL which share orthographic features with the to-be-named non-word; these pronunciations are then modified and concatenated. Thus the *ave* segment of *tave* will be pronounced not by the application of grapheme-to-phoneme rules but by analogy with the pronunciation of the *ave* segments of words which are represented in the reader's VIL system. In brief, there is a single route to pronunciation with grapheme-to-phoneme conversion accomplished by retrieval of phonological features from the lexicon.

Marcel (1979) reaches an essentially similar conclusion (a) from the observation that impaired whole word reading-to-name is usually accompanied by impaired orthographic reading, and (b) from an analysis of pronunciation errors of surface dyslexic patients which, although typically classified as failures in grapheme–phoneme conversion (see Marshall and Newcombe, 1973), show some lexical tendencies such as grammatical class and word-frequency effects.

We are now faced with the question of how to decide how much of the dyslexic child's reading is performed by means of whole word (VIL) and how much by orthographic (VILLL) strategies. The key notions which allow an answer to this problem are: (a) orthographically irregular words can reliably be pronounced correctly only if specified in the lexicon; (b) the orthographic strategy necessitates the involvement of articulatory and AIL mechanisms before the word can be understood; (c) reading by the VIL strategy shows frequency effects whereby high frequency words are named faster than low frequency words; and (d) non-words cannot be represented in the VIL and can thus be read only by a VILLL strategy. Seymour and Porpodas (1979) manipulated these variables in order to investigate lexical and orthographic reading in four dyslexic boys. They found that when reading orthographically regular non-words their subjects were considerably slower than either chronological-age-matched or reading-age-matched controls, and that the longer the non-word the greater the difference. Since non-words can be read only orthographically, Seymour and Porpodas conclude that 'dyslexic children . . . rely on a slow and somewhat defective operation of grapheme–phoneme translation when reading'. In addition, when they investigated dyslexic children's ability at naming orthographically regular words they found that naming time was essentially the same as it was when the stimuli were non-words. This again suggests the primary operation of an orthographic reading strategy, since normal readers (who presumably use mainly a whole word strategy) are able to name words more quickly than they can name non-words (Frederiksen and Kroll, 1976). Since, however, these dyslexic subjects to some extent showed frequency effects, their dependence on an orthographic strategy could not have been total.

Seymour and Porpodas (1979) therefore conclude that there is some whole-word reading in dyslexic children but that this is impaired both with regard to the time required for translation and the range of vocabulary covered by the VIL system. They also claim that the reading of dyslexic children is primarily performed by means of an orthographic (VILLL) strategy but that this strategy, too, is defective in comparison with that of chronological-age-matched controls in terms of speed and accuracy and in comparison with that of reading-age-matched controls in terms of speed. A comparison between the performance of dyslexic children and that of reading-age-matched controls at orthographic reading of non-words was also made by Snowling (1980), who found that in the case of normal readers the use of grapheme–phoneme correspondences increased with reading age (from 7–10 years) but not in the case of the dyslexic subjects. She concludes, like Seymour and Porpodas, that dyslexic children have a special difficulty in orthographic reading.

Evidence which further supports these conclusions can be found in studies of acquired dyslexic patients (see Meudell, Chapter 4 of this volume). The two most studied classifications of acquired dyslexia are deep dyslexia (Marshall and Newcombe, 1973) or phonemic dyslexia (Patterson and Marcel, 1977; Shallice and Warrington, 1975) and surface dyslexia (Marshall and Newcombe, 1973). The most notable features which characterise phonemic dyslexia are (a) an almost total inability to read non-words, (b) an inability to decide whether written words rhyme (*hope: soap*, for example), (c) greater success at reading concrete words than at reading abstract words, (d) the presence of grammatical category effects in their reading whereby nouns are read better than verbs and both are read better than function words, and (e) the presence of semantic paralexic errors in their reading (see Section III and also Meudell, Chapter 4 of this volume). It has been argued that these characteristics reflect an almost total inability at orthographic reading and a dissociation between VIL and OL such that the only available naming route is VIL–semantic system–OL (hence the semantic errors and the grammatical class effects). (Compare also Coltheart, 1979; Marcel, 1979; Marshall and Newcombe, 1973; Patterson and Marcel, 1977; Shallice and Warrington, 1975). In terms of Model B this would be represented by the absence of a direct link between VIL and OL.

The reading of surface dyslexic patients is characterized by words being understood, if at all, only on the basis of laborious, and often erroneous, application of an orthographic reading strategy. Success at naming appears to be less affected by grammatical class or word frequency (Hécaen and Kremin, 1976) than in the case of phonemic dyslexic patients, although Marcel (1979) questions this disassociation. The theoretical interpretation of these symptoms is that they reflect an almost total inability at whole-word reading coupled with an additional deficiency in orthographic reading. In other words the VIL system is almost totally non-existent and the VILLL system slow and malfunctioning in operation (Marcel, 1979; Marshall and Newcombe, 1973).

Now, since patients with acquired dyslexia could read prior to the trauma which resulted in their deficiency, the VIL system had presumably been developed and its connections to the semantic system and OL system were presumably intact. The essential difference between surface and phonemic dyslexic patients thus appears to be that the former have lost the function of the VIL (and VILLL) system almost entirely, whereas the latter have retained their VIL (and presumably VILLL) system and its connection to the semantic system but have lost the link between VIL and OL.

If we consider the development of the reading of an alphabetic language, the following appear to be the typical stages. The child has developed a heard vocabulary whereby there is a route from AIL to semantic system and one from AIL to OL. Visual symbols are than placed before him and either their spoken equivalent is sounded out for him (if the method is 'look and say') or he is taught orthographic strategies which allow him to sound the correct word himself. The route to meaning is thus initially mediated by the AIL system, and his internal speech makes understanding possible, this route being VIL–OL–articulatory code–AIL–semantic system. In other words the eventual development of direct VIL–semantic system associations is preceded by, and contingent upon, the development of VIL–OL associations. In patients with acquired dyslexia both associations had been formed and both routes were functional before trauma. The evidence shows that one function (VIL–OL) can be thereafter lost without the other (VIL–semantic system). If, however, the development of the VIL system proceeds from VIL–OL through to eventual VIL–semantic system, then it follows that retarded VIL development or retarded VIL–OL development cannot occur in the absence of associated VIL–semantic system development. Thus it would be expected that the VIL deficiency in developmental dyslexia would involve both the passage of information to the OL system and the passage of information to the semantic system. The deficiency would thus be similar to that found in surface dyslexia rather than to that found in phonemic dyslexia where the dissociation is between VIL and OL.

It is worth noting that both Holmes (1973) and A. W. Ellis (1981) reach the conclusion that the reading errors made by developmental dyslexic children are 'of a piece' with those made by surface dyslexic adults, and they extend the above interpretation of surface dyslexia to cover developmental dyslexia. Marcel (1979) even goes so far as to suggest that the same interpretation can be extended to all beginner readers.

The similarities with the phenomena of surface dyslexia, coupled with the evidence cited both in the present subsection and in Section II, give strong support to our central thesis that there is impaired VIL and VILLL functioning in developmental dyslexia.

If we now take stock of the evidence so far presented, it is reasonable to conclude that dyslexia involves deficiencies in the VIL, VILLL, P-to-L, AL and OL systems and that it is the VIL, VILLL, and P-to-L systems which are most seriously affected. If this is so, however, then it is clearly correct to think in terms of a 'disconnection' (see Geschwind, 1974) between visual pattern-recognition systems and the internal lexicon. In addition a further possible link suggests itself between the functional deficiencies described in this chapter and the phenomena relating to hemispheric specialization. In summarizing the evidence in this area (in so far as it relates to dyslexia) Beaumont and Rugg (1978) conclude that, while in dyslexic subjects there is normal hemispheric specialization for auditory language, as inferred from right-ear advantage in dichotic listening tasks, there is also a tendency when verbal material is presented visually for the right visual field advantage to be smaller in dyslexic subjects than in controls. The fact that there are these links with the 'disconnection syndrome' and with the phenomena of hemispheric specialization gives further support to the view that the typically dyslexic person is primarily handicapped at tasks which require the processing of visually presented verbal material.

V   CONCLUDING REMARKS

In Sections I and II of this chapter a simple model of the functions involved in visual information processing was developed, and the ability of developmental dyslexic children at each of these functions was assessed. Since they performed normally at pre-lexical levels it was concluded that they were displaying a language disorder which involved the failure to access easily the lexical representations of sensory inputs. Since this model was clearly an over-simplification, we attempted in Section III to develop a more accurate and complete description of the functions involved. When the information-processing ability of dyslexic children was interpreted along these new lines it was concluded that there was some generality of the lexical encoding deficiency across input and output modalities. The evidence suggested that the children in question behaved as a homogeneous group in showing some relatively small impairment in the lexical encoding of auditory input material (that is, in the AIL) and in accessing the lexical representations necessary for articulatory output (that is, in the OL). By far the largest and most consistent impairment, however, was shown to be in the lexical encoding of visual events: both the P-to-L system and the VIL system were shown to be slow in operating, with comparatively fewer words available for use, while the VILLL system was both slow and inaccurate.

The age-factor may well be important. The experiments carried out by Ellis and Miles (1978a and b) involved children in the age range 10–14; and it does not therefore follow that there is similar homogeneity of symptoms in younger children.

The lexical encoding of visual stimuli has been demonstrated to be a complex blend of many functions. Not only must visual pattern-recognizers for words be formed, but links must be also forged between them and the semantic system and between them and the systems for expressive speech, the development of such systems being itself contingent upon efficient auditory receptive mechanisms. If an orthographic reading strategy is learned, then a complex interaction between VILLL, OL, articulatory, phonological and AIL mechanisms and the semantic system is involved; and it is therefore not at all surprising that there should be varying sorts of limitation at different ages. Moreover, it seems *prima facie* likely that a deficiency in one area of functioning will result in deficiencies elsewhere. In this connection it must undoubtedly be of significance that prelingually deaf children, whose inability to receive speech results in relative failure at speech production, have been shown to be like dyslexic children in that they are poor readers and are impaired at digit-span tasks involving visual presentation, despite having the same span as hearing children 'when the material to be remembered consists of shapes that do not readily have names' (Conrad, 1972a, p. 226; compared also Blair, 1957; Furth, 1964; Olsson and Furth, 1966). Similarly it is not at all surprising that some young dyslexic children should be found to have 'visuospatial and perceptual problems' (Boder, 1971), nor that those with developmental receptive aphasia (involving retarded AIL development), developmental expressive aphasia (involving retarded OL development), and developmental dysarthria and developmental articulatory apraxia (involving retarded articulatory encoding) are all said to show later reading problems (Morley, 1972). These differences are alike in that they all result in some degree of inadequacy in the area where sensory events are linguistically represented; and, if this is correct, it follows that developmental dyslexia is one of a 'family' of deficiencies having various elements in common with each other.

Further discussion of this point, however, will be deferred until the end of Chapter 9. Our next task is to show how the lexical encoding deficiency hypothesis makes sense of the many interesting features of developmental dyslexia which have been observed clinically.

ACKNOWLEDGEMENT

The authors would like to express their gratitude to Dr A. D. Baddeley for some particularly helpful discussions about the contents of this chapter.

REFERENCES

Allport, D. A. (1968) The rate of assimilation of visual information. *Psychonomic Sci.*, **12**, 231–232.

Allport, D. A. (1973) Recognition units in reading: backwards masking experiments (unpublished).

Allport, D. A. (1978a) On knowing the meaning of words we are unable to report: the effects of visual masking. In S. Dornic (ed.) *Attention and Performance 6* Hillsdale, NJ: Erlbaum Associates.

Allport, D. A. (1978b) Word recognition in reading: a tutorial review. In H. Bouma, P. A. Kolers and M. Wrolstad (eds.), *Processing of Visible Language* New York: Plenum Publishing Company.

Audley, R. J. (1976) Reading difficulties: the importance of basic research in solving practical problems. *Presidential Address to the meeting of the British Association for the Advancement of Science.*

Baddeley, A. D. (1966) Short-term memory for word sequences as a function of acoustic, semantic and formal similarity. *Q. J. Exper. Psychol.*, **18**, 362–365.

Baddeley, A. D. (1968) How does acoustic similarity influence short-term memory? *Q. J. Exper. Psychol.*, **20**, 249–264.

Baddeley, A. D. (1976) *The Psychology of Memory.* New York: Basic Books, Inc. Harper International.

Baddeley, A. D. (1979) Working memory and reading. In H. Bouma, P. A. Kolers and M. Wrolstad (eds.) *Processing of Visible Language*, Proceedings of a conference held at the Institute for Perception Research, IPO, Eindhoven (1977).

Baddeley, A. D., Ellis, N. C., Miles, T. R. and Lewis, V. (1981). Developmental and acquired dyslexia: a comparison. *Cognition*, in press.

Baddeley, A. D. and Hitch, G. (1974) Working memory. In G. H. Bower (ed.) *The Psychology of Learning and Motivation*, vol. 8. pp. 47–90, New York: Academic Press.

Baddeley, A. D. and Hitch, G. (1978) Working memory and information processing. Open University Cognition Course D303.

Bakker, D. J. (1967) Temporal order, meaningfulness and reading ability. *Perceptual and Motor Skills*, **24**, 1027–1030.

Bakker, D. J. (1972) *Temporal Order in Disturbed Reading.* Rotterdam: Rotterdam University Press.

Baron, J. and Strawson, C. (1976) Use of orthographic and word-specific knowledge in reading words aloud. *J. Exper. Psychol.: Human Perception and Performance*, **2**, 386–393.

Bartlett, F. C. (1932) *Remembering.* Cambridge: Cambridge University Press.

Beaumont, J. G. and Rugg, M. D. (1978) Neuropsychological laterality of function and dyslexia. *Dyslexia Rev.*, **1** (1).

Birch, H. G. and Belmont, L. (1965) Auditory–visual integration, intelligence and reading ability. *Perceptual and Motor Skills*, **20**, 295.

Blair, F. X. (1957) A study of the visual memory of deaf and hearing children. *Amer. Ann. Deaf*, **102**, 254–263.

Blank, M. and Bridger, W. H. (1966) Deficiencies in verbal labelling in retarded readers. *Amer. J. Orthopsychiat.*, **36**, 840–847.

Blank, M., Weider, S., and Bridger, W. H. (1968) Verbal deficiencies in abstract thinking in early reading retardation. *Amer. J. Orthopsychiat.*, **38**, 823–834.

Boder, E. (1971) Developmental dyslexia: prevailing concepts and a new diagnostic approach. In H. R. Myklebust (ed.) *Progress in Learning Disabilities,* vol. II New York: Grune and Stratton.

Bouma, H. and Legein, Ch. P. Visual recognition experiments in dyslexia (Chapter 7 of this volume), 1980.

Bousfield, W. A. and Sedgewick, C. H. (1944) An analysis of sequences of restricted associative responses. *J. Gen. Psychol.*, **30**, 149–165.

Bradley, L. and Bryant, P. E. (1978) Difficulties in auditory organisation as a possible cause of reading backwardness. *Nature*, **270**.

Cashdan, A. (1977) Backward readers—research on auditory visual integration. In J. F. Reid and H. Donaldson (eds.) *Reading: Problems and Practices.* London: Ward Lock Educational.

Cohen, R. L. and Netley, C. (1977) Short-term memory deficits in poor readers, under conditions of minimal rehearsal. *Paper presented at Canadian Psychology Association meeting, Ottawa, June 1977.*

Coltheart, M. (1972) Visual information processing. In P. C. Dodwell (ed.) *New Horizons in Psychology II*, pp. 62–85, Harmondsworth: Penguin.

Coltheart, M. (1979) Mysteries of reading in brain defects. *New Sci.*, **81** (1141), 368–370.

Coltheart, M., Patterson, K. E. and Marshall, J. C. (eds.) (1979) *Deep Dyslexia.* London: Routledge and Kegan Paul.

Conrad, R. (1964) Acoustic confusion in immediate memory. *Brit. J. Psychol.*, **55**, 75–84.

Conrad, R. (1972a) Speech and reading. In J. F. Kavanagh and I. G. Mattingley (eds.) *Language by Eye and by Ear.* Cambridge, Mass.: M.I.T. Press.

Conrad, R. (1972b) The developmental role of vocalizing in short-term memory. *J. Verbal Learning and Verbal Behav.*, **11**, 521–533.

Critchley, M. (1970) *The Dyslexic Child*, London: Heinemann Medical Books.

De Hirsch, K., Jansky, J. J. and Langford, W. S. (1966) *Predicting Reading Failure*, New York: Harper and Row.

De Leeuw, M. and De Leeuw, E. (1969) *Read Better, Read Faster*, Harmondsworth: Penguin.

De Renzi, E. and Vignolo, L. A. (1962) The token test: to detect receptive disturbances in aphasics. *Brain*, **85**, 665–679.

Denckla, M. B. (1972) Color naming in dyslexic boys. *Cortex*, **8**, 164–176.

Denckla, M. B. and Rudel, R. (1974) Rapid 'automized' naming of pictured objects, colours, letters and numbers by normal children, *Cortex*, **10**, 186–202.

Denckla, M. B. and Rudel, R. (1976) Naming of object-drawings by dyslexic and other learning disabled children. *Brain and Language*, **3**, 1–15.

Done, D. J. and Miles, T. R. (1978) Learning, memory and dyslexia. In M. M. Gruneberg, P. E. Morris and R. N. Sykes (eds.), *Practical Aspects of Memory*, London: Academic Press.

Ellis, A. W. (1981) Developmental and acquired dyslexia: some observations on Jorm (1979). *Cognition*, in press.

Ellis, N. C. (1979) A model for the reading/short-term memory span correlation. *Paper presented to the British Psychological Society (Cognitive Section) Conference on Cognitive Models, City of London Polytechnic, December 1979.*

Ellis, N. C. (1980) Functional analysis of reading and short-term memory in dyslexic children. Doctorate dissertation, University of Wales.

Ellis, N. C., Baddeley, A. D., Miles, T. R. and Lewis, V. (in preparation). Limitations in reading ability and short-term memory span.

Ellis, N. C. and Miles, T. R. (1977) Dyslexia as a limitation in the ability to process information. *Orton Soc. Bull.*, **XXVII**, 72–81.

Ellis, N. C. and Miles, T. R. (1978a) Visual information processing as a determinant of reading speed, *J. Reading Res.*, **1**, (2), 108–120.

Ellis, N. C. and Miles, T. R. (1978b) Visual information processing in dyslexic children. In M. M. Gruneberg, P. E. Morris and R. N. Sykes (eds.) *Practical Aspects of Memory* London: Academic Press.

Ellis, N. C. and Miles, T. R. (in preparation). Individual differences in lexical encoding efficiency.

Firth, I. (1972) Components of reading disability. Unpublished doctorate dissertation, University of New South Wales, Australia.

Frederiksen, J. R. and Kroll, J. K. (1976) Spelling and sound: approaches to the internal lexicon. *J. Exper. Psychol.: Human Perception and Performance*, **2**, 361–379.

Fry, D. B. and Whetnall, E. (1954). The auditory approach in the training of deaf children. *Lancet*, **1**, 583.

Furth, H. G. (1964) Research with the deaf: implications for language and cognition. *Psychol. Bull.*, **62**, 145–164.

Geschwind, N. (1974) *Selected Papers on Language and the Brain*, Boston studies in the Philosophy of Science, Vol. XVI, Dordrecht: D. Reidel Publishing Co.

Gibson, E. J. and Levin, H. (1975) *The Psychology of Reading*, Cambridge, Mass.: MIT Press.

Gleitman, L. R. and Rozin, P. (1977) The structure and acquisition of reading I: relations between orthographies and the structure of language. In A. S. Reber and D. L. Scarborough (eds.) *Towards a Psychology of Reading*, Hillsdale, NJ: Erlbaum.

Glushko, R. J. (1978) The organization and activation of orthographic knowledge in reading aloud. *Occasional papers No. 1.* Center for Human Information Processing, University of California, San Diego.

Goldberg, H. K. (1968) Vision, perception and related factors in dyslexia. In A. H. Keeney and V. T. Keeney (eds.) *Dyslexia*. St. Louis: C. V. Mosby.

Haber, R. N. (1973) Visual information storage. In National Research Council. Division of Behavioural Sciences: *Visual Search: Symposium conducted at the Spring Meeting 1970.* Washington, DC: National Academy of Sciences.

Head, H. (1920) *Studies in Neurology.* vol. II, Oxford: Oxford University Press.

Hécaen, H. and Kremin, H. (1976) Neurolinguistic research on reading disorders resulting from left hemisphere lesions: aphasic and 'pure' alexias. In H. Whitaker and H. A. Whitaker (eds.) *Studies in Neuro-linguistics*, vol. 2, New York: Academic Press.

Hermann, K. (1959) *Reading disability.* Copenhagen: Munksgaard.

Hinshelwood, J. (1917) *Congenital Word Blindness.* London: H. K. Lewis and Co.

Holmes, J. M. (1973) Dyslexia: a neurolinguistic study of traumatic and developmental disorders of reading. Unpublished PhD thesis, University of Edinburgh.

Indow, T. and Togano, K. (1970) On retrieving sequence from long-term memory. *Psychol. Rev.*, **77**, 317–331.

Jansky, J. and de Hirsch, K. (1973) *Preventing Reading Failure.* New York: Harper and Row.

Jorm, A. F. (1979) The cognitive and neurological basis of developmental dyslexia: a theoretical framework and review. *Cognition*, **7**, 19–33.

Landauer, T. K. (1962) Rate of implicit speech. *Perceptual and Motor Skills*, **15**, 646.

Lesèvre, N. (1964) Les movements oculaires d'exploration. Thèse de Paris. Cited in Critchley, M. (1970) *The Dyslexic Child.* London: Heinemann Medical Books.

Liberman, I. Y., Shankweiler, D., Liberman, A. M., Fowler, C., and Fischer, F. W. (1977) Phonemic segmentation and recoding in the beginning reader. In A. S. Reber and D. Scarborough (eds.) *Towards a Psychology of Reading*, Hillsdale, NJ: Erlbaum.

MacMeeken, M. (1939) *Ocular Dominance in Relation to Developmental Aphasia.*

London: University of London Press.

Mackworth, J. F. (1963) The relation between the visual image and post-perceptual immediate memory. *J. Verbal Learning and Verbal Behav.*, **2**, 75–85.

Mackworth, J. F. and Mackworth, N. H. (1974) How children read: matching by sight and sound. *J. Reading Behav.*, **6** (3), 295–303.

Marcel, A. J. (1976) Unconscious reading—experiments on people who do not know that they are reading. Paper given to the British Association for the Advancement of Science, September 1976.

Marcel, A. J. (1979) Surface dyslexia and beginning reading—a revised hypothesis of the pronunciation of print and its impairments. In M. Coltheart, K. E. Patterson and J. C. Marshall (eds.), *Deep Dyslexia*. London: Routledge and Kegan Paul.

Marcel, A. J. Conscious and unconscious reading: the effects of visual masking on word perception (in preparation).

Marcel, A. J., Katz, L. and Smith, M. (1974) Laterality and reading deficiency. *Neuropsychologia*, **12**, 131–139.

Marcel, A. J. and Patterson, K. (1978) Word recognition and production: reciprocity in clinical and normal studies. In J. Requin (ed.) *Attention and Performance VII*, Hillsdale, NJ: Erlbaum.

Marshall, J. C. and Newcombe, F. (1973) Patterns of paralexia: a psycholinguistic approach. *J. Psycholinguistic Res.*, **2**, 175–199.

McCarthy, J. J. and Kirk, S. A. (1961) *Illinois Test of Psycholinguistic Abilities*. Urbana, Ill: Institute for Research in Exceptional Children.

Miles, T. R. (1978) *Understanding Dyslexia*. London: Hodder and Stoughton.

Miles, T. R. and Wheeler, T. J. (1977) Responses of dyslexic and non-dyslexic subjects to tachistoscopically presented digits, *IRCS. Med. Sci.*, **5**, 149.

Mitchell, D. C. (1976) Buffer storage modality and identification time in tachistoscopic recognition. *Q. J. Exper. Psychol.*, **28**, 325–337.

Mittler, P. and Ward, J. (1970) The use of the Illinois Test of Psycholinguistic Abilities on British four-year-old children. *Brit. J. Educ. Psychol.*, **40**, 43.

Morley, M. E. (1972) *The Development and Disorders of Speech in Childhood, 3rd edition,* Edinburgh: Churchill Livingstone.

Morton, J. (1964) The effects of context upon speed of reading, eye-movements and eye-voice span, *Q. J. Exper. Psychol.* **16**, 340–354.

Morton, J. (1969) The interaction of information in word recognition, *Psycholog. Rev.*, **76**, 165–178.

Morton, J. (1970) A functional model of memory. In D. A. Norman, *Models of Human Memory*. New York: Academic Press.

Morton, J. (1978) Facilitation in word recognition: experiments causing change in the logogen model. In H. Bouma, P. A. Kolers and M. Wrolstad (eds.) *Processing of Visible Language*, New York: Plenum Publishing Company.

Morton, J. (1979) Word recognition. In J. Morton and J. C. Marshall (eds.) *Psycholinguistics Series 2:Structures and Processes*, London: Elek.

Murrell, G. A. and Morton, J. (1974) Word recognition and morphemic structure. *J. Exper. Psychol.*, **102**, 963–968.

Naidoo, S. (1972) *Specific Dyslexia*. London: Pitman Press.

Neisser, U. (1954) An experimental distinction between perceptual process and verbal response. *J. Exper. Psychol.* **47**, 399–402.

Neisser, U. (1967) *Cognitive Psychology*. New York: Appleton-Century-Crofts.

Neisser, U. (1976) *Cognition and Reality*. San Francisco: W. H. Freeman and Co.

Newell, A. (1973) You can't play 20 questions with nature and win. In W. G. Chase (ed.) *Visual Information Processing*. New York: Academic Press.

Newton, M. and Thomson, M. (1976) *The Aston Index: a Classroom Test for Screening and Diagnosis of Language Difficulties.* Cambridge: Learning Development Aids.

Oldfield, R. C. (1954) Memory mechanisms and the theory of schemata. *Brit. J. Psychol.*. **XLV**, 1, 14–23.

Oldfield, R. C. and Wingfield, A. (1965) Response latencies in naming objects. *Q. J. Exper. Psychol.*, **17**, 273–281.

Oldfield, R. C. and Zangwill, O. L. (1942, 1943) Head's concept of the schema and its application in contemporary British Psychology. *Brit. J. Psychol.*, 1942, **XXXII**, 4, 267–286; **XXXIII**, 1, 58–64; 2, 113–129; 3, 143–149.

Olsson, J. E. and Furth, H. G. (1966) Visual memory span in the deaf. *Amer. J. Psychol.*, **79**, 480–484.

Orton, S. T. (1937) *Reading, Writing and Speech Problems in Children.* London: Chapman and Hall.

Osgood, C. E., and Miron, M. S. (eds.) (1963) *Approaches to the Study of Aphasia,* Urbana: University of Illinois Press.

Patterson, K. E. (1978) Phonemic dyslexia: errors of meaning and the meaning of errors. *Q. J. Exper. Psychol.*, **30**, 587–601.

Patterson, K. E. and Marcel, A. J. (1977) Aphasia, dyslexia and the phonological coding of written words. *Q. J. Exper. Psychol.*, **29**, 307–318.

Pavlidis, G. Th. (1978) The dyslexics' erratic eye movements: case studies. *Dyslexia Rev.*, **2** (1), 22–28.

Perfetti, C. A. and Hogaboam, T. (1975) The relationship between simple word decoding and reading comprehension skill. *J. Educ. Psychol.*, **67**, 461–469.

Phillips, W. A. (1974) On the distinction between sensory storage and short-term visual memory. *Perception and Psychophys.*, **16**, 283–290.

Phillips, W. A. and Baddeley, A. D. (1971) Reaction time and short-term visual memory. *Psychonomic Sci*, **22**, 73–74.

Phillips, W. A. and Christie, D. F. M. (1977) Components of visual memory. *Q. J. Exper. Psychol.*, **29**, 117–133.

Posner, M. I. (1969) Abstraction and the process of recognition. In J. T. Spence and G. Bower (eds.) *The Psychology of Learning and Motivation, Vol. 3* London: Academic Press.

Rabinovitch, R. D., Drew, A. L., De Jong, R. N., Ingram, W., and Withey, L. I. (1954) A research approach to reading retardation. *Research Publication of the Association for Research in Nervous and Mental Disorders*, **34**, 363.

Rozin, P. and Gleitman, L. R. (1977) The structure and acquisition of reading II: the reading process and the acquisition of the alphabetic principle. In A. S. Reber and D. L. Scarborough (eds.) *Towards a Psychology of Reading*, Hillsdale, NJ: Erlbaum.

Rugel, R. P. (1974) WISC subtest scores of disabled readers. *J. Learning Disabilities*, **7**, 48–55.

Savin, H. B. (1972) What the child knows about speech when he starts to learn to read. In J. F. Kavanagh and I. C. Mattingly, *Language by Ear and by Eye*, Cambridge, Mass: M.I.T. Press.

Selfridge, O. G. (1959) Pandemonium: a paradigm for learning. In *Proceedings of a Symposium on the Mechanization of Thought Processes*, London: HMSO. Reprinted in L. Uhr (ed.), *Pattern Recognition*, New York: Wiley (1966).

Seymour, P. H. K. (1973) A model for reading, naming and comparison. *Brit. J. Psychol.*, **64**, 35–49.

Seymour, P. H. K. and Porpodas, C. D. (1979) Lexical and non-lexical processing of spelling in developmental dyslexia. In U. Frith (ed.) *Cognitive Processes in Spelling*, London: Academic Press.

Shallice, T. and Warrington, E. K. (1975) Word recognition in a phonemic dyslexic patient, *Q. J. Exper. Psychol.*, **27**, 187–200.

Silver, A. A. (1968) Diagnostic considerations in children with reading disability. In G. Natchez (ed.) *Children with Reading Problems*, New York: Basic Books.

Smith, E. E. and Spoehr, K. T. (1974) The perception of printed English: a theoretical perspective. In B. H. Kantowitz (ed.) *Human Information Processing: Tutorials in Performance and Cognition*. Hillsdale, NJ: Erlbaum.

Snowling, M. J. (1980) The development of grapheme–phoneme correspondence in normal and dyslexic readers, *J. Exper. Child Psychol.* **29**, 294–305.

Spache, G. D. (1976) *Investigating the Issues of Reading disabilities*, Boston: Allyn and Bacon.

Sperling, G. (1963) A model for visual memory tasks. *Human Factors*, **5**, 19–31.

Sperling, G. (1967) Successive approximations to a model for short term memory. *Acta Psycholog.* **27**, 285–297.

Spring, C. (1976) Encoding speed and memory span in dyslexic children. *J. Spec. Educ.*, **10**, 35–46.

Spring, C. and Capps, C. (1974) Encoding speed, rehearsal, and probed recall of dyslexic boys. *J. Educ. Psychol.*, **66**, 780–786.

Stanley, G. and Hall, R. (1973) A comparison of dyslexics and normals in recalling letter arrays after brief presentation. *Brit. J. Educ. Psychol.*, **43**, 301–304.

Stinchfield, S. N. and Young, E. H. (1938) *Children with Delayed and Defective Speech*. London: Oxford University Press.

Supramanian, S. and Audley, R. J. (1976) The role of naming difficulties in reading backwardness. Paper presented to the British Association for the Advancement of Science Annual Conference.

Torgesen, J. and Goldman, T. (1977) Verbal rehearsal and short-term memory in reading-disabled children. *Child Develop.*, **48**, 56–60.

Treisman, A. (1960) Contextual cues in selective listening. *Q. J. Exper. Psychol.*, **12**, 247–248.

Underwood, G. (1978) Concepts in information processing theory. In G. Underwood (ed.) *Strategies of Information Processing*. London: Academic Press.

Underwood, G. and Holt, P.O'B. (1979) Cognitive skills in the reading process; a review. *J. Res. Reading*, **2**, 82–94.

Vellutino, F. R. (1977) Alternative conceptualizations of dyslexia: evidence in support of a verbal-deficit hypothesis. *Harvard Educ. Rev.*, **47**, 334–354.

Vellutino, F. R. (1978) Towards an understanding of dyslexia: psychological factors in specific reading disability. In A. L. Benton and P. Pearl. *Dyslexia: an Appraisal of Current Knowledge*, New York: Oxford University Press.

Vellutino, F. R. (1979) *Dyslexia: Theory and Research*. Cambridge, Mass: M.I.T. Press.

Venezky, R. (1970) *The Structure of English Orthography*. The Hague: Mouton.

Vernon, M. D. (1971) *Reading and Its Difficulties*, Cambridge: Cambridge University Press.

Warrington, E. K. (1967) The incidence of verbal disability associated with reading retardation, *Neuropsychologia*, **5**, 175–179.

Warrington, E. K., Logue, V. and Pratt, R. T. C. (1971) The anatomical localization of selective impairment of auditory verbal short-term memory, *Neuropsychologia*, **9**, 377–387.

Wechsler, D. (1949) *Wechsler Intelligence Scale for Children*. New York: Psychological Corporation.

Wilkinson, A. M. (1971) *The Foundations of Language*. London: Oxford University Press.

Winnick, W. A. and Daniel, S. A. (1970) Two kinds of response priming in tachistoscopic recognition. *J. Exper. Psychol.*, **84**, 74–81.

Dyslexia Research and its Applications to Education
Edited by G. Th. Pavlidis and T. R. Miles
© 1981 John Wiley & Sons Ltd.

CHAPTER 9

A Lexical Encoding Deficiency II : Clinical Observations

T. R. MILES AND N. C. ELLIS

INTRODUCTION

Evidence was put forward in Chapter 8 in support of the thesis that dyslexic subjects display a limitation at the level of lexical encoding. In the present chapter we shall try to show how this idea makes sense of many of the dyslexic phenomena which have been observed clinically by those involved in assessment and teaching.

For convenience we shall begin by recapitulating some of the main features of the model which was proposed. One of its central features was the suggestion that each individual can be thought of as equipped with an internal lexicon or dictionary which provides standards against which incoming stimuli can be matched. The energy changes which stimulate the receptors (eyes, ears, etc.) are assumed to be represented in the nervous system in the form of engrams or traces, and lexical encoding is the name of the process by which 'codes' (that is, representations of relevant features of these traces) are matched to entries in the lexicon. Logogens are thought of as pattern-recognition mechanisms as a result of which the appropriate entries are activated, the logogens themselves being responsible for the activation of whole words or morphemes, and lower level logogens being responsible for the activation of word parts (for example single letters, digraphs, and syllables). In addition to the visual input and auditory input logogens and the output logogens it is necessary to postulate a semantic system which makes possible the recognition of meaning and which, on the basis of contextual information, permits an assessment of what is the most likely word in a particular context.

A deficiency at the level of lexical encoding implies some degree of failure in the activation of entries in the lexicon; and if such a failure is central to dyslexia one would expect *tasks which involve verbalisation* to be the ones which dyslexic subjects (unless they work out appropriate compensatory strategies) will

217

find most difficult. This is in fact what the clinical evidence shows.

The arguments presented in the last chapter were based on the results of controlled experiments and were intended to be logically rigorous. In the present chapter we have allowed ourselves the luxury of being somewhat more speculative, since from their very nature clinical observations are less 'secure' than the results of systematic experimentation. We believe, nonetheless, that such observations have their part to play and that the lexical encoding deficiency hypothesis *makes sense* of phenomena which would otherwise seem disparate and puzzling.

Section I of this chapter is concerned with reading and spelling, Section II with the notions of directional confusion, mirror images, and handedness, Section III with the performance of dyslexic subjects at intelligence tests, Section IV with their performance at reciting tables, Section V with a puzzling facet of their behaviour which can be described as 'the need for concrete representation', Section VI with cross-cultural studies of dyslexia, Section VII with teaching programmes, and Section VIII with the unity and diversity of dyslexic phenomena. Our central aim is to show how the behaviour of dyslexic subjects can be interpreted—or, perhaps better, reinterpreted—in the light of the lexical encoding deficiency hypothesis.

I   READING AND SPELLING

Many writers with educational interests have treated the concept of 'reading' as central (see, for example, Moyle, 1968; Reid, 1972; Vernon, 1971); but as far as the understanding of dyslexia is concerned statistical calculations based on 'reading age' are of limited value. Like many everyday concepts, 'reading' has no doubt provided a starting point for psychological investigation in much the same way as have concepts such as 'learning', 'memory', and 'attention'; but one cannot in general assume that a concept which is convenient for workaday purposes necessarily holds the key to any major scientific advance. Indeed it is noticeable that any investigator who attempts to write comprehensively about reading is immediately driven to say that reading difficulties can arise from many different causes. In general we believe that research into language skills has suffered through the lack of a concept with sufficient unificatory power and that the concept of a deficiency in the mechanisms for lexical encoding can make a significant contribution towards meeting this need.

An important function of this concept is to suggest links between the difficulties experienced by dyslexic subjects over reading and spelling and their difficulties at a variety of other tasks where language is involved. Although derivations are sometimes misleading (for example that of 'hysteria' implies a disease of the womb), in this particular case the suggestion of difficulty with *lexis*—language—is remarkably apposite.

The evidence cited by Ellis and Miles (1978a) can be interpreted to mean that speed of lexical encoding is a limiting factor in determining any person's reading speed; in other words, so long as there is slowness in the mechanisms for lexical encoding there cannot be fast reading, or at any rate not accurate fast reading. To say this is not, of course, to deny that speed of lexical encoding can be increased with practice, as happens, for instance, when an English speaker becomes progressively more proficient at reading Russian or Chinese or when a child who has been absent from school makes up for lost ground; but a likely conclusion from the data is that those in whom there is some constitutional limitation in the mechanisms for lexical encoding (including the dyslexic population in particular) will not easily be able, even after considerable practice, to combine fast reading with accuracy. There are no doubt many other components necessary for successful reading; but if one assumes random variation in the dyslexic population as far as these other components are concerned, then our hypothesis predicts a *tendency* for dyslexic persons to be relatively weak readers while accommodating the facts (a) that some of them learn to read fairly well and (b) that some non-dyslexic people read badly. In connection with (a) it is of interest to note that Naidoo (1972) found it convenient to distinguish 'reading retardates' (that is, those dyslexic children who were retarded at both reading and spelling) from 'spelling retardates' (those dyslexic children who were retarded at spelling only). It is also important to note that dyslexic persons of all ages may continue to be *slow* readers even though their performance on some standardized tests—particularly those where accuracy rather than speed is at a premium or where intelligent use can be made of contextual information—is not necessarily far, if at all, behind the norm. Because of the absence of precision timing the conventional reading test cannot be all that sensitive an instrument as far as dyslexia is concerned, though our hypothesis would of course become very uncomfortable if persons were found who displayed other dyslexic signs but who at no time in their lives had had any problems with reading.

Moreover a deficiency at the level of lexical encoding explains very much more than weakness at reading. As we shall show later, it accounts for a whole range of other dyslexic manifestations, including weakness at spelling, at digit span tasks, and so on. It seems, therefore, that the concept of 'reading difficulty' covers both too much and too little; it covers too much in that other factors, including of course environmental as opposed to constitutional ones, can be contributory causes and too little in that the relationship with other dyslexic manifestations is ignored. In contrast, the concept of a lexical encoding deficiency offers a change of emphasis by encouraging a different system of classification.

One consequence of this change is that reading and spelling difficulties, when they occur in those who are dyslexic, need to be regarded as manifestations of a wider deficiency which is likely to show itself whenever the handling of verbalizable material is involved. Because of their social importance these difficulties are the most noticeable effects of the lexical encoding deficiency but they are not the only ones.

An important consequence of the deficiency is that there is a slow rate of assimilation of verbal material. If it is also assumed (compare p. 185) that decay rate of information in dyslexic persons is normal, these two factors in combination would explain why reading and spelling present them with such difficulty in the early stages. At first glance it might seem that the time-intervals involved are not large enough to cause any major handicap. Thus Ellis and Miles (1977) report that a group of 41 dyslexic children, aged 10–14, needed on average 1331 msec (or about $1\frac{1}{3}$ sec) for correct recall of a string of five digits in backwards masking conditions, compared with 289 msec in the case of an age-matched control group; and on the face of it a difference of about 1 sec seems very little. It is a matter of familiar experience, however, that an adult who can recall a string of six digits with no difficulty may be quite unable to recall the first six digits from a string of, say, fifteen; there is just too much happening for him to 'keep track'. One suspects that something similar must be happening when the young dyslexic child first attempts to read. The correct strategy for the adult is to note the first six digits and ignore the others, but this is not easy. Similarly it would be correct for the young dyslexic child to try to assimilate a few stimulus properties (for example, the shapes of certain letters) and ignore the rest; but because he is overloaded it is very difficult for him to do so. The result is the familiar fact that in the early stages of learning to read he often fails to recognize the same word on two different occasions; indeed he is just not noticing the details which the non-dyslexic child is picking up automatically. A further consequence is that he does not know—as does the non-dyslexic child—that a certain combination of letters (such as *rsg* for *ask*) is not a possible word; and if he is then told by an adult to 'try harder' and avoid 'silly' mistakes, he does not easily learn how to set about doing so or how to tell when a mistake is 'silly'. Reading is of course easier for him than spelling since it involves recognition of letters or combinations of letters rather than their generation (compare the situation where we cannot remember a name but can instantly say 'That's right' when the name is presented to us); but both involve the noticing of detail, and there is too much detail to be noticed in the time available.

There is the further finding (Done and Miles, 1978) that in a paired-associate learning task dyslexic children needed more trials than age-matched controls to learn 'names' (three-letter nonsense words) for meaningless shapes. It could be said that this experiment involves a replication of the situation where a child initially learns the names for letters and figures; each of these is a 'meaningless shape' in the first place, and, since lexical encoding is required if these meaningless shapes are to be given names, dyslexic children need more 'trials' (that is, need longer time in class) before they make the necessary associations. The 8 or 9-year-old dyslexic child typically knows the names of individual letters (Miles, 1970), but parents often report lateness in achieving even this.

Two further well-known phenomena connected with reading can conveniently be discussed at this point: (a) the so-called 'proof reader's error', and (b) the tendency observed in some children to 'bark at print'. With regard to (a), it is well known that minor misprints in the spelling of a word often go undetected; and where this happens one could say that the 'evidence' from the semantic system is stronger or more influential than the 'evidence' relating to the visual characteristics of the letters. In the case of (b), it is sometimes found that even when a child has correctly spoken the words in front of him (whether by recognizing them as wholes or by sounding out individual letters) it may still be clear from numerous small cues—for example nuances in his tone of voice—that he has not understood their meaning. This phenomenon appears to be the precise opposite of the proof reader's error, since the 'evidence' about the visual characteristics of the letters is more influential in determining the response than is 'evidence' from the semantic system.

Finally, it may be helpful at this point to call attention to the biological advantages which accrue from naming. Verbalization is of particular use when the organism has to deal with what is not actually present or when what is present is too complex for the recording of detail. Familiarity with the visual features of words and letters is no doubt increased during the process of learning to read; but if we had to rely on visual features only, then memorization of letters would be very difficult. Thus, adapting the example given elsewhere by Miles (1970, p. 21), one might say that the Hebrew word for 'wilderness', if presented to a reader unfamiliar with Hebrew, is no more than a series of marks whose complexity is too great to be reproduced after a single showing. In the light of our present theory it may be suggested that once these marks become lexically encoded (or once visual stimulus/lexical entry associations are built up), the complexity becomes much more manageable and small differences in the physical properties of the stimulus, due for instance to different scripts or to individual differences in handwriting, can be discounted. It follows that his lexical encoding deficiency puts the dyslexic child in a position which is somewhat like that of a reader unfamiliar with Hebrew who meets the Hebrew word for 'wilderness' for the first time. Moreover, since what we obtain from vision is of far greater complexity per unit time than what we obtain from the other senses, a means of lexically encoding visual material is of particular advantage. Dyslexic-type difficulties do not occur only when visual stimuli are involved, as is plain from the weakness which dyslexic subjects show in recalling auditorily presented digits, but the old description of dyslexia as 'word-*blindness*' was not as for wide of the mark as some have supposed. A dyslexic person shows some degree of 'blindness' to any visual stimuli which are complex enough to require lexical encoding.

II DIRECTIONAL CONFUSION, MIRROR-IMAGES, AND HANDEDNESS

It is commonly asserted that dyslexic children show 'directional confusion' (MacMeeken, 1939) and that they tend to produce the 'mirror-image' of the correct answer, for example by confusing *b* and *d* or *p* and *q*, by saying *left* when they mean *right* and by writing for example, *was* for *saw* or *on* for *no*. Orton's (1937) concept of 'strephosymbolia' (literally 'twisting of symbols') gives a central place to such errors and offers an account of them in terms of the non-elision of 'engrams' from the two halves of the brain. It is also widely believed that there is an association between dyslexia and unusual patterns of handedness and eyedness. Such patterning might include simple left-handedness at a variety of tasks, crossed laterality (that is, left-handedness coupled with right-eyedness or right-handedness coupled with left-eyedness), or—what some people regard as more important—a failure to be strongly right-handed or right-eyed. In what follows we shall, for convenience, refer to anyone who is not conventionally right-handed and right-eyed as displaying 'UHE' (= unusual handedness or eyedness).

No detailed review of the literature on handedness and eyedness will be attempted here. It seems safe to say, however, that the evidence for an association between UHE and dyslexia—let alone a direct causal relationship—is anything but strong. Indeed Spache (1976, pp. 201–2), after reviewing 34 studies, goes so far as to conclude that there is no relationship at all; and while this may be going too far (compare Naidoo, 1972, p. 73; Zangwill, 1962, pp. 109–111) it is certainly the case that many dyslexic children and adults (probably at least 50%, to judge from Naidoo's figures) are straightforwardly right-handed and right-eyed.

Possible reasons for the inconsistencies in the literature may be (a) different criteria for selection of subjects, and (b) different criteria for handedness and eyedness. However that may be, the area is certainly untidy; and it seems to us that any attempt to invoke UHE as an explanation of dyslexia or even as an associated phenomenon should be viewed with considerable caution.

Some other facts, of course, are not in dispute. Thus there is a clearly established link between handedness and hemispheric specialization (see, for example, Zangwill, 1962, p. 106), and it is also virtually incontrovertible that there is specialization by one hemisphere, the left more often than the right, in the production of language. In addition it is widely accepted that some dyslexic children continue to confuse *b* and *d*, both in reading and spelling, at an age when non-dyslexic children (if indeed they ever confused them at all) have ceased to do so. It is also a matter of common experience that a dyslexic person is more liable to go wrong than a non-dyslexic person when given instructions involving left and right.

The significance of these undisputed facts, however, is by no means clear. That dyslexia should involve a failure in language-processing and that there is specialization by a single hemisphere in the production of language can scarcely be unrelated phenomena; but it by no means follows that poorly established dominance or crossed laterality are major causal agencies in generating dyslexic behaviour. Moreover the fact that some people confuse *b* and *d* may be quite unrelated to the fact that the two cerebral hemispheres are for the most part mirror-images of each other.

If it is indeed true that UHE in some form is more common in dyslexic subjects than in controls (and this is by no means firmly established), one possibility could simply be this: *any* left-handed, left-eyed or cross-lateral person has difficulty in writing or in scanning print in the correct direction; and if UHE is *superimposed* on dyslexia (that is, superimposed on the deficiency over lexical encoding) the difficulties become aggravated. Observant teachers may then have noticed a child's struggles in moving his left hand from left to right across the page, or the extra effort in checking with his left eye what he has written, and perhaps too readily jumped to the conclusion that the left-handedness or left-eyedness was sufficient to explain most of his difficulties. It is also worth noting that when the hand of a left-handed writer moves across the page this may obscure part of what he has written and thus make monitoring more difficult. We are not totally convinced that the difficulties which confront a left-handed person and those which result from a lexical encoding deficiency are one and the same phenomenon even though the effects may be aggravated when the two phenomena occur in conjunction.

The question still arises, however, as to why *left* and *right* should be any different from any other confusable pair of terms, such as *up/down, before/after, blue/red*, or *triangle/circle*. *Before/after* confusions occur from time to time in dyslexic subjects (Critchley, 1970, pp. 80–1) but *up/down* confusions, if they occur at all, are certainly rarer than *left/right* confusions. In this connection Quinault (1972) has offered an interesting 'cross-association' model in which he calls attention to the ease with which we confuse one member of a pair of terms with the other, such as *clockwise/anticlockwise, anode/cathode, port/starboard, stalagmite/stalactite*, etc., and he calls attention to the regular use of mnemonics as a means of telling which member of the pair is which. Now it seemed to us *prima facie* possible that an instruction such as 'Touch my left hand with your right hand' is no more and no less complicated than, for instance, 'Put the blue circle on the red triangle'. It has been found, however (Ellis *et al.*, in preparation), that dyslexic subjects are only marginally less effective than controls at the latter task; and some other explanation of the distinctive difficulty of *left* and *right* is therefore necessary.

A further suggestion, perhaps more plausible, is that *left* and *right* are a unique or almost unique pair of terms because of the lack of consistency with which they are applied. To use a somewhat problematic expression, they fluctuate in their 'referents', or, in other words, they do not necessarily 'tag on' to the same aspect of a situation as it occurs on two separate occasions. For example, as a person walks through a room the fireplace is on the right only if he is facing a particular direction, and the same fireplace would be on the left if he started to face the other way; in contrast *up* remains up and *down* down whichever way he is facing. On this terminology one might say that *left* and *right* have fluctuating referents whereas *up* and *down* do not. It is also the case that the personal pronouns *I* and *you* have fluctuating referents since the referent of *I* varies whenever there is a change of speaker and the referent of *you* varies whenever there is a change of listener, though in this case there may be less difficulty for a dyslexic person since from his own point of view *I* always refers to himself and *you* to someone else. In contrast, the colour of objects remains relatively constant, and when it changes the colour-word changes also (for example, when a green table is painted blue or the mountains change colour in the evening sun). Shape-words, too, such as *triangle* and *circle*, have none of the uncertainty associated with *left* and *right*: it is fortunate that if one walks in the opposite direction triangles do not have to be called circles!

One possibility, therefore, is that where there is some kind of weakness in the activation of entries in the internal 'lexicon', words which fluctuate in their referents are likely to cause more difficulty than words which do not; and if this is correct it would explain why dyslexic subjects are more likely to make mistakes over *left* and *right* than over, for examples *red* and *green* or *circle* and *square*.

Can the same explanation make sense over difficulties with points of the compass? We know of no controlled research in this area, but on the basis of clinical evidence it seems likely (a) that dyslexic children have distinctive difficulty over learning the points of the compass, and (b) that east west confusions are more common than north south confusions (and indeed may sometimes occur in non-dyslexic persons).

Now the points of the compass have fluctuating referents in the sense that if one is walking forwards there is no knowing whether one is going north, south, east or west: there is no invariant relationship with the direction of one's bodily movement. Nor is, say, Salisbury cathedral always to the north; it is so only if one is looking at it from the south! On the other hand, once an association is built up between, say, a particular view from one's home and the word 'south', this can be the basis for the future learning of all of the points of the compass. (Nor is it necessary that the words *north, south, east,* and *west* should be written on the horizon; this might be an extra aid to learning but clearly we can manage without it!)

Now it is possible that awareness of the points of the compass develops significantly when children start to look at maps, and this awareness may well be strengthened if implicitly they make use of the verbal instructions, 'North is at the top' and 'West is on the left'. In that case, however, the non-dyslexic child is in a position to absorb both sets of instructions, whereas the latter, 'West is on the left', may be a source of confusion to the dyslexic child because of his uncertainty over left and right, while the former, 'North is at the top', generates less confusion since *top* and *bottom* do not fluctuate in their referents in the same way as do *north* and *south*. Indeed, in the case of an object which has a standard way up, such as a clock, it does not have to be given a new name just because someone turns it upside down. In general, therefore, it could be suggested that small differences in the ways in which the referents of a word-pair fluctuate may make large differences to the ease with which the members of that pair are distinguished. In addition, it should be remembered that non-standard methods of distinguishing are available to a dyslexic person, that is, those which we call 'compensatory strategies', for example remembering that a particular hand is one's right hand because of a scar.

The dyslexic child can at least take comfort from the fact that the same direction is not referred to as *north* on Mondays and *south* on Wednesdays. There are different kinds of fluctuation, and we suggest that the difficulties which occur in dyslexia may vary with both the nature of the fluctuation and the possibility of a compensatory strategy. This could be tested in the laboratory with artefact concepts which fluctuated in different ways. As things are, the fact that *left* and *right* have fluctuating referents, combined with the fact that knowledge of left and right can contribute to knowledge of east and west, could be an explanation of why those with a lexical encoding deficiency have more than average difficulty with both pairs of terms.

It remains to discuss the well-known confusion between *b* and *d*. This can occur both in reading (as when a child is given a word beginning with, say, *d* and starts with a *ber*-sound) and in writing, as when a child writes *hab* for *had*. It is believed to occur in non-dyslexic children in the early stages of learning to read and spell and is almost certainly prevalent among slow learners. As far as dyslexic children are concerned, however, it sometimes persists until quite a late age, in some cases 12 or 13, and is occasionally found in dyslexic adults; moreover it can occur even in those of very high intelligence.

It is a puzzling phenomenon. It is often said that the child is writing 'mirrorwise'; and while this expression is harmless as a description there are potentially misleading theoretical overtones. It is *in fact* the case that *b* is the mirror-image of *d*, and if a child writes *b* when he should have written *d* it is therefore true to say that the end product was the mirror-image of *d*. But it is unproven to suggest any kind of mechanism which is susceptible to mirror-image confusion; and indeed if the reference to mirror-writing is intended as in some sense an *explanation* of the substitution of *b* for *d* it is at best speculative. Similarly if a child writes *on* for *no* it is in fact the case that he has written the mirror-image of the correct word; but since a possible explanation is that he knew that the letters *n* and *o* were needed but did not know the correct order (perhaps because he had failed to grasp basic principles of sound–letter correspondence), it is a gratuitous assumption to postulate a brain mechanism which inverts traces or engrams in a mirrorwise fashion. Moreover, if a child writes *was* for *saw* this cannot be a straightforward mirror-image error, since *was* and *saw* are not mirror-images. Indeed, in the interests of accuracy it seems to us that one should not say that the child wrote (the word) *was* for (the word) *saw* but wrote the letters *w-a-s* when he should have written the letters *s-a-w*.

It is interesting in this connection that Orton (1937, p. 150) distinguishes what he calls 'static' reversals from 'kinetic' ones. On this terminology, substitutions of *b* for *d* or *p* for *q* are called static reversals, since the letters have the same form but opposite orientation, whereas writing *was* for *saw* is a kinetic reversal since it is thought to involve progression through the letters of a word in a right-to-left order. Orton was of course well aware that it was symbols, not objects, which tended to be reversed; and there is nothing absurd in the idea of a limitation which selectively affects the ability to operate with the one and not the other. Not all later writers have been as cautious, however, and there has been a tendency to speak of *was-saw* and *b-d* confusions as though they were the same kind of phenomenon—an assumption which seems to us open to question. Indeed, it is perhaps as a result of Orton's influence that too much emphasis has been placed on directional difficulties in dyslexia and too little on naming difficulties. We believe him to have been nearer a correct explanation when he wrote (1937, p. 145): 'The record left by previous exposures to the same word is not sufficiently clear to suffice for its recognition, as in reading, and still less for its reproduction, as in spelling'.

It is even possible that the visual characteristics of *b* and *d* are not as important in explaining *b–d* confusion as has sometimes been supposed. It is known that short-term memory is subject to phonemic confusions and that the sounds of the letters *b* and *d* are phonemically confusable (Conrad, 1964); and it may simply be that these confusions occur in any child at a young age but persist in a dyslexic child because of the connection between dyslexia and a limitation in short-term memory. Moreover, if the fact that *b* is visually the mirror image of *d* were the only factor in the confusion it would not be easy to explain mistakes over the capital letters, *B* and *D*, which undoubtedly occur from time to time. Nor would it be easy to explain the relative lack of frequency with which Ƨ is written for *S*, a mistake which is common in 5–6-year-olds but which is very rare among typically dyslexic older children. It may be more relevant to point out that when a person has to distinguish *b* and *d* it is necessary for an association to be formed between one of two visually confusable shapes and one of two acoustically confusable sounds; and where there is this dual confusability the possibility of cross-checking is non-additively reduced.

Indeed, if mirror-images were as important in this connection as some people have supposed, it is hard to see why dyslexic children do not sometimes walk away from objects which they wish to approach (as Alice found was necessary in looking-glass world); yet there is no evidence that they do. Nor is there any reason for thinking that they make the left–right equivalent of the mistakes reported by Stratton (1897) when he wore up-down inverting spectacles; if they did, one might suppose the obvious remedy would be counterinverting spectacles which corrected half the visual field in each eye, and this is surely a *reductio ad absurdum*. The importance of mirror analogies for the understanding of dyslexia has, we believe, been exaggerated (compare also Elaine Miles, Chapter 10 of this volume).

It may also be suggested, albeit speculatively, that the lexical encoding deficiency hypothesis can accommodate the fact (if indeed it is one) that dyslexic children are more likely than controls to display finger agnosia. It should be said at once that the evidence in this area is inconclusive (compare Naidoo, 1972), and it follows that there may indeed be nothing to explain. On the assumption, however, that Hermann and Norrie (1958) are right in associating finger agnosia with dyslexia, one might offer the following tentative suggestion. Because of weakness at building up lexical code associations, a dyslexic person would be expected, unless he works out a suitable compensatory strategy, to have difficulty in performing any task where particular fingers have to be *identified by name*; in that case the failure to respond correctly would be the result of a naming difficulty and not, as Hermann and Norrie imply, a manifestation of some more general disorder of body-schema. This, however, is speculation; and the very concept of a Gerstmann syndrome, involving writing difficulties and disorders of the body-schema, has been called into question (Critchley, 1970, p. 84).

It is widely reported, too, that dyslexic persons of all ages are more than usually liable to become 'tied up' in saying words aloud. Frequently cited examples are *par cark* for *car park* and *beelwharrow* for *wheelbarrow*; and Miles (1978, pp. 51–2) has reported consistent difficulty over *preliminary, statistical, philosophical,* and *anemone*. Figures presented by Miles (1979) confirm that, although these words are difficult for many 9-year-olds and 10-year-olds whether they are dyslexic or not, there is significantly more 'stumbling' among dyslexic subjects than among controls. Here, too, it is tempting to offer an explanation in terms of a difficulty over ordering, in this case temporal as opposed to spatial. If the lexical encoding deficiency hypothesis is correct, however, one must assume that the difficulty arises not with *things* (objects) but only with items which are lexically encodable, in other words, symbols. Over 50 years ago Head (1926) described aphasia as a 'disorder of symbolic formulation and expression'; and it was no doubt Head's influence which led Miles (1961, p. 68) to say: 'I am not of course suggesting that there is any failure of integration when *things* lie side by side, but only when symbols lie side by side'. One might therefore tentatively offer an explanation of the stumbling of dyslexic persons over *car park, preliminary,* etc. in terms of 'slow processing coupled with phonemic confusability'. Thus if the lexical encoding of the *w* sound in *wheelbarrow* is slow, the *b* sound is upon the person before he is ready for it, and, since the two sounds *ber* and *wer* are phonemically confusable, there is serious risk of the wrong one being substituted for the correct one. Incidental observation has shown that if a dyslexic adult *goes slowly enough* over the words *preliminary, anemone,* etc. he can say them without difficulty. It also seems likely that it is phonemic confusability rather than length of word which is the important factor. In that case one would explain the errors over *car park* by the confusion of the two *ar* sounds, the difficulties over *preliminary* and *anemone* by the close proximity of the *m* and *n* sounds, the difficulty over *statistical* by the presence of three *t*s, two *s*s and two *a*s, and the difficulty over *philosophical* by the presence of two *phs* and two *l*s. In contrast, the word *contemporaneous*, which is also used in clinical assessments, creates relatively less difficulty despite the larger number of syllables; this could be because the component sounds in this word are not readily confusable with each other. If there were a verb to *bedeedy* and another to *de-bedeedy*, one may surmise that the past tense of the latter, *de-bedeedied* would be particularly difficult for dyslexic persons (and perhaps others) to say. Indeed phonemic confusability is a common characteristic of the components of many familiar tongue-twisters, such as 'She sells sea shells on the sea shore'. Our suggestion is that the mistakes of dyslexic subjects over repeating words arise because phonemic confusability in the stimulus is superimposed upon slowness at lexical encoding in the organism.

There is a possible parallel in the visual sphere when reading is involved. Unless the person deliberately goes very slowly, difficulty will arise if material which is later to be lexically encoded is superimposed upon material at present being lexically encoded; and the unusual eye movements which have been shown by Pavlidis (Chapter 6 of this volume) to be characteristic of dyslexic subjects may occur because part of the visual input has not 'registered' and it is therefore necessary for the eyes to 'flit' from later to earlier material in order to determine what point has been reached. The situation has the character of a re-enactment, below the level of consciousness (since we are largely unconscious of our eye movements), of the familiar situations when a dyslexic person in reciting his tables asks 'Where have I got to?' (Miles, 1978, p. 53). There is also a parallel in some of the arithmetical errors made by dyslexic subjects. Thus the number which he says and thinks of as 'sixteen' the dyslexic child may write as '61'. In this case he has not 'written sixty-one for sixteen' any more than he has written 'was' for 'saw' (see above): rather he has written sixteen as 'six-one'. The risk of confusion is no doubt greater when the conventional order of writing the two digits (tens first, units second) is at variance with the order in which the components of the number are said, as happens in the 'teens' in the English number system; and if it is the case, as it may well be, that dyslexic subjects make more ordering errors when writing two digits if one of these digits is a 1 this could be explained by this special characteristic of the 'teens' and would not have occurred if, for instance, instead of 'sixteen' we spoke of 'one-ty six' (compare Griffiths, 1976).

Now if a limitation at the level of lexical encoding is a central feature in dyslexia, this predicts that in tasks which involve orientation *without* lexical encoding dyslexic subjects will perform no differently from controls. An experiment which bears upon this point was carried out by Ellis and Miles (1978b) who required their subjects to respond 'same' or 'different' to pairs of meaningless shapes, some of them 'mirrorwise' inverted; in these conditions only minimal differences were found between dyslexic subjects and controls, the dyslexic subjects being no slower and making only marginally more errors (10% as against 5%). This is a further argument for saying that the tendency to confuse mirror-images is not as important for the understanding of dyslexia as many people have supposed.

If left–right confusions are not (save incidentally) mirror-image confusions, what are they? One possibility is that they occur in dyslexic subjects only when the *names* 'left' and 'right' are involved (compare Vellutino, 1978, p. 73). Thus a dyslexic individual who is giving directions to a pedestrian or motorist may know perfectly well which way that person should turn (in the sense, for example, of being able to correct him if he went wrong) but may still say 'Turn left' when he should have said 'Turn right'. It has been noted (Miles. 1979) that when given a task such as 'Touch my right hand with your left hand' dyslexic subjects may need longer time or be more subject to error than controls; and if the lexical encoding deficiency hypothesis is correct one can interpret the situation by saying that the retrieval of the action-*name* association is deficient in dyslexic subjects. Since, however, the sensory input decays as rapidly in dyslexic subjects as in controls (Ellis and Miles, 1978b), it follows that they are more likely to become lost and/or to need the 'props' to memory which all of us use on occasions. These include requests to have the question repeated (for example, 'Could you say that again, please?'), echoing the question (for example, 'Your right with my left, was it?'), and what grammarians call *epanalepsis*, that is, the taking up of what one has said earlier so as to get 'on track' again, for example, if a child is hesitating over seven sixes he may deliberately revert to an earlier part of the table by saying, for example, 'Five sixes are thirty', so as to give himself a fresh start. These hesitations and the use of 'props' can be understood in terms of loss of instructions from short-term memory; and if, as has been suggested by Ellis (1980) and by Ellis *et al.* (in preparation), the span of short-term memory for verbal material is dependent upon efficiency in the forming of associations between the lexical code and its articulatory representation, then those whose lexical representation is deficient would be expected to show a greater degree of hesitation and have a greater need for 'props'. There need not, of course, be total failure, and indeed there is not; but, as in many areas, dyslexic subjects (and presumably those who are slow at lexical encoding for other reasons) are more at risk.

Despite the general trend of the above arguments we are not disputing that dyslexic subjects may have a genuine directional difficulty *additional to* their slowness at tasks which involve naming. In this connection we are grateful to Helen Arkell, who has taught dyslexic pupils for many years, for the following observations:

(1) when dyslexic pupils are given exercise books without margins they are often unsure which side the margin goes, or if they rule too broad a margin they become confused as to which side of it they should write;

(2) even after considerable writing practice they may place the loop of the letter *a* on the left instead of the right;

(3) when making corrections they sometimes put the caret mark above the line and the additional letters below it, for example

rem˘ ber

em

(4) some of them are unsure at which end of an exercise book to start writing.

It would, of course, be possible to argue that implicit verbalization is needed if these tasks are to be adequately carried out and that all directional mistakes by dyslexic persons (such as laying knives and forks on the table incorrectly) are the result of inadequate labelling. This, however, is not firmly established, and the precise relationship between 'directional confusion' and 'difficulty with naming' remains at present a matter about which we think it wisest to reserve judgement.

III   INTELLIGENCE TESTS

A considerable amount of evidence is available about the performance of poor readers and/or dyslexic children on the subtests of the WISC (Wechsler Intelligence Scale for Children). There may, of course, be methodological difficulties if, without suitable precautions, one tries to compare dyslexic and control children on subtest scores after preselection for matched intelligence based on such scores, but the two groups can be matched in terms of social background (compare Naidoo, 1972) and in addition a child's score on a particular subtest can be rated as 'higher' or 'lower' than his average score on the subtests as a whole. Much of the relevant evidence has been summarized by Rugel (1974, pp. 51–3) and by Spache (1976, p. 140); and if in addition to these two sources we take into account the data presented by Naidoo (1972, p. 56) the following comparisons between dyslexic and control subjects on the Wechsler Intelligence Scale for Children subtests seem legitimate:

(1) *No differences*	(2) *Occasional reports of differences*	(3) *Consistent reports of differences*
Comprehension	Similarities	Information
Picture Completion	Vocabulary	Arithmetic
Picture Arrangement	Block design	Digit Span
Object Assembly		Coding

This means in effect that if a hypothetical group of dyslexic subjects were matched for 'intelligence level' with a group of controls on the basis of their results on the Comprehension, Picture Completion, Picture Arrangement, and Object Assembly tests then the great majority would score lower than the controls on Information, Arithmetic, Digit span and Coding, with possibly some slightly lower scores on Similarities, Vocabulary and Block Design.

Not all the placings are incontrovertible. For instance one of the 26 sources cited by Spache found poor readers lower on the Comprehension subtest, but this is offset by the fact that one of the eleven sources cited by Rugel actually found them higher on this test (in a context where poor readers and controls were matched for full-scale IQ). In the case of Block Design, Naidoo's reading retardates, but not her spelling retardates, were marginally lower than their controls but a similar result is found in only one of Spache's 26 sources, while just the opposite is reported in two out of Rugel's eleven sources. Differences on the Similarities test occur only in the case of Naidoo's reading retardates and in two of Spache's 26 sources. The genuineness of these differences is therefore perhaps open to question.

In contrast, virtually all studies consistently show the poor readers to be weaker on Information, Arithmetic, Digit Span, and Coding and equal (or stronger, according to the method of comparison) at Picture Completion, Picture Arrangement, and Object Assembly. A relative weakness at Vocabulary is reported in some studies but not by any means in all of them.

It seems to us likely that not all the differences are connected with dyslexia as such. Thus one might expect that *any* poor reader, whether dyslexic or not, would score lower than a good reader on the Information test for the simple reason that much of the relevant knowledge will in fact have been acquired from books, of which he will have read fewer. It is possible, though this is less certain, that the small differences sometimes reported in the Vocabulary and Similarities tests are also the result of the lesser amount of reading done by the dyslexic subjects; their vocabulary might be expected to be less wide, and failures at the Similarities test could be the result of failure to know the meaning of key words such as *liberty* and *justice* which are found at the difficult end of the scale. The fact that Naidoo's reading retardates, but not her spelling retardates, scored lower than their controls on the Vocabulary and Similarities subtests gives some extra support to the view that absence of reading experience was affecting the results. We can offer no convincing explanation of the occasional reports of differences on the Block Design subtest, and since they are so rarely reported there may indeed be nothing of permanent importance to be explained. What is of more interest is that this test seems *prima facie* to involve some kind of directional awareness, since it is all too easy to place a block 90, 180 or 270 degrees 'out'; and on the thesis that 'directional confusion' is the central concept in dyslexia it is surprising that *more* dyslexic children do not find the Block Design test difficult. It seems reasonable to assume that most children, in matching the blocks to the patterns on the cards, are in effect relying on the visual features of each without attempting to verbalize; but it would be interesting to find out whether the result was different if they were encouraged to describe aloud what they were doing, for example whether a verbalization such as 'This is 90 degrees out' resulted in any faster completion of the task.

The three remaining subtests where differences are consistently found (Arithmetic, Digit Span and Coding) are ones which directly involve lexical encoding. Thus in the case of the Arithmetic subtest one would expect the main successes of the dyslexic child to come only in the early items; here the counting can be done by 'concrete aids'—blocks in the case of the original test and trees in the case of the WISC (R)—and only minimal holding in mind of instructions is needed. In contrast all the later items require lexical encoding—in this case rapid verbalization of the number-words which form part of the auditory stimulus. Moreover many of these later items are particularly difficult for those who do not know their tables (see pp. 234–5 below), however intelligent they may be in other ways. Similar verbalization is needed in the case of Digit Span; and the lexical encoding deficiency hypothesis predicts that dyslexic subjects will have severe difficulty with this subtest, which indeed they do. It should be noted, however, that compensatory strategies are not totally impossible, for example grouping in the case of 'digits forward' and saying them forwards *sotto voce* in the case of 'digits reversed' (compare Miles and Wheeler, 1974).

In the case of the Coding test the following marks are used:

$$\div\ )+\vdash\ \neg\ \lor\ (\ \div\ \dashv$$

The subject is first shown how each mark is paired with a digit and then, in the test proper, where digits are presented on their own with an empty space under each, he has to supply the missing mark, his score being determined by the number of correct marks made in 2 minutes. What one cannot know—and what doubtless varies from subject to subject—is whether a particular mark is acting as a symbol or whether it is simply a meaningless shape. Thus—suggests, but is not identical with, a division sign; + is presumably often verbalized as a 'plus' sign; ∨ is rather like the letter V, and so on. We therefore do not know which of the stimuli result in a visual-pattern-to-visual-pattern match and which result in a visual-pattern-to-name match. Vellutino *et al.* (1975) have shown that dyslexic subjects are no less efficient than controls at the former but have considerably more difficulty with the latter (a result which fits well with the lexical encoding deficiency hypothesis). With the test in its present form it would seem that all the digits and an unknown number of marks are lexically encoded; and on our hypothesis the relatively low scores of the dyslexic subjects occur because their slowness at lexical encoding results in less being done in the time available. It should be noted that on this test there is seldom a complete 'flop' on the part of the dyslexic child. Thus a subject whose scaled scores on some of the other tests come out as 13 or more may well score around 10 (average for age) on Coding. To be slow at a task does not mean that one cannot do it at all.

With regard to the Picture Arrangement subtest, it is interesting that Rugel (1974, p. 53) regards it as 'misplaced' among tests of sequencing (compare Bannatyne, 1968). Certainly the cards have to be arranged in a correct sequence so that they tell a coherent story; but the task is unlike that involved in Coding in that pictures rather than digits or symbols are involved, and is unlike Digit Span both in this respect and in the fact that all the elements of the situation (cards) are co-present and do not have to be 'held in mind' as do auditorily presented digits. Thus it would seem that *rapid* lexical encoding is not really needed, in which case any slowness in the postulated mechanism would not be a significant handicap. Now in fact there is no evidence of weakness by poor readers/dyslexic subjects at this subtest either in the 26 studies reported by Spache or in the eleven studies by Rugel, nor was it found in either of Naidoo's two dyslexic groups; and if dyslexic subjects were weak at all tasks which involve 'sequencing' the *absence* of difference on this subtest would be surprising. As things are, the observed results are compatible with the existence of a lexical encoding deficiency but not with any view which treats dyslexia as a sequencing problem without qualification.

Our hypothesis also makes sense of the high scores obtained by dyslexic subjects on the Raven Advanced Matrices test (Raven, 1965; compare Miles, 1978, p. 99). This test does not call for any reading of words, and the only writing involved is the recording of answers on the score sheet. The subject does not have to deal with any series length greater than 3 (since the stimulus is always a 3×3 set of patterns with one pattern missing whose characteristics have to be deduced) and the patterns do not for the most part represent familiar symbols which a non-dyslexic person would more rapidly encode. It would be rash to say that no lexical encoding is needed at all, since some or all subjects may find it convenient to verbalize parts of the patterns as 'squiggle', 'triangle', 'oblique line', etc.; but in a task of this sort which lasts for 40 minutes, much of which is spent on the very difficult later items, it seems unlikely that slowness at lexical encoding would have any decisive influence on the results, which depend far more on the subject's ability to reason logically.

It should also be noted that many group tests require the ability to hold in mind items in a series. For example, in one such test the subject is required to put crosses on 'the one that should come first' and 'the one that should come last' in the series 6, 8, 2, 10, 4. This is clearly a dyslexia-laden item. Even if a particular dyslexic child has come to terms in general with the notion of a series he still needs in this case to be able to operate with five different items at once if he is to work out their correct order, and this may be too much for him. Moreover, even if he gets round his memory limitation by means of some compensatory strategy (for example by comparing the numbers two at a time and putting marks on the paper) this procedure is likely to take extra time, and in a timed test he will therefore be penalized. According to his personality make-up he may try to hurry through all the items with resultant loss of accuracy or he may go slowly and complete only a small number of them; but in either case his score will not do justice to his intelligence level. If it is argued that speed at handling serially ordered verbal material is itself an important component of 'intelligence'—in the sense of being something which needs to be investigated if one is to assess the child's general reasoning ability—it is still important to point out that a total score based on results of test-items which are dyslexia-laden and test-items which are not must necessarily be an unsatisfactory hybrid.

Finally, mention should be made of the 'Memory for Sentences' items in the Terman–Merrill test. One of the present authors has met dyslexic children who, when presented with the sentence, 'At the summer camp the children get up early in the morning to go swimming', could paraphrase it correctly but had striking difficulty in repeating it verbatim even when it was repeated back to them six or more times. This finding is precisely what would be predicted if one assumes that the semantic system of a dyslexic person works normally but that his logogen system is deficient.

That the two systems work independently and that one can sometimes be more efficient than the other should perhaps be taken into account by those who assume that 'intelligence' is a unitary concept. From an information processing point of view there can be no doubt that traditional intelligence tests tap many different functions. Even, therefore, if one discounts the special difficulties which arise in assessing the intelligence of a dyslexic child, there is still a case for saying that those who are searching for measures of 'intelligence' should devise items which require the operation of fewer functions at a time.

IV   ARITHMETICAL TABLES

It is widely agreed that almost all dyslexic children and adults have difficulty in learning and reciting tables. Documentation of some of their typical responses is given by Miles (1978), and evidence cited by Miles (1979) shows that in a sample of 107 dyslexic subjects aged 9–12, 99 (93%) satisfied the criteria for dyslexia-positive compared with 112 out of 227 controls (49%). Detailed discussion of this evidence will not be attempted here, but the most likely conclusions seem to be:

(1) that many children nowadays do not know their tables,

(2) that dyslexic children have distinctive difficulty,

(3) that for dyslexic children some degree of 'learning overlay' is possible, though their hesitations and the types of error which they make (for example, losing the place or changing to the 'wrong' table) are evidence for at least a residual handicap, and

(4) that a distinction needs to be drawn between (a) those who because of absence of opportunity (possibly as a result of school policy) do not know their tables but possess the potential to learn them and (b) those who despite every opportunity still find the learning of tables difficult.

On this showing dyslexic children belong in the latter group, and it is therefore appropriate to examine how the hypothesis of a lexical encoding deficiency might explain their failure.

If any units are to be arranged in a coherent series then a knowledge of the requisite order is needed as well as a knowledge of the units themselves. Weakness at tables on the part of dyslexic subjects is thus 'of a piece' with their weakness at saying the months of the year, their uncertainty over the seasons, and their difficulty in the recall of auditorily presented digits. The hypothesis of a lexical encoding deficiency suggests that when a unit is 'fed' into the system the relative deficiency in the forming of a lexical code, coupled, of course, with normal decay rate, makes difficult the representation not only of the units themselves but of the relationship between them. It is no doubt the loss of such information which causes dyslexic subjects to 'lose the place' when reciting tables, for example by asking 'Where have I got to?' (Miles, 1978, p. 53) or by changing to the wrong table. Learning overlay makes it possible for most of them to recite the 5, 10 and 11 times table without serious error, while some of them can say the 9 times because they have learned that the two digits combined always add up to 9. A very interesting phenomenon in this connection is the request which some dyslexic subjects make to leave out what may be called the 'preamble' (for example, 'one seven is . . ., two sevens are . . .' etc.). Some in fact ask, 'Can I just say "six", "twelve", "eighteen"?' or in other ways indicate that the preamble adds to their difficulty. It would seem that having to keep track of the preamble is in some cases just sufficient to make the load too heavy, though of course if they were permitted to write the preamble down the task would immediately become easier.

V   THE NEED FOR CONCRETE REPRESENTATION

There is one further strategy which is regularly adopted by dyslexic subjects and which again can be understood if we think in terms of a deficiency in lexical encoding. Many dyslexic children, even at age 11 or over, and a number of dyslexic adults cannot count without some kind of 'concrete representation' of the numbers being counted. This usually takes the form of counting on fingers or putting dots on paper, and it is particularly needed if, for example, in a subtraction sum, the number to be subtracted is more than about 5. The same phenomenon can be observed when the more intelligent dyslexic subjects attempt the Terman–Merrill Enclosed Boxes test, where the instruction is, for example, 'Suppose this box has four smaller boxes inside it and that each of the smaller boxes contains four tiny boxes, how many boxes altogether?' Many of them represent the boxes by marks on paper, and by counting the dots they are able to arrive at the correct answer. It seems to us that a likely explanation of the phenomenon is that a mark on paper is a substitute for a unit in the mechanism for lexical encoding; it is 'there' (on the paper), available for future use, and will not 'run away'. The mechanism is therefore freed for the activation of other lexical code associations and there is thus avoidance of what would otherwise be an impossible overload.

Another very interesting phenomenon is that when given a task such as 'Touch my right hand with your left hand' (as they sit face to face with the tester) some dyslexic subjects actually turn in their seats, and even when there is no overt turning there are slight turning-movements or a report of 'I pretended to turn'. Similarly, when given the 'Direction' items from the Terman–Merrill test, such as 'Which way would you have to face so that your *left* hand would be towards the *east*?', many dyslexic subjects actually draw the points of the compass on paper (and in view of the interesting results it is legitimate, with suitable safeguards, to depart from the instructions in the test manual and permit them to do so). Some actually rise in their seats and orientate their bodies so as to make the required calculation; and since at this age most of them have acquired a strategy for working out which is their left hand, they are regularly able, if they proceed slowly, to come up with the correct answer. As often happens in the case of tasks given to a dyslexic person, one receives the impression that they are using all sorts of ingenious ways to compensate for a disability. Often it seems that they need to *do something with their bodies*; and this can be understood as an attempt to lighten the load of material which has to be lexically encoded. It seems to us, therefore, that a useful formula for the understanding of some types of dyslexic response is to say that *doing, real or imagined, is a substitute for naming*. We say 'real or imagined', since some subjects report that they *pretend* to turn round, take up a pencil, etc. or *imagine themselves* doing so, and it seems that for their purposes an imagined 'doing' can be as effective as a real 'doing'. We know of no evidence that dyslexic subjects are weak at imagining things or at 'supposing' such-and-such to be the case.

In our opinion these 'doing' responses, which are regularly found in the behaviour of dyslexic children and adults, have not so far received the attention which they deserve, though it is interesting that Spring and Capps (1974, p. 782) point out, correctly in our opinion, that dyslexic persons 'evidence no dramatic inability to function in an environment of concrete stimuli'.

VI CROSS-CULTURAL DIFFERENCES IN LITERACY SKILLS

The hypothesis of a lexical encoding deficiency also offers a possible interpretation of some of the cross-cultural comparisons of literacy skills. Thus Makita (1968) has pointed out that the prevalence of dyslexia in Japan (0.98%) appears to be some ten times lower than that found in Western countries, while in contrast Jansen (1973) reports that 15–18% of Danish children receive remedial teaching for reading retardation.

Now it is said that young Japanese children start to read using the Hiragana script, which is a 46-symbol syllabic script where the name of each symbol corresponds exactly to its pronunciation. It is not surprising, therefore, that in these circumstances the building up of lexical code associations take place easily even in the case of those potentially dyslexic persons who might have had difficulty with the familiar western alphabetic system. In contrast Danish is agreed to be a language in which the sound—letter correspondences are highly irregular.

Nothing, of course, follows from this about the influence of genetic factors on dyslexia. For example it is still possible that there are many more people in Japan who for genetic reasons would have displayed dyslexic-type difficulties if they had been tested by an equivalent of the Wechsler Digit Span test or had been exposed to brief presentation of nameable material in a tachistoscope. From the research point of view, therefore, it would have been interesting if cross-cultural comparisons had been available on language-skills other than reading and spelling. Meanwhile the coherence of the lexical encoding deficiency hypothesis with existing evidence on cross-cultural differences is worth recording.

VII TEACHING METHODS

In this section we shall examine the relationship between the lexical encoding deficiency hypothesis and the practical aspects of teaching dyslexic children. Marcel (1978) has expressed doubts as to whether any information processing model can be of help to the practising teacher except possibly in so far as it suggests 'substitute' procedures in the case of the brain-damaged. Such models 'may say that a person lacks x or has an impaired y. But they do not tell you what to do about it other than substitution' (p. 536). Marcel seems unaware, however, of the fact that successful programmes for teaching specifically dyslexic children are already in existence (compare Elaine Miles, this volume, Chapter 10; Naidoo, this volume Chapter 11, and Hornsby and Miles, 1980).

It is true, of course, that these methods have evolved as a result of work by gifted individuals who were influenced little or not at all by the findings of experimental psychologists. Such findings, however, not merely make sense of why the methods in question have been successful; in addition they can help teachers to determine which among possible procedures are likely to be the more effective and thus contribute to the elimination of time-wasting and the evolution of improved techniques. In brief, the value of such research is that it demonstrates the nature of the functional deficiencies shared by all those who are dyslexic. This being the case, the offering of substitute methods seems rather like offering a wheelchair—which substitutes a functionally different type of locomotion—to a person who could walk adequately if given massage! In contrast we should like to suggest that the most obvious next step after diagnosing a deficiency is to attempt to remedy it rather than offer the person some kind of substitute procedure.

Now the methods which have been found to be most successful with dyslexic children are those which are 'structured sequential, cumulative, and thorough' (Rawson, 1970; compare Rawson, this volume, Chapter 2, and Naidoo, this volume, Chapter 11). These include schemes by Gillingham and Stillman (1956),

Cotterell (1970), Miles (1970), Hornsby and Shear (1977), Miles and Miles (1975), Smelt (1972, 1976), Hickey (1977), Allan (1978), and Pollock (1978). Although there has been some degree of 'cross-fertilization' in recent years, it is worth noting that many of these schemes evolved independently. Gillingham and Stillman's work in the United States had considerably influence on Hornsby and Shear and on Hickey; the schemes of Cotterell, Miles, and Allan were developed in the United Kingdom, though Cotterell also advocates use of the Edith Norrie Letter Case which was developed in Scandinavia. Smelt did her work in Australia, while Pollock was influenced by both British and Scandinavian ideas. Not only did these schemes evolve partly independently in different parts of the world; their success is no accident. In all cases there is the abandonment of the traditional 'Look and Say' method, which in any case is aimed at helping reading rather than spelling, and in its place there is the substitution of a structured phonic programme in which the associations between word-parts (including single letters, digraphs, blends, and syllables) and their corresponding sounds are progressively learned. In some cases (such as Gillingham and Stillman, 1956; Hickey, 1977) routine *drills* are carried out to ensure that such learning takes place.

Now according to our hypothesis the dyslexic person has an underdeveloped system for finding the appropriate 'match' between incoming stimuli and entries in the lexicon, and, as has in effect been shown by the Done and Miles (1978) study, he does not easily acquire one. This means not only that special drills are needed but that those associations should be taught which are of most use. It is a drawback of the 'Look and Say' method, however, that a separate association has to be formed for every word that is to be read. In contrast, phonic methods capitalize on the alphabetical nature of the English language. Thus the development of a relatively small number of 'matches' between lower level logogens and entries in the internal dictionary, provided these 'matches' are coupled with appropriate skills in blending, will enable the dyslexic child to attack many new words using orthographic reading strategies and to capitalize on his substantial heard vocabulary.

Our model also explains why the learning of the dyslexic pupil needs to be 'multisensory' (compare Naidoo, this volume Chapter 11). It is widely agreed by teachers who are experienced in the dyslexia field that links need to be forged between inputs from the three different sensory modalities, vision, hearing and kinaesthesis, and that the pupil has to learn to associate together (a) a particular movement of the hand as he writes, (b) a particular sound, and (c) a particular mark seen on the page. In terms of our model one might say that development of extra input routes facilitates lexical access. We suggested earlier (p. 226) that the mistakes which many children make over *b* and *d* could perhaps be the result of the combined influence of the auditory and visual confusability of these letters. In contrast, one never finds substitution of *f* for *s* (or vice versa) despite their auditory confusability, presumably because the use of a visual input route provides clear distinguishing features. In general one may surmise that easily distinguishable inputs, and in particular inputs via different sensory modalities, contribute to the activation of the appropriate entry in the lexicon. This, at any rate, is a possible theoretical justification for the policy of 'multisensory learning'.

It is also worth noting that the lexical encoding deficiency hypothesis leads to the active *dis*couragement of certain teaching practices. For example, as has been pointed out by De Leeuw and De Leeuw (1965), training in making more rapid eye movements is unlikely to improve comprehension, and it seems likely that the unusual eye movements associated with dyslexia are at most a manifestation rather than the initial cause of their information-processing deficiency (compare p. 179). Nor, it seems, is anything distinctive gained if dyslexic children are given practice at shape discrimination as a precursor to learning to read: if shapes are matched without naming, dyslexic children are no less efficient than controls, and if naming takes place it is clearly more economical that they should learn to name letters of the alphabet from the start. There are perhaps similar objections to teaching dyslexic children by means of the Initial Teaching Alphabet (i.t.a.), since further matching between visual shapes and entries in the lexicon will be needed when the child has to deal with traditional orthography. Some teachers encourage their poor readers to play pelmanism and other games which are alleged to 'train the memory', but it is by no means clear that practice at memorizing, for example, the position of playing cards on a table will do anything to help the building up of appropriate associations between incoming stimuli and entries in the lexicon. Finally, since the lexical encoding deficiency hypothesis involves a shift of emphasis away from the study of mirror-images and handedness and towards the study of information processing as a key for understanding dyslexia, it gives no support to the use of those training methods which, on the basis of decidedly speculative neurology, attempt to change a child's cerebral dominance by discouraging the use of his left hand and left eye (compare the comments of Critchley, Chapter 1 of this volume). All the techniques mentioned in this paragraph are regarded as unsatisfactory by experienced teachers of dyslexic children, and the lexical encoding deficiency hypothesis both supports their judgement in this matter and is itself rendered more probable on grounds of coherence.

With regard to the improvement of techniques, although for convenience people speak of 'a' (single) teaching programme, an actual lesson for a dyslexic pupil (or indeed any other pupil) comprises hundreds of subtle interactions between teacher and child. To say that a teacher is following a programme therefore means only that certain types of procedure predominate; it does not follow that the programme cannot be modified. Thus if for purposes of argument one assumes that a lesson comprises a hundred 'procedural units' chosen largely by the teacher (where a 'unit' might be, for example, 'Notice the "e" at the end of the word', 'Say whether the vowel is short or long', etc.) it will be difficult in practice for a teacher to be sure which 'procedural units' are most important even when the programme overall is successful. In that case, however, the lexical encoding deficiency hypothesis (or, indeed, any other development in cognitive psychology) might quite well give him grounds for preferring one 'procedural unit' to another. The fact that teachers have achieved some degree of success without being influenced by the lexical encoding deficiency hypothesis does not therefore mean that no further successes will be possible under its influence.

We conclude, therefore, that our hypothesis not only explains why existing practices in the teaching of dyslexic children are successful but may contribute in the future towards helping these practice to evolve.

VIII   THE UNITY AND DIVERSITY OF DYSLEXIC PHENOMENA

A general advantage of the lexical encoding deficiency hypothesis is that it explains both the unity and the diversity of dyslexic phenomena. It is not surprising that those who assess and teach dyslexic children regularly report the same pattern of difficulties, since the underlying unity is obvious to anyone who knows what to look for. The word 'syndrome' is useful here since, without implying a unitary cause, it emphasizes that certain manifestations belong together. Moreover the fact that in controlled conditions (see, for example, Ellis and Miles, 1978a and b, and elsewhere) older dyslexic subjects consistently behave as a group is further evidence for thinking in terms of a unity. On the other hand the amount of 'learning overlay' which a particular individual can achieve will of course depend on his personal circumstances, for example his motivation, his intelligence level, and the opportunities which he has for receiving skilled remedial help. It follows that if a particular task is said to be difficult for a dyslexic person one should not expect every dyslexic person to fail at it and every non-dyslexic person to succeed at it. On the one hand a dyslexic person may have been able to devise an effective compensatory strategy, while on the other hand a non-dyslexic person may be slow at lexical encoding through lack of familiarity with the material, or sometimes he may make errors (for example, slips of the pen and tongue) through what is ordinarily called lack of attention or concentration. Any brain mechanism can be temporarily out of action and it is not at all surprising that the non-dyslexic person makes seemingly dyslexic errors from time to time.

We are not claiming that the lexical encoding deficiency is always itself due to the same cause. As was noted in the previous chaper, the dyslexic manifestations displayed by prelingually deaf children could be the result of a deficiency in lexical encoding which is a direct consequence of the deafness; and, indeed, when children who have had relatively mild hearing loss display dyslexic manifestations (as sometimes happens), this could again be because the hearing loss has affected the mechanism for lexical encoding. Moreover, when dyslexic manifestations occur as a result of acquired injury, one may surmise that the lexical encoding mechanism has been similarly affected, along, of course, with other mechanisms if the injury has been severe. The existence of more diffuse damage would of course explain why some mentally handicapped children (although not others) make dyslexic-type mistakes. If, however, we limit ourselves to a consideration of the so-called 'pure' cases of dyslexia—those who display typical dyslexic difficulties but no other relevant handicap—the most common cause appears to be a genetic one; and one must conclude that deficiences in the lexical encoding mechanism can sometimes be genetically determined. Where the mechanism is only mildly affected one may get the 'formes frustes' of dyslexia mentioned by Critchley (see Chapter 1 of this volume and, for further details, Critchley and Critchley, 1978) which are sometimes found in relatives of more severely affected persons.

We conclude that dyslexic manifestations are both a unity and a diversity. They are a unity in that they are all the consequence of a deficiency in the mechanism for lexical encoding; they are a diversity both because individuals vary in the compensatory strategies available to them and because the mechanisms for lexical encoding can be deficient for different reasons.

ACKNOWLEDGEMENT

The Psychological Corporation is the copyright owner of the WISC(R).

REFERENCES

Allan, B. V. (1978) *Logical Spelling*. Glasgow and London: Collins.

Bannatyne, A. (1968) Diagnosing learning disabilities and writing remedial prescriptions. *J. Learning Disabilities*, **1** (4), 28–35.

Conrad, R. (1964) Acoustic confusion in immediate memory. *Brit. J. Psychol.*, **55**, 75–84.

Cotterell, G. C. (1970) Teaching procedures. In A. W. Franklin and S. Naidoo (eds.) *Assessment and Teaching of Dyslexic Children*, pp. 49–70. London: Invalid Children's Aid Association.

Critchley, M. (1970) *The Dyslexic Child*. London: Heinemann Medical Books.

Critchley, M. and Critchley, E. A. (1978) *Dyslexia Defined*. London: Heinemann Medical Books.

De Leeuw, E. and De Leeuw, M. (1965) *Read Better, Read Faster*. Harmondsworth: Penguin.

Done, D. J. and Miles, T. R. (1978) Learning, memory and dyslexia. In M. M. Gruneberg, P. E. Morris and R. N. Sykes (eds.). *Practical Aspects of Memory*, London: Academic Press.

Ellis, N. C. (1980) Functional analyses of reading and short-term memory in dyslexic children (Doctorate dissertation, University of Wales).

Ellis, N. C., Baddeley, A. D., Miles, T. R. and Lewis, V. (in preparation) Limitations in reading ability and short-term memory span.

Ellis, N. C. and Miles, T. R. (1977) Dyslexia as a limitation in the ability to process information, *Bull. Orton Soc.*, **XXVII**, 72–81.

Ellis, N. C. and Miles, T. R. (1978a) Visual information processing as a determinant of reading speed, *J. Reading Res.*, **1** (2), 108–120.

Ellis, N. C. and Miles, T. R. (1978b) Visual information processing in dyslexic children. In M. M. Gruneberg, P. E. Morris and R. N. Sykes (eds.) *Practical Aspects of Memory*, London: Academic Press.

Gillingham, A. and Stillman, B. E. (1956) *Remedial Training for Children with Specific Disability in Reading, Spelling and Penmanship*. Cambridge, Mass.: Educators Publishing Service Inc.

Griffiths, J. M. (1976) Dyslexia and dyscalculia. Unpublished paper delivered at a conference organised by the University College of North Wales Dyslexia Unit.

Head, H. (1926) *Aphasia and Kindred Disorders of Speech*. London: Macmillan.

Hermann, K. and Norrie, E. (1958) Is congenital word-blindness a hereditary type of Gerstmann's syndrome? *Psychiat. Neurolog.*, **136**, 59–73.

Hickey, K. (1977) *Dyslexia. A Language Training Course for Teachers and Learners*, 3 Montague Road, London SW19.

Hornsby, B. and Miles, T. R. (1980) The effects of a dyslexia-centred teaching programme. *Brit. J. Educ. Psychol.*, **50**, 236–242.

Hornsby, B. and Shear, F. (1977) *Alpha to Omega*. London: Heinemann Educational.

Jansen, M. (1973) In J. Downing (ed.) *Comparative Reading*. New York Macmillan, pp. 285–307.

MacMeeken, M. (1939) *Ocular Dominance in Relation to Developmental Aphasia*, London: University of London Press.

Makita, K. (1968) The rarity of reading disability in Japanese children, *Amer. J. Orthopsychiat.*, **38**, 599–614.

Marcel, A. (1978) Prerequisites for a more applicable psychology of reading, In M. M. Gruneberg, P. E. Morris and R. N. Sykes (eds.) *Practical Aspects of Memory*, London: Academic Press.

Miles, T. R. (1961) Two cases of developmental aphasia. *J. Child Psycholog. Psychiat.*, 48–70.

Miles, T. R. (1970) *On Helping the Dyslexic Child*, London: Methuen Educational.

Miles, T. R. (1978) *Understanding Dyslexia*. London: Hodder and Stoughton.

Miles, T. R. (1979) Dyslexia as a limitation in short-term memory. Unpublished talk delivered at St Bartholomew's Hospital, London.

Miles, T. R. and Miles, E. (1975) *More Help for Dyslexic Children*. London: Methuen Educational.

Miles, T. R. and Wheeler, T. J. (1974) Towards a new theory of dyslexia. *Dyslexia Rev.*, **11**, 9–11.

Moyle, D. (1968) *The Teaching of Reading*. London: Ward Lock Educational.

Naidoo, S. (1972) *Specific Dyslexia*. London: Pitman Press.

Orton, S. T. (1937) *Reading, Writing and Speech Problems in Children*. New York: W. W. Norton and Co.

Pollock, J. (1978) *Signposts to Spelling*. London: Helen Arkell Dyslexia Centre.

Quinault, F. (1972) Cross associations, opposites and reversibility. Unpublished paper, University of St Andrews.

Raven, J. C. (1965) *Advanced Progressive Matrices, Sets I and II*. London: H. K. Lewis and Co.

Rawson, M. B. (1970) The structure of English: the language to be learned. *Bull. Orton Soc.*, **XX**, 103–123.

Reid, J. (ed.) (1972) *Reading: Problems and Practices*. London: Ward Lock Educational.

Rugel, R. P. (1974) W.I.S.C. sub-test scores of disabled readers. *J. Learning Disabilities*, 7, 48–55.

Smelt, E. D. (1972) *How to Speak, Read and Spell*. Melbourne: Melbourne YMCA.

Smelt, E. D. (1976) *Speak, Spell and Read English*. Victoria, Australia: Longman Australia Pty Ltd.

Spache, G. D. (1976) *Investigating the Issues of Reading Disabilities*. Boston: Allyn and Bacon.

Spring, C. and Capps, C. (1974) Encoding speed, rehearsal, and probed recall of dyslexic boys. *J. Educ. Psychol.*, **66**, 780–786.

Stratton, G. M. (1897) Vision without inversion of the retinal image. *Psychol. Rev.*, **4**, 341–360. Cited in R. J. Herrnstein and E. G. Boring (eds.) *A Sourcebook in the History of Psychology*. Cambridge, Mass.: Harvard University Press, 1965.

Vellutino, F. R. (1978) Towards an understanding of dyslexia: psychological factors in specific reading disability. In A. L. Benton and D. Pearl (eds.) *Dyslexia: An Appraisal of Current Knowledge*. New York: Oxford University Press.

Vellutino, F. R., Harding, C. J., Phillips, F. and Steger, J. A. (1975) Differential transfer in poor and normal readers, *J. Genetic Psychol.*, **126**, 3–18.

Vernon, M. D. (1971) *Reading and Its Difficulties*. Cambridge: Cambridge University Press.

Zangwill, O. L. (1962) Dyslexia in relation to cerebral dominance. In J. Money (ed.) *Reading Disability*. Baltimore: Johns Hopkins Press.

Dyslexia Research and its Applications to Education
Edited by G. Th. Pavlidis and T. R. Miles
© 1981 John Wiley & Sons Ltd.

CHAPTER 10

A Study of Dyslexic Weaknesses and the Consequences for Teaching

ELAINE MILES

If we look at the written work of dyslexic children we find that its most striking characteristic is the lack of correspondence between the letters on the page and the sounds made in saying the words. Similarly we find that when they read there is a mismatch between the sounds which they say and the letters or combinations of letters which appear in the book. Their weakness in literacy skills is thus of a particular kind—a weakness in the coding and decoding aspects of reading and spelling.

In many cases it seems that they have not picked up even basic spelling conventions, their matching of letters to sounds being crude at best. This can be seen, for example, by reference to Figure 10.1 which shows the performance on the Schonell S1 spelling test of a boy aged $8\frac{1}{2}$, reported as having a full-scale IQ of 135, and of a girl aged 15 whose verbal IQ was given as 120. The boy has added *ll* to the end of the word *four*, although there is no *l* sound in that word, and has written the same vowel for *lid* as for *let*. The girl has transposed, omitted, and substituted letters, particularly in the ninth and tenth rows, and for *through* has produced what seems to be a mix-up of the letters of *through* and *threw*, with the *r* out of order near the end. Even at the age of 15 she is unable to spell the word *talk*. Both children have written *b* for *d*, thus in fact writing a letter that represents the wrong sound. (That *b* is a mirror-image of *d* is another issue, which will be discussed later in this chapter).

The writing of *pes sasne* for *police station* (by a girl aged 10, IQ given as 116 +) is an example of the same tendency. In this case, despite some attempt at phonetic representation, she has left out the *l* in *police* and and *t* from the blend, *st*, in *station*.

Sometimes there are even more extreme cases of mismatching. The following mistakes were made by three different children:

    eged   *(edge)*,   *lil*   *(ill)*,   *witer*   *(write)*

Here the letters written are the correct ones, and after the event it seems almost as

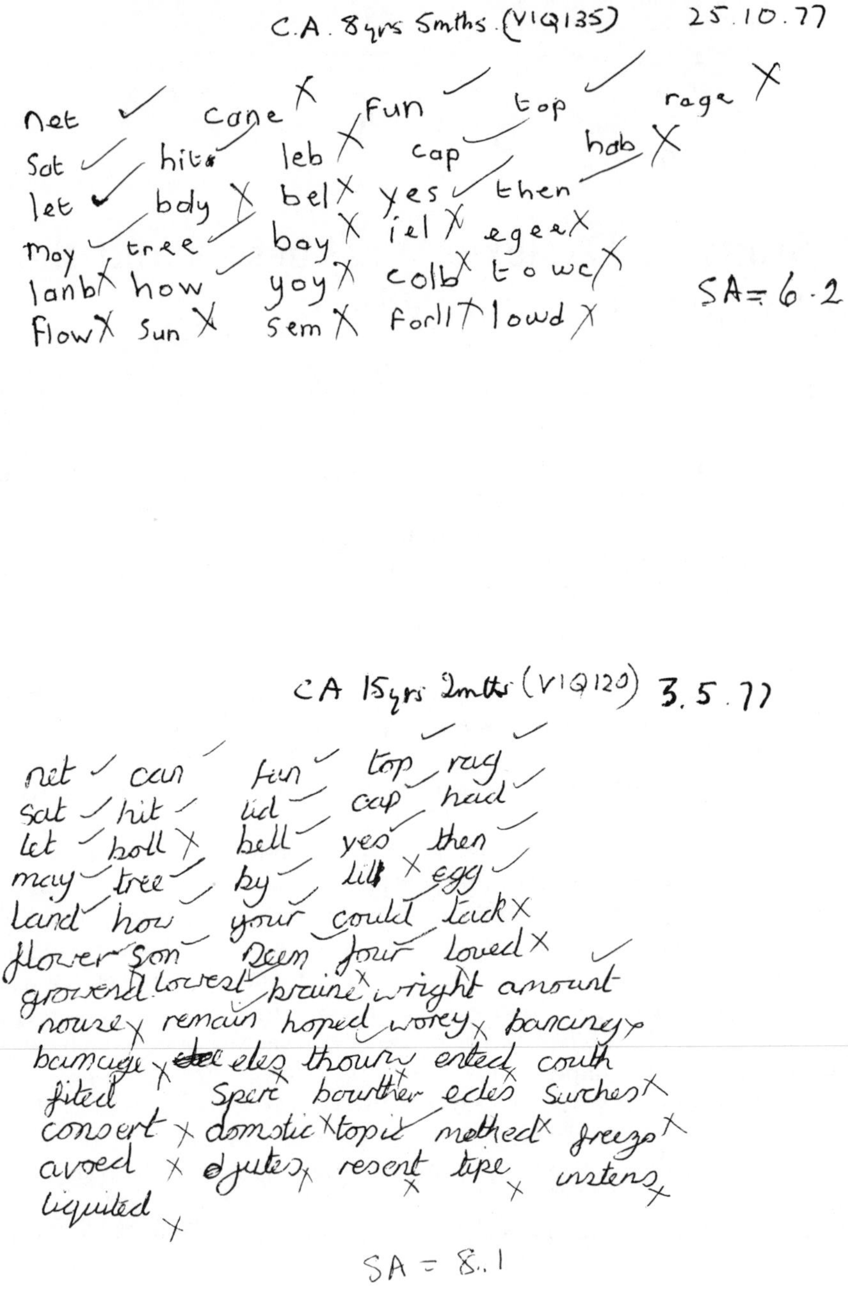

C.A. 8yrs 5mths. (VIQ 135)   25.10.77

net ✓   cane ✗   fun ✓   top ✓   rage ✗
Sat ✓   hit   leb ✗   cap ✓   hab ✗
let ✓   bdy ✗   bel ✗   yes ✓   then ✓
moy ✓   tree ✓   boy ✗   iel ✗   egea ✗
lanb ✗   how ✓   yoy ✗   colb ✗   to wc ✗
flow ✗   sun ✗   sem ✗   forll ↑   lowd ✗

SA = 6·2

CA 15yrs 2mths (VIQ 120)   3.5.77

net ✓   can ✓   fun ✓   top ✓   rag ✓
Sat ✓   hit ✓   lid ✓   cap ✓   had ✓
let ✓   boll ✗   bell ✓   yes ✓   then ✓
may ✓   tree ✓   by ✓   lilt ✗   egg ✓
land ✓   how ✓   your ✓   could ✓   lack ✗
flover ✗   son ✓   deem ✓   four ✓   loved ✗   ✓
groverd ✗   lovest ✓   braine ✗   wright ✓   amount ✓
nourse ✗   remain ✓   hoped ✓   worey ✗   bancing ✗
bamage ✗   eleg ✗   thoury ✗   ented ✓   couth ✗
fited ✓   spare ✓   bowther ✗   edles ✗   surches ✗
consert ✗   domstic ✗   topic ✗   methed ✗   freizp ✗
avoed ✗   djutes ✗   resent ✗   tipe ✗   unstens ✗
liquited ✗

SA = 8.1

Figure 10.1

if the writer might have known how to spell the word but got the order wrong in putting down the letters. However this was not the impression given to an observer at the time: the children wrote haltingly, and both the *d* at the end of *eged* and *r* at the end of *witer* were added after a pause, as an afterthought; they seemed to write *ege* and *wite*—and then to realize that there should have been a *d somewhere* and an *r somewhere* without being able to place them correctly.

Spelling of this sort has been termed 'bizarre' (Miles, 1970) and is rather different from 'poor' spelling by non-dyslexic children, who in general get the odd letter wrong in places where they cannot check by sound but know perfectly well where the letter should go, such as *discription* for *description* and *seperate* for *separate*. They tend to use an English spelling pattern which is possible and is in fact correct in some other word for the same sound combinations. For instance, in the last two examples, *dis* is a common English prefix found in, for instance, dis*continue* and dis*perse*, but it is the wrong one for *description* since the *s* belongs to the second half of the word (*scription*) and the prefix is in fact *de*; likewise *-erate* is a perfectly possible English spelling pattern found in *mod*erate and *lit*erate, but is the wrong pattern for *separate*, where the *p* belongs not with the prefix *se*-but with the second half, *-parate* (also found in *disparate*). The spelling therefore is wrong but plausible. Thus it is apparent that in the case of non-dyslexic children a basic knowledge of spelling patterns is revealed even in the errors.

When they read, dyslexic children sometimes fail to say the word which is actually on the page; instead they say another word of similar meaning often having some phonetic elements in common with the correct word. One source of difficulty is the fact that the stress in English is usually on the first syllable of a word, and since dyslexic children are seldom very flexible in their approach they find it difficult to adapt when the stress is elsewhere. Thus one of my pupils read *probably* for *particularly*, while many have difficulty, when doing the Schonell R1 test, over *canary* and *heroic*. I remember an intelligent boy who, faced with *heroic*, said to me, 'I know that word—it means "brave", doesn't it?, but he still could not *say* the right word. (The corresponding noun, *hero*, where the stress is on the first syllable, is, of course, much more familiar in conversation and may have interfered with the response).

Sometimes there is partial decoding but the pupil is ultimately defeated by some phonetic difficulty. Thus a clever 11-year old, reading a book which was somewhat too hard for him, made the following mistakes: *Sunday* for *Saturday*, *his mother* for *Mrs Jones* (when Mrs Jones was the mother in the context), *said* when the word in the book was *replied* or *asked*, and *pins and needles* for *aches and pains in his legs*. It seems likely, in the case of the word *Saturday*, that the *ur* in an unstressed syllable, which has to be pronounced as a 'schwa', was a source of difficulty to him, and that knowing that a day of some sort was needed he substituted another day also beginning with *s*. Similarly the written word *Mrs* does not seem to correspond with the sound of *mother*, but it could have suggested the word, since he knew the kind of person the word stood for. In the case of both *replied* and *asked* it seems as though he knew that both words denoted speech in the past tense; the phonetic difficulties, however, defeated him: in the word *replied* the stress is shifted to the second syllable and *asked* is in fact a one-syllable word but does not look like one. The final example is particularly interesting. The words *aches and pains* were at the end of a line in the book, the rest of the phrase being on the next line. It seemed to me likely, as I observed him, that he had understood the sense of the sentence but had failed to decode *aches* (a difficult word), had then slightly misinterpreted *pains* (as *pins*), and, running his eyes frantically to and fro along the next line, had got the sense of the kind of aches and pains involved and then produced something which made sense.

This situation is different in some ways from that in which a brain-damaged patient makes a so-called 'semantic' error, such as *crocus* for *tulip* (compare Coltheart, 1979). There is no particular *phonetic* problem over *tulip*, nor is it phonetically similar to *crocus*. The patient in question, like my own pupil, must have had some idea of the correct semantic category to which the word belonged, and he may even have been helped by visualization, since a crocus has a similar shape to a tulip, but he seems to have made no attempt at decoding. In contrast the dyslexic pupil does not *totally* lack decoding skills; it is rather that they are poorly developed.

Errors such as those described above are sometimes described as 'sequencing difficulties'. This description, however, encourages us to think in purely visual terms and thus ignores the essential feature of what has gone wrong.

Imagine for a moment that I am springcleaning a room, and that when I start to put the furniture back I leave the table upside down, the mirror facing the wall and the hearthrug draped over the mantelpiece. My mistakes *could* be described as errors in ordering or arrangement. It is more important, however, to indicate that I have put the pieces back in positions where they cannot perform their proper functions. So it is with letters in a word, which are there to perform a function—that of representing the sounds of speech. Writing a word (spelling) is not just a visual sequencing activity; the serial order is determined at the auditory–vocal level (Bannatyne, 1973), and indeed I shall later put the point that it is at that level that the difficulty may well first manifest itself. For now, I merely want to stress, like Bannatyne, that the only connection between the written letters in a word is in their auditory reference, and that it is misleading to describe the jumbled letters of a dyslexic pupil's spelling in exclusively visual terms.

The term 'mirror-writing' is another case of a misleading, purely visual, description which has perhaps been used somewhat uncritically. Even if what a child has written on his book looks totally or in part like what you see when you hold ordinary writing up to a mirror, this description bears no relation to the process of producing it. Although such cases intrigued Dr Orton and influenced his theories, it is rare to find a dyslexic pupil who sets out methodically and consistently to write from right to left. I remember teaching one such child, a girl of $8\frac{1}{2}$, who was left-handed and wrote letters starting from the right, doing so quite naturally and legibly. As a result, however, she was at odds with the class and showed many signs of frustration. It was a hard battle, even at this age, to train her to make the necessary change; but when this was achieved she was able to make progress in both reading and spelling, and the isolation and feelings of frustration began to disappear. These extreme cases are rare, however; and most of the examples of so-called 'mirror-writing' are produced by children who are not very well coordinated and who, lacking the help which they need over letter production, have started letters in the wrong place; this can result in some of these letters coming out backwards or even upside down. The mistakes appear to be somewhat accidental, and the child himself is often confused, particularly if a different letter emerges from the one intended, *b* for *d*, for instance. (Since *d* is the only letter with an upright which does not start at the top, the mistake is easily made: starting at the top begins a confusion which then becomes general.) Whereas in writing a child may evade the issue by using capitals, he cannot evade it in reading. Alas, in this confused state he may arrive at that traumatic stage in primary school when he has to switch to 'double writing' and change the starting place of the letter again to include a preliminary upstroke from the line, when he becomes still more unsure as to what he is trying to achieve.

It is also unfortunate that another term, 'reversal', is frequently used to refer, without distinction, to two different situations—one in which there is incorrect orientation of individual letters such as I have described and the other in which the letters of a word are transposed, as when *brian* is written for *brain*. Underlying the latter sort of mistake is a misunderstanding of spelling convention or sound–symbol correspondence. Thus it is probable that the writer of *brian* does not understand that *ai* is a representation of a long *a* sound. In fact the first letter of this vowel combination indicates the overall vowel category; this is common practice in English and finds expression in the tag 'Where two vowels go walking, the first does the talking'; *ia*, on the other hand, is a combination of two separate vowels, as in *dial*, and is never a vowel digraph. Misunderstanding of the way in which letters in a word correspond to its sound is a different problem from letter production, even if some children have both problems.

Failure to observe the distinction between these different situations is once more the result of an exclusively visual approach to the child's errors. It is helpful as a corrective to take into account the research on audiovisual integration in reading (for details see Bryant, 1975) and the already quoted work of Bannatyne (1973) in which the importance of the auditory–visual link is always kept in mind. As has been stressed, the whole basis for the correct visual ordering of the letters is the pattern of sounds to which they are related, and the dyslexic child often seems to fail to make the necessary associations. It seems from more recent research described by Bryant that retarded readers are equally deficient at making associations intramodally; however, the association to be made in spelling and basic reading skills is, of course, an audiovisual one.

It is possible that the reason why dyslexic children have not built up such associations is a failure to do some kind of verbal labelling of incoming data, similar to that suggested to retarded readers by Fearn in his modification of Birch and Belmont's auditory–visual integration task (Cashdan, 1977). Fearn found that to say 'That was two taps and then two taps' helped such children to make the match between an auditory pattern and a visual pattern in front of them, thus improving their performance to a level nearer that of good readers of similar age and intelligence. One can hardly avoid the conclusion that the good readers were spontaneously 'labelling' in some such way.

My initial description of dyslexic weaknesses has been confined to the characteristics noticeable in their reading and writing. The question next arises whether it is possible to widen this description so as to include other difficulties. There is some relevant evidence on this point in a research study undertaken at the Word Blind Centre (Naidoo, 1972).

Naidoo reports that the scores of both dyslexic groups (reading retardates and spelling retardates) were significantly lower than the control groups on certain items of the Wechsler Intelligence Scale for Children: Information, Arithmetic, Digit Span, and Coding. Perhaps the score on Information, particularly low in the case of reading retardates, is only to be expected, since an important source of information is cut off for those who cannot attempt any reading beyond the level of a school graded reader. In the case of one dyslexic pupil whom I taught, a low score on both Vocabulary and Information had brought his Verbal IQ score down to 100, compared with a Performance IQ score of 125, when he was tested at the age of $13\frac{1}{2}$ years. Yet he did not seem at all the sort of boy to have that balance of abilities, being noticeably unmechanical and uninterested in craft work; and in the course of time he manifested a passion for reference books. However, when originally tested his reading age had been only just over 6 years; and the absence of a normal family life (he was in a children's home) might well also partially explain his poor vocabulary. Thus a low Information score need not necessarily indicate a distinctively dyslexic weakness, although low scores on the other three tests may possibly do so.

In a recent talk on tape in a Short Talk Series (Vernon, 1978) Professor Vernon discussed the two main types of severely backward reader that were extracted from a cluster analysis of scores on various tests in the case of 98 dyslexic boys at the Word Blind Centre (there was considerable overlap between groups). One group (6%), which Vernon describes as being deficient in performing visual tasks, she lists as having the following characteristic weaknesses: difficulty 'in analysing and constructing complex visual forms' and 'in remembering forms presented sequentially one after another'; 'directional confusion' (exemplified in confusion over reversible letters and words), and 'difficulties in grasping other kinds of direction' (exemplified in an inability to point with the left hand to the right eye of someone facing them).

Some of these features appear also in Johnson and Myklebust's (1967) list of characteristics of those whom they call 'visual dyslexics', although the last two are not included there.

On a closer examination, however, it is by no means certain that the *specific* point of difficulty in all these cases is essentially a visual one. Dyslexic pupils do not seem to be inferior at all visual discrimination tasks, but only at certain kinds. Thus, according to Ellis and Miles (1978), when pairs of capital letters were exhibited tachistoscopically, or pairs of geometrical straight-lined figures of the same or different orientation, dyslexic children were on average not appreciably slower than controls in saying whether the members of the pair were the same or different; but when one capital and one lower case letter were used, so that something more than a visual match was involved, the differences between the groups were much greater. In another experiment (Done and Miles, 1978), dyslexic subjects were significantly slower than controls at arranging digits or pictures in the correct order but both groups were almost equally slow when nonsense shapes were used. Moreover Done and Miles report that when verbal labelling was largely eliminated by the technique known as 'articulatory suppression' (the subjects having to say the word 'the' aloud while the stimuli were being presented) differences between the two groups became minimal. On the other hand Myklebust says that those whom he grouped as 'visual dyslexics' were poor at performing the sort of visual discrimination task in which the twin of a lower case letter given at the beginning of a row has to be identified among a whole row of lower case letters (for an example of a similar task see Figure 10.2). Here, however, some 'carry over or retention in the mind of the original letter is clearly needed and this could require verbal labelling as well as visual recognition.

It has also been doubted whether the sort of directional confusion involved in being unable to point with one's left hand to the right eye of someone facing is a purely visual matter, or rather the result of the complex memory load involved in making the adjustments (Miles and Wheeler, 1974). It might then be a similar difficulty to that involved in reciting tables, when the progression of the multiplicand has to be kept in mind as well as the progression of the answers to the multiplication sums. As I have said, Myklebust does not mention this sort of left–right confusion among deficiencies of what he terms 'visual dyslexics', and indeed when Shute and Graham (1977) did a cluster analysis of 99 boys at a school in Sussex, they found 'directional difficulties' to be closely related to 'poor auditory ability', both being among the core features, while 'poor visual ability' came in a different and more peripheral group. It has already been pointed out that *b* and *d* confusion is not a purely visual matter but is connected with letter production in writing and that such errors in orientation of letters are different in kind from writing the letters of a word in the wrong order. Reading or writing *was*

b	p b d g p b q
u	v u m u n w u
a	o d a c a e o
h	t h n k h l k
o	a c a e o c e
d	p d g d p d p
k	h t k l f k h
m	m n w u m h u
l	k i l t h f l

Figure 10.2.

(Reproduced by permission of London Borough of Barking Schools Psychological Service)

for *saw* is a transposition of letters just as is writing *lil* for *ill*. If the transposition results in a recognized word it is more likely to be accepted by the writer, but that does not make it a 'visual' error as such; it might rather be a reason for judging the pupil to be less severely dyslexic than the writer of a jumble of letters which do not represent the sounds of any word at all. There is no necessity to interpret reading *was* for *saw* as a *directional* confusion.

Another example of a restrictively visual approach is the glib use of the term 'visual memory' in relation to matters which are far from purely visual. I once set out to drive through the North Wales mountains from home, a route that I knew, as they say, 'by heart', since it is the direct route into England. On this occasion, however, for the first time, I wanted to post a letter. Vivid though my visual memory of the route seemed to be, rich in detail of bridges, winding roads, villages and isolated farmhouses, I searched it in vain for a recollection of a letterbox! Letterboxes had never been significant to me on previous trips because I normally posted my letters at home before I left and I therefore had not noticed them. In a similar way a child who writes *together* and *aside* as separate words may be doing so because grammatical distinctions which made the sentence nonsense as written were not significant to him, and in that case it is misleading to say just that he has a poor visual memory. It is possible that he did not understand the difference between an infinitive such as *to gather* (two words) and an adverb *together*, or between *aside* (adverb) and *a side*. These differences are in fact reflected by slight differences of stress in speech; for instance in the sentences, 'He turned aside' and 'He turned a side of amateurs into the top team in the country', we say *aside* differently from *a side*. It is possible, then, that failure to notice when *aside* is written as one word betrays *cognitive* deficiencies, and that these could in fact have been exhibited in listening as well as in looking. Similarly if a pupil reads *walking* for *walked* a contributory factor may be that he is not conscious of the difference in function between *-ing* and *-ed* endings.

With regard to a second, larger group of difficulties mentioned by Professor Vernon (31% of the World Blind Centre dyslexic pupils), it is to be noted that she does not call them 'auditory difficulties' but 'deficiencies in language' even though listening is clearly involved in reproducing speech. However, in auditory discrimination and visual discrimination there is always a cognitive element, which often goes unrecognized. When, for instance, we listen to the sounds of the letters *c* and *g* in their 'hard' pronunciation, there are always slight differences according to what vowels follow. For instance the *c* in *scatter* is pronounced further forward in the mouth than the *c* in *scuttle*. Such differences we learn to ignore, although they can be heard, and we expect both *c*s to be judged to be virtually the same sound and the difference from *g* to be thought of as the only significant one. However a Welsh-speaking child sees words which originally begin with a *c* constantly changed to begin with a *g* (soft mutation). In Welsh, too, a *c* is pronounced with an explosive burst which *g* does not have, and *sc* and *sk* are represented by *sg* in words derived from English (for example *sgriw* for *screw* and *sgyrt* for *skirt*), possibly because the English *c* lacks that explosive burst and the sound is therefore felt to be nearer to a *g*. Is the *sg* then the same sound as the English *sc* or *sk* equivalent or not? Obviously the Welsh child's *expectations* when listening to a *c* or *g* are rather different and his judgement of sounds will be influenced by this.

Expectations may also be affected by what a child has seen. Thus he may not have noticed that he is saying *lickle* while others say *little* until his attention is drawn to the *t*s in the word in front of him.

Indeed, many factors seem to be involved in poor performance at so-called 'auditory discrimination' tests. I once watched a severely dyslexic child with obvious articulatory deficiencies being asked in a lesson (not in test conditions) whether pairs of words ended in the same sound or not. On several occasions he hesitated, and this hesitation resulted in his losing his recollection of the sounds. He seemed to need to repeat the words to himself first, and once, when these were difficult to pronounce, he cried out in exasperation 'But I can't *say* those words'—and that seemed to make it impossible for him to answer. A momentary lapse of concentration could well have interfered more than once. If a child gives the wrong answer in such tests this does not establish that a weakness is involved which is specifically auditory.

Yet the simple labels given to some of these tests may mislead us into thinking that they sum up all the factors involved. The titles given to the 'Visual Sequential Memory Test' and the 'Auditory Sequential Memory Test' in the Illinois Test of Psycholinguistic Abilities (I.T.P.A.) (McCarthy and Kirk, 1961) imply that the only differences between them are in the sensory channel used, although this is not so. In the auditory test the items are given over intervals of time, whereas in the visual test they are all presented simultaneously and removed together; but, as Spache (1976, p. 159) points out, these tests are widely used as a basis for distinguishing what are supposed to be auditory and visual disabilities.

There are certainly differences of severity among dyslexic pupils, and the more severe cases often have histories of delayed speech and/or current minor speech defects. They perform poorly when asked to say whether, for example, *bat* and *pat* are the same or different, and they may often be difficult to distinguish from children with known past auditory problems. (However the latter seem to progress much more rapidly, as if their problems are in the past and the deficiency not permanent). Any child who has had difficulties on his earlier matching task, matching his own speech to the speech which he hears, is necessarily handicapped when he comes to learn to read and write, since it is on that foundation that the early skills of reading and spelling are built. Wisbey (1979) has put forward the point that appreciation of pitch is vital: 'The ability to learn pitched sounds is vital for language development because the very language we must learn is made up of varying-pitched sounds. All vowels are in fact musical chords'.

For severely dyslexic children it may even be necessary to begin with whole-word labelling of pictures of objects to establish the one-to-one relationship of single word and single object. This, however, is because they have not reached the stage at which they recognize that speech is made up of units which we call 'words'; and in that case what they need is work at a more basic stage rather than a 'different method'. Even if tuition starts at this level, however, such children must in the end come to phonic analysis, although it may be hard to convince them that analysis and syllabification are the necessary road to success. It is in fact noticeable that many of these severely dyslexic children are reluctant to do phonic work or oral spelling even though they are ready to chatter away about their own outside activities. One such pupil recently said to me that he could spell better by writing down words than by saying the letters orally, and so, he said, could his father. When I tested this theory, however, it turned out to be mistaken. He certainly found it easier to write down a succession of letters, without giving them any serious thought, than to say letters aloud, but he could not correct his mistakes. I found it best, therefore, to encourage him to write the word and then to study it carefully with a view to spelling it back to me aloud, since in these conditions he gave the analysis his full attention and did some precise oral work besides.

It appears that all children, not just dyslexics, may learn better in one modality than in another. Field trials with the Mills Learning Methods Test and the experimental Peabody Differential Learning Test are said by Spache (1976,

p. 104) to have shown that 'the most effective modality can be established for many but not all children (the modality seeming to be of little importance among children of high mental ability, and the auditory seeming to be least effective among low-ability pupils)'. It is possible therefore that dyslexic children are particularly weak in their non-preferred modality without necessarily having a specific limitation in one modality.

It may be that even in cases where there is no recorded history of speech delays or evidence of speech defects the difficulties in reading and spelling were preceded by deficincies over spoken language. In a recent study of twenty adolescent dyslexic boys Stirling (1978) found evidence, even at this age, of linguistic uncertainty, mispronunciation, wrong use of words and failure to complete sentences. The boys nevertheless succeeded in making themselves fully understood and could give just as many correct answers on the technical names of parts of objects (the tooth of a comb, for example) as did a control group.

In short, the weaknesses of dyslexic children may not be specifically auditory or visual; it may rather be that the more severe cases are related to more severe language deficiencies. As Professor Vernon (1978) puts it, 'It seems possible therefore that the fundamental deficiencies in severely backward readers lie not in visual and auditory memory as such, but in the reasoning processes which are necessary to acquire the visual and auditory associations on which reading is based'.

Weaknesses in performing a mental operation while holding another in mind could be due to a failure to do some sort of verbal labelling (compare Miles and Ellis, Chapter 9 of this volume). This might account for low digit span, poor performance in reciting tables, and even possibly poor performance in tests which involve 'carrying over' a symbol for comparison with another one some distance away as in Myklebust's task (see p. 251) and in the exercise illustrated in Figure 10.2.

The system of association between the sounds of speech and the written symbol is indeed a complex one, especially in an irregular language like English. The following inconsistencies, which most of us have managed to master tolerably well, are a real source of bewilderment to dyslexic children.

(1) Vowels as visual symbols have no distinguishing visual feature from consonants, yet they perform a different function, appearing usually in the middle of a syllable, with consonants closing them in on either side. There must in fact be a vowel in every syllable. Vowel letters are not differentiated by differences in their production as are vowel sounds in speech and we have to learn to use them differently from consonant letters and to uderstand the relationship between vowels and consonants in the structure of a word.

(2) Some consonant letters are paired to represent a sound (for example, *th*, *ch*, *sh*), yet there is nothing to indicate that they are forming a pair rather than functioning as separate letters, as they may do elsewhere. Thus the *th* in *bother* has a different function from the adjacent *t* and *h* in *penthouse*.

(3) Some vowel letters, too, are paired to represent a single sound, yet the same letters may elsewhere be functioning separately. Thus the *ea* in *meat* has a different function from the adjacent *e* and *a* in *create*, while the *ea* in *manageable* is different again.

(4) Some pairs of vowels are split by a consonant in writing, so that the order no longer reflects the order in speech which has the consonant sound last. Thus the *a* and *e* in *gate* are separated by the *t*, unlike the *a* and *i* in *gait*.

(5) Some combinations represent a number of different sounds on different occasions, for instance, *bear, hear, heart, hearse*.

(6) Sometimes consonants appear in writing which do not represent any sound in the original word, for instance *knife, wrong, pneumatic*; and sometimes a consonant can influence a vowel sound even when not pronounced itself. For example the silent *g* in *sign* is preceded by a long *i* sound, in contrast with the short *i* which appears before the *g* in *signal*.

(7) In an unstressed syllable, particularly at the end of a word, a vowel may lose its full value in speech (becoming a 'schwa') yet is still represented by a variety of vowels in writing, for instance *butt*on, *tart*an, *batt*en, *rais*in.

(8) In an unstressed syllable, particularly at the end of a word, corruption of the sound may bring it about that a consonant–vowel combination in writing stands for a purely consonantal sound, as if it were a consonant diagraph, such as *pa*tient, *sol*dier, *na*ture.

These subtleties of correspondence are absorbed for the most part by a normal child in the course of time, and he makes his own rough generalizations. In the case of dyslexic children, however, they have to be 'spelled out' in detail. The English spelling system is very complicated and difficult for a dyslexic child to master, whether for reading or writing purposes.

Yet it is necessary for the talented dyslexic child to master it to the standard needed for success in an O level or at least a CSE form if he is to make use of his other abilities, and he needs to be at quite a high level of literacy from the moment he enters secondary school. To reach this level quickly he must necessarily be taught in the most economical and purposeful way, since, because he is retarded, he has to advance at a faster rate than his peers even though he is handicapped and they are not.

The advantage of a structured phonic programme is that it takes account of his weaknesses and uses his strengths. In particular he is almost certain to be weak at rote learning yet is often very strong in reasoning; and a programme of this sort eliminates the need for the one while enabling him to make good use of the other. Then since his ideas on sound–letter correspondence are confused, he needs a programme which is systematic and proceeds logically, with reading and spelling supporting each other. Finally, because such a programme involves an ordered series of stages, the rate at which he proceeds can be controlled to suit his individual needs.

Various additional aids have been devised to help the assimilation of the spelling complexities which I have described above. One of these is colour-coding. Colour can be valuable in stressing fundamental distinctions, such as that between vowels and consonants, but if the colour-code is complex it involves memorizing the significance of a large number of colours, which defeats the objective. This is perhaps the difficulty in Gattegno's (1962) system, *Words in Colour*. The International Teaching Alphabet (i.t.a.) similarly has a large number of symbols to memorize, with their corresponding sounds, and this has often defeated severely dyslexic children; traditional orthography has fewer symbols and the system can be built up gradually. Although shifting to traditional orthography from I.T.A. may not be hard for the normal child, it can be confusing for the dyslexic child in that it involves building up a new system of associations. Pictures may help, when used sparingly, but only if they are genuinely making the bridge between sounds and letters and helping to build up the associations; after that they need to be discarded. A programme which constantly underlines the characteristics of the spoken word is perhaps most helpful of all. Phonic programmes have specific devices for stressing the links between the letters and the sounds in the form of routine phonic drills or 'linkages' as in the Gillingham and Stillman (1956) programme. Teachers of such programmes ask for dictated sentences to be repeated back by the pupil before they are written and to be read aloud after they were written; and they require pupils to respond with phonemes to the graphemes on cards (letters, digraphs, and blends). In this way they constantly require the pupil to make the necessary links between sound and symbol.

To appreciate what has to be specifically taught to the pupil the teacher may often have to try to think his own thought processes aloud, making explicit the steps which he himself takes for granted. I recently taught a boy of 9 years old, of average ability, who had failed to read or spell any words from the Schonell tests. In 4 years at school he had not grasped the principles either of consonant digraphs or vowel digraphs but only of single letters corresponding to single sounds. Although he soon learned the *th* sound, he was still at a loss immediately afterwards when he met *Th*, despite the fact that he knew in principle when to use capital letters and how to write them. (Indeed it is reasonable to wonder why it is not *TH* that is written). An adult literacy teacher once wrote to say that a pupil about 20 years old had now mastered three-letter words, but could not read *the*. I suggested that she should explain to him the consonant digraph *th* and call his attention to the facts (a) that vowel sounds are different at the end of a word, and (b) that we say *the* and *a* so frequently that we do not pronounce them fully, except when we are emphasizing them (as in '*the* book on the subject is . . . '). That was an extreme case, but it is common to find adult illiterates preoccupied with the names of the letters, having never come to grips with sound–symbol correspondence.

The teacher needs to be clear and explicit about irregular words. Far from being words from another planet, as sometimes seems to be suggested, and not comparable with regular words, they are constructed just like regular words and have a clear system of sound–symbol correspondence. The pattern is just less common in some respects that that in so-called 'regular' words, and it is helpful to make clear in what respect this is so. Thus the word *laugh* is not just a fortuitous combination of letters: it begins with a consonant, *l*, followed by a vowel digraph *au*, and ends in a consonant digraph, *gh*; *gh* for *f* is not unique but occurs in a few other words of Anglo-Saxon origin, for instance *cough* and *rough*, while *au*, though usually sounded like *aw*, occasionally represents *ah* as in this case and in the word *draught*. It is a word which has to be learned specially, but it need not be learned without understanding, for intelligent children remember better if they understand. Similarly in the word *people* everything is perfectly regular except the vowel digraph used for the long *e* sound: the word as a whole is not irregular.

Handwriting is involved on only one side of the double process which comprises reading and writing, but it is an essential prerequisite for literacy that the letters can be written down easily and fluently. If the child cannot do this he cannot give his attention to what he is using the letters to represent, and the discrepancy between what he writes and what he sees on the page is too great for him to have any clear concept of a letter's shape. Normally then, and especially with young children, it is vital to get the letter production correct very early on.

In planning a structured phonic programme, sophisticated linguistics are not always the best guide. This is because precision of scientific description is not what is needed. But development of a methodical way of thinking in the child. Although it may be linguistically and historically correct to describe the vowel sound in *game* as a long single vowel *a* (with the *e* simply having a function), Gillingham and Stillman (1956) seem on much sounder pedagogical ground in teaching, it as a whole pattern—what they call the 'vowel-consonant-e situation' (p. 63). In the same way learned derivations can be more confusing than enlightening if they are seen as important in themselves. What matters in English in learning to write prefixes is not what was the form of the original preposition in Latin or Greek from which the prefix is derived but what is the form actually found in English, with any variations due to assimilation.

This point can be illustrated by the following tables of variations in three prefixes:

con-	*com-*	*corr-*	*coll-*
syn-	*sym-*		*syll-*
in-	*im-*	*irr-*	*ill-*

Set out in this way with appropriate examples the similarities of behaviour of three English prefixes ending in *n* become plain. Telling the pupil that the original prepositions from which the prefixes came were *cum*, *sun* and *in*, which have different vowels and even different end consonants, only emphasizes the differences and makes for confusion (although of course it may be of interest to point out that the first two prefixes have much the same meaning of 'togetherness', the one occurring in Latin words, the other in Greek words).

On all these points the purpose of conveying to the pupil a clear picture of the English spelling system is paramount.

When considering the techniques that may help the dyslexic child, one cannot ignore the claims of the Fernald (1943) technique. In stipulating that the word should be said aloud as the child repeatedly traces the letters this method seems to be insisting on a link between sound and symbol. There is no doubt that the method is successful and that it greatly encourages children in the spelling of quite long words. However it has a wider remedial application, since it was not intended specifically for dyslexic children but for any failing pupil, for example the older child who has not succeeded when young for many and various reasons. Perhaps some of these pupils, when once handed the key, can go on to open the door to literacy for themselves, not having a specific hadicap. But the dyslexic pupil needs more attention to detail than this. Another drawback for him is that the Fernald technique deals with just one word at a time; it cannot teach the principles of spelling which will apply to many examples. If one can start with a dyslexic child in primary school before his needs have so far outstripped his abilities that he is resistant to going back to first principles, he obviously has more to gain by following a systematic programme than by learning one word at a time, and he will be more interested also, for children of average and above average intelligence soon begin to find the process of tracing words and saying them aloud a mindless mechanical activity and become bored with it.

At the other extreme to a systematic structured phonic programme is the approach suggested by Goodman (1967) who says: 'Efficient reading does not result from precise perception and identification of all elements but from skill in selecting the most productive cues necessary to produce guesses which are right the first time. . . . Teaching for more precise perception may actually impede the child's reading development.'

Goodman argues that 'miscues', as he calls the reader's slips in accuracy, are not just 'errors' but stages in a process of learning.

It is true, as we have seen (p. 247), that substitutions may reflect an understanding of the grammatical status of the original word and even a partial success in decoding. Spontaneous progress from that point, however, depends on the ability of the reader ultimately to make phonic corrections, which is not necessarily guaranteed by the fact that he has partial insight already.

'Incidentally, he reveals here that he can use a phonic letter–sound strategy when he wants to', says Goodman of a 9-year old pupil reading from a basic school book of 11-year level. This is just what is not true, however, of a dyslexic child. The selection of cues in higher-level reading depends on a prior ability to study a word in detail and distinguish the vital ones from the superfluous. The dyslexic child is not yet ready to raise his reading to that higher level and probably will not be ready until he has reached about an 11-year reading standard. That is not to say that his phonic programme will keep him on a letter-by-letter basis; on the contrary it needs to progress from letters to digraphs and blends and then to syllables, so that at a later stage he is able to select relevant cues. The risk that he will be merely 'barking at print'—that is, reading accurately but without understanding—is minimal since typically he is a child of good comprehension but inaccurate word attack. If, therefore, he is reading without understanding it is probably because the phonic difficulties of that particular text are so great that he cannot consider the meaning as well as make the right sounds. In that case he should be reading something easier.

There seem to be close parallels between teaching the basic skills of reading and spelling and teaching music. Although practising scales is not music in the full sense that playing a Chopin nocturne is music, nobody can play such pieces with fine musicianship without having scale-work at his finger tips. ('Scales', said Paul Tortelier during a *Master Class* on television, 'are the food of music'.) A pianist who has practised chromatic scales will recognize at a glance that a particular pattern of notes *is* a chromatic scale and thereafter he can operate on 'minimal cues' Similarly with reading: the non-dyslexic child without much explicit tuition readily picks up the equivalent of scales, that is, an understanding of phonics, and is thus likely to have little difficulty in using 'minimal cues' in more advanced reading. However the dyslexic child is different. He needs to practise phonic skills as diligently as a music pupil practises scales. This is because he does not naturally rehearse and develop these skills with an active curiosity as do non-dyslexic children. Not long ago I came on a 5-year old girl, book in hand, happily sounding out, letter by letter, 'l-ŏ-v-ĕ'; these sounds she instantly transferred correctly into the word 'love', making an immediate transition from the individual letter sounds to the word as a whole, despite its phonetic irregularities. I do not think that one would ever catch a dyslexic child talking aloud to himself in this way—working things out explicitly. To encourage a dyslexic child to use 'minimal cues' is like discouraging a musician from practising scales. Moreover, phonic skills are needed not only for reading but for writing too. At a later stage the dyslexic adolescent or adult may well be able to operate with 'minimal cues' here also; in other words he may be in a position to put his ideas on paper without having to give all his attention to the question of what letter to write next. He will be able to do so, however, only if he has at some time acquired the basic phonic skills.

REFERENCES

Bannatyne, A. (1973) *Reading—An Auditory Vocal Process*. San Rafael, Cal.: Academic Therapy Publication.

Bryant, P. E. (1975) Cross-modal development and reading. In D. Duane and M. B. Rawson, (eds.) *Reading, Perception and Language*, pp. 195–213, Baltimore, Md.: Orton Society.

Cashdan, A. (1977) Backward readers—research on auditory-visual integration. In J. M. Morris, S. F. Reid and H. Donaldson (eds.) *Reading: Problems and Practices*. London: Ward Lock Educational.

Coltheart, M. (1979) Mysteries of reading in brain defects. *New Sci.*, **81**, 368–370.

Done, D. J. and Miles T. R. (1978) Learning, memory and dyslexia. In M. M. Gruneberg, P. E. Morris and R. N. Sykes (eds.) *Practical Aspects of Memory* pp. 553–560, London: Academic Press.

Ellis, N. C., and Miles T. R. (1978) Visual information processing in dyslexic children. In M. M. Gruneberg, P. E. Morris, and R. N. Sykes (eds.) *Practical Aspects of Memory* pp. 561–569, London: Academic Press.

Fernald, C. (1943) *Remedial Techniques in Basic School Subjects*. New York: McGraw-Hill.

Gattegno, C. (1962) *Words in Colour*. Reading: Educational Explorers Ltd.

Gillingham, A. and Stillman, B. W. (1956) *Remedial Training for Children with Specific Disabilities in Reading, Spelling and Penmanship*. Cambridge, Mass.: Educators Publishing Service.

Goodman, K. S. (1967) Reading: a psycholinguistic guessing game. *J. Reading Specialist*, **4**, 126–135.

Johnson, D. T., and Myklebust, H. R. (1967) *Learning Disabilities*. New York: Grune and Stratton.

McCarthy, J. J., and Kirk, S. A. (1961) *Illinois Test of Psycholinguistic Abilities*. Urbana, Ill.: Institute for Research in Exceptional Children.

Miles, T. R. (1970) *On Helping the Dyslexic Child*. London: Methuen Educational.

Miles, T. R. and Wheeler, T. J. (1974) Towards a new theory of dyslexia. *Dyslexia Review*, **10**, 9–11.

Naidoo, S. (1972) *Specific Dyslexia*. London: Pitman.

Shute, H. and Graham, N. (1977) *Reading Disability: A School Based Study in Dyslexia*. Aston Educational Enquiry Monographs and Occasional Papers. Birmingham: University of Aston.

Spache, G. D. (1976). *Investigating the Issues of Reading Disabilities*, Boston: Allyn and Bacon.

Stirling, E. G. (1978) Naming and verbal fluency in dyslexic boys, Unpublished MEd thesis, University of Wales.

Vernon, M. D. (1978) *Dyslexia*, Short Talk Series, Centre for the Teaching of Reading, School of Education, University of Reading (on cassette).

Wisbey, A. (1979) Music as a source of learning. *Music Teacher*, **58**, 2.

Dyslexia Research and its Applications to Education
Edited by G. Th. Pavlidis and T. R. Miles
© 1981 John Wiley & Sons Ltd.

CHAPTER 11

Teaching Methods and their Rationale

S. NAIDOO

INTRODUCTION

Since literacy became a desirable universal goal, methods and ideas concerning the teaching of reading have not remained static. Although one or other method may find particular favour at any one point in time, over the years distinct changes are discernible. In Great Britain, individual schools enjoy considerable freedom in their choice of method, reading schemes and materials, so that not only does the method in popular use change from one period to another, but different methods also coexist at any one time.

It is remarkable that whatever method is in use, most children learn to read, to spell and to write without undue difficulty. Yet teaching methods are often blamed for the very poor progress of some children. Whole-word and 'Look-and-Say' methods are condemned by the adherents of phonic methods, and phonics are regarded as stumbling blocks by those concerned primarily with reading for meaning. It is interesting to note that two large surveys in geographically different parts of the country and separated by more than 30 years should find such similar percentages (approximately 4%) of children with severe and specific reading retardation (Rutter, Tizard, and Whitmore, 1970; Schonell, 1942). Dyslexic children, whose reading and spelling problems are not the direct result of low intelligence, emotional disturbance, sensory deficiency or environmental disadvantage, have been and continue to be identified irrespective of which teaching method is in vogue. At the Invalid Children's Aid Association's Word Blind Centre, a varied background of teaching methods and conditions was apparent in the children who came for treatment and indeed many had had what would generally be regarded as good but conventional remedial help. But all had failed to make progress where their classmates had succeeded.

Given ordinary school conditions, what normal readers are able to do, despite the presence or absence of particular method, is to deduce for themselves the rules and constraints which govern the system whereby oral language has been visually coded. The process of discovery and mastery may be aided by sound phonic teaching at the right time. That it does take place without such assistance was evident in a longitudinal study by the author (unpublished) of more than 60 normal children aged 6 to 10 years in six different schools. The children were examined and observed in reading and spelling at 6-monthly intervals, their teachers using several methods including purely whole-word, purely phonic, and combinations of both. All but a few children learned to read and to spell competently whatever the method. The few who had difficulties were not restricted to one or other class or school. This is not to say that teaching methods are unimportant. The opposite is true especially for those to whom reading is a problem. But to blame a method of teaching or even a lack of method for the difficulties of dyslexic children is to overlook and misunderstand the nature of their condition.

BASIC PROBLEMS AND REQUIREMENTS

The written forms of all Indo-Aryan languages are based on sets of symbols, letters representing the sounds of which words are comprised. Such systems, phonic in nature, require the learner to form permanent associations between sounds and symbols, which are not arbitrary but conform to rules which can be abstracted and generalized. This applies even to English words, some 85% of which obey rules of phonic regularity. Although the dyslexic child may have no difficulty in grasping scientific or mathematical concepts for example, unlike the normal reader he does not readily forge the necessary cross-modal links or deduce the phonic rules. Critchley (1970) suggests that the primary problem may be of a specific cognitive nature affecting the linking of one percept with another. Vernon (1975) sees the problem as one of poor conceptualizing ability where cross-modal integration and generalizations are concerned. Cotterell (1970) underlined the dyslexic child's failure in these respects when she said 'I have learnt not to expect a dyslexic to know anything which he has not been specifically taught'. A first requirement in teaching dyslexic children is to leave nothing to chance, to place no reliance on spontaneous learning but to make sure that all sound/symbol associations, and all the rules governing their use, are taught.

Phonically based coding systems demand competence in a wide range of subskills which include the discrimination, perception, memory and reproduction of single sounds, of the sequences of sounds within words, of single letters and of strings of letters. Delayed or defective development in one or more of these areas has been reported in numerous investigations such as those referred to in Naidoo (1971) and Newton, Thomson, and Richards (1979). Although no single set of symptoms has been found to characterize all dyslexic children, a very common finding is poor performance on tests of short-term auditory memory, and Miles and Wheeler (1974) have proposed that an important feature in dyslexia is 'the inability to retain complex information over time'. In practice, in the remedial situation, the dyslexic child is notorious for his ability to forget what has recently been taught. The laborious slowness with which he learns to read and write contrasts strongly with the speed with which he may learn in other fields, and this is often difficult for both teachers and parents to understand. A second important requirement in any teaching programme is therefore the provision of ample opportunity for repeated practice in each small step until it is firmly fixed.

To achieve literacy a child must learn to read, write and spell. The dyslexic child's difficulty in learning this visual coding system affects both reading and spelling and indeed the latter is often the major problem. It is therefore imperative that writing and spelling as well as reading be taught. What is needed is integrated instruction in decoding and encoding right from the start so that an understanding and mastery of the one sheds light on and reinforces the other. A further reason is that together reading and spelling provide a multisensory approach which utilizes auditory, visual and kinaesthetic modalities. Any weakness of function in one modality can be compensated for by the concentrated use of others.

In devising any teaching programme, one must first decide upon what is to be taught, in other words, the syllabus, and second how the information or facts comprising the syllabus are to be presented. The *what* (or syllabus) is determined by ultimate goals, by the very nature of the corpus of information to be conveyed and by the needs of the learner—how much or little of the syllabus he needs. All syllabuses designed for dyslexic children include the phonic data necessary to master the code. Strictly speaking, the term 'method' should be applied only to *how* the material is presented. In practice, in the conventionally recognized 'methods' of teaching reading and spelling, the content of the teaching programme is often inextricably bound with the way in which it is presented. It is important to be aware, however, that content and method are not necessarily interdependent and that one can use different methods to teach the same syllabus. Programmes for dyslexic children have been constructed on the basis of very definite ideas about the nature of dyslexia. They nonetheless evolved from and in reaction to conventional methods which have been or are in current use. Some features of conventional methods have been retained, some rejected and new ideas introduced. The fact that those meeting programmes for dyslexic children for the first time may recognize some familiar elements and practices in no way detracts from the highly specialized character of the programmes as a whole.

Why some ordinary methods are deemed to be unsuitable and why some aspects of others are viewed favourably might best be explained by reference to the major present and past methods of teaching reading.

BRIEF OVERVIEW OF CONVENTIONAL
TEACHING METHODS

Methods for teaching reading are limited in number and kind by the very nature of the coding system and by those features peculiar to the oral linguistic system which is coded. As Goodacre (1972) has pointed out, different methods are not generally diametrically opposed to one another; rather, each emphasizes a particular facet of the total reading process.

In learning to read, a child has to abstract two kinds of information from print. The first concerns the way in which sounds and symbols are related, and the rules which govern how certain letters or strings of letters should be sounded. Such information is needed to crack the code, to be able both to read and to spell.

The second kind of information relates to the meaning of what is printed. This is of course the ultimate object of reading. Competent abstraction of the first kind of information without the second results in 'barking at print'. But there cannot be truly competent abstraction of the second semantic type without considerable information about grapho-phonemic relationships. When this is unreliable or patchy, the reader may make *apparent* sense of what is read, but read inaccurately and make mistakes such as substituting *king* for *knight*, *a* for *the* and other errors such as those described by Elaine Miles (Chapter 10 of this volume). Clearly the ability to abstract both kinds of information is essential for true, fluent reading and spelling and writing.

Teaching methods tend to fall into one of two groups; one emphasizing the rules of coding, the other the meaning of the text. Into the first category fall alphabetical and phonic methods as well as those which use diacritical markings and/or colour. These aim to indicate fairly precisely what sounds are to be attached to single letters, strings of letters or letter orders. The second category includes the whole-word and sentence methods and those based on oral language experience.

Methods based on decoding

Alphabetical

By the alphabetical method, very popular during the eighteenth century, pupils were taught the names of letters, and each new word was spelled out and then read. Since the sound of a series of letters spelled out by name, for example *bee-ae-tee* bears little resemblance to the sound of the word *bat*, one can only surmise that teachers must often have provided the whole word. However, the alphabetical method has the advantage of directing attention to the sequence of letters in a consistent left-to-right direction, and the repetition of letters in correct order was, and still is, an aid to spelling for many children. As will be seen below, the alphabetical method continues to find a place in some programmes designed for children with reading disorders, although otherwise it is rarely encountered.

Phonic

By the end of the nineteenth century the alphabetical method, widely used for 200 years, was giving way to the phonic method, which provided a much more helpful key to the coding system. Moyle (1970) tells us that a brilliant teacher, Nellie Dale, has been credited with the invention of this method in which letters are associated, not with their name but with their sound. Phonics were in fact being used before her time, but she introduced some new ideas, in particular where children were encouraged to listen to words and to identify sounds within them, thus becoming aware of the phonic elements. This is an important contribution. Nellie Dale realized that a phonic approach requires a facility which most young children just learning to read do not have, namely an ability to understand that words are composed of sounds (Reid, 1972). The process of blending sounds together is even more difficult, and one with which many dyslexic children have great difficulty. She also introduced colour coding as an aid to the recognition of the sound value of letters. Black was used for voiced and blue for unvoiced consonants; red for vowels, and yellow for silent letters. Children were thoroughly grounded in single letter–sound associations, and slowly introduced to short phonically regular words. In the security of these, and the practice given in reading and writing such words, it was expected that phonic rules would be understood and applied. But phonics badly presented are no more an aid to breaking the code than the alphabetical method. *Hcu-a-tuh* is as unhelpful as *see-ae-tee* in triggering *cat*. The child who wrote *bt* for *butter* was acting in a very logical manner. Again, although most English words conform to a regular phonic pattern, the remainder includes many of the most frequently used words, and children must simply learn these as a whole. Teaching words as wholes must be introduced quite early in a child's school career.

Other decoding methods

Other methods which are based on sound–symbol associations include colour-coded systems such as those of Gattegno (1962). Although most logically evolved, these systems have not gained popularity either in ordinary or special education. They include so many colours that some children have considerable difficulty in distinguishing some from others. Moreover, the colours themselves introduce a distracting element, some attracting attention more readily than others and interfering with a consistently left-to-right direction. For children with reading difficulties and whose memories are weak, learning colour-sound associations as well as symbol–sound associations adds unnecessary difficulties.

The Initial Teaching Alphabet (i.t.a.) attempts to overcome the problem of representing by a mere 26 letters the much greater number of phonemes in the language. While the phonic regularity of i.t.a. may help the normal reader to master the coding system, regularity in itself is of limited assistance to the dyslexic child. Transfer must be made to traditional orthography, usually before the age of 8 years (when the dyslexic child is usually floundering). Having ultimately to learn two sets of sound–symbol associations again increases unnecessarily the dyslexic child's learning load.

Methods based on reading for meaning

Whole-word

A whole-word approach to reading had been proposed by Comenius in the seventeenth century, but it did not become an established popular method until well into the nineteenth century in the United States, and not until the third and fourth decades of this century in Great Britain. Two movements, one psychological, the other educational, encouraged the growth of a method in which the basic unit is the word, a semantic instead of a coding unit. Gestalt psychology with its focus on the perception of whole forms assumed that, as far as written language was concerned, the shape (particularly the outline) of a word constituted a whole. It became important in devising suitable texts not to juxtapose two words with a similar outline, such as *cat* and *mat*. In education there was increasing commitment to the provision of interesting, active environments in which children would be self-motivated towards learning. The use of the whole-word method, leading to the fairly rapid acquisition of a sight vocabulary, meant that children could be reading with meaning very much sooner than with methods which worked on the coding system itself.

The term 'whole-word' should really refer only to the content of the teaching/learning material, to *what* is taught. This is a vocabulary of words from which the text of readers, such as the Ladybird Series, is composed and which is usually drawn from lists of words most frequently used by young children and therefore familiar to them. Sometimes the term 'Look-and-Say' is used interchangeably with 'whole-word'. The former in fact describes the method whereby a sight vocabulary is usually established. Each word, printed on a flashcard, is shown to the children by the teacher who says the word. The children *look* at it *and say* the word. By much repetition of this procedure children learn to recognize and read words.

Attractively illustrated readers were produced, the pictures being intended to provide linguistic clues to the text. The language itself, freed from the constraints of phonically regular words, could employ those used most frequently by children themselves. Attractive, interesting material may help to create and sustain a desire to learn; but learning itself requires repetition. Moreover only a limited number of words can be learned at a time. As a result, the texts of many whole-word schemes are as stilted and unnatural as any found in phonic readers. Very often, too, the pictures bear only the slightest relevance to the text.

Sentence method

Linguistically sounder is the sentence method, whereby for their first reading material children compose wheir own sentences usually to accompany the pictures which they draw. By repetition, sentence matching, and 'reading' without the aid of the picture several sentences are established, albeit rather shakily. From the beginning children respond to print with natural intonation and phrasing. Solving new words is a matter of intelligent guesswork from language cues, vocabulary and syntax. Semantic acceptability, though not reading accuracy, is fostered and a child will happily read 'wall' for 'window' if either one makes sense. Sentences composed by the children will not ensure exposure to a sufficient number of repetitions for learning. The sentence method generally gives way to a whole-word scheme although *Breakthrough to Literacy* (Mackay, Thompson, and Schaub, 1970) provides continuing opportunities for children to construct their own sentences using a vocabulary which can be limited and controlled by the teacher.

A language-experience approach

In education today, a child-centred approach is generally encouraged. This is particularly so in activities which foster the development and enrichment of language. There is a general movement towards using a child's own experiences as the basis for written as well as spoken language; thus, written material is produced and read which the child himself fully understands. In practice, a language-experience approach is not too dissimilar from the sentence method.

Comment

All methods which concentrate primarily on reading for and with meaning from the beginning leave to chance the learning of the code itself. Children cannot become independent readers, able to give sound to unknown printed words, unless they master the code. Many children will deduce the code and its rules for themselves. But as Southgate (1972) rightly points out, there are many others who will fail to learn to read without specific guidance and instruction from the teacher on the phonic structure of words. The dyslexic child without such instruction has little chance of achieving literacy.

Apart from their effect on different aspects of the reading process, methods which aim to teach the coding system itself, and those which aim at reading with meaning from the start, differ in other important respects. They involve differing aspects of speech, linguistic, perceptual, discriminatory, memory and cognitive processes. The decoding methods depend heavily upon word analysis into sounds, the blending of sounds into words, the ability to recall and remember sounds and in correct order, the discrimination of sounds and their reasonably accurate reproduction in speech. Reading for meaning systems demand oral linguistic competence, a well-developed ability to discriminate and identify and match quite complex visual patterns and to recognize, recall and remember these. While most children function so effectively in all areas that no difficulty is created whichever methods are used, this is not so with dyslexic children, a point to which I shall return later.

HISTORICAL BACKGROUND AND RATIONALE OF PROGRAMMES FOR DYSLEXIC CHILDREN

The last 15 years have seen a sudden increase in the number of publications devoted to the teaching of dyslexic children. The methods, techniques and approaches they describe have been specially evolved to meet the dyslexic child's particular problems. Individually and together they provide much that is new and unique, although many of the elements of the programmes are, or have been, in use in normal education.

Dyslexia, or congenital word-blindness as it was first known, was identified at the end of the nineteenth century. During the first two decades of the twentieth century the term 'word blind' was applied only to the most severely affected, such children being recognized on both sides of the Atlantic. At this time the most popular method for teaching reading both in the United States and in Britain was phonic. In the United States, however, the whole-word method was rapidly coming into vogue, a movement which did not experience a similar impetus until the 1930s and 1940s in Britain. Around the 1920s, as indeed now, word-blind children needed some method other than those from which they had failed to profit.

Although Orton (1937) and his colleagues, especially Bessie Stillman and Anna Gillingham, are often credited with devising the first specifically designed schemes for teaching dyslexic children, Dr Grace Fernald's work in this field preceded theirs, and indeed some of her ideas were incorporated in their later programmes.

At her clinic in Los Angeles, Dr Fernald developed her auditory–kinaesthetic method for word-blind pupils who had failed to respond to conventional phonic and whole-word methods. The method was evolved with blind and deaf Helen Keller (Fernald and Keller, 1921) who had learned to write utilizing the kinaesthetic modality, until then little employed in education outside Montessori schools. A word, written in cursive script, is traced over with the pupil's forefinger (not with a pencil). As he traces, the pupil slowly enunciates the word at which he is also looking, thus creating a multisensory image. The tracing is repeated until the kinaesthetic image is firmly established and available for word recognition and for writing (Fernald, 1943). This is essentially a whole-word method and does not itself offer instruction in grapho-phonemic association. It is still in use in some remedial centres. As a way of starting off children with very severe auditory and visual perceptual and memory difficulties, and to reinforce the learning of phonically irregular words, it has much to commend it.

The first very detailed and fully comprehensive programme for teaching dyslexic children was written by Anna Gillingham and Bessie Stillman (1969). Their manual was developed over many years, taking in several editions and reprintings. Agnes Wolff (1970) who worked with Gillingham and Stillman, tells us that her 'manual' in 1932 consisted of two quarto pages of typescript with much personal explanation and demonstration by the authors.

I believe it is true to say that no other work has had such a monumental influence over the teaching of dyslexic children. Subsequent programmes and ideas, if they have not grown directly from this initial work, have certainly had to take it into account. The rationale for both the content and of the methods described in the manual is firmly rooted in Orton's (1925, 1929, 1937, 1939) observations, findings and theories.

Orton, a neurologist and psychiatrist, had noted that the reading, spelling and writing disorders which prompted the referral of so many children to his clinics, were frequently accompanied by other, less prominent features. These included the delayed onset of speech, defective articulation, immature language, clumsiness and directional confusions. Unilateral dominance had frequently not been established, the children being neither definitely right nor left-handed. These, although common, were not so common as other 'symptoms', and this led Orton to conclude that they were characteristic of the condition. These were confusions between lower case letters such as *b* and *d*, *p* and *q*; uncertainty in reading words like *was* and *saw*, *not* and *ton*, *on* and *no*; a tendency to transpose letters in words, for example *gary*, for *gray*, *tarshin* for *tarnish*, *twomorrom* for *tomorrow*; and a greater facility than usual for reading via a mirror and often a facility for mirror-writing. These confusions to which Orton gave the term 'strephosymbolia' (twisted symbols) were, he believed, due to a failure in the establishment of complete unilateral cerebral dominance. His argument, based on the neurological knowledge of the 1920s, for linking incomplete cerebral dominance and wholly or partially reading or writing mirror images went thus: the neural pathways are such that images transmitted by macular or central vision (used when reading and writing) pass to both cerebral hemispheres; now the two halves of the body are mirror copies of each other, this applying for example to the arrangement of muscles, joints and to groups of cells in the spinal cord. Moreover, if anatomically identical writing movements are made by the right and left hands simultaneously, one hand must produce mirror-writing. Orton (1929) thought:

it seems therefore highly probable that the engrams which are stored in the silent areas of the non-dominant hemisphere are opposite in sign, i.e. mirrored copies, of those in the dominant. If then these opposite engrams are not elided through establishment of consistent selection from one hemisphere, we would expect them to evince themselves by errors or confusion in direction and orientation . . .

Orton's hypothesis relating to the faulty elision of mirror or opposite engrams from the non-dominant hemisphere lies at the heart of his concept of word-blindness. The hypothesis has received equivocal support from later research and is still open to question. Orton's theories, however, led him to very definite views on teaching, views to which his colleagues and later many writers of remedial programmes have adhered almost religiously. Any method which depended upon or emphasized the visual aspects of reading and writing was strongly condemned because 'visual' methods would result in the implantation of paired engrams, and increase the problems of children whose incomplete cerebral dominance gave rise to the faulty elision of mirror engrams. Thus sightreading methods were likely to create serious obstacles to the child with strephosymbolia. It was because the visual aspects of the necessary associations between sounds and their symbols was deemed to be so weak and unreliable that Orton commended the use of a third sensory modality, the kinaesthetic, to facilitate and reinforce the auditory–visual links. Indeed he recommended tracing and writing with eyes averted to exclude the unreliable visual element and to strengthen the kinaesthetic bond. Thus Orton was advocating working to strengths, using normally functioning modalities, auditory and kinaesthetic, to fortify associations which involved the fallible visual one. Orton (1939) also recommended flexibility in treatment, to be decided on full examination and analysis of problems in fields relating to but other than reading and writing, such as speech, language, and movement. He estimated that in much less than 50% of cases seen in his clinic was the reading disorder unaccompanied by other problems. The total picture determined treatment. Orton leaves us in no doubt, however, about the basic necessity in remediating reading and writing disorders which arise from deviant, not pathological, neurological processes; namely, a multisensory method which establishes sound–symbol associations and which systematically builds up words from letters thus eliminating the guesswork inherent in sight methods.

TRAINING PROGRAMMES AND AIDS FOR DYSLEXIC CHILDREN

To those educators and parents who seek to provide or find help for dyslexic children, it soon becomes evident that more of what is normally available in schools is not enough. There is a continuing demand for instruction and materials and for courses for teachers specifically designed to meet the needs of the dyslexic child. Several training programmes have now been published, some forming the basis of courses for teachers. All can be read and studied with profit by the experienced teacher. Only some are mentioned here, in order to convey to the reader those features of content, method and general principle deemed to be of primary importance in the past or present. To the first, already referred to briefly above, those that follow owe an enormous debt.

Remedial training for children with specific disability in reading, spelling and penmanship (Anna Gillingham and Bessie Stillman, 1969)

This highly structured phonic programme sets out in great detail the precise methods to be used and the procedure to be followed. The theoretical rationale is described in the previous section.

There are two alternative Manuals, a Green and a Red. The information which follows is taken from the Red Manual (5th edition, 1969). Both Manuals provide remedial programmes for teaching reading, spelling and writing to children who have achieved little or nothing, for teaching spelling to those with some competence in reading but whose primary problem is spelling and for writing itself.

The training procedures aim to establish decoding and encoding skills which rest securely on enduring associations between sounds and symbols and upon a thorough knowledge of the structure of written language. The multisensory procedures for establishing bonds between sounds and symbols constitute one of the unique features of the method. First learned are letters, which, as they are mastered, are used to build words. Each new phonogram is learned by eight linkages which include the creation of links between auditory, visual and kinaesthetic input and output. As teachers of dyslexic children quickly realize, the learning of new structures must be reinforced by frequent repetition.

Phonic drills and constant revision are built into this programme, and there are eight linkages for teaching new phonograms, as follows:

Linkage 1

A card with a letter is presented: pupil looks while teacher gives the name of the letter; pupil repeats.

Once the name is known the procedure is repeated but now the teacher gives and the pupil repeats the sound of the letter (visual–auditory: auditory–kinaesthetic).

Linkage 2

The letter is made by teacher. Its formation, orientation, where to start, and the direction of movement is discussed; pupil then traces over the letter, copies, writes it from memory and then with eyes averted (visual–kinaesthetic: kinaesthetic–visual).

Linkage 3

The letter is shown: pupil names; teacher may move pupil's hand passively to form letter (visual–auditory: kinaesthetic–auditory).

Linkage 4

Teacher dictates the letter name: pupil writes (auditory–kinaesthetic: auditory–visual)

Linkage 5

The letter is presented: pupil gives its sound (visual–auditory).
 This is the important linkage for reading.

Linkage 6

Teacher gives the name of phonogram: pupil gives its sound (auditory–auditory).

Linkage 7

Teacher gives the sound, pupil gives the name of the phonogram (auditory–auditory).
 This is the important linkage for oral spelling.

Linkage 8

Teacher gives the sound, pupil writes it (sometimes with eyes averted) and gives the name (auditory–kinaesthetic: auditory–visual).
 This is the important linkage for written spelling.

 As the children become proficient, only Linkages 5 (for reading), 7 (for oral spelling) and 8 (for written spelling) are retained for revision and reinforcement drills.

 After a few letters have been thoroughly learned, pupils are taught to blend sounds into words and to analyse words into their component sounds. Thus quite rapidly a child is reading and spelling phonically regular words. His knowledge of letters steadily increases. He is introduced to polysyllabic words, being taught how to divide words into syllables for ease of reading and how to build syllables into words. As yet only sounds having one symbol and symbols having one sound have been used with the aim of achieving insight into and mastery of the basic code, and also creating a real feeling of security when using it. The order in which letters, phonograms, and other structures are learned ensures that the programme is cumulative and a child is not asked to read or spell or write anything which introduces an unknown factor.

Once they have learned to analyse words into their component sounds, children learn to spell by means of a four-point programme. The teacher says the word: the child then (1) repeats the word, (2) names the letters, (3) writes, naming each letter as it is written, (4) repeats the word.

The technique of Simultaneous Oral Spelling (SOS) relies heavily on the auditory recall of a sequence of letter names. This is a deliberate attempt to provide an alternative to recalling the visual pattern of words since it is assumed that visual recall is poor.

There comes a point, 'a momentous event', when pupils must be introduced carefully and systematically to spellings which have more than one sound, such as **ea** as in *great, meat, bread,* and to sounds which have multiple spellings, such as c*a*t, k*i*te, ch*ri*stmas, *bla*ck. Generalizations, some of which can be expressed as rules, are applicable to most apparently irregular words and these generalizations and rules are explained, learned and applied, again to reduce reliance on faulty visual perception and recall. At this juncture, instruction in reading and spelling diverge, as they must, since information about some structures relate only to reading and some only to spelling. This is not to say that they become quite separate activities; both continue to be included in the daily routine, and reading, spelling and writing continue to be regarded as integral parts or aspects of the coding system.

The manual provides a wealth of helpful teaching points which cannot be absorbed in a single reading. The chapters on aids to the pronunciation of polysyllables and on using a dictionary are particularly valuable. The programme may appear to be dull and unattractive to the reader who has not taught in this structured, rather formal, and systematic manner. Such an impression is misleading. Children with learning disorders are delighted to succeed in tasks at which they have previously failed. Success itself becomes the motivating force. If there is boredom over drills and repetition, it is more often experienced by the teacher who has failed to understand a characteristic feature of this problem. Although it does not follow chronologically, the next programme is probably the most direct descendant of this one, the first to be published in Great Britain.

Dyslexia: a language training course for teachers and learners (Kathleen Hickey, 1977)

This British publication has its roots in Gillingham and Stillman's work and also in the Language Training Programmes developed at the Scottish Rite Hospital in Dallas, Texas by Dr Lucius Waites and Aylett Cox.

Like its predecessors, the training course is based on a recognition of the dyslexic child's need for instruction in the structures of written language to enable him to come to grips with both decoding and encoding aspects of the coding system. Thus the syllabus of this programme also begins with the smallest unit, the letter, carefully differentiates consonant and vowel, proceeds to word building and then cumulatively and systematically works towards polysyllabic words, both phonically regular and irregular, read and spelled.

Again, the method is based on multisensory techniques with well-defined drills for learning phonograms and later words. The alphabetical names of letters are used for spelling. There are, however, a few important points of difference in the training procedures, which while not altering the fundamental similarity to the Gillingham and Stillman programme, do give this one a slant and breadth missing from the first. Recognizing, as indeed did Orton and his colleagues, that some dyslexic children show particularly outstanding weaknesses in auditory and/or visual perception and memory, Hickey includes in her regular training procedures suggestions for improving these functions. The exercises are very sensibly directly related to the reading and spelling tasks which they accompany and not, as so often happens in remedial work, carried out quite separately usually employing non-verbal material, such as patterns, shapes and non-verbal sounds which have not been shown to carry over to reading. Much of the material is self-correcting, thus enabling a child to work on his own after initial instruction from the teacher. The programme is designed so that it can be used with children individually or in small groups of two to four. Hickey recommends Fernald's auditory–kinaesthetic technique (see above, page 270) for the learning of phonically irregular words. The manual includes many illustrative word lists, the vocabulary being more modern and much more suited to both young and older English children than American lists. Once familiar with the manual, the general layout and the colour coding for different sections make this an easy book to use.

On helping the dyslexic child (T. R. Miles, 1970) **and more help for dyslexic children** (T. R. Miles and Elaine Miles, 1975)

These two volumes together present an outline of a systematic phonic programme. The authors take a refreshingly optimistic view which in no way detracts from their sound understanding of the problems facing the dyslexic child and adult. Their attitude gives hope to situations which are often filled with despair. Something *can* be done about the problem. Recognized and faced, confidence can be created through a true appreciation of the individual's total gifts and worth, and of course by the right kind of teaching to overcome, if not cure, the difficulties.

Their programme is based on the recognition that the dyslexic child is usually well able to comprehend but fails to make the correct associations between sounds and symbols. The problem lies in mastering the coding system itself. What is described in these two volumes is a thorough and detailed syllabus which starts with letters, consonants and vowels, builds up words and systematically covers all the phonic elements, blends, work on syllables, rules for spelling and so on. It is designed and constructed so that a thorough understanding of the structure of words is achieved. Nothing is left to chance, and the student progresses in the security of a cumulative programme which does not suddenly present him with a problem which cannot be solved because it is totally unfamiliar. The student is trained to apply the knowledge needed to operate the coding system in both its decoding and encoding aspects. Unfortunately the second volume does not follow on from the first, so a teacher has to jump from one to another. The syllabus in use at the Dyslexia Unit itself follows a logical systematic sequence of cumulative steps.

This programme is more flexible than others so far referred to. It contains fewer 'musts' and 'shoulds' and leaves much more to a teacher's own discretion. In particular, little is laid down with regard to method, and one word which is notable by its absence is 'multisensory'. Few references are made to sensory modalities, strengths or weaknesses. Apart from giving due credit to Orton's important contribution to the recognition of this disorder and to our understanding of it, no mention is made of his neurological theories which gave earlier programmes their rationale for methods as well as syllabus. Reading and spelling are taught side by side because they are different aspects of the coding process and understanding structures for spelling helps and reinforces understanding reading structures, and both are essential for literacy.

Learning the alphabetical names of letters is regarded as an extra complication, and alphabetical spelling is discouraged as putting too great a load on children who find it difficult to hold in mind a sequence of sounds. Several suggestions are made for checking on and improving a child's discrimination of sounds, and for helping him to articulate speech sounds which are unclear. The volumes contain a wealth of helpful ideas on teaching; the latter in particular includes a most useful chapter on arithmetic, which many dyslexic children find difficult. The problem relates to calculation, for example to remembering tables and number combinations, and not necessarily to mathematics, and of course the dyslexic child is as likely to reverse and transpose numbers as letters.

Alpha to omega (Beve Hornsby and Frula Shear, 1975)

This programme for the teaching of reading, writing and spelling owes much, as its authors acknowledge, to Anna Gillingham and Bessie Stillman, and Edith Norrie (see below). It is quite comprehensive and takes teacher and pupil from the beginnings of reading, writing and spelling up to an adult level.

Designed specifically for dyslexic children, it could be profitably used for any child or adult with reading difficulties. This applies to most programmes–while remedial programmes which have not been designed with dyslexic children in mind are of limited benefit to them, those for dyslexic children have in general much wider application. This programme is aimed also at students learning English as a foreign language making some of the exercises inappropriate for children.

The syllabus reflects the combined knowledge and skills of speech therapy and teaching, a particularly fruitful combination. It begins with individual letters, their sounds and alphabetical names, and works towards word building and the construction of sentences for reading and writing. Consonants are introduced according to the developmental sequence of their acquisition. Short vowels, so often a source of confusion, are taught in pairs in an order which best contrasts them and makes discrimination less difficult; for example, *a* and *o* are paired. Sentences, too, follow in general the developmental sequence of usage, beginning with Simple Active Affirmative Declarative (SAAD) types. Although some of these sentences conform to a pattern which Crystal, Fletcher, and Garman (1976) identify as occurring much later than others, it is unlikely that the dyslexic, but linguistically normal, child would experience any difficulty with their comprehension or construction.

By concentrating on short phonically regular words to begin with, sound–symbol associations and a familiarity and competence with the basic coding system is established. 'Odd' (irregular) words are introduced gradually and are very usefully listed below the table of *Contents* with the number of the page on which they are introduced. As in all programmes for dyslexic children, the need for overlearning is fully recognized. Lists of words for reading and especially writing follow new teaching points, and the syllabus is liberally interspersed with well-thought-out sentences for dictation, which illustrate and recap what has recently been learned. As in the Gillingham and Stillman Manual, there is a definite drill for giving dictation which emphasizes the pupil's repetition of a sentence with the object of improving auditory memory, and encouraging the transfer by the pupil himself from spoken to written language.

The method for establishing sound–symbol associations is multisensory. Each consonant digraph and consonant blend, as well as each letter, has a key picture which unlocks the sound. The drill for learning these includes both alphabetical name and sound, and is clearly described. Once all the single letters have been learned, lists of short, and a few two-letter long, vowel words are written and read. Thereafter reading and spelling proceed hand in hand, ensuring the integration of hearing, saying, seeing and feeling. Rhymes, many of which incorporate a mnemonic, have been compiled as an aid to remembering rules. I am not at all sure, however, whether children who have difficulty in remembering rules will remember rhymes more readily if longer than a line or two. Homonyms are presented together, and this does create problems for many children who know there are two ways of spelling *pāl* for example, *pail* and *pale*. When to use which, however, often remains a lasting source of confusion. Much better to teach *pale* in relation to that concept and then after a considerable lapse of time teach *pail*. Attention is given to punctuation and literary skills from the beginning. Comprehension, letter, précis, story and essay writing are not neglected.

The index is particularly helpful, especially to the teacher of older or more advanced pupils, who can read and spell reasonably but need to refer to relevant items of information and practise exercises to fill in any gaps in knowledge.

Check list of basic sounds and phonic reference cards (Gill Cotterell)

These aids are the fruit of four years' experience as senior remedial teacher at the Invalid Children's Aid Association's Word Blind Centre for Dyslexic Children, London and later as remedial advisory teacher with a local authority. Record keeping can be laborious and time-consuming, and it is not always easy to find the information one wants quickly. The *Check List* is a welcome aid to recording the errors made in spelling and reading in terms of phonic structure, both at the beginning of tuition when one wishes to check what is known and unknown, and during teaching as errors occur. It also serves as a record of what is taught and what is learned. It includes single letters, diphthongs, digraphs, consonant blends, other letter strings which form syllables or other sound units, spelling rules both easy and hard, prefixes, suffixes and some common root words. It is in effect a syllabus as well as a record sheet, the teacher deciding the order in which sounds are taught. Each letter, etc., has a small box at the side in which is entered a cross when an error is made relating to that sound or symbol, a triangle when the point has been taught, and a tick when this is deemed to have been learned. This distinction between what is taught and what is learned is very important, and one which too many teachers fail to make. The *Check List* thus provides at a glance what needs to be taught next, what has been taught and learned and, dyslexic children being what they are, what should be revised.

The *Phonic Reference Cards* grew out of the lists of words compiled while teaching, to illustrate and teach specific structures. Neatly housed in a sturdy box are 110 alphabetically indexed cards, which altogether cover almost 200 phonic patterns which largely correspond to those in the *Check List*. The words on each card are listed in an order of phonic difficulty, this being based on Miss Cotterell's own considerable teaching experience. The lists are not exhaustive as it is intended that they should be added to by the teacher and pupil. Moreover, the author recommends that only those words which are within a child's comprehension should be selected. This recommendation reflects an important principle, namely that reading and spelling activities should always be meaningful. There are no lists of nonsense words.

The *Check List of Basic Sounds* and the *Phonic Reference Cards* do not in themselves constitute a full programme, but they are an integral part of an approach which is structured and systematic yet flexible, and child rather than programme-centred. The order in which sound–symbol associations are to be taught is not indicated. The first objective is to establish a confident ability in reading and writing two- or three-letter regular words, creating a competence to represent a short string of sounds by a short string of letters. This achieved, further teaching points are determined by errors made by the child, the teacher, where necessary, deciding which are the most profitable on which to work first. In the very informative booklet which accompanies the *Reference Cards*, Miss Cotterell specifies a number of important teaching principles, which include training pupils to vocalize while writing, and to say long words in syllables, teaching phonic structures *en bloc* for overlearning and reinforcement, training children to notice the 'tricky part' (or irregular element) of a word and always to use a multisensory approach in which reading, writing and spelling are learned together.

The Edith Norrie Letter Case (Arkell, 1970)

This system was devised by a Dane, Edith Norrie, who was herself dyslexic. Trained as a speech therapist, she brought to the teaching of dyslexic children insights from both personal and professional experience. The *Letter Case* is an aid rather than a programme or method, but its manner of organization reflects a commitment to a phonic approach enriched by the application of knowledge about the perception and reproduction of speech sounds and their symbols.

The letters of the alphabet, digraphs, and punctuation marks are printed separately on small rectangular cards. Vowels are printed in red, voiced consonants in green, and unvoiced consonants in black. Consonants are divided into three groups, dental, labial and palatal, each occupying a separate section of the box. A small mirror is provided. Children are shown how to produce each sound and can see by watching their mouths into which group a sound falls. Thus *b* and *d* cannot be confused since the former is labial and the latter dental.

The box lends itself to many uses. For example, a word or sentence constructed by the child with letters can be worked on to perfection by teacher and pupil before pencil is put to paper. For the child who is uncertain about the form of some letters, to recognize the letters he needs in the box is easier than to write them from memory. When put together to form a word, their rectangular shape avoids the creation of large spaces around each letter, and physically putting letters together or separating them provides a visual aid to oral blending and syllabification. The letter cards are, however, rather small to handle and the clumsy child may find it difficult to put them together neatly.

Other programmes and aids

Patterns of Sound (Gertrude Baldwin, 1968) was not designed specifically for the dyslexic child but for young children learning to read and for any child who is experiencing difficulty. Particularly helpful to the teaching of dyslexic children is the author's technique for ridding consonants of the unwanted 'schwa' (added -*er* sound) which interferes with effective blending. The technique also encourages distinct articulation and the subsequent kinaesthetic feedback from the organs of speech. Children are shown how to form consonants in a rather exaggerated way, the position of lips, tongue, etc., being humorously illustrated wherever possible. Consonants are never sounded in isolation but are, from the beginning, used as signals for saying a vowel. A procedure for getting the mouth ready to say a consonant—GET READY—then GO INTO a vowel sound is established for word building. Sound blending is never easy, but once acquired this technique facilitates word building. The shape of letters, digraphs and blends is used to create a picture, the name of which is associated with the sound, the picture itself picking out the outstanding features of the visual form. Thus shape and sound are linked to a picture to aid recall.

The technique of creating a picture from the shape of a letter, etc., has been expanded and developed in Lyn Wendon's *Pictogram System*, a comprehensive programme for teaching the structures of language. Picture characters drawn on the basis of letter shapes are accompanied by a story, rhyme or comment to illustrate and act as a prop for remembering the sound of a symbol and the rules or other principles governing its use. Some children do not remember spelling rules easily, and the pictograms have been devised as an *aide-memoire*. Another approach to aiding the recall of rules is by mnemonics. These are incorporated to supplement the spelling guides, which form the content of Pollock's (1978) *Signposts to Spelling* with its humorous and effective drawings as a further aid.

Spelling rules receive much attention in programmes for dyslexic children. Their purpose is to remove much of the apparent irrational, arbitrary spelling of words, most of which do in fact follow a regular pattern. Rules are intended to substitute reason for guesswork based on faulty memory. Indeed this message is conveyed in the very title of *Logical Spelling* (Allan, 1977) written by a former teacher at the Word Blind Centre for Dyslexic Children, London. The programme is comprehensive and can be used with both children and adults. The rules are clearly explained, illustrated and each is accompanied with exercises for practice. The layout of the contents page make this a very easy book in which to find precisely what is wanted.

A booklet which provides opportunities for developing some of the subskills which make for fluent decoding is *Attack-A-Track* (Lewis, 1976). The exercises, not for beginners, can be used for alphabet tracking and putting words into alphabetical order. Most are devised to practise breaking words into closed and open syllables, which contain a range of digraphs and diphthongs, the words then being read. The alphabet is clearly printed at the top of every page, a boon to the dyslexic who rarely knows which letters follow or precede others; a consistent left-to-right-direction must be maintained. The exercises are repeated at least once, and by recording the time taken to complete them the pupil can compete against himself. No concession is made to comprehension, the reading involved whether of nonsense or of real words being purely of a translating symbol-into-sound nature. A very profitable 5 to 10 minutes could be spent on such exercises at the right time in the programme of pupils who are achieving a fair degree of competence.

Common features

The programmes and aids referred to above do not nearly exhaust those now available. But the similarities between these few are found in all. The fact that so many experienced teachers are in such agreement does itself tell us much about the nature of dyslexia.

There is general agreement that the dyslexic child's basic problem lies in matching, associating, and fitting together the sounds of oral language and the symbols of written language. The dyslexic child presents an opposite picture to the dull child who frequently barks at print most effectively but who fails to understand what he reads. The dyslexic child has great difficulty in deciphering print, but understands with ease if someone else will read to him. It is, then, instruction in the coding system which all programmes give, instruction in both the decoding and encoding aspects which is needed. Reading, writing and spelling are learned one with the other. I doubt whether in any 'reading' lesson paper and pencil are ever absent. Only a small part of the daily lesson is usually devoted to 'reading' as such.

Some programmes place greater explicit emphasis on multisensory techniques than others, but all by virtue of their integrated reading, writing and spelling schemes of teaching practise such procedures.

All employ a phonic approach and all eschew whole-word methods. For some, their reasons hark back to Orton's theories propounded at a time when the whole-word method was escalating in America. But there is a general awareness that teaching by whole-word methods leaves children to deduce the coding system for themselves, and this of course is what the dyslexic child finds so difficult. All follow traditional phonic methods which start with the smallest sound–symbol unit, namely single letters, and proceed to build words 'brick by brick'.

All syllabuses are comprehensive and detailed. Some explicitly specify or strongly recommend a particular order for teaching structures, thereby ensuring cumulative progress. Others permit greater flexibility. But all stress that all structures must be covered. The teacher of dyslexic children must take it for granted that little or nothing will be deduced or 'picked up'. Should this happen it is a bonus.

Without exception the dyslexic child's facility for forgetting is recognized, this being of a specific nature which particularly affects rote learning for he may have an excellent memory for events. It is not enough to teach a structure, but imperative to set up an effective learning and reinforcing situation; hence the accent on linkage drills and continual revision. The teacher's slogan might well be Teach, Learn, Test and Revise until a structure is securely established.

Dyslexic children are not very good at making generalizations about graphophonemic associations. They are slow to realize that if they can read and write *ill* and *hill*, they can also manage *fill*, *till*, *mill* and *sill*. Lists of words to illustrate and

to practise each teaching point are necessary stocks-in-trade, and are supplied in all the above programmes, a great boon to teachers who know too well the hours of laborious work entailed in compiling such lists.

The teaching programmes of course differ in minor respects, though the broad principles are the same. They have been evolved by very experienced teachers and I doubt whether there is any such teacher who, thoroughly understanding her subject and the needs of her pupils, does not add to, modify or omit from whatever scheme she uses. All are structured and systematic, multisensory and thorough and leave nothing to guesswork or chance.

MEETING THE NEEDS OF INDIVIDUAL CHILDREN

There is then, general agreement about the information which must be conveyed to dyslexic children. It has also been generally supposed that the only way to present this information is by starting with letters and building words 'brick by brick'. The emphasis given by the earliest workers in this field to such a phonic approach was based on the assumption that the dyslexic child's major weakness lay in the visual aspects of the coding process. These early pioneers worked on the principle that greater reliance must be placed upon modalities which function most effectively, hence the stress on the auditory–kinaesthetic components. Later workers, while not necessarily subscribing to early theories of cerebral dominance, have pursued similar approaches in teaching. This would be quite acceptable if one could be certain that all dyslexic children learn in the same way.

During the last 15 years or so, considerable attention has been paid to the possibility that within the dyslexic population different types or subgroups exist. It has been suggested that one type, an auditory dyslexia, is characterized by difficulties in recalling sounds and words, by a very poor short-term auditory memory, by difficulties in rhyming, of auditory discrimination and sound blending—in short, showing weakness in those subskills of importance in learning by phonic methods. In a second type, visual dyslexia, the problem is related primarily to faulty visuospatial functions and it is thought that this type is often accompanied by clumsiness. The types are described fully by Johnson and Myklebust (1967) and an unsuccessful attempt to identify them statistically was made in the research carried out at the Word Blind Centre (Naidoo, 1972). One cannot conclude from these negative findings that individual variations in learning style do not exist among dyslexic children. Indeed one finds quite frequent reference to specific problems experienced by some but not other children in the manuals of Gillingham and Stillman (1969) and of Hickey (1977). Recent research suggests that of greater difficulty than tasks of a visuospatial nature are those of an auditory–verbal one and that tasks involving verbal labelling are a particular problem (Done and Miles, 1978; Ellis and Miles, 1978; Richardson, 1978; Shute and Graham, 1977). In a conventional 'Look-and-Say' method, it is verbal labelling which is the requested response. The basic repetitive

technique for learning letters in the programmes described above, is to ask a child to LOOK at a grapheme AND SAY its sound and/or name (see linkages and drills in the Gillingham and Stillman, and Hickey manuals). Thus although the syllabus is phonic, the method of learning is 'Look-and-Say', and whether it is a letter or word which must be labelled verbally the child with marked sound or word-labelling difficulties is at a disadvantage.

Again, word building, a blending synthetic process, requires a child to hold in mind a sequence of sounds in correct order while he decodes from the beginning to the end of a word. As has been shown many times, short-term auditory memory as measured by tasks such as the WISC Digit Span is often very weak as is performance on tests of blending.

If it is found that a dyslexic child has major problem in these areas, should not this influence the method of teaching? Should not greater emphasis be placed on the visual and kinaesthetic modalities if greater strengths are demonstrated there? It would be a great mistake to assume that by encouraging a more visual approach one was advocating conventional whole-word methods with their consequent lack of instruction on the structure of written language. Nothing could be further from the truth. What is suggested is a technique which utilizes visual strengths and whereby the phonic structure of words is taught by working from the whole word to its constituent sounds.

The building up of a small sight vocabulary is a first necessity not as a gentle start to the more serious business of phonics but as a deliberate way of learning about word structure. There is no reason why initially a language experience approach should not be employed to determine which words are first learned. Indeed using words produced by a child himself is more likely to increase motivation. The method for learning is not 'Look-and-Say' but what I have called 'Say-and-Look'. By discussion, drawing, picture labelling, etc., a first association is made between three or four oral and written words. These now have to be learned. Each word is printed on a flashcard and all, but not more than four or five at any one time, are placed in front of the child. The teacher then asks 'Which word SAYS . . . ?' and the pupil LOOKS and points. The procedure is repeated until recognition is perfect. The pupil now copies and says the word after pointing. Only after the teacher thinks that the bond between the oral and written word is firm does she ask the pupil to 'Look-and-Say' when shown a flashcard.

Sounds should be worked on independently beginning with the first sound of a word, in games such as 'I spy' or listing children whose names begin with a particular letter. Having identified the first sound of a group of words beginning with for example, *m*, the written symbol is then associated with the sound. Three or four letters are introduced in similar manner; these must now be learned, again by the 'Say-and-Look' method just described.

All the phonic structures must be taught but as word building is usually easier from syllables or 'chunks' (the memory load is lessened) the order of teaching has

to be modified. Thus one might work from three whole words, such as *hit, sit, bit,* discover visually the common part **it**, and proceed to build *fit, kit, pit.*

Another teaching point which calls for modification to meet the needs of a few children is the learning and use of short vowels for word building right at the beginning of a teaching programme. Some dyslexic children experience considerable difficulty in discriminating short vowels particularly, *a* and *e* and *i*. Only Hornsby and Shear (1975) make a positive recommendation to get round this problem by pairing short vowels such as *a* and *o* which give the greatest contrast. I would go further and suggest in cases of major difficulty that long vowel sounds be introduced first. These have the advantage, not only of being easier to identify, but permit exaggerated mouthing which adds a further kinaesthetic dimension in making the basic sound–symbol association. By using only one spelling, for example *ee, oo,* the necessary one-to-one correspondence between sound and symbol can be retained to facilitate an understanding of the coding system.

Spelling rules form an important part of all programmes, some of which require them to be learnt by heart. As explanations, as a means for creating rational order and regularity out of seeming chaos and irregularity, they are invaluable and must certainly be known by the teacher. For the pupil to have to *learn* them, along with the invariable exceptions, adds enormously to the memory load. Knowing the spelling rules may help to *correct* at least some errors but the effect on spontaneous spelling is open to doubt. It is very difficult when writing to concentrate both on the content and on the spelling. A quotation from a dyslexic university student illustrates the point: 'Personally I find spelling rules and their exceptions more confusing than the direct tasks of reading and spelling. They have no immediacy for me; rather they put a functional (and sometimes conceptual) block between my vocabulary and my use of the words' (Gauntlett, 1978). My own advice to the dyslexic taking external examinations is to concentrate on content, and arrange for the relevant certificate explaining the reason for the poor spelling to be sent to the appropriate examining body.

Choosing a programme

Teaching dyslexic children is no easy teaching option. Even the most experienced teacher of normal children becomes a novice once more when she starts to tackle the problems of dyslexia. Wisdom and knowledge come with experience, but until that is gained, it is advisable to follow in the footsteps of those who have paved the way. Programmes such as those described above provide the necessary structured, systematic and thorough approach. Their success has been demonstrated by Homsby and Miles (1980) who examined the effect of tuition in three dyslexia centres, each using one of the programmes described above (Hornsby and Shear, 1977; Miles, 1970, and Miles and Miles, 1975: and Hickey, 1977). Reading gains averaged 1.91 years per year and spelling gains 1.94 years per year compared with averages of 0.53 and 0.32 respectively in the pre-teaching period.

At the same time, every effort should be made to adapt methods and materials to the needs of individual pupils. How this was done at the Word Blind Centre for Dyslexic Children is described by the author elsewhere (Naidoo, 1970). Following a well-thought-out and detailed programme does not make teaching an easy, routine matter. Each child brings some new problem which the teacher has to solve. The task of teaching dyslexic children is endlessly challenging.

REFERENCES

Allan, B. V. (1977) *Logical Spelling*. London: Collins.
Arkell, H. (1970) The Edith Norrie Letter Case. In A. W. Franklin and S. Naidoo (eds.), The *Assessment and Teaching of Dyslexic Children*. London: ICAA
Baldwin, G. (1968) *Patterns of Sound*. London: Chartwell Press.
Cotterell, G. (1970) Teaching procedures. In A. W. Franklin and S. Naidoo (eds.) The *Assessment and Teaching of Dyslexic Children*. London: ICAA.
Cotterell, G. (1973) *Diagnosis in the Classroom*. Reading: The Centre for the Teaching of Reading, School of Education, University of Reading.
Cotterell, G. *Phonic Reference Cards*. Wisbech, Cambs.: Learning Development Aids.
Cotterell, G. *A Check List of Basic Sounds*. Wisbech, Cambs.: Learning Development Aids.
Critchley, M. (1970) *The Dyslexic Child*. London: Heinemann Medical Books.
Crystal, D., Fletcher, P., and Garman, M. (1976) *The Grammatical Analysis of Language Disability*. London: Edward Arnold.
Done, D. J., and Miles, T. R. (1978) Learning, memory and dyslexia. *Dyslexia Rev.*, **1**, 2, 13–14.
Ellis, N. C. and Miles, T. R. (1978) Visual information processing in dyslexic children. *Dyslexia Rev.*, **1**, 2, 10–12.
Fernald, G. M. (1943) *Remedial Techniques in Basic School Subjects*. New York: McGraw-Hill.
Fernald, G. M., and Keller, H. (1921) The effect of kinaesthetic factors in the development of word recognition in non-readers. *J. Educ. Res.* **4**. Quoted by D. Moyle (1970), in *The Teaching of Reading*. London: Ward Lock Educational.
Gattegno, C. (1962) *Words in Colour*. Reading: Educational Explorers Ltd.
Gauntlett, D. A. (1978) In another's shoes. A case study of a mature dyslexic. *Dyslexia Rev.*, **1**, 2, 23–27.
Gillingham, A., and Stillman, B. W. (1969) *Remedial Training for Children with Specific Disability in Reading, Spelling and Penmanship. 5th edn*. Cambridge, Mass.: Educators Publishing Co.
Goodacre, E. J. (1972) Methods of teaching reading. In A. Melnik and J. Merritt (eds.) *The Reading Curriculum*. London: University of London Press.
Hickey, M. (1977) *Dyslexia: A Language Training Course for Teachers and Learners*. 3, Montague Road. London, SW19.
Hinshelwood, J. (1917) *Congenital Word Blindness*. London: Lewis.
Hornsby, B., and Miles, T. R. (1980) The effects of a dyslexia-centred teaching programme. *Br. J. of Educ. Psychol.*, **50**, 236–242.
Hornsby, B. and Shear, F. (1975) *Alpha to Omega*. London: Heinemann Educational Books Ltd.
Johnson, D. J. and Myklebust, H. R. (1967) *Learning Disabilities*. New York: Grune and Stratton.
Lewis, L. (1976) *Attack-A-Track*. Bath: Better Books.

Mackay, D., Thompson, B., and Schaub, P. (1970) *Breakthrough To Literacy*. London: Longman for the Schools Council.

Miles, T. R. (1970) *On Helping the Dyslexic Child*. London: Methuen Educational Ltd.

Miles, T. R. (1978) *Understanding Dyslexia*. London: Hodder and Stoughton.

Miles, T. R., and Miles, E. (1975) *More Help for Dyslexic Children*. London: Methuen Educational Ltd.

Miles, T. R., and Wheeler, T. J. (1974) Towards a new theory of dyslexia. *Dyslexia Rev.*, **11**, 9–11.

Moyle, D. (1970) *The Teaching of Reading*. London: Ward Lock Educational.

Naidoo, S. (1970) Remedial re-education. In A. W. Franklin and S. Naidoo (eds.) *The Assessment and Teaching of Dyslexic Children*. London: The Invalid Children's Aid Association.

Naidoo, S. (1971) Specific developmental dyslexia. *Brit. J. Educ. Psychol.*, **41**, 1, 19–22.

Naidoo, S. (1972) *Specific Dyslexia*. London: Pitman.

Neville, M. H. (1978) Learning to Read in Japan. *Reading*, **12**, 1, 21–28.

Newton, M., Thomson, M. E., and Richards, I. J. (1979) *Readings in Dyslexia*. Wisbech: Bemrose U.K. Ltd.

Orton, S. T. (1925) 'Word-Blindness' in school children. *Arch. Neurol Psychiat*, **14**, 581–615.

Orton, S. T. (1929) The 'sight-reading' method of teaching reading, as a source of reading disability. *J. Educ. Psychol.*, 135–142.

Orton, S. T. (1937) *Reading, Writing and Speech Problems in Children*. London: Chapman and Hall.

Orton, S. T. (1939) A neurological explanation of the reading disability, with some remarks as to the value of this explanation in treatment. *Educ. Record*, **Supplement No. 12**, 58–68.

Pollock, J. (1978) *Signposts to Spelling*. London: Helen Arkell Dyslexia Centre.

Reid, J. F. (1972) Learning to think about reading. In A. Melinik, and J. Merritt (eds.) *Reading: Today and Tomorrow*. London: University of London Press.

Richardson, G. (1980) *The development of some aspects of visual perception, serial verbal learning and oral language in good readers and children with specific reading difficulties in the age range 8–12 years*. PhD thesis, University of Cambridge.

Rutter, M., Tizard, J., and Whitmore, K. (1970). *Education, Health and Behaviour*. London: Longman.

Schonell, F. J. (1942) *Backwardness in the Basic Subjects*. Edinburgh: Oliver and Boyd.

Shute, H. and Graham, N. (1977) *Reading Disability*. Aston Educational Enquiry Occasional Paper No. 2, The University of Aston in Birmingham.

Southgate, V. (1972) The importance of structure in beginning reading. In A. Melnik and J. Merritt (eds.) *The Reading Curriculum*, London: University of London Press.

Vernon, M. D. (1975) Comments on 'Towards a new theory of dyslexia'. *Dyslexia Rev.*, **14**, 21–22.

Wendon, L. *The Pictogram System* (from Pictogram Supplies, Barton, Cambridge).

Wolff, A. G. (1970) The Gillingham and Stillman Programme. In A. W. Franklin and S. Naidoo (eds.) *The Assessment and Teaching of Dyslexic Children*, London: ICAA.

Author Index

289

Subject Index

Sequence (*contd.*)
 reverse, 145
 words in, 116
Sequencing, xii, 135, 139, 145, 203, 233, 248
 automatic, 26, 136
 difficulties in, xii, xiii, 58, 68, 101, 119, 248
 errors, 54, 96
 linear, 26
 problem, 142, 233
 temporal tasks of, 91
 tests of, 232
Sequential activity, 136
Sequential auditory pattern, 60, 141
Sequential behavioural problems, 101
Sequential control, 137
Sequential deficits, 141, 142, 143, 145
Sequential disability, 143, 144, 145, 153, 154
Sequential experience, 26
Sequential fixation, 117, 119, 141, 142
Sequential illumination of lights, 146, 148, 152, 153
Sequential malfunction, 146
Sequential memory, 27, 139
Sequential order, 126, 136, 137, 138, 139, 141, 143, 145, 153, 154, 155, 156
 hypothesis, 155
Sequential ordering, 133, 135, 137
 deficits in, 138, 153, 154, 155, 156
 dyslexics, problem in, 143, 153
 skill, 138
Sequential performance, 136
Sequential presentation, 250
Sequential problems, 101, 126, 144, 154, 155, 156
Sequential processing, 138, 139, 166
Sequential requirements, 153
Sequential skills, 119, 136, 138, 144, 157
Sequential structures, 138
Sequential tasks, 101, 137, 142, 143, 144, 153
Sequential test, 254
Sequential visual patterns, 141, 254
Serial order, 248
Serial position, 88, 90
Somaesthetic visual and auditory data, 39
Somaesthetic area, 45
Somaesthetic information, 51

Somaesthetic input, 53
Somatosensory area, 36
Spatial abilities, 64, 118
Spatial disorders of orientation, 117
Spatial order, 88, 227
Spatial problems, 67, 70, 71
Spatial separation, 170
Spatial skills, 62, 63
Spatial superiority, 22, 63
Speech, 102, 201, 272
 aspects of, 269
 code, 166, 181, 191
 encoding, 187
 implicit, 181, 186, 204
 muscles, 183
 order in, 256
 organs of, 280
 output, 77, 199
 production, 209
 recoding phase of, 172, 174
 spontaneous, 77
 telegrammatic, 79
Spelling, xii, xiv, 9, 28, 55, 60, 70, 77, 101, 170, 205, 218–221, 222, 226, 237, 245, 247–250, 256, 257, 259, 260, 264–266, 276, 278, 279, 280, 282
 bizarre, 101, 120, 247
 difficulties, x, xiii, xiv, xv, 2, 14, 22, 56, 102, 174, 255, 263, 271
 erratic, xiii, xv, 1, 8, 103
 instruction in, 275
 linkage for written, 274
 omissions, 120
 oral, 254
 patterns, 204, 247
 poor, 247
 retardation, 231
 rules for, 276, 281, 285
 schemes, 282
 simultaneous oral, 275
 spontaneous, 285
 teaching of, 273
 weakness, 219
Spoonerisms, 22
Strephosymbolia, 102, 222, 271, 272
Syntactic deficiencies, 191
Syntactic skills, 71
Syntactic structure, 77, 136

Tactile recognition, 64
Tactile stimuli, 63